The International Handbook on Financial Reform

The International Handbook on Financial Reform

Edited by

Maximilian J.B. Hall

Professor of Banking and Financial Regulation, Loughborough University, UK

Edward Elgar

Cheltenham, UK • Northampton, MA, USA

Published by
Edward Elgar Publishing Limited
Glensanda House
Montpellier Parade
Cheltenham
Glos GL50 1UA
UK

Edward Elgar Publishing, Inc.
136 West Street
Suite 202
Northampton
Massachusetts 01060
USA

A catalogue record for this book
is available from the British Library

Library of Congress Cataloguing in Publication Data
The international handbook on financial reform / edited by Maximilian J.B. Hall.
p. cm.
1. Financial services industry—Case studies. 2. Financial institutions—Case studies. 3. Banks and banking—Case studies. 4. Monetary policy—Case studies. I. Hall, Maximilian.

HG173 .I573 2003
332.1—dc21

2002034679

ISBN 1 84064 063 4

Printed and bound in Great Britain by Biddles Ltd, *www.biddles.co.uk*

Contents

Figures

Tables

Contributors

Kevin Davis, Commonwealth Bank Group Chair of Finance, Department of Finance, University of Melbourne, Australia.

Klaus Gottwald, Economist, Department of Economic Development and International Economics, Goethe University Frankfurt, Germany.

D.H. Gowland, Senior Teaching Fellow, University of Birmingham and Research Co-ordinator of Banking and Finance, European Business School, London, UK.

Maximilian J.B. Hall, Professor of Banking and Financial Regulation, Economics Department, Loughborough University, UK.

Y.C. Jao, Honorary Professor and Honorary University Fellow, School of Economics and Finance, University of Hong Kong.

Rainer Klump, Professor of Economics, Department of Economic Development and International Economics, Goethe University Frankfurt, Germany.

Akio Kuroda, Professor of Money and Finance, School of Political Science and Economics, Meiji University, Japan.

Andy Mullineux, Professor of Global Finance, Department of Accounting and Finance, Birmingham Business School, University of Birmingham, UK.

Victor Murinde, Professor of Finance, Birmingham Business School, University of Birmingham and Hallsworth Senior Research Fellow, IDPM, University of Manchester, UK.

Kee Jin Ngiam, Senior Fellow, Regional Economic Studies, Institute of Southeast Asian Studies (ISEAS), Singapore.

Marco Onado, Professor, 'Paolo Baffi' Centre for Monetary and Financial Economics, Universita Commericale Luigi Bocconi, Italy.

Adisorn Pinijkulviwat, Chief Officer, Department of Examination and Supervision, Bank of Thailand, Bangkok, Thailand.

Beate Reszat, Head of Research on International Financial Markets, Hamburg Institute of International Economics (HWWA), Hamburg, Germany.

Margot Schueller, Senior Research Fellow, Institute of Asian Affairs, Hamburg, Germany.

Pierre L. Siklos, Professor, Department of Economics, Wilfrid Laurier University, Waterloo, Ontario, Canada.

Roberto Luis Troster, Chief Economist, Febraban and Professor of Economics, Pontificia Universidade Católica, São Paulo, Brazil.

Introduction

Maximilian J.B. Hall

Under the combined pressure arising from the common trends of financial globalization, conglomeration, diversification, innovation and intensification in competition, countries around the globe have been forced to refashion the way they regulate and supervise their financial services industries. Such financial reforms typically embrace central bank reform, financial liberalization, supervisory reform and enhanced consumer protection.

On the central banking front, the clear trend is towards enhancement of central bank independence – although countries differ in the precise models chosen for adoption – and the narrowing of operational responsibilities to ensure a clear focus on monetary policy. In connection with the latter, inflation targeting is in the ascendancy, with open market operations the preferred means of securing the policy objectives. As in the UK, central banks are being stripped of their supervisory roles (although the Federal Reserve Board has so far successfully fought off any moves in this direction in the USA); yet, possession of the lender of last resort facility, ensures they retain at least some responsibility for ensuring overall financial stability.

Wide-scale financial deregulation has also become a global phenomenon as countries seek to maximize economic efficiency and meet the international challenge arising from such moves overseas (the European 'universal banking' model eventually forced both the US and Japanese administrations to abandon their long-held segmentation barriers). Typically, such deregulation embraces the liberalization of financial markets (money, capital, foreign exchange, derivatives, commodities and so on), the abolition of interest rate controls, liberalization of the scope of business activity (involving both the dismantling of segmentation barriers and restrictions on geographical areas of operation) and the abandonment of exchange controls (as currently required, for example, of all European Economic Area member states, other than in crisis situations although, even then, prior agreement in principle has to be received before their temporary reactivation).

Financial liberalization has, in turn, created acute pressures for supervisory reform, the need for which has been accentuated by a dramatic increase in the pace of financial innovation (for example, the emergence of new markets, financial products and corporate structures) and a fast-changing finance industry landscape, due to changes in the legal environment and market pressures for mergers, consolidation and demutualization. The supervisory reforms themselves typically embrace changes in the institutional organization of supervision – the trend is towards the integration and centralization of supervision and away from specialization, a path adopted by the present UK government when it created the Financial Services Authority – as well as changes in the style and *modus operandi* of supervision. The latter are needed to accommodate implementation of the ever-changing international 'rules of the game', as set out, for example (as far as banks are concerned), in the Basle Capital Accord, the Basle Concordat, the Basle Committee's Core Principles for Effective Banking Supervision and the related European Union directives, and to raise economic efficiency and improve cost-effectiveness in a very dynamic environment.

Finally, under pressure from both governments, whose ultimate goal is financial stability, and the consumer protection lobby, various measures have been widely adopted to enhance the protection afforded the consumers of financial products. Typically, these embrace the introduction/improvement of deposit insurance and compensation schemes, the tightening of anti-money laundering measures, improved self regulation (achieved, for example, through the introduction of industry 'codes of conduct') and the toughening of legal sanctions (to deter fraud, malpractice, market abuse, and insider trading, for example).

These developments, then, are the subject matter of this 'Handbook', which seeks to provide an up-to-date, authoritative, analytical and comprehensive account of financial reforms adopted around the globe (with an emphasis on the banking industry). The Handbook, which features both developed and developing economies, contains contributions from acknowledged area specialists covering selected countries from Western Europe, North America, South America and Australasia.

1. Financial reform in Australia*

Kevin Davis

1 INTRODUCTION

The process of reform of financial regulation in Australia provides a valuable case study of the interaction between the development of economic ideas, political constraints and commercial realities. Australia was one of the first countries to embrace financial deregulation in the late 1970s and by the mid-1980s had largely liberalized its financial markets. However, that approach was premised on a belief that capital and product market forces would generate an efficient and stable financial system, without examining whether the necessary preconditions for such an outcome were in existence. Official regulation was not replaced by adequate market monitoring and capital market discipline, and management systems and governance practices within financial institutions were not adequate for the new competitive environment. Excessive credit expansion led to an asset price bubble, excessive corporate borrowing, and a minor financial crisis in the late 1980s. Subsequent developments have focused upon strengthening the regulatory infrastructure and ensuring that information, incentives and accountability are adequate to ensure that market mechanisms operate effectively.

This chapter reviews the financial reform process in Australia, focusing primarily on the past 20 years. In Section 2, a brief historical overview of financial reform is presented, and this is followed in Section 3 by an outline of the current regulatory structure. Section 4 addresses the types of reform which have occurred and compares the current state of financial regulation in Australia with international practice. Section 5 considers some of the effects which financial reform has had on the Australian financial sector, and Section 6 provides a brief assessment of the current regulatory approach and concluding comments.

2 FINANCIAL REFORM: A BRIEF HISTORICAL OVERVIEW[1]

For some 30 years following the Second World War, the Australian financial system, and regulation thereof, changed relatively little – certainly when judged by the experiences of the subsequent 30 years. Until the latter part of the 1970s, the regulatory structure was one reliant on direct controls (of interest rates, allowable activities, portfolio structure, entry and so on) imposed by the central bank upon the (small number of) banks, which dominated the financial sector. That approach, which evolved out of the wartime experience and *ad hoc* responses to subsequent market developments, had a strong institutional focus. It was oriented primarily towards monetary control considerations rather than prudential objectives – the latter being handled indirectly through restrictions on entry into banking and controls limiting the risk-taking activities of banks. Information flowing to the public, from both the authorities and the banks, was relatively scarce, with (for example) accounting and reporting requirements enabling banks to maintain substantial secret reserves. Outside of the banking sector, the 1901 Constitution had created a division of responsibilities between the federal and state governments which led to a fragmented approach by individual states to regulation (or lack thereof – as in the case of general insurance) of non-bank financial intermediaries and securities markets.

The 1970s

By the 1970s, the inherent weaknesses in the regulatory structure were becoming clearly apparent. Non-bank financial institutions, operating outside the Reserve Bank's sphere of control, had grown rapidly since the 1950s. While some of those institutions (money market corporations, building societies and so on) were competitors with the banks, others, such as bank-owned finance company subsidiaries, provided a means for the banking groups to evade controls. Financial innovation, such as the development of the bank-accepted commercial bill market, provided another way for banks to evade lending controls and the implicit taxes which direct controls imposed on deposit-based financing. The Reserve Bank's stated preference for reliance on 'market-oriented' monetary policy measures rather than direct controls was thwarted by the absence of an active bond market, and monetary policy was further stressed by the development of large government fiscal deficits. The emergence of high inflation highlighted the distortions and costs of direct controls, and the breakdown of the Bretton Woods system of fixed exchange rates saw the emergence of a managed exchange rate system and associated problems of such a system for macroeconomic management.[2]

For a time, and reflecting the ideological position of the Whitlam Labor government of 1972–75, the possibility of an extension of controls to non-bank financial institutions looked possible.[3] The Financial Corporations

Act, passed in 1974, provided for such a possibility, but the relevant section was never put into effect. Instead, the Fraser Liberal government (elected in late 1975) took small *ad hoc* steps along the deregulatory path for several years until the announcement in 1979 of the first full-scale review of the Australian financial system (the Campbell Inquiry) since the Royal Commission of some 40 years earlier.[4]

The 1980s

The Campbell Committee did not report until November (Committee of Inquiry into the Australian Financial System, 1981), but the government did not wait for the report to begin deregulating the financial system. A capital shortage of one smaller bank (due to losses incurred by its finance company subsidiary, highlighting weaknesses in extant prudential arrangements) saw a takeover by a larger bank arranged. Subsequently, other bank mergers were permitted and approval of a new entrant signalled a relaxation of the previous official entry barrier. Initial steps towards reform of the bond market were taken with new primary market issue techniques introduced and 'captive market' asset-holding requirements on banks, which limited secondary market activity, watered down.

The removal of most interest rate ceilings on bank deposits in December 1980 marked the start of a massive process of deregulation, subsequently endorsed by the Campbell Report. Surprisingly (since the party platform had, until a few years earlier, contained a call for bank nationalization) the process was accelerated by the Hawke Labor government which was elected in March 1983. Over the first half of the 1980s, direct controls over banks were largely abolished (except for some asset portfolio restrictions retained for prudential reasons), foreign bank entry permitted, and the exchange rate floated. The stockbroking industry was reformed in 1984 and fixed brokerage rates abolished, stockbrokers being allowed to advertise and permitted to operate as incorporated companies rather than as partnerships. Banks were permitted to take an equity interest in stockbrokers.

Although the possibility of increased competition from new banks was created, the existing banks were largely freed of the shackles which had encumbered them, and permitted to engage, via subsidiaries, in securities market and wholesale money market activities as well as more traditional deposit markets. But banks remained different from other institutions through their control of the domestic payments mechanism and through public perceptions of an implicit government guarantee of deposits.

The outcome of this process was a rapid increase in credit creation by banks and other financial intermediaries, contributing to significant asset price inflation. While reintermediation (particularly towards banks) and thus rapid, but largely benign, growth in credit aggregates had been expected to occur as a result of deregulation, the reality was somewhat different. Increased competition, coupled with inadequate internal control mechanisms and a lack of stock market (and regulatory) discipline, saw a relaxation of credit standards by banks and other financial institutions, which (assisted by the stock market crash of October 1987) culminated in a minor financial crisis at the end of the 1980s. Several state government-owned banks experienced horrendous losses (and were, ultimately, taken over by other banks), several non-bank financial institutions collapsed, and several of the major banks posted losses which made them, for a time, vulnerable to takeover.

During the second half of the 1980s, other financial and economic reform measures, which were to have major effects on the financial system – in particular, facilitating the subsequent growth of securities markets relative to intermediation – proceeded apace. Tax reform, particularly the introduction of a dividend imputation tax system, increased the attractiveness of equity finance relative to debt finance for Australian companies. Government policy promoting the growth of superannuation (pension) schemes contributed to the expansion of the managed funds industry and demand for marketable securities. Reform of federal–state government fiscal relationships and state government borrowing techniques saw the emergence of an active 'semi-government' (state government) bond market alongside the market for federal debt. The earlier deregulation of the stock market (1984) and creation of a unified national stock exchange (1987) facilitated growth of the securities markets, although the domestic corporate bond market remained in its infancy, with corporate borrowers reliant on bank lending or, for major companies, international bond markets.

The 1990s and the New Millennium

The 1990s financial reform experience can be viewed as having three overlapping phases. First, there was a 'mopping up' exercise following the problems which had emerged in the latter part of the 1980s, leading to an increased emphasis on prudential regulation and regulatory arrangements. The Reserve Bank had introduced risk-weighted capital requirements for banks in 1988 (too late to constrain the excesses permitted by deregulation), and this was followed by the introduction of on-site inspections in the early 1990s. The Insurance and Superannuation Commission (ISC) had been established in 1987, and its supervisory powers (over life and general insurance and superannuation funds) were enhanced in legislation of 1993 and 1995. The Australian Financial Institutions Commission (AFIC) was created as a national coordinator of state supervisors of building societies and credit unions in 1992, following agreement among the state governments to adopt common regulation.[5] The Australian Securities Commission (ASC) was created in 1991 as a national regulator of companies and securities markets, succeeding the National Companies and Securities Commission which had attempted to coordinate state government based regulation and enforcement. The Council of Financial Supervisors was formed in 1992 to facilitate coordination among these regulators. A new accounting standard (AAS32) was introduced in 1996 setting out required standards for disclosure by financial institutions of information relating to liquidity, solvency and degrees of risk associated with various activities.

The second phase of the 1990s experience involved general economic reform[6] aimed at facilitating competition, marked by the adoption in 1996 of the National Competition Policy. The reforms included: strengthening trade practice laws; a requirement for competitive neutrality between government and private sector competitors; a review of laws which restrict competition; introduction of a national access regime to ensure fair terms for access to important national infrastructure; and specific reform (leading to privatization) of industries such as gas, electricity, water and transport. The Australian Competition and Consumer Commission (ACCC), responsible for consumer protection and oversight of mergers and anti-competitive practices, was created by merging the previously separate Prices Justification Tribunal and the Trade Practices Commission. More emphasis was given by regulators to ensuring increased information flows and more attention given to consumer protection. Industry codes of practice were developed and the Uniform Consumer Credit Code introduced.

Major institutional restructuring of the financial sector occurred over this period, with governments generally exiting from the provision of financial services (as part of a wider privatization agenda), numerous cases of demutualization, and mergers and takeovers aplenty. Bancassurance emerged and universal banking, through the integration of commercial banking and securities market activities, became the norm. Securitization, mortgage originators, managed investments and corporate bond issues all increased in significance as the role of securities markets relative to intermediation expanded. Notably, however, other than through equity holdings via trustee (nominee company) arrrangements, funds management arms, or work-outs of distressed borrowers, a degree of separation of banking and commerce still existed – as much due to habits of banking practice as to regulation.

The final phase of the 1990s experience, merging into the new millennium, is the completion of a government agenda of putting in place a regulatory infrastructure consistent with efficient financial and capital markets, in which regulation hinges not upon enforcement of rigid rules, but upon disclosure, supervision and private sector monitoring. Beginning in the mid-1990s, attention was given to a reform of Corporate Law, initially focusing on simplification, but later broadened to the Corporate Law Economic Reform Program (CLERP). Improvements in accounting and disclosure, clearer articulation of directors' duties and expected standards of corporate governance, and improvements in regulation of fund-raising, takeovers and financial advisers form the basis of this programme. In 1996, the Wallis Inquiry into the financial system was announced and its report in 1997 led to the restructuring of regulatory agencies as they exist today.

3 AUSTRALIAN REGULATORY INSTITUTIONS AND RESPONSIBILITIES

The current structure of financial regulation in Australia was introduced in 1998, following the recommendations of the Wallis Inquiry, through a restructuring and reallocation of regulatory responsibilities. The Wallis Inquiry placed great emphasis on the need for a functional approach to regulation. The restructuring (based upon the Wallis recommendations) can be interpreted as an attempt to divide regulatory responsibilities along functional lines,[7] although it retains significant features of an institutional approach. Table 1.1 summarizes the current regulatory structure and responsibilities.

The Reserve Bank of Australia (RBA) no longer has responsibility for prudential regulation, but a specific responsibility for systemic stability (reflecting the possibility of market failure arising from spillovers and externalities), monetary policy and efficiency and stability of the payments system. (A separate Payments System Board has been established within the Reserve Bank.) The Australian Prudential Regulation Authority (APRA) was formed by combining the prudential regulation activities previously undertaken by the Reserve Bank, AFIC and the ISC. It has responsibility for supervision of financial institutions which issue liabilities with a high 'intensity of promise' (a concept underpinning the Wallis approach) and for which market failure arising from imperfect information might be significant. The Australian Securities and Investment Commission (ASIC) took over consumer protection responsibilities for insurance and superannuation from the ISC and for the financial sector generally from the ACCC. Allied with its responsibilities for ensuring market integrity and the operation of company law, inherited from its predecessor (ASC), its responsibilities can

Table 1.1 Australian financial regulation at the start of the twenty-first century

	Regulatory institutions			
	Reserve Bank	APRA	ASIC	ACCC
Responsibilities	• Systemic stability • Monetary policy • Payments system	• Prudential regulation	• Integrity of (primary and secondary) securities markets • Investor/financial claimant protection	• Consumer protection (excluding financial sector) • Competition policy
Financial institutions supervised		• Banks • Other ADIs • Insurance • Large superannuation funds	• Fund managers • Securities firms • Investment advisers	
Techniques	• Market operations (in bonds, repos and forex swaps) to achieve announced cash interest rate target • Lender of last resort and discount window operations for system stability purposes • Determining rules for access to, and setting efficiency and safety standards for, designated payments systems	• On- and off-site inspections • Formulation of policy • Risk-weighted capital requirements	• Enforcement of company law • Ensuring adequate disclosure • Dealing with consumer issues • Promotion of industry codes of conduct and self-regulation	• Enforcement of trade practices and prices surveillance acts • Conduct of inquiries and monitoring of market behaviour • Provision of information

be viewed as reflecting the possibility of market failure from misconduct by market participants. The ACCC's involvement with the financial sector arises from its role in preventing market failure through anti-competitive behaviour, reflected in its responsibilities for oversight of mergers and pricing behaviour.

This institutional structure of the regulatory sector attempts to provide a clear delineation of each regulator's responsibilities and achieve minimal overlap or duplication and comprehensive coverage of areas requiring regulation. Where there are areas of common interest, such as between the Reserve Bank and the ACCC regarding the payments system, memoranda of understanding have been signed. The RBA, APRA and ASIC comprise the Council of Financial Regulators (which supplanted the Council of Financial Supervisors) and there is some cross-representation on governing boards.

This Australian approach to the structure of regulatory arrangements has been asserted by Australian government ministers as being 'a benchmark for countries around the world' (Hockey, 2001 p. 1). While the structure appears to be working well, there are several features of it which warrant note. First, it does not achieve a clear functional division of responsibilities. An institutional distinction is used to determine which institutions are supervised by APRA and those supervised by ASIC. Second, by removing prudential regulation from the central bank, it is hoped that public expectations of automatic government support for failing institutions will be prevented, and private sector monitoring enhanced. The explicit eschewing of any deposit insurance or government guarantee scheme (or similar scheme for claimants on other regulated institutions), means that Australian financial regulators face a difficult task in managing public expectations when financial institutions face difficulties and in facilitating orderly exit of such institutions.[8]

The Reserve Bank of Australia

The Reserve Bank in 2001 is a very different institution from that of 20 (or more) years ago. One difference is that its direct involvement with the banking sector has declined markedly. Historically, the use of direct controls over the banking sector (until the mid-1980s) and development of techniques of prudential regulation since the 1980s, together with the provision of clearing and settlement services, meant that the central bank and commercial banks had a close, if not always, comfortable relationship. Now, that involvement is largely limited to the payments clearing and settlements systems.

A second relationship which has changed is that with the government.

While the RBA was established in 1959[9] with its own Board, its degree of independence was questionable. Policy was nominally determined by the Board, and any decision by the treasurer to overrule the Board had to be reported to parliament. None ever were, and to outsiders the fact that the secretary of the treasury sat on the Board suggested that independence was in name only. That changed in August 1996 when the appointment of the current governor was marked by release of a statement from the government giving explicit recognition of the 'independence' of the RBA, and an explicit statement of the responsibility and procedures for policy formulation and resolution of disagreement.

The RBA has also changed markedly in terms of its degree of transparency and accountability. Information flows to the public have improved markedly.

This change in transparency is also reflected in the conduct of monetary policy. After a period of experimentation with monetary targets from 1976 to 1985, followed by a 'checklist' approach, the RBA in 1990 commenced its current practice of making explicit announcements of a short-term (cash) interest rate target as the basis for the operation of monetary policy. Subsequently, in the August 1996 'Statement on the Conduct of Monetary Policy', an inflation target for monetary policy of 2–3 per cent on average over the business cycle was agreed by the government and the RBA, although an implicit inflation target had been in operation since 1993. Concurrent with that, regular six monthly presentations by the Reserve Bank governor to a parliamentary committee on the conduct of monetary policy began. Reflecting the continuing decline in commonwealth government securities outstanding (due to fiscal surpluses), the RBA commenced using repurchase agreements involving semi-government debt in 1997 and more recently has increased its use of foreign exchange swaps for monetary management purposes.

The change in the RBA's functions has also affected its structure and size. With the passing of direct control techniques, loss of the prudential regulation function, loss of banking business previously conducted for state governments, and labour-saving technological change impacting on both account keeping/clearing/settlement and note issue functions, the size of the bank's workforce has shrunk considerably.

The objectives for the RBA have also been updated. While its statutory objectives, as given in the 1959 Reserve Bank Act, remain (a) the stability of the currency of Australia; (b) the maintenance of full employment in Australia; and (c) the economic prosperity and welfare of the people of Australia, its mandate is now focused explicitly upon monetary policy, overall financial system stability, and regulation of the payments system.

Australian Prudential Regulation Authority

Australia's new regulatory structure specifically locates responsibility for prudential regulation of a specific set of financial institutions with a government statutory authority (APRA), governed by a board appointed by the government for fixed terms (and with provision for a majority of private sector members). APRA is accountable to parliament and funded by levies on the financial institutions supervised. Its mission statement is 'to establish and enforce prudential standards and practices designed to ensure that, under all reasonable circumstances, financial promises made by institutions we supervise are met within a stable, efficient and competitive system'.[10]

Several features of this mission and role are worthy of note. First, institutions supervised are banks, other approved deposit institutions (ADIs) such as building societies and credit unions, friendly societies, life and general insurers, and large superannuation funds[11] – that is, those judged, on some basis, to be institutions for which the 'intensity of promise' is high. The approach adopted in Australia of an 'integrated' prudential supervisor (rather than a number of prudential supervisors for different types of institutions) is one which has increased in popularity internationally in recent years. Notably, however, finance companies which raise money by debenture, money market corporations (investment banks) and fund managers are outside this net. When such institutions are owned by a bank or an insurance company, their activities are included in APRA's consolidated supervision of the group, but they are not supervised as such. APRA supervisory responsibilities thus range from large diversified conglomerates to small specialized institutions and across both banking and insurance. Second, APRA has quite strong powers enabling it to intervene in the case of troubled institutions, and a good deal of regulatory discretion about when and how to do so. Third, APRA has no resources of its own available, nor is there a deposit insurance scheme in existence to ensure that claimants at failed financial institutions do not suffer loss. Fourth, supervision of 'consumer issues', such as information provision, advice and quality of service of APRA-supervised institutions, is not a responsibility of APRA, but of ASIC.

Australian Securities and Investment Commission

ASIC is an independent government body headed by government-appointed commissioners and reporting to parliament through the treasurer. Its responsibilities can be summarized as involving first, the protection of investors and financial claimants (such as superannuants, depositors and insurance policy holders), and second, the regulation and enforcement of laws that promote honesty and fairness in financial markets, products and services and in Australian companies. In sum, these responsibilities with regard to the financial sector can be referred to as 'investor protection and market integrity'. In pursuing these objectives, the approach followed is based upon ensuring that adequate information is available for consumers and investors to make informed decisions rather than a rule-based approach of setting standards for products and services.

ASIC has explicit responsibility for the regulation of a group of financial institutions – money market corporations, finance companies, public unit trusts – which are excluded from APRA's ambit on the grounds that investors in securities issued by such institutions are expected to be aware of the market and credit risks involved. ASIC does not undertake prudential regulation of such institutions, but ensures that they comply with legal requirements regarding fund raising and securities licensing requirements.

Organized securities exchanges in Australia, most notably the Australian Stock Exchange (ASX) and the Sydney Futures Exchange (SFE), are also subject to oversight by ASIC and in turn play a role in self-regulation of financial markets through their listing requirements and rules for member organizations. For example, in 1994, the ASX introduced its continuous disclosure regime for listed companies.

Australian Competition and Consumer Commission

The ACCC is not generally regarded as a financial regulator, although its activities impinge on financial institutions and markets in (at least) two ways. First, given its role as a regulator of mergers and takeovers under competition objectives, it can have a significant influence on the structure of the financial system. Second, its role in determining the justifiability of prices in markets where there are concerns about the degree of competition, means that it has had important influence on the pricing of payments services and on other fees and charges of financial institutions.

4 CHANGES IN AUSTRALIAN REGULATORY PRACTICE

This section examines in more detail the changes which have occurred in the conduct of financial regulation in Australia, and relates them to best practice as advocated by international bodies such as the Basle Committee. In doing so, a classification of reform areas into (a) financial price and quantity distortions, (b) impediments to competition, (c) financial infrastructure and (d) strengthening of financial institutions as presented in Cull (2001) is adopted. Table 1.2 provides an overview of key dates.

Financial Price and Quantity Distortions

As the brief historical overview in Section 2 indicates, most regulatory impediments to market-determined prices and quantities in Australian financial markets were removed by the mid-1980s. Foreign exchange market liberalization occurred in December 1983, with the floating of the exchange rate and removal of foreign exchange control regulations. Interest rate controls on banks were progressively abolished, with the interest rate on housing loans being the last rate deregulated in 1986. Restrictions on the composition of asset portfolios of financial intermediaries have also been largely abolished. 'Captive market' restrictions on banks and life offices which required minimum holdings of government debt were removed in the 1980s, and quantitative lending directives issued to the banking sector by the Reserve Bank were discontinued in the early 1980s. The practice of paying below-market interest rates on required bank reserves persisted[12] (except for a short period) until minimum reserve ratios were replaced in 1998 by the requirement that an agreed, satisfactory, liquidity management policy be in place. Restrictions on bank involvement in property development and ownership have been replaced by prudential standards for the treatment of equity associations (which link such investments to capital requirements). 'Blanket' portfolio restrictions on 'specialist' institutions such as credit unions have been replaced by requirements that institutions

Table 1.2 Financial reform in Australia: some major events

1980 (Dec.)	Interest rate ceilings on many bank deposits removed, new bank entry permitted
1981	Campbell Inquiry Report released
1982	Maturity controls on bank deposits relaxed, lending restrictions abolished, some asset portfolio restrictions relaxed, bond tender system introduced
1983 (Dec.)	Australian dollar floated and exchange control regulations largely abolished
1984	40 new foreign exchange dealers authorized, interest rate prohibition on cheque accounts removed, deregulation of stockbroking, portfolio deregulation of life offices
1985	16 foreign banks given banking licences, interest rate ceiling on 'small' bank loans (other than housing loans) removed, Liquid and Government Securities (LGS) convention abolished

1986	Interest rate ceiling on bank home mortgage loans removed, Non Bank Financial Institutions (NBFIs) permitted to participate in payments system
1987	ISC established, dividend imputation tax system commenced
1988	Risk-weighted capital requirements introduced for banks
1989	Banking industry ombudsman scheme introduced
1990	'Six pillars' policy on bank mergers introduced
1991	Part privatization of Commonwealth Bank, ASC established, life and general insurance complaints schemes introduced
1992	Foreign bank entry as a branch permitted, AFIC established, risk-weighted capital requirements applied to building societies and credit unions. Council of Financial Supervisors formed, bank on-site inspections commenced
1993	Banking code of practice released
1994	General insurance code of practice released, continuous disclosure regime introduced by ASX for listed companies, first 'bancassurance' group created
1995	Life Insurance Act passed and life insurance code of practice released, risk-weighted capital requirements applied to life companies, ACCC created
1996	Wallis Inquiry announced, Uniform Consumer Credit Code introduced, central bank independence affirmed, National Competition Policy adopted, Accounting Standard AAS32 addressing disclosure standards for financial institutions released
1997	Wallis Inquiry reports, 'four pillars' policy towards bank mergers adopted, CLERP announced
1998	Bank capital requirements for market risk introduced, APRA created, ASIC created, Payments System Board established within Reserve Bank, Council of Financial Regulators replaces Council of Financial Supervisors, Financial Sector Reform Act passed, Financial Sector (Shareholdings) Act passed, Payments System (Regulation) Act passed, RTGS introduced
1999	CLERP Act passed, replacement of minimum liquidity requirements for banks with 'agreed liquidity policy'-based approach, access to exchange settlements account facilities at RBA widened
2000	Uniform prudential standards for ADIs announced by APRA
2001	Financial Services Reform Bill passed

have appropriate risk-management policies and practices in place for the types of activities undertaken. Risk-weighted capital adequacy requirements, introduced for banks in 1988, have been argued by some to lead to distortions in pricing and credit allocation, with a significant expansion in home mortgage lending by banks in the 1990s sometimes being attributed to the lower risk weight accorded to these assets.

In the tax arena, the introduction of the dividend imputation tax system in 1987 has largely removed the tax distortion favouring debt over equity finance – although complicating the tax analysis of international financing choices (and business activities). Likewise, the introduction of explicit capital gains tax in 1996 (as a tax on inflation-adjusted gains, later changed in 1999 to a tax on 50 per cent of nominal capital gains) has gone some way to removing tax distortions on both real and financial investment decisions. Some transactions taxes on financing activities have also been ameliorated, with significant reductions in stamp duty and the abolition of the Financial Institutions Duty imposed by state governments on deposit transactions in July 2001 and eventual removal (2005) of the bank accounts debit tax. Tax concessions to sectors believed to be not adequately financed by free markets or adversely affected by usual tax arrangements, such as small venture capital and large infrastructure projects, have also occurred.

Impediments to Competition

Until the start of the 1980s, new entry into banking in Australia was generally thought to be not possible. In 1981, the first new domestic entrant was permitted and a limited number of foreign entrants were permitted to establish local bank subsidiaries in 1985.[13] (Foreign banks could previously only operate as merchant banks.) That quantitative limit has since been removed. Foreign banks wanting involvement in retail deposit markets must do so by establishment of a subsidiary, while those that limit activities to wholesale markets can operate as branches of the foreign parent.

Those changes have altered the face of the Australian banking sector which at the start of the 1980s comprised four major banks, several smaller private banks, three long-standing foreign banks (with very small operations) and a number of government-owned banks. During the 1980s and 1990s, significant numbers of building societies demutualized and became banks – reflecting the fact that the deregulation of the early 1980s had, if anything, reversed the tilt in the playing field to now favouring banks. Significant numbers of foreign banks have established a presence. Now, entry is possible for any organization which meets fairly standard criteria of minimum capital, expertise and so on, although policy guidelines limit allowable structures for financial conglomerates.[14]

The extent to which product market competition and efficiency are enhanced by pressures from the market for corporate control is somewhat less obvious. Privatization of government banks (or their sale to private competitors) has meant that all banks operating in Australia are either listed on the local stock exchange or foreign owned.[15] There are, however, restrictions on ownership shares and takeovers. First, there is a maximum limit (which can only be exceeded with permission of the treasurer) of 15 per cent on the ownership stake which any one party can have in an Australian bank, except in the case of subsidiaries of foreign-owned banks. Second, the Australian government has in place a 'four pillars' policy towards the market structure of the banking system which precludes mergers between the big four local banks, and creates uncertainties about their susceptibility to foreign takeover. While this can be seen as an attempt to ensure that an adequate number of competitors exist, it can also be interpreted as a measure which inhibits cost-saving rationalizations in the banking industry.

Despite a significant number of new entrants, there has also been a degree of consolidation in the financial sector. Some of the 'regional banks', which emerged in the 1980s from the demutualization of building societies (as well as a 'bankassurance' group formed through takeover of a state government bank by a demutualized life office), have been taken over by the larger banks. While permitted by the competition watchdog (the ACCC), and justified on the grounds of cost savings and greater efficiency arising from increased scale and scope, these events have certainly decreased the number of competitors operating in retail deposit markets. For while foreign banks have been active participants in the wholesale markets they have largely eschewed the retail market, and a marked reduction in the number of other non-bank ADIs has occurred through mergers. Numerous commentators have suggested, and popular opinion is of like mind – prompted by high bank profits and growth in explicit bank fees and charges – that the degree of competition in retail deposit and transactions services markets has been less than optimal.[16] In contrast, competition in wholesale markets and at the retail level in securities markets (evidenced by unit trust/mutual fund charges and brokerage charges for direct equity investments) appears more intense.

Strengthening of Financial Infrastructure

The restructuring of Australia's regulatory bodies, which has clearly delineated their responsibilities and powers, has been outlined in Section 3. Central bank independence (and that of other regulators) has been accepted, and specific attention paid to the importance and regulation of payments, clearing and settlement schemes. As part of those latter changes, significant changes have been made to arrangements for daily, system-wide, liquidity management (including abolition of the 'authorised short term money market dealers') – making such activities more transparent and efficient. Also relevant to the goal of assuring systemic stability has been the introduction of a real time gross settlements system (RTGS) in 1998 for interbank settlements.

The reform of prudential regulation arrangements has also been outlined previously. Underpinning those arrangements is the view articulated by the Wallis Inquiry that financial claimants should have confidence that promises made by issuers of certain liabilities will be kept. However, and an important distinguishing feature of the Australian approach, the government has eschewed the introduction of any form of deposit insurance scheme. The argument underlying this approach, recommended by the Wallis Inquiry, is that explicit recognition of depositor priority in the event of liquidation coupled with adequate disclosure, monitoring and supervision, is sufficient to maintain depositor confidence. In this regard, several question marks hang over the Australian approach.

First, depositor preference over other creditors does not overcome the problem of potential for runs by depositors arising from the 'first come first served' nature of bank deposits – which makes intra-depositor priority dependent on timing of withdrawal. Second, although the prudential regulator APRA has been explicitly structured to make it clear that it has no resources available to it to compensate claimants on a failed institution, it is far from clear that public expectations reflect the intention that *caveat emptor* applies for customers of regulated institutions. While improved disclosure, accountability and transparency of regulated institutions has occurred, the extent to which private sector monitoring will supplement supervisory activity is open to question. Third, the Australian system retains a distinction between 'banks' and other ADIs. The logic of such a distinction, which suggests something special about one subgroup of institutions (when all are subject to similar regulation), can be questioned – although restrictions on use of the label 'bank' are consistent with the Basle core principles. Fourth, one of the potential merits of an explicit deposit insurance scheme is that it can have benefits for competition, by offsetting possible advantages of perceived safety of large institutions arising from perceptions of 'too big to fail'. Fifth, prudential regulation reflects both the desire to control the risk characteristics of certain products or services such as deposits, long-term savings schemes, insurance products and payments services, as well as to ensure orderly exit of insolvent institutions from the marketplace. The dilemma is that the relevant products and functions are provided by institutions and, in practice, it is difficult to prevent the image of protection of products and services (justifiable only for a subset of activities) from also being attached to the institution involved and extending across its entire range of activities. The institutional approach to prudential regulation adopted in Australia has this weakness.

A further important component of financial infrastructure strengthening has been the government's commitment to reform of corporate law, which has found expression in the Corporate Law Economic Reform Program (CLERP) announced in 1997. Prior developments in the 1990s had focused upon simplification of company law, which had become unwieldy and complicated. CLERP was premised on the view that efficient financial markets require: market freedom (subject to appropriate regulation); access to appropriate information to ensure investor protection; a need for transparency through adequate disclosure; cost-effective regulation; regulatory neutrality and flexibility; and a fostering of high standards of business practices and ethics.[17] Subsequent changes, including the CLERP Act (1999), have focused upon: corporate accounting and reporting standards; articulation of directors' duties and improvements in standards of corporate governance; improving efficiency of the regulatory approval process for fund-raising documents while ensuring adequate provision of information; and improvements in takeover mechanisms (see Table 1.3 for a summary). The latest stage of the process involves the

Table 1.3 CLERP Act 1999: an overview of changes

Fundraising	• Four types of disclosure document (prospectus, short-form prospectus, profile statement, offer information statement) provided for • Certain exemptions to need for disclosure documents • Seven-day preview period for prospectuses for non-quoted securities replaced prospectus registration
Directors' duties	• Duty of care and diligence requirements clarified • Protection of directors clarified by introduction of business judgement role and specification of acceptable reliance on information and delegation
Statutory derivative action	• Enables shareholders (with leave from the court) to bring action on behalf of company, supplementing common law rights
Financial reporting system	• New Financial Reporting Commission introduced to oversee standard-setting process
Takeovers	• Corporations and Securities Panel to hear disputes • Compulsory acquisition provisions strengthened • Disclosure requirements made more consistent with fundraising requirements • Allowable offer period extended to 12 months

Financial Services Reform Bill, passed in 2001, which seeks to implement a uniform regime across the whole financial sector for licensing arrangements for the sale of financial products and provision of financial advice.

The ACCC and other regulators have paid particular attention to the role of information provision in financial markets and this has led to the development of codes of banking practice, the consumer credit code, greater disclosure requirements and so on. There is little doubt that a major change in recent decades has been in the extent of information provision to users of financial services and customers of financial institutions. In the case of banks, that can be seen from the growth of information contained in annual reports. Between 1987 and 1998, the average number of pages given to providing risk-related information in the annual reports of the four major banking groups increased from five to 110 (Thompson and Gray, 2000).

Strengthening Institutions

At the start of the 1990s, the Australian financial sector was characterized by a significant number of institutions in weak financial positions. Following the deregulation of the 1980s, the expansion of credit and asset price inflation, and subsequent collapse of asset prices and some large corporate borrowers, a significant portion of the banking sector needed recapitalization. Several building societies collapsed, as did some merchant banks and life offices, while inadequacies in the structure of several unit trusts were shown up – leading to an imposed freezing of funds in unlisted (open-ended) property trusts pending their eventual conversion to listed (closed-end) form.

Gizycki and Lowe (2000, p. 181) comment that Australia was 'probably fortunate that it did not experience a more profound episode of financial instability' and resolution of banking sector problems proceeded relatively smoothly, with sell-offs of state government banks, and equity raisings by major banks which had posted large losses.[18] The Reserve Bank commenced on-site inspections of bank credit systems in 1992 (and of their market risk systems in 1994), improved reporting of impaired assets was required, and the role of auditors and directors regarding risk management was clarified. Building societies, credit unions and friendly societies were brought under a consistent national regulatory scheme and supervision increased in intensity. Risk-based capital standards were introduced for building societies and credit unions in 1992, official vetting of risk-management policies was introduced, and amalgamations involving smaller and/or weaker institutions were encouraged. The ISC introduced risk-based capital requirements for life insurance offices in 1995.

Consequently, there was a major increase in the capitalization of financial firms in Australia, together with a significant degree of financial innovation in terms of developing alternative financial instruments to straight equity which meet capital adequacy requirements.

The introduction of risk-based capital adequacy requirements has had a major influence upon the activities of financial institutions. In particular, in conjunction with deregulation, it has caused them to focus upon the appropriate pricing of various financial products to ensure an adequate expected return for the risk involved, and encouraged the development of risk-based performance measures and capital management policies.

Greater focus on corporate governance practices also occurred. It has already been noted that the problems following the deregulation of the early 1980s reflected the fact that regulatory constraints were removed from management of financial institutions and not immediately replaced by effective market-based monitoring and control mechanisms. Improvements in disclosure and internal management systems, and better articulation of directors' duties and accountability, are among the changes which have occurred to supplement the existing legal framework which protects the rights of shareholders.

Australia and Comparative International, and Best-practice Financial Regulation

International organizations such as the Basel Committee, the International Organization of Securities Commissions (IOSCO), International Association of Insurance Supervisors (IAIS), the Organization for Economic Cooperation and Development (OECD), the International Monetary Fund (IMF) and the World Bank have been active in recent years in producing checklists and guidelines for good regulatory practice in financial markets. The Basel Committee, for example, has released documents setting out 'core principles' (Basel Committee, 1997), and articulated a 'three pillars' policy (Basel Committee, 1999) for financial regulation involving minimum capital requirements, the supervisory review process and an enhanced disclosure framework.

The Basel Committee has set out its view on preconditions for effective regulation which can be summarized as: sound macroeconomic policies; well-developed public infrastructure; effective market disciplines; and mechanisms which provide systemic protection. The comparison between Australia at the start of the twenty-first century and the deregulatory period of the 1980s could not be starker.

In the 1980s, macroeconomic policies were undermined by continued fiscal imbalance and inadequate monetary indicators, although labour market policies had contributed to the containment of inflation. Now, monetary policy has a clear inflation objective and a *modus operandi* of market operations (including foreign exchange swaps) to achieve an announced target for the short-term interest rate, conducted by an independent Reserve Bank. Fiscal stability is in place, with ongoing budgetary surpluses and clearly articulated arrangements for government-financing activities, including a Charter of Budget Honesty and introduction of accrual accounting. In these regards, Australian experience parallels international developments in central banking over the past 25 years, noted by the BIS (1997, p. 143) as involving 'a greater emphasis on transparency, market incentives and the credibility of policies', with the last of these factors reflected in greater central bank autonomy and accountability, and specification of clearer goals for policy.

In the 1980s, the supervisory structure was inadequate, although accounting standards and the legal infrastructure were adequate (although capable of improvement). Now, the supervisory structure has been reformed, the CLERP reforms are in train (focused upon legal and accounting reform) and disclosure and reporting by financial institutions greatly improved. Market discipline has increased through activities of ratings agencies and because capital market assessment of performance is now applicable to a far greater proportion of the financial sector, due both to changes in organizational forms to listed companies and to greater use of debt market funding.

Kane (2001) provides comparative international information on relevant indicators of financial system integrity. On the 'quality of economic information' criteria, based on accounting standards, levels of corruption and press restrictions, Australia scores relatively well among high-income countries. (These figures relate primarily to the first half of the 1990s.) Similarly, on indicators of counterparty protection, Australia again rates well.

Systemic stability responsibility is specifically allocated to the Reserve Bank which has lender of last resort powers and system liquidity management ability, although management of the exit of troubled institutions is the responsibility of APRA. Although these arrangements have not been put to the test, the ability of the Australian financial system to come through the Asian financial crisis of 1997–98 largely unscathed was a positive sign that the reforms of the 1990s had strengthened the financial system. In that respect, Australia was perhaps doubly fortunate, since absence of a deposit insurance scheme would have been viewed negatively by the IMF, which regards explicit deposit insurance as a necessary feature for a well-functioning financial system (Garcia, 2000).

APRA has conducted a self-assessment exercise against the core principles for banking supervision articulated by the Basle Committee, and believes that Australia is non-compliant on only two of the 25 principles.

Those areas of non-compliance involve the absence of a 'fit and proper' test for bank directors and managers (which is planned for introduction) and lack of supervisory oversight of foreign banks operating as merchant banks (who cannot take retail deposits without a prospectus) in Australia. In terms of regulatory standards and approach, APRA adheres quite closely to the Basle (and IAIS) standards of risk-weighted capital requirements, a two-tier approach to risk measurement and management (relying on agreed use of acceptable internal models for risk management and specification of a required method otherwise), and emphasis on disclosure, accountability and governance.

The Payments System Board (2000) also undertook a stocktake of Australia's high-value payments system against a separate set of 'core principles' for systemically important payments systems (CPSS, 2000) and concluded that it scored high. Particularly important for meeting those principles was the introduction of the RTGS in July 1998 and associated legal changes under the Payments System and Netting Act (1998). In the area of foreign exchange settlement arrangements, Australia is participating in the Continuous Linked Settlement (CLS) initiative, which aims to further reduce settlements risk.

Barth et al. (2001) illustrate vividly that regulatory systems differ markedly around the world, and have constructed several indices characterizing regulatory systems. It is noticeable that Australia ranks very high on their index of 'private monitoring' reflecting partly the absence of a deposit insurance scheme, and the assumption that this provides incentives for such monitoring. Also noticeable are the relatively high rankings on 'overall capital stringency' (reflecting the incorporation of some market valuation information into capital requirements), 'overall official supervisory power', and 'restructuring power'. In contrast, the ranking is low on the index of 'prompt corrective action' (since there is no legally imposed solvency trigger which requires action) and high on an index of 'forbearance and discretion'. The overall impression is that, internationally, APRA has a relatively high degree of authority and freedom to exercise discretion in the use of that power.

On Barth et al.'s (2001) index of 'overall bank activities and ownership restrictiveness' (based on 1999 data) Australia appears as a moderately restrictive regime by international standards. This reflects a combination of prudentially based restrictions on bank involvement in property development and direct equity interests in non-financial activities, some impediments to takeovers (the four pillars policy), maximum shareholding restrictions, preclusion of foreign banks from retail deposit markets unless a subsidiary is created, and restrictions on financial conglomerate structures[19] and on conglomerates involving both finance and commerce. Since then, APRA has released guidelines on allowable organizational forms and activities for financial conglomerates and replaced restrictions on property and business activities with prudential standards for equity associations which permit such activities and link them into the risk-weighted capital requirements approach. The ranking on this index has thus probably already changed.

5 ASSESSING THE EFFECTS OF FINANCIAL REFORM IN AUSTRALIA

Financial reform is undertaken (presumably) because it is believed to be in the social interest – although it is hard to ignore the multiplicity of private self-interests which influence the reform process and direction. In that regard, the public examination of past experience and assessment of alternative future directions by major official inquiries (Campbell, Wallis and several other less-comprehensive reviews) is a positive characteristic of the reform process in Australia. However, in reviewing the outcome, costs and benefits of regulatory reform may be hard to identify precisely and harder still to quantify.

The Financial Supervisory Authority in the United Kingdom has placed great emphasis on undertaking cost–benefit analysis of regulatory reform. Alfon and Andrews (1999) suggest six main impacts of regulatory change which can generate costs and/or benefits. These are: direct costs; compliance costs; product quantity adjustments; product quality adjustments; product variety changes; and changes in the efficiency of competition.

Where wholesale regulatory reform has been undertaken, such as in Australia, the ability to utilize such techniques is limited. Cost–benefit analysis of a change to one piece of legislation is feasible, but when many regulations are being changed the interrelationships between them make calculations infeasible. Consequently, it is necessary to look to more general indicators of costs and benefits. Among such indicators might be such things as growth of the financial sector, improvements in operating efficiency of the financial sector, evidence of increased competition, evidence of increased innovation and absence of systemic problems.

Unfortunately, interpretation of movement in such indicators of improved financial sector performance as evidence of the effects of financial reform is confounded by the effects of ongoing technological change, real sector developments and so on. Nevertheless, it is worth perusing such indicators for evidence consistent with the hypothesis that financial reform has had beneficial effects.

Battellino (2000) examines four broad areas consistent with those mentioned above in which it would be expected that financial reform would affect the financial sector and bring social benefits.[20] First, growth and increasing financial sophistication of the financial sector could be expected as the repressive effects of regulation were removed and opportunities for profitable innovation (other than that to evade regulations) were increased. There are no simple indicators of 'financial sophistication' or 'innovativeness' available, but there are numerous examples of a more innovative and sophisticated system. These include an explosion in the range of retail financial products available, introduction of innovative corporate securities, growth of securitization, funds management and mortgage origination, strong growth in futures and derivatives markets, and development of sophisticated risk-management techniques within financial institutions.

The second indicator which might be considered relevant is that of an increased size of the financial sector relative to the economy. Figure 1.1 and

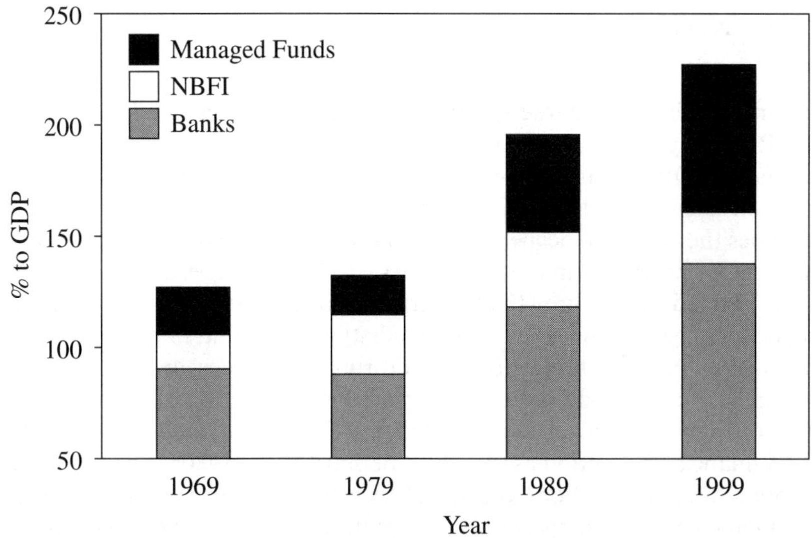

Sources: RBA, 'Australian Economic Statistics 1949–50 to 1996–97', Occasional Paper No. 8, http: //www.rba.gov.au/Statistics/op 8_index.html; RBA, *Reserve Bank Bulletin*, Table B01, http: //www.rba.gov.au/Statistics/Bulletin/index.html#table_b.

Figure 1.1 Financial institutions: total assets as a percentage of GDP

Table 1.4 provide such information. As shown in Figure 1.1, the total assets of financial institutions have increased relative to GDP quite markedly since the start of the 1980s, with the growth coinciding with the process of financial reform. Table 1.4 indicates that similar growth in activity has

Table 1.4 Financial market turnover

	A$m. per day	
	1985	1999
Equities	50	1,000
Equity futures	100	2,000
Bonds	1,000	4,000
Bond futures	100	7,000
Money market securities	600	7,000
Money market futures	1,000	30,000
Repurchase agreements	200	15,000
Foreign exchange	5,000	77,000
Memo item: Nominal GDP (A$m. pa)	230,000	600,000

Source: Battellino (2000).

occurred in financial markets, with turnover increasing markedly relative to GDP. Among developed nations, Australia's ratio of financial institution assets to GDP is in the mid-range, while financial market turnover ratios are consistent with the size of the economy.[21] Other relevant evidence includes the 'financial deepening' evidenced in the growth in size of household sector portfolios in the 1990s (see Gizycki and Lowe, 2000).

A third indicator is growth of securities market financing techniques and funds management relative to intermediation, reflecting improvements in disclosure, investor protection, monitoring techniques and consequent willingness of ultimate savers to bear market and credit risk. This can be seen in Figure 1.1, which shows the increased share of funds managers in total financial institution assets since the start of the 1980s. Again relative to other developed nations, the mix of securities markets versus intermediary financing is mid-range. However, significant recent growth in corporate bond financing, mortgage origination and securitization, together with increased emphasis on private provision for retirement saving, suggest that securities markets will grow further in relative importance.

Finally, financial reform could be expected to have led to increased efficiency within the Australian financial sector, with competitive pressures reducing costs and profit margins. The evidence on this score is mixed, and confounded by changes in risk taking by financial institutions following deregulation and consequent changes in required rates of return (profit rates) to compensate for such risk taking. To the extent that efficiency gains from financial reform in the banking sector have occurred, those benefits appear to relate primarily to the latter half of the 1990s. Gizycki and Lowe

(2000, p. 180) looking back at writings from 1991 comment that 'At the time, there was a sense that liberalisation had promised much, but delivered relatively little, other than a speculative property boom and a lot of wasted assets'. More recently, there is some evidence of declining margins in banking, although rates of return on equity remain high.

An alternative perspective on efficiency changes can be gained from an examination of Figure 1.2. Employment in the financial sector has

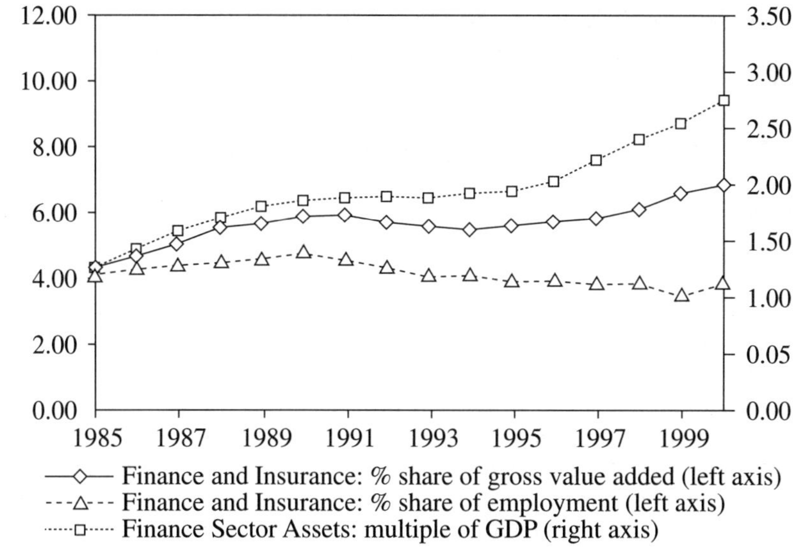

Sources: Australian Bureau of Statistics, *Australian National Accounts: National Income, Expenditure and Product*, Cat. No. 5206.0, Table 15: Industry Gross Valued Added, Australian Bureau of Statistics, *Labour Force Employed – Industry – Australia – Quarterly*, Cat. No. 6291.0, Table 9I: *Labour Force – Employed Persons – Australia – Total – Industry*, RBA, *Reserve Bank Bulletin*, Table B1: Total Assets of Financial Institutions, RBA, 'Australian Economic Statistics 1949–50 to 1996–97': Occasional Paper No. 8, 3, Table 4a: *Total Assets of Financial Institutions*.

Figure 1.2 Indicators of finance sector importance

declined, despite massive growth in financial sector assets. Such improved labour efficiency is consistent with financial reform increasing competitive pressures, but also reflects improvements in technology and communications which have dramatically affected the methods of delivery of financial services. Also shown is the contribution of the financial sector to GDP. This has increased much less than the increase in the asset size of the financial sector. Such an outcome could be interpreted as reflecting the effects of increased competition and technological improvements and declining costs and usage of labour in the sector, with efficiency gains being passed on to customers via improved prices, rather than showing up as increased profits and value added.

6 CONCLUSION

Financial reform in Australia has occurred on a grand scale since the start of the 1980s. Initially focused on (primarily bank) deregulation and in the absence of the necessary preconditions for reliance on market mechanisms, the experience of the 1980s was less than satisfactory. In the past decade, those inadequacies have been systematically rectified, enabling the development of a 'contract-based' rather than 'rule-based' approach[22] which increasingly underpins contemporary thinking on optimal regulatory approaches. By international standards, the Australian regulatory system appears to accord closely with world 'best practices' espoused by international agencies. Nevertheless, there are a number of distinct features of the Australian approach which have been identified in this chapter, and which constitute potential weaknesses warranting continued scrutiny.

First, the Australian approach (like that of New Zealand[23]) is marked by the absence of explicit deposit insurance and explicit disavowal of government guarantees of bank deposits – despite the apparent acceptance that it is important that some 'risk-free haven' should exist for unsophisticated investors. Separation of the prudential regulator (APRA) from the central bank is partly premised on a view that such a structure will reduce public perceptions of government guarantees. It is not clear that explicit deposit insurance is the appropriate form of 'safety net' in all circumstances (Kane, 2001), although this is the IMF view of best practice (Garcia, 2000). Its absence, however, can be argued to be a potential impediment to competition if market monitoring is weak or if perceptions of 'too big to fail' persist despite government denials of ultimate support for failing institutions.

In that regard, the continuing distinction between banks and other ADIs even though both are subject to the same regulation raises concerns about the implications for competition. Use of the label 'bank' is restricted to larger institutions (Tier 1 capital in excess of A$50 million is required). Accepting that such a label is valuable (that is, that it signifies something special to the general public) thus creates a distinction between larger and smaller depository institutions which could be inimical to the entry and activities of smaller institutions and thus have adverse competitive effects.

Second, there is an interesting juxtaposition in the approach to prudential regulation of substantial regulator discretion (regarding when and how to take action over troubled institutions) and absence of regulatory fiscal responsibility for losses incurred from regulatory forbearance. The implications of such arrangements for regulatory incentives towards forbearance warrant further study.

Third, arrangements for dealing with cases of systemic stability create potentially interesting problems. Institutions viewed as solvent by APRA, but facing systemic liquidity crises, would presumably get access to discount window facilities and lender of last resort loans at the RBA. This suggests the possibility of some interesting regulatory interrelationships if the market value of assets of the institution receiving support turned out to be less than initially thought. Lender of last resort loans would presumably be secured against particular assets of the troubled institution, but would also presumably rank behind depositor claims. In that regard, lender of last resort loans could turn out, *ex post*, to be little different from the put option over a bank's assets which depositors hold under a system of government guarantees. The critical difference, of course, is that access to that put option would be conditional on APRA (and the RBA) misjudging the underlying worth of the bank's assets and liabilities.

Fourth, the Australian approach involves a mix of both functional and institutional approaches to regulation. Prudential regulation is premised on the view that certain economic functions or financial products are worthy of protection, but the regulatory focus is upon the health of the institutions which provide those products. The extension of benefits and costs of official supervision to the whole of the institution's activities, rather than just those activities warranting attention, would seem to be unnecessary when other alternatives (such as 'narrow banking' proposals) could be considered.

Fifth, the Australian approach is marked by a somewhat cautious approach to the likelihood of a competitive environment emerging from an unrestricted entry and ownership policy in financial markets. Whether such restrictions as currently exist are socially benign, since interested parties can typically undertake the desired activities through some alternative institutional arrangements, or whether they inhibit competitive forces and the ability of institutions to exploit economies of scale or scope, is an open question.

Finally, the Australian system appears somewhat atypical internationally in that the prudential regulator (APRA) is financed by levies upon the institutions it regulates.[24] The merits of such an approach to regulatory financing, in particular the implications for whether the level of funding provided for supervision is optimal (or socially preferable to those which would arise from other funding mechanisms), have yet to be fully explored.

NOTES

* I am grateful to the editor, Christine Brown, and officials of the Reserve Bank of Australia for comments on an earlier version.
1. Detailed analyses of the development of the Australian financial system and its regulation can be found in Lewis and Wallace (1997) and previous books in that series. See also: Grenville (1991), the Wallis Inquiry (1997), Edey and Gray (1996), Battellino (2000) and Gizycki and Lowe (2000).
2. Davis and Lewis (1980) provide an overview of monetary policy and developments in the financial system over this period.
3. Regulation of the previously unregulated general insurance company sector, in which 16 institutions collapsed between 1970 and 1973, occurred with the passage of the Insurance Act in 1973.
4. Lewis (1997) provides a useful historical overview of inquiries into the Australian financial system.
5. Its responsibilities were extended to include friendly societies in 1997.
6. Tax reform was also a major issue, culminating in the introduction of a 10 per cent Goods and Services Tax in July 2000.
7. Goldsworthy et al. (2000) interpret the new regulatory structure in this way, although their definition of 'functional', which relates to causes of market failure (as used in the paragraph below), differs from the more common usage of that term as popularized by Merton (1995).
8. This difficulty is apparent in public reaction to the failure of a general insurance company (HIH) and expectations of the regulator's responsibilities. See APRA (2001).
9. Prior to that time, central banking functions had been undertaken by the government-owned Commonwealth Bank of Australia which also conducted trading and savings banking activities in competition with the rest of the banking sector.
10. APRA's Objectives and Funding, http://www.apra.gov.au/CorporateInfo/APRA objectivesfunding.pdf.
11. The Australian Tax Office is responsible for regulating small, self-managed, superannuation funds.
12. This practice was sometimes justified on the grounds that it was a substitute for bank licence fees and/or compensation for the cost of prudential supervision and resultant benefits to the banking sector.
13. Sixteen applicants were given approval (although only four or five licences had been expected to be granted) and 15 of the successful applicants took up the licences.
14. A conglomerate group including an ADI must be either headed by an ADI or a non-operating holding company, or by an approved foreign entity, and can involve non-financial activities.
15. Government insurance businesses have also been privatized.
16. A joint investigation by the RBA and ACCC into interchange fees and access arrangements for credit and debit cards concluded that competition and pricing practices were less than optimal (RBA, 2000).
17. See Treasury (2001).
18. Several smaller banks experienced significant deposit outflows which were stemmed following Reserve Bank pronouncements about the financial strength of those institutions.
19. Historically, life insurance companies were allowed by the ISC to engage in other (non-financial) activities, whereas the RBA put strict limits on banking groups doing so. The RBA also adopted an 'umbrella' approach to bank-holding company structure, requiring the bank itself to be the holding company.
20. Davis (1997) also provides an overview.
21. Battellino (2000) provides information on turnover figures on a 'world league table' basis.
22. 'At the risk of gross over-simplification, there are two general and alternative approaches to regulation. At one end of the spectrum the regulator lays down fairly precise regulatory requirements that are applied to all regulated firms. While there may be limited

differentiations within the rules, the presumption is for a high degree of uniformity. At the other end of the spectrum is . . . Contract Regulation. Under this regime, the regulator sets down a clear set of objectives and general principles. It is then for each regulated firm to demonstrate to the regulator how these objectives and principles are to be satisfied by its own chosen procedures.' (Llewellyn, 1999 p. 49).

23. See Davis (1999) for a comparison of Australian and New Zealand financial reform.
24. The Reserve Bank, on the other hand, is financed by seigniorage from the note issue, trading profits, and fees from provision of banking services, and is required to remit a dividend to the government.

REFERENCES

Alfon, I. and P. Andrews (1999), 'Cost–benefit analysis in financial regulation – how to do it and how it adds value', Financial Services Authority Occasional Paper Series 3, September.

Australian Prudential Regulation Authority (APRA) (2001), 'HIH insurance – APRA's role revisited', Media Release, Friday 20 April, No. 01.13 http://www.apra.gov.au/mediareleases/01_13.htm.

Bank for International Settlements (BIS) (1997), *67th Annual Report, 1st April 1996–31st March 1997*, Basel: Bank for International Settlements, 9 June.

Barth, J.R., G. Caprio Jr and R. Levin (2001), 'The regulation and supervision of banks around the world: a new database', World Bank Working Paper 2588, http://econ.worldbank.org/view.php?type=5&id=1697.

Basel Committee (1997), 'Core principles for effective banking supervision', Basel Committee Publications No. 30, Basel: Bank for International Settlements, http://www.bis.org/publ/bcbs 30a.htm.

Basel Committee (1999), 'A new capital adequacy framework', Basel Committee Publications No. 50, Basel: Bank for International Settlements, http://www.bis.org/publ/bcbs 50.htm.

Battellino, R. (2000), 'Australian financial markets: looking back and looking ahead', *Reserve Bank of Australia Bulletin*, March, 16–25, http://www.rba.gov.au/Speeches/2000/bu_0300_3.pdf.

Committee of Inquiry into the Australian Financial System (1981), *Australian Financial System: Final Report of the Committee of Inquiry* (K. Campbell, Chairman), Canberra: AGPS.

Committee on Payment and Settlement Systems (CPSS) (2000), 'Core principles for systemically important payment systems', CPSS Publications No. 34, Basel: Bank for International Settlements, http://www.bis.org/publ/cpss 34e.htm.

Cull, R. (2001), 'Financial-sector reform: what works and what doesn't', *Economic Development and Cultural Change*, **49** (2); 269–91.

Davis, K. (1997), 'Financial Restructuring in Australia', *Economic Papers*, **16** (2), June, 1–18.

Davis, K. (1999), 'Reform of Australian and New Zealand financial markets', Chapter 11 in G. de Brouwer and W. Pupphavesa (eds), *Asia Pacific Financial Deregulation*, London and New York: Routledge, 241–64.

Davis, K. and M.K. Lewis (1980), *Monetary Policy in Australia*, Melbourne: Longman Cheshire.

Edey, M. and B. Gray (1996), 'The evolving structure of the Australian financial system', Reserve Bank of Australia Research Discussion Paper RDP9605.

Garcia, G. (2000), 'Deposit insurance and crisis management', International Monetary Fund Working Paper WP/00/57, http://www.imf.org/external/pubs/ft/wp/2000/wp 0057.pdf.

Gizycki, M. and P. Lowe (2000), 'The Australian financial system in the 1990s', in *The Australian Economy in the 1990s*, Sydney: Reserve Bank of Australia.

Goldsworthy, B., D. Lewis, and G. Shuetrim (2000), 'APRA and the financial system Inquiry', APRA Working Paper 3, http://www.apra.gov.au/policy/research/working_papers/wp 0003.pdf.

Grenville, S. (1991), 'The evolution of financial deregulation', in I. Macfarlane (ed.), *The Deregulation of Financial Intermediaries*, Sydney: Reserve Bank of Australia, http://www.rba.gov.au/FinancialSystemStability/financial_publications.html.

Hockey, J. (2001), 'MP Minister for Financial Services and Regulation Addressing the CEDA luncheon', 2 February, Melbourne, http://www.minfsr.treasury.gov.au/content/speeches/2001/002.asp.

Kane, E. (2001), 'Financial safety nets: reconstructing and modeling a policy metaphor', National Bureau of Economic Research Working Paper 8224, http://dsl.nber.org/papers/w8224.pdf.

Lewis, M.K. (1997), 'The Wallis Inquiry: its place in the evolution of the Australian financial system', *Accounting Forum*, **21** (2), September, 229–53.

Lewis, M.K. and R.H. Wallace (eds) (1997), *The Australian Financial System: Evolution and Practice*, Melbourne: Addison-Wesley Longman.

Llewellyn, D. (1999), 'The economic rationale for financial regulation', Financial Services Authority Occasional Paper Series 1, April.

Merton, Robert C. (1995), 'A functional perspective of financial intermediation', *Financial Management*, **24** (2), Summer, 23–42.

Payments System Board (2000), *Annual Report*, Sydney: Reserve Bank of Australia, http://www.rba.gov.au/PublicationsAndResearch/Annual_Reports/Payments_System_2000/index.html.

Reserve Bank of Australia (RBA) (2000), 'Debit and credit card schemes in Australia: a study of interchange fees and access', http://www.rba.gov.au/PublicationsAndResearch/Occasional_Papers_And_Other_Publications/Interchange_Fees_Study.pdf.

Thompson, G. and B. Gray (2000), 'Supervising financial institutions and conglomerates', in C. Cassidy (ed.), *Risk and Capital Management: Proceedings of a Conference*, Sydney: Australian Prudential Regulation Authority, http://www.apra.gov.au/policy/conference_papers 1/ConfVol.pdf.

Treasury (2001), 'Corporate law economic reform program: policy framework', http://www.treasury.gov.au/publications/Bills,ActsAndLegislation/CorporateLawEconomicReformProgram/index.asp#Policy Framework.

Wallis Inquiry (1997), *Final Report*, Canberra: Australian Information Service, http://www.treasury.gov.au/publications/FinancialSystemInquiry(WallisReport)/index.asp.

2. Price stabilization, the banking crisis and financial reform in Brazil

Roberto Luis Troster

1 INTRODUCTION

This chapter focuses on the influence of stabilization policy on Brazilian banking in the 1994–98 period and the financial reforms that accompanied it. A new stabilization plan, *Plano Real*, rapidly curbed inflation from 40 per cent a month in early 1994 to less than 2 per cent a year in 1998. Besides stopping the price spiral, Plano Real promoted a considerable change in the economy. All sectors were deeply affected by it. My aim is to analyse what happened to the banking sector.

Following the fall in inflation, the country as a whole endured a significant structural change. One of the sectors most affected was the banking sector. Before the plan, Brazil had 243 banks; afterwards, 42 were liquidated by the central bank, 34 had their control transferred, or their assets sold, and 28 lost their banking charter. In other words, roughly 43 per cent of all existing banks before stabilization either changed hands or ceased to exist in a time span of less than five years. Besides that, there were changes in the structure of the banking sector.

It is my understanding that stabilization, *ceteris paribus*, contributes to banking sector development, but even so, Brazilian banking faced its worst crisis just after stabilization. The main conclusion is that a considerable part of the obstacles faced were due to an inappropriate banking policy, and even though many of the problems have been solved, some remain. The purpose of this chapter is to throw some light on to this subject. Understanding what happened is important to avoid repeating some of the problems in the future.

The rest of this chapter is subdivided as follows. Section 2: Background – the macroeconomic and banking background and an overview of the system and recent changes; Section 3: Stabilization issues – the effects of stabilization on banking, the overbanking issue and how to measure it; Section 4: The three waves of the banking crisis – what happened to the banking system; and Section 5: Reactions to the crises and the aftermath – what was done to correct the problems and what happened afterwards. Section 6 offers some concluding remarks.

2 BACKGROUND

Macroeconomic Background

Economic volatility has been present in Brazil since its foundation. Cycles of impressive growth have been followed by deep recession and are common throughout the history of the country, although, after the late 1970s, the upsides of the cycles were very limited. At the end of the 1960s, GDP increased in the 10 per cent per year range, and in the whole decade of the 1980s it practically stopped. The economic performance of the country in the early 1970s, called the 'Brazilian Miracle', was notorious. It was followed by what is known as the 'Lost Decade', the 1980s. In the early 1990s, the economic accomplishments were also poor. (See Table 2.1.)

Table 2.1 GDP growth in Brazil

	1987	1988	1989	1990	1991	1992	1993	1994
GDP growth % p.a.	3.50	−0.10	3.20	−4.35	1.03	−0.54	4.92	5.85

Source: Instituto Brasileiro de Geografia e Estatística (IBGE), 1994.

The main reason for the poor performance was the government's inability to control the price spiral. Brazil has experienced double-digit inflation during the last 30 years – in some years there was triple-digit inflation and in others it was above 1,000 per cent a year (see Table 2.2). On 1 July 1994, Brazil issued its seventh stabilization plan in less than a decade, which succeeded in bringing down inflation from a level of 40 per cent per month in June 1994 to 1.4 per cent in 1998. Inflation in the whole year of 1998 was smaller than in some single days in 1994. The price stabilization was welcomed by Brazilians, and was the basic reason for the re-election of President Fernando Cardoso in 1998.

Plano Real represented a sharp change in economic policy. Even though the introduction of a new currency, the real, took place in July 1994, there were some changes before that. The first important modification took place on 9 September 1993; the transferring of responsibility for external debt from the central bank to the treasury. That was needed to give more operational independence to monetary policy.

Table 2.2 Inflation: consumer price index (CPI) in Brazil

	1992	1993	1994	1995	1996	1997	1998	1999
CPI – Year %	965	1,920	2,149	67.3	16.5	6.4	1.4	8.0

Source: Fundação Instituto de Pesquisas Econômicas (FIPE).

The next step was the introduction of a constitutional amendment, on 24 February 1994, to change some aspects of fiscal legislation in order to achieve a fiscal accounts balance. Immediately afterwards, the URV (Unit of Reference Value) was introduced. This was a combination of existing indices of inflation, and its purpose was to synchronize all price readjustments. It existed from 1 March to 30 June 1994. On 1 July, the real was introduced, displacing the cruzeiro real at a fixed rate of R$1= CR$2,750.00.

The inflation on the new currency was markedly lower than before. But even so, a firm monetary policy was a characteristic of the plan during the following years; interest rates were always high in the period after 1994, to prevent inflationary pressures, or to avoid exchange rate devaluation demands, or even to fight off speculative attacks. In most countries the basic interest rates have recently been under 10 per cent a year; in Brazil, the average basic rate has always been over 20 per cent a year since the beginning of *Plano Real*. (See Table 2.3.)

Table 2.3 Basic interest rate in Brazil

	1994	1995	1996	1997	1998	1999
Basic rate (CDI*) p.a. %	51	35	21	35	31	25

Note: *CDI stands for the interbank deposit rate.

Source: Banco Central do Brasil.

Fiscal policy was also tight, but only in the first year. The fiscal results for 1994 showed an improvement over the previous year. The result was obtained with an impressive growth in government revenues. From 1995 on, the budget deficit increased, in spite of the numerous announcements of fiscal tightening (although, in 1999, things changed after the devaluation crisis).

In 1994, a revaluation of the national currency was needed to brake inflation and discourage indexation. As a result of the revaluation of the real, combined with the increase in economic activity and a lowering of tariffs, imports grew and the trade balance registered a deficit that increased over the following years. Exports showed a very modest performance, but imports registered explosive growth (see Table 2.4). The medium-term result of the currency appreciation and rising fiscal deficits was the external crisis at the beginning of 1999.

Table 2.4 Trade balance in Brazil (US$ million)

	1994	1995	1996	1997	1998	1999
Trade balance	10,466	−3,352	−5,554	−8,357	−6,430	−1,213
Exports	43,545	46,506	47,747	52,990	51,120	48,011
Imports	33,079	49,858	53,301	61,347	57,550	49,224

Source: Banco Central do Brasil.

The most convincing payoff of the *Plano Real* was the complete deindexation of the economy. Until July 1994, almost every price or contract had an index attached to it. Although the official currency was the cruzeiro, prices were expressed in a variety of indexes. In spite of a legal prohibition, the dollar was used as a reference for many prices and budgets; even government figures were expressed in American dollars. The innovative combination of indexing all prices to one index – the URV – the appreciation of the real (depreciation of the dollar) and changes in the existing regulation eliminated, in a short span of time, three decades of indexation. The market now sets even long-term contracts, such as salaries and rents.

The almost five years of gradualism of *Plano Real* were punctuated by three shocks. The first shock was rather mild and came from a spillover of the Mexican devaluation on 20 December 1994. The second was a reflection of the Asian crisis in the second half of 1997; and the third started in August 1998 with the Russian default and caused the strong devaluation of the real in January 1999. They should not have come as a complete surprise, for some economic analysts had been warning about the effects that could result from the combination of turmoil in the international markets combined with the leniency of Brazilian fiscal and external policies.

Nevertheless, Brazil has shown positive results since 1994: inflation has ended, investment has increased, the country has enjoyed moderate growth, many enterprises have been privatized, there has been an opening up of the economy and market mechanisms now play a more important role. On the other hand, the solutions to substantial problems, such as the labour, social security and tax reforms, have been postponed.

Banking in Brazil

The first Brazilian banks were established in the early 1800s, and until 1964 were basically focused on typical short-term commercial banking activities. The number and economic importance of financial institutions was determined by the level of economic activity in the rest of the economy. Economic booms came hand in hand with rising banking activities, and were followed by recessions and financial crises. In 1964, a new regulation changed the basic characteristics of banking in the country. Brazil was to have a segmented financial system and a regulatory structure similar to the United States, with some adaptations: a special role for the state banks, a bigger-banks bias and a closed system.

An important event for the future of banking took place in 1988, when the new Constitution for Brazil, in its Article 192 stated that from that date there would be no barriers to entry in the financial sector. Until then, each type of institution, branch and permitted activities had a set number of 'points' that had to be 'purchased' to enter the system. The total number of points was fixed. The system functioned as an oligopoly, where entrance and exit had a price set by the cost of gaining the points. Banks enjoyed a goodwill that was their authorization to function; branches were bought and closed sometimes merely for the right to open a branch elsewhere. As the new constitution abolished the points system, the barrier to entry was taken away, and the number of banks rose rapidly. While in 1988 there were 106 banks, two years later the number of banks had more than doubled, to 216 (see Table 2.5).

Table 2.5 Number of banks in Brazil

Year	No. of banks	Year	No. of banks	Year	No. of banks
1964	336	1980	112	1992	234
1966	313	1982	115	1993	243
1968	231	1984	110	1994	246
1970	178	1986	105	1995	242
1972	128	1988	106	1996	231
1974	109	1989	179	1997	217
1976	106	1990	216	1998	203
1978	107	1991	225	1999	193

Source: Banco Central do Brasil.

The table reflects the transformation the system had undergone after the stabilization programme. The Brazilian banking system had, on 31 December 1997, a net worth of R$45.3 billion (US$1 ≈ R$1.7) and comprised 217 banks, of which one-fifth were foreign banks, one-sixth were state banks, and the remaining were private banks. The system had 24,671 branches and it employed 463,330 people directly. It also had 42.4 million sight deposit accounts and 52.1 million savings accounts. By December 1998, the number of banks had fallen to 203, and over 1,000 branches were closed in 1998.

On the other hand, Brazil has a very dynamic and sophisticated financial system. Its futures trading exchange (Bolsa Mercantil e de Futuros: BM&F) is, by contract volume, the fourth largest in the world, and it has a payment system, on real time, which links the whole country instantly. On the other hand, the market share of public banks is very high, and the system is inefficient. Besides the formal banking system, Brazil also has an informal system of credit through pre-dated cheques.

The banking system is mostly focused on retail banking, where public banks play an important role. Productivity comparisons are, however, a little distorted; as wages are comparatively lower in Brazil than in other countries, activities are more labour intensive than in other countries. (See Table 2.6.)

Table 2.6 Selected indicators of banking systems

	Country			
Indicator	Netherlands	Korea	USA	Brazil
Public banks' deposit share (%)	0	12	0	60
Top 3 banks' deposit share (%)	77	14	10	57
Retail banking employment (%)	48	55	60	92
Banked population (%)	76	70	74	20–23
Banking labour productivity (%)	148	71	100	40
Non-electronic transactions (%)	12	72	71	81
Clients per branch	2,500	1,600	2,350	1,300/1,950

Source: McKinsey Global Institute (1998).

3 STABILIZATION ISSUES

Analysis of the effects of stabilization policies – to reduce inflation – on the banking system is central to understanding what happened after July 1994 in Brazil. There are basically three points to discuss: (i) what the effects are; (ii) how they are to be measured, and (iii) whether Brazil underbanked or overbanked before stabilization.

The central bank stated explicitly that stabilization would shrink the banking system and that Brazil was overbanked. According to this diagnosis, it was necessary to smooth the transition through regulations that would foster a contraction of the banking sector. On the other hand, if the central bank was wrong, the new regulations would displace banks unnecessarily from the market, and this might trigger a financial crisis. A wrong policy response would cause perverse effects.

The government's diagnosis implied that the number of banks in Brazil had to diminish and that the participation of banks in GDP would shrink with stabilization. The basis for the diagnosis was the correlation of financial participation in GDP on the previous years (see Table 2.7), and the fall in the number of banks in the stabilization process in the late 1960s.

Table 2.7 Financial participation in GDP in Brazil

	1988	1989	1990	1991	1992	1993	1994	1995
Financial participation GDP (%)	16.8	26.5	12.8	10.5	12.1	15.6	12.4	6.94
Inflation (% p.a.)	628	1,304	2,737	416	969	1,996	2,240	77

Source: Instituto Brasileiro de Geografia e Estatística (IBGE).

Financial participation in GDP increased when inflation rose, and fell when the price spiral dropped. Thus, if price stabilization were to be achieved then the number of banks had to fall.

There are two misconceptions in the above reasoning, in that the number of banks and bank participation in GDP are poor estimators of banking sector size. Based upon these misconceptions, the banking policy adopted promoted a shrinkage of the system, thus triggering a banking crisis at a time when vigorous growth was expected.

Number of Banks

The first misconception is that the question of what is the optimal number of banks a country should have is poorly formulated. Even though there may be a positive correlation between size and the number of companies of a sector, there are other variables that have to be considered. The quality and quantity of services and products offered by the sector is what is relevant. Banking structures vary so much in different countries over time and even classifications of banking structures can vary (see Wilson, 1986).

The number of banks is not directly related to economic variables – while the United States has around 10,000 banks, in Brazil there are only 203 (as at December 1998), 50 times less. But Brazil has roughly the same territory as the United States, a little over one-tenth of its GDP and more than half its population. Banking has specific scopes in different countries. The number of banks is thus a combination of several factors: the size of the sector, scale and scope economies, regulation, technology, demographic factors, income distribution, location of economic activity, openness of the economy, cultural patterns of the population and so on. In other words, a correlation between the number of banks and inflation, and other economic variables is not meaningful.

Banking Anomaly in the National Accounts

The second point of this section is that in Brazil, bank participation in GDP is a poor indicator of its size. Some analysts argue that the Brazilian banking system was 'swollen' by inflation. They refer to the fact that national account statistics show that the financial system was responsible for 7.7 per cent of GDP in 1995, and that participation of the financial system in GDP reached 25 per cent in 1989, the appropriate number being assumed to be lower. Since interest – just like profits, rents and wages – is a payment for a productive factor, there is a distortion in the national accounting, known as the 'banking problem' or 'banking anomaly'.

The wrong interpretation gives rise to the misunderstandings in the Brazilian case. It is a very important issue, so important that the latest report on national accounting (CEC, IMF, OCDE, UN and World Bank, 1993) set, as an immediate priority, the development of practical procedures to allocate financial services in the national accounts. Basically, money and banks have very peculiar characteristics that distort the accounts. For a deeper analysis, see Troster, 1996; Mamalakis, 1987; Banco Central de la Republica Argentina (1994); Als, 1988; and Rymes, 1985 and 1986).

We shall illustrate the problem with just two imaginary sectors (Tables 2.8–11). From Table 2.8, it can be seen that:

Value added in GDP = Sales – Inputs = 1,000 – 200 = 800;
Value added in GDP = Factor payments = Wages + Rent + Net interest + Profits
= 200 + 200 + 200 + 200 = 800.

Table 2.8 Value-added calculations I

Restaurant 'Good Food'	Statement of income
Sales	1,000
(–) Inputs – Purchases of salt, bread . . .	200
(–) Wages	200
(–) Rent	200
(–) Net interest payments*	200
= Profits	200

Note: * Interest expense minus interest income (national accounts perspective).

Supposing that interest rates went up (Table 2.9), we would have the following figures:

Value added in GDP = Sales – Inputs = 1,000 – 200 = 800;
Value added in GDP = Factor payments = Wages + Rent + Net interest + Profits
= 200 + 200 + 300 + 100 = 800.

Table 2.9 Value-added calculations II

Restaurant 'Good Food'	Statement of income
Sales	1,000
(–) Inputs – Purchases of salt, bread . . .	200
(–) Wages	200
(–) Rent	200
(–) Net interest payments*	300
= Profits	100

Note: *Interest expense minus interest income (national accounts perspective).

We have the same result.

Making the same calculation for a bank (see Table 2.10) we have the results below:

Value added in GDP = Sales – Inputs = 0 – 20 = –20;
Value added in GDP = Factor payments = Wages + Rent + Net interest + Profits
= 200 + 200 – 600 + 180 = –20.

Table 2.10 Value-added calculations III

Bank 'Good Money'	Statement of income
Sales	0
(–) Inputs – Purchases of paper, clips . . .	20
(–) Wages	200
(–) Rent	200
(–) Net interest payments*	–600
= Profits	180

Note: *Interest expense minus interest income (national accounts perspective).

If interest rates rose (see Table 2.11), participation would remain the same:

Value added in GDP = Sales – Inputs = 0 – 20 = –20;
Value added in GDP = Factor payments = Wages + Rent + Net interest + Profits
= 200 + 200 – 700 + 280 = –20.

Table 2.11 Value-added calculations IV

Bank 'Good Money'	Statement of income
Sales	0
(−) Inputs − Purchases of paper, clips . . .	20
(−) Wages	200
(−) Rent	200
(−) Net interest payments*	700
= Profits	280

Note: *Interest expense minus interest income (national accounts perspective).

The example highlights an established fact in national accounting. Banking participation is calculated creating a virtual sector and then deducting it from the estimated GDP. The wrong analyses arise when the value of the virtual sector created is considered as real without the deductions. The point is that national accounting methodology cannot measure banking participation in GDP. In our examples, interest rates varied, profits changed but the banking participation remained the same and negative.

Banking Sector Size

As just argued, the number of banks and banking participation in GDP should not be used as an indicator of the size of the sector. As financial institutions are basically producers of services related with intermediation, the value of their assets – deposits, loans, total assets, net worth and so on – is used as a proxy for the sector's size. The economics literature, macroeconomic and microeconomic, uses a wealth variable to measure the size of the banking sector (see Santos & Troster, 1993 for a survey). The use of the wrong size indicator misleads the central bank in its diagnosis on the appropriate policy response after stabilization.

Using stock variables (credit, assets and so on) it can be seen that the Brazilian banking system was small when compared to other countries. Table 2.12 shows that, comparatively, Brazil has a low value for banking credit/GDP.

Inflation and Banking

The third point is the effect of inflation on banking. It is a popular belief that inflation benefits banks. Even though it is true in some contexts and for some specific sectors of banking intermediation, it is totally false in most situations and for most segments of its industry.

Table 2.12 Banking credit/GDP (%) 1991–1993

Country	Banking credit/GDP	Country	Banking credit/GDP	Country	Banking credit/GDP
Brazil	17.9	Venezuela	20.9	Singapore	63.2
China	99.0	Japan	139.1	Argentina	22.5
India	53.6	USA	80.5	Chile	60.8
Colombia	18.6	Indonesia	48.8	Thailand	75.5
Mexico	36.1	Malaysia	83.7	Korea	55.2

Source: Bank for International Settlements (1995).

It is important to stress that the impact of inflation on banks is not the same for all banks. Inflation dynamics vary, and impose different adaptations and distortions – indexation, overbranching, regulatory scale economies, distributive issues, monetary policy effectiveness and so on. The literature on the distortions caused by inflation on the financial system is vast (see Moraes, 1989 and Troster, 1995). The main point is that the relation between inflation and the size of the banking sector is not simple. There is a Laffer curve (see Figure 2.1) for banking and inflation, where benefits diminish after a certain level or duration of inflation (see Kiguel and Neumeyer, 1995). On the one hand, inflation increases floating rates but diminishes the amount of banking assets. On the other hand, a fall increases

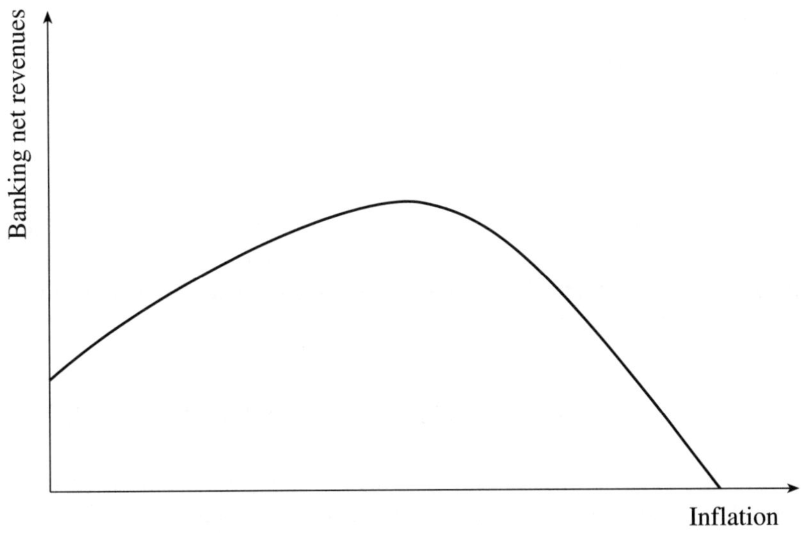

Figure 2.1 Laffer curve: inflation and banking

assets and diminishes floating rates. Stability reduces some risks and increases some revenues. The question is, what is the net effect of inflation?

There are positive and negative effects of inflation on banking. The net effect is the result of several factors. It is reasonable to assume that a mild unexpected inflation would be advantageous for banks. As banks have demand deposits that pay no interest rate, and as nominal interest rates on assets rise with higher inflation, bank profits should increase. But that is a short-term effect only. Over the long term, other factors such as volatility, shorter investment horizons and the lack of non-interest-bearing liabilities have a strong negative effect on banks.

Table 2.13 shows the correlation between broad money supply/GDP growth rates and inflation rate changes for some selected countries. It shows a negative correlation. In these countries, price stability fostered the growth of the banking sector and instability retarded it. It is a fact that there are a number of factors explaining banking sector growth – technology, regulation, economic growth and so on. It is beyond the scope of this chapter to develop this discussion further.

Table 2.13 Correlation: broad money supply/GDP and inflation rate change, 1974–1993

Country	Correlation	Country	Correlation	Country	Correlation
Germany	−0.63	Denmark	−0.94	Switzerland	−0.56
Indonesia	−0.51	Equador	−0.67	Austria	−0.79
Turkey	−0.52	Luxembourg	−0.50	Chile	−0.72
Finland	−0.82	S. Korea	−0.51	Canada	−0.53
Japan	−0.73	S. Africa	−0.68	Kuwait	−0.83

Source: World Bank (1995).

Considering that the country was underbanked at the time of stabilization (July 1994), and considering as well that stabilization fosters banking, the question is, why did Brazil experience a crisis right after stabilization? This is the subject of the next section.

4 THE THREE WAVES OF THE BANKING CRISIS

After July 1994 (*Plano Real*) the Brazilian banking sector faced its worst crisis. The question is why, in spite of being underbanked, and receiving the positive effects of stabilization, banks had problems. The answer is in the inadequate use of instruments of policy. I shall describe the three waves of the crisis caused by: (a) the raising of minimum capital; (b) the liquidity squeeze; and (c) the delay in supervision action. It is important to bear in mind that the banking crisis was not a consequence of diminishing expectations of the banking sector. Diminishing expectations would cause a gradual adjustment, never a dramatic one.

The First Wave: Size Exclusion

The first wave of bank failures after *Plano Real* was caused by a policy adopted to reduce the number of banks. This was made clear in official documents and even a member of the cabinet, Ministro Sérgio Mota, stated that Brazil should have only 70 banks compared with the existing 246 at the time.

On 17 August 1994, together with the regulation implementing the Basle leverage limits, the central bank raised the absolute levels of capitalization, leading to the first wave of banking problems since the plan was introduced (see Table 2.14). The Brazilian central bank adopted regulations that favoured bigger banks as an attempt to mitigate the impact, while accelerating the process of consolidation. The process would be through mergers, acquisitions and the closing down of banks.

Table 2.14 Increases in operating capital requirements introduced under Resolution 2.099

Operating requirement for	Increase (%)
Multiple bank – commercial activities	60
Multiple bank – investment activities	60
Multiple bank – development activities	722
Multiple bank – consumer financing	135
Multiple bank – real estate	174
Commercial bank	60

Source: Central Bank Resolution 2.099 (1994).

The restrictions introduced were: (a) a fixed capital detachment for bank branches; (b) minimum capital requirements for different types of assets; (c) an increase in the absolute level of the minimum capital requirement for financial institutions; and (d) the imposition of a very short time for small banks to adjust – less than nine months. Because the restrictions were especially severe for small banks, they faced adverse selection problems; some had to close their doors. In a short time, 11 banks were liquidated, and only two had a net worth above the new standards set.

Banks that were economically viable on 16 August 1994 suddenly became non-viable on account of the new legislation. They had to find another institution to merge with or a buyer, close or increase their capital. One of the alternatives had to be completed in less than nine months.

There are other reasons, however, why having big banks was an objective of the Brazilian government. Before 1988, the banking systems development depended on a 'point' system. That meant that for a branch of a bank to be opened, another one had to be closed. There was a barrier to entry in the system and to open a new bank, an existing one had to be sold. Even though, in 1988, the new constitution took away the barrier to entry for the financial system, in 1994 new barriers were adopted immediately after stabilization.

Both regulations, either using 'points' as before 1988 or raising the minimum amount of capital in 1994, promote bigger banks. There are many examples of this. One relates to the opening of branches. A bank with a higher capital base can open more branches than one with a smaller base. That has implications for social welfare, since it restricts the number of agencies the public will have and promotes the opening of agencies only by big banks. Instead of ensuring that branches had levels of risk proportional to the bank's capital, irrespective of the size of the branch, Regulation 2.099 set an absolute value of capital. In December 1998, the five largest banks in Brazil held 53.11 per cent of all the branches (16,060) in Brazil (see Table 2.15).

Table 2.15 Bank branches in Brazil, December 1998

Bank	Branches
Banco do Brasil	2,828
Bradesco	2,090
Caixa Econômica Federal	1,602
Itaú	1,019
HSBC – Bamerindus	991
Rest of the banking system	7,530
Banking system total	16,060

Source: Banco Central do Brasil.

There are other explanations why the government promoted bigger banks, of which the first might be due to the existence of economics of scale and of scope. If scale and scope economies were a fact, then bigger and more diversified banks would be more profitable. The reasons for scale and scope economies can be many: high fixed technology costs, research, financial and so on. Promoting big conglomerated banks would then be the same as promoting efficiency.

It is evident that if a minimum level of absolute capital were needed on account of the existence of economies of scale, there would be a need for definite empirical evidence concerning the setting of the levels. It is also important to emphasize that the evidence should include all banking sectors and segments. In addition, it is important to mention that banking has characteristics of a contestable market; barriers to entry – absolute minimum capital – would take away those contestability characteristics and that means losing efficiency.

Another motivation would be to promote financial stabilization: an oligopolistic banking market structure promotes the earning of extraordinary economic profits. Those profits survive intense competition among different banks and act as buffers to absorb shocks. Big banks would also have more stable profits than small banks. A system with small banks might exhibit more mobility, and depositors could regard that as a sign of instability. Depositors would regard bigger banks as safer, able to avoid bank runs. Nevertheless, it is difficult to accept that extraordinary economic profit is needed to promote stabilization in the banking system. On a longer time horizon, an oligopolistic market structure might have the opposite effect.

A third purpose might be to increase international competitiveness for Brazilian banks. Big Brazilian banks would be able to 'face' foreign banks; if they were too small, it would be difficult for them to obtain funds from abroad. International banks would prefer to negotiate with big banks. All banks would have the capacity to obtain funds abroad.

To open a bank in Brazil, the initial capital is several times larger than in other countries such as the United States. In addition, with big banks there is the issue of the 'too big to fail' problem. International experience shows that problems with big banks are often more difficult to handle than those with small ones.

The Second Wave: The Liquidity Squeeze

To understand the second wave, one has to bear in mind that the demand for financial services increased with stabilization. The increase in broad money supply (M4), which totalled 31.0 per cent of GDP by the end of July 1994, reached 49.9 per cent by the end of 1998. The second wave of banks had all the symptoms of a liquidity crisis.

Solvent and economically feasible enterprises with temporary liquidity problems became insolvent. There was also a domino effect and the rise in delinquency rates was strong – it almost doubled in less than six months. It is important to stress that what was observed was not a crisis derived from a change in economic conditions (oil price shock, raising of interest rates, currency devaluation and so on) but a typical crisis of liquidity drainage (see Calomiris and Kahn, 1991; Goodhart, 1989; and Diamond and Dybvig, 1983).

The question is, how can one have a liquidity crisis if broad money supply was rising at a fast pace? The answer lies in the reserve requirements imposed on financial institutions by the central bank, which rose by 249 per cent in the first six months of the plan (see Table 2.16). In the first year, the central bank had more than 40 new rules on these compulsory deposits. The requirements were such that for a loan of R$100.000 the bank needed funding of R$168.000. In addition, requirements on demand deposits in some cases went up to 100 per cent.

Table 2.16 Reserve requirements of financial institutions (R$ million)

Date	Compulsory deposits
June 1994	13,536
July 1994	20,732
September 1994	22,842
October 1994	31,151
November 1994	39,627
December 1994	43,131
January 1995	47,225
February 1995	50,992
March 1995	52,953
April 1995	50,629

Source: Banco Central do Brasil.

The effects were lagged and the problem was worsened by other factors: (a) the discount window facilities in Brazil were very limited at the time; (b) the adverse selection that small banks were facing due to Resolution 2.099; (c) the operating restrictions that banks had to face – limits on the number of instalments for credit and a prohibition on the discounting of cheques; (d) shrinkage of the credit assignment market; and (e) crowding out of banking liabilities by government bonds. Table 2.17 shows the dramatic impacts of these forces on bank's balance sheets.

The Third Wave: Delayed Prudential Actions

The third crisis involved three of the ten largest banks in Brazil – Econômico, Bamerindus and Nacional. The origin of the problems was a

Table 2.17 Loans in arrears and non-performing for the private sector financial system (%)

Date	Bad loans (% total)
January 1995	8.528
February 1995	8.807
March 1995	9.426
April 1995	10.648
May 1995	11.499
June 1995	12.157
July 1995	15.258
August 1995	17.341
September 1995	16.140
October 1995	17.104

Source: Banco Central do Brasil.

combination of poor management – in one of the cases plain fraud – and poor supervision, prior to 1994. It is important to stress that the problems had existed for some time already (see World Bank, 1989, explicitly recommending an improvement in the quality of credit supervision), and that the central bank failed to intervene to solve the problems.

In all three cases the problems of the banks had existed for many years. With the worsening conditions caused by the liquidity squeeze, the situation of the banks became unbearable. They could hardly find any financing in the market, and had to rely on the central bank for rolling over their liabilities. Due to poor supervision of the quality of their assets, and to delay in prudential action, the cost of the intervention was extremely high; the three together had losses of over US$10 billion.

5 REACTIONS TO THE CRISES AND THE AFTERMATH

The elimination of the three banks with problems improved the overall financial condition of the banking system. Many funds were channelled to improve the situation of state banks, and some advances were made. There were also changes induced by economic factors such as: (a) increasing competition of foreign banks; (b) price and interest rate stability; (c) cheaper and better bank technology; (d) opening of the Brazilian markets to international investors; (e) longer planning horizons; (f) evolving patterns of responsibility and transparency; and (g) demographic changes.

The central bank of Brazil acted on several fronts to improve banking: (a) it provided fiscal incentives and a special credit line – PROER – to finance the restructuring of distressed banks; (b) it introduced deposit insurance; (c) it loosened the requirements for foreign banks entering the Brazilian banking system; (d) it introduced new market risk regulations; (e) it reformulated supervision and increased its intervening capacity; (f) it passed new accounting and transparency requirements; and (g) it set up a central bank bureau of credit risk information.

The central bank also made significant advancements in improving the public banks. In 1996, it created a credit line, the PROES (Programa de Incentivo à Redução do Setor Público Estatal na Atividade Bancária), with funds for the states to privatize, or convert into a development agency, or liquidate state banks. Since then, 16 state banks have been converted into development agencies, ten liquidated, seven privatized, six taken over by the central government, and five restructured by the states. Of the 49 state banks existing at the end of 1995, 44 were reorganized. On the other hand, very little has been done with the three big federal banks – Banco do Brasil (BB), Caixa Econômica Federal (CEF) and Banco Nacional de Desenvolvimento Econômico e Social (BNDES).

In January 1999, the banking system had a significant boost in its net income with the devaluation of the real. With the exception of two small private banks, FonteCindam and Marka, and perhaps some public banks that had a shortage of dollars, the rest of the banking system was either neutral or had a sufficiency of dollars. The profits made by banks as a result of the devaluation were substantial. In contrast to other countries, the devaluation of the real was expected by the banks to occur at any moment. In the months prior to the devaluation, the central bank's reserves were daily being transferred from Brazil in nine-figure amounts, and it was evident for the market that it had to devaluate. The result of the devaluation on the banking sector was positive and very significant. Even though the system was sound, the outcome for banks of the devaluation was the result of an announced event, and bore no relation to the stability or efficiency of the banking system.

The banking system is now comparatively more efficient, competitive and stable than it was when the stabilization was introduced. Many changes have taken place in the last few years, but there is room for more improvement. Brazil is underbanked and its financial intermediation is very inefficient when compared to other countries.

6 CONCLUSION

Brazilian banking experienced its worst crisis at a time when it was expected to grow. Many of the obstacles faced were due to the adoption of an inappropriate banking policy. Even though corrective action was taken, and many problems solved, others still remain, such as high minimum capital requirements and high reserve deposit ratios. There are other structural problems still to be solved, such as the taxing of financial activities, better liquidity mechanisms, high compliance costs, the crowding out of private institutions' liabilities and an inefficient public banking sector. However, it remains to be seen how soon these problems will be addressed.

REFERENCES

Als, G. (1988), 'The nightmare of economic accounts in a small country with a large international banking sector', *Review of Income and Wealth*, **34** (1), 101–10.

Banco Central do Brasil, Reports (various).

Banco Central de la República Argentina, 'Determinacion del Nível de Actividad del Sector Financiero: Periodo 1980–92', mimeo.

Bank for International Settlements (1995), *65th Annual Report*, Basle: Bank for International Settlements.

Calomiris, C.W. and C.M. Kahn (1991), 'The role of demandable debt in structuring optimal banking arrangements', *American Economic Review*, **81** (3), 497–513.

Commission of the European Community (CEC), International Monetary Fund (IMF), Organization for Economic Cooperation and Development (OECD), United Nations (UN) and World Bank (1993), *System of National Accounts 1993*, Brussels/Luxemburg, New York, Paris, Washington, DC: CEC/IMF/OECD/UN/World Bank.

Diamond, D.W. and P.H. Dybvig (1983), 'Bank runs, deposit insurance, and liquidity', *Journal of Political Economy*.

Goodhart, C.A.E. (1989), *Money, Information and Uncertainty*, 2nd edn, London: Macmillan.

Instituto Brasileiro de Geografia e Estatística (IBGE) (1994), *Contas Consolidadas para a Nação – Brazil 1980–1993*, Rio de Janeiro: IBGE.

Kiguel, M.A. and P.A. Neumeyer (1995), 'Seigniorage and inflation: the case of Argentina', *Journal of Money Credit and Banking*, **27** (3), 672–83.

Mamalakis, M.J. (1987), 'The treatment of interest and financial intermediaries in the national accounts the old "bundle" versus the new "unbundle" approach', *Review of Income and Wealth*, **36** (2).

McKinsey Global Institute (1998), 'Productivity – the key to an accelerated development path for Brazil', São Paulo, Washington (mimeo).

Moraes, P.B. (1989), 'Inflação e o número de intermediários financeiros', Rio de Janeiro: PUC Discussion Paper No. 204.

Rymes, T.K. (1985), 'Inflation, nonoptimal monetary arrangements and the banking imputation in the national accounts', *Review of Income and Wealth*, **32** (4), 425–42.

Rymes, T.K. (1986), 'Further thoughts on the banking imputation in the national accounts', *Review of Income and Wealth*, **31** (1), 85–95.
Santos, J.C.S and R.L. Troster (1993), 'Um estudo econométrico do setor bancário', São Paulo: FIPE Discussion Paper No. 26/93.
Troster, R.L. (1995), *Brazilian Banking Regulation*, London: London School of Economics, Financial Markets Group.
Troster, R.L. (1996), 'Overbanking in Brazil', FIPE–USP: Relatório Final (mimeo).
Troster, R.L. (1999), 'Brazilian banking and stabilization', *Journal of Financial Regulation and Compliance*, **7** (2), 105–13.
United Nations (1994), 'National Accounts Statistics: Main Aggregates and Detailed Tables, 1992', New York: United Nations.
Wilson, J.S.G. (1986), *Banking Policy and Structure: A Comparative Analysis*, New York: New York University Press.
World Bank (1989), 'Brazil: Selected Issues of the Financial Sector, Report No. 7725–BR', World Bank: Country Department I, Trade, Finance and Industry Division, Latin America and Caribbean Regional Office.
World Bank (1995), *World Tables 1995*, Washington, DC: World Bank.

3. Financial reform in Canada: past, present and future

Pierre L. Siklos*

1 INTRODUCTION

The development and reform of the Canadian financial system represents an interesting case study as it reflects the continuing impact of its British origins with an eye to ever-present US influences, by far Canada's largest trading partner in the post-Second World War era. Indeed, the Canadian experience has often served as a means of evaluating the relative efficiency of the US financial system and economy-wide responses to various shocks over time (for example, Bordo et al., 1994; Siklos, 2000b).

The present study explores major developments in the Canadian financial sector since the 1950s with an emphasis on the present state of affairs, together with a brief analysis of prospects for reform in the near future.

Section 2 deals with the central bank, the Bank of Canada. In several respects, the Canadian experience is instructive to a wider international audience not only because the Bank of Canada is at the forefront in the latest trend to adopt and maintain inflation control targets but also because it presents an important historical illustration of political pressures on monetary policy.

Section 3 outlines the development of the commercial banking sector. Here too the Canadian experience is of interest because of the continuing influence of the federal system of politics on financial sector reform and the reactions of the financial industry under such circumstances.

Section 4 then examines the system of deposit insurance and how events over the last two decades have led to considerable discussion about the need to reform the deposit safety net and the role of bank supervision.

Section 5 concludes.

2 THE BANK OF CANADA

Past

The Bank of Canada is a relative newcomer among central banks having been created in 1935, following a favourable report issued by the MacMillan

Commission, set up to investigate the possibility of establishing a central bank. Although there has been some debate about the forces which led to its creation, political forces, coupled with the abandonment of the gold standard, are the most likely explanations for its creation (Bordo and Redish, 1987). In addition, the need to coordinate policies in an increasingly international environment required an institution such as a central bank.

At first, the Bank was a private institution but it ceased to be so quite early in its history when it was nationalized in 1936. The immediate post-war period was marked by the need to return the Canadian economy to some semblance of normality, coupled with the problem of managing the large debt accumulated as a result of the war. However, a first milestone in the Bank's history came at the end of the 1950s when monetary policy clashed with fiscal policy, resulting in what has been called the Coyne Affair (Rymes, 1994; Muirhead, 1999). James Coyne, governor of the Bank from 1955 until he resigned in 1961, pursued a high interest rate policy which was at odds with government policy that aimed at expansion in a period when the Canadian economy was mired in recession. Attempts by the federal government of the day to fire him were unsuccessful and, feeling vindicated, Coyne resigned.

This led to what is today referred to as the Rasminsky Directive, later enshrined in the 1967 revision of the Bank of Canada Act. The importance of the directive lies primarily in its role as clarifying responsibility for monetary policy. Hence, 'if the Government disapproves of the monetary policy being carried out . . . it has the right and the responsibility to direct the Bank as to the policy which the Bank is carrying out' (Muirhead, 1999, p. 176). Far from making the Bank less autonomous, as some critics suggested at the time[1] (see the analysis in Rymes, 1994), the directive actually enhanced the autonomy of the Bank since the minister of finance would have to disagree publicly with the governor, presumably at a higher political price.

The 1970s and part of the 1980s were marked by the monetary targeting experiment, as in other industrial countries, in the wake of the breakdown of Bretton Woods. Canada's experience with this strategy for monetary policy was fairly quickly abandoned relative to other countries (Bernanke and Mishkin, 1992; Howitt, 1986; and Courchene, 1981). Indeed, it was in part the failure of existing monetary policy strategies which led to another milestone in the Bank of Canada's history, namely the pursuit of price stability, eventually via inflation targets.

Present

In January 1988, former Governor John Crow gave a now famous speech – the Hanson Memorial Lecture – in which he advocated that the Bank of

Canada pursue 'a policy aimed at achieving and maintaining stable prices' (Crow, 1988, p. 3). Thus began a period of transition of sorts (see Laidler and Robson, 1993) during which time the governor advocated inflation targets following the lead of the Reserve Bank of New Zealand which had by then adopted this strategy. However, it was not until the federal government's budget of 1991 that formal inflation targets were announced. As in other countries with inflation targets, gradual reductions in inflation were expected during the targeting regime (see Siklos, 1997, 1999). Figure 3.1 shows the annual inflation rate in consumer prices, based on quarterly data, since the introduction of inflation targets, as well as the inflation target control ranges. Inflation fell quickly and has remained very near the bottom of the target range. The Bank aims for the mid-point of the range but, for a time, it appeared to be indifferent to inflation performance which put changes in the cost of living firmly at the bottom of the range. It should be noted, however, that whereas the targets are expressed in terms of the overall consumer price index (CPI), the Bank 'focuses on the CPI excluding food, energy, and the effect of indirect taxes' (Bank of Canada 1999a, p. 4), that is, core inflation. The targets were renewed in 1995, 1998, and were revived in 2001 until at least 2006. At that time the government and the Bank plan to decide what target is consistent with price stability. Again, it bears pointing out that such a decision was to have been reached by 1998 but has since been postponed. In the ensuing discussion over the impact of these targets, much has been written about whether the type of monetary policy strategy can, by itself, lead to desirable economic outcomes. After all, such targets were introduced at a time of worldwide disinflation and they have yet to be severely tested by an economic downturn (Siklos, 1999).

As Canadian banks are not required to hold reserves, the Bank of Canada has signalled monetary policy intentions since 1994 via the overnight market.[2]

The Bank sets a band for overnight interest rates of 0.5 per cent such that overdrafts at the Bank of Canada are charged at the upper limit of the band (that is, the mid-point of the band plus 0.25 per cent) while surplus balances earn interest at the bottom of the band (that is, the mid-point of the band less 0.25 per cent).

As Canada is a small open economy where exchange rate influences are important, it is clear that any restrictive monetary policy achieved via higher interest rates would also prompt the Canadian dollar to appreciate against the US dollar in particular. These effects could, at least potentially, cancel each other. Consequently, the Bank of Canada pioneered the concept of a Monetary Conditions Index (MCI) which represents a linear combination of a short-term interest rate and a trade-weighted exchange rate. Experience and empirical research suggest that interest rate changes

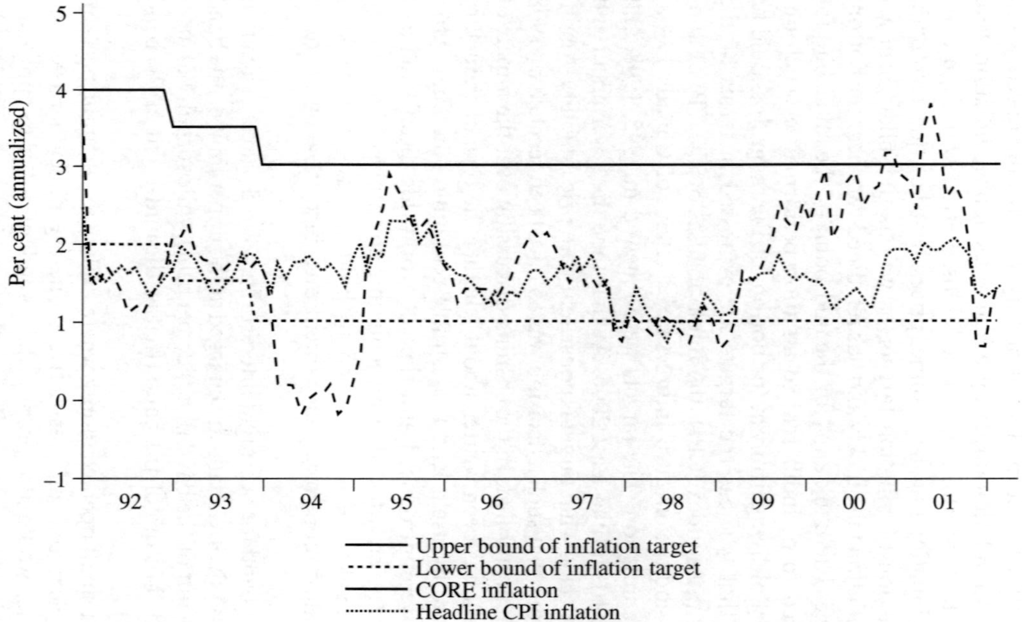

Notes: Plot is based on monthly data. Core regulation includes food, energy, and indirect taxes.

Sources: Data are from the Bank of Canada 1992–2000. Siklos (1997, 1999) provides details about the inflation control target ranges and their history.

Figure 3.1 Annual inflation rate in consumer prices and inflation target control ranges

have a relatively larger impact on output than do exchange rate changes. Hence, the object of the MCI is as a device to indicate the direction of current monetary policy and thus provide the central bank, and financial markets, with potentially useful information about how higher expected inflation, for example, can be forestalled via a change in the current stance of monetary policy.

Usage of the MCI has spread to several central banks (see Siklos, 2000a, and reference therein), although there have also been a number of criticisms levelled at this measure (again, see Siklos, 2000a; and Grant, 1997). While a thorough analysis is beyond the scope of this study, suffice it to note that many observers tend to forget that interpretations of the ease or tightness of policy is relative to some benchmark which is not publicly announced. Hence, the MCI can occasionally confuse markets about the degree of ease or tightness in monetary policy. Indeed, the Bank of Canada has felt obliged to publicly reiterate its meaning and relevance in the conduct of monetary policy (Bank of Canada, 1998a).

Future

At the time the second set of inflation targets agreed to between the minister of finance and the governor of the Bank of Canada were to expire in 1998, a discussion began about the costs and benefits of price stability, as well as whether the Bank of Canada Act should enshrine some form of price stability in its preamble. The current act calls on the central bank to be all things to all people (see Laidler, 1997; and Bank of Canada, 1998b).

Rather, the benign level of inflation and the recovery of the Canadian economy, together with a decision to postpone the definition of price stability, pushed the question of the role of the Bank of Canada off the national agenda. Instead, the continued weakness of the Canadian dollar, which accelerated sharply in the summer of 1998, has recently led to suggestions that Canada pursue monetary union with the United States (for example, see Courchene and Harris, 1999; Laidler, 1999). It is, of course, too early to tell what the outcome of these proposals will be, but the widespread belief that the Canadian dollar is severely undervalued and the continuance of this state of affairs will no doubt further highlight dissatisfaction with the current monetary regime. Nevertheless, it should be emphasized that there exist formidable political and economic obstacles to such a monetary union. It should also be mentioned that the Canada–US situation cannot be compared with the pressures and events leading up to the adoption of European Monetary Union, especially as the relative influence of Canada in a North American monetary policy is likely to be small to trivial and barriers to labour mobility, despite an existing free trade agreement, are likely to remain.

3 THE COMMERCIAL BANKING SECTOR AND FINANCIAL INNOVATION[3]

Past

In the nineteenth century, policy makers in Canada, and elsewhere, believed it was unsound for banks to lend other than for 'productive' uses. This reflected the 'real bills' type of philosophy which prevailed at the time. Another convention of the time was the requirement that any joint-stock company (what one would call a corporation today) obtain a charter from the appropriate legislation. Hence, banks in Canada came to be known as chartered banks. The name persists to this day, although the significance of the charter has diminished considerably. Early charters permitted banks to issue their own notes and, in common with parts of the US and the UK, Canada experienced an era of free banking which lasted for only a brief time.

What was to prove to be one of the salient differences between US and Canadian commercial banking is the authorization for banks to open branches across the country, if they so wish.

Unfortunately, the conservative nature of banking regulations would prove to have perhaps unintended consequences for the development of the banking industry, broadly speaking. The Constitution Act of 1867 would grant the federal government monopoly powers over banking and currency issue. Unfortunately, the governing legislation, namely the Bank Act, left undefined what banking meant and, furthermore, outlined what chartered banks could not do, that is, it did not provide for contingencies or activities outside the legislation, considered forbidden territory (the legal term is *ultra vires*). As a result, banking-type institutions such as credit unions, trust companies and mortgage loan companies, created to satisfy the deposit and finance needs of non-commercial borrowers and lenders, emerged largely under provincial jurisdiction. Therefore, as the Second World War ended, regulation of the financial sector in Canada would involve not only the federal government but also individual provinces as well. It is only during the 1980s that federal and provincial governments began an attempt to rationalize regulation and supervision of the financial sector (see the next subsection).

Among financial institutions, chartered banks are the largest. In 1997, over 40 per cent of industry assets were held by banks, followed by life insurers and pension fund managers, distant second and third place holders (McKinsey & Co., 1998, Exhibit 2–1). This market position has not changed much during the 1990s (Siklos, 2001, ch. 3).

The post-war period in chartered banking is marked by the widening scope of operations. Indeed, from institutions involved solely in commercial-type activities chartered banks have become the dominant players in residential mortgages and consumer loans, in addition to their historical dominance in personal deposits and commercial loans (banks still made 84 per cent of all such loans in 1997). Table 3.1 provides the relevant data. Thus, by the 1960s, chartered banks were permitted free access to the mortgage lending field, while the 1980s saw banks enter the financial leasing, data processing, brokerage and trust services. Limitations continue on certain forms of finance (for example, automobile leasing) and insurance, thereby preventing chartered banks from becoming the universal banks some of their European counterparts are (also see subsection 'Future', below). These developments reflect the general trend to deregulate the banking industry, leading to an easing of the restrictions on obtaining a charter. As a result, by 1981, subsidiaries of foreign banks could obtain a bank charter, although separate treatment of domestic and foreign banks persisted. The former are referred to as Schedule I banks while the latter are called Schedule II banks. As of 1999, there are 54 chartered banks in Canada, 11 of which are domestic banks (Canadian Bankers Association, 1999).

Table 3.1 Principal activities of financial institutions, 1997

	Type of activity		
Type of institution	Personal deposits	Residential mortgages	Consumer loans
Chartered banks	61.7	60.1	69.3
Trusts	8.6	6.6	9.8
Credit unions/ *caissis populaire*	16.1	13.9	10.6
Life insurance	7.9	5.8	2.9

Source: McKinsey & Co. (1998, Exhibit 2–24).

Although the Bank Act was intended to be revised every ten years, a chronology (Siklos, 2001, Table 19.1) reveals that crisis and financial innovations often meant that an existing Bank Act was occasionally outdated even before it was enacted.

The latest Bank Act (2001) favours the creation of equal or near-equal competition among chartered and non-chartered financial institutions although, for example, some barriers to entry, such as in the insurance field, remain. Consequently, whereas institutions used to fit neatly into four categories – the four pillars as they were known (chartered banks, trust companies and near-banks, insurance companies and investment dealers) – these divisions began to crumble under the weight of regulatory reform and increased competition. Another important barrier, at least in so far as the chartered banks are concerned, is the regulation which requires them to be 'widely held', that is, a single shareholder cannot acquire majority interest in a chartered bank. By contrast, trust, mortgage loan and insurance companies can continue to be 'closely held' (also see subsection 'Future', below).[4]

In 1987, the Canadian and US federal governments completed the Free Trade Agreement (FTA), extended in 1992 to include Mexico and since called NAFTA or the North American Free Trade Agreement. Essentially, NAFTA ensures that any federal regulation in the signatory countries does not discriminate against 'foreign' banks by the US, Canadian or Mexican banks. However, as the retail side of the Canadian financial sector, for example, is very well served by the various types of existing banking firms, there has been little direct impact on Canada's financial industry as a result of NAFTA. Second, provincial (in Canada) and state (in the US) regulation and involvement in the financial sector remains significant and is outside the purview of the FTA and NAFTA agreements.

Siklos (2001, chs 17, 19–21), provides a comprehensive account of the development and reform of the Canadian financial sector from its earliest years to the present. A new Bank Act along the lines discussed in this section and below received Royal Assent in October 2001.

Present

There are three sources of influence on the present position of commercial banks in particular. They are: financial innovation, the regional and small business loans problem, and bank consolidation. To some extent, all countries' financial systems face these forces but some have a distinctly Canadian flavour to them.

While the branch banking system has meant wide access to a full range of banking-type services, the recent trend has been to open 'mini' branches at large supermarkets or retailers. Perhaps even more interesting is the appearance of the 'virtual bank'. Wells Fargo, a US bank, began to offer commercial loans and other banking services to Canadian customers across the border but without any physical Canadian presence. This type of banking activity was not, of course, contemplated by existing legislation. After much discussion, the government passed into law an amendment to the Bank Act dealing with foreign bank branching (Department of Finance, 1999a). Essentially, 'virtual banks' are now permitted to set up shop in Canada but are limited to accepting deposits over CDN $150,000.

However, perhaps the most important development in recent years has been the growth in banking conducted in a cashless setting, via phone lines and the internet. A particular area of growth has occurred in the form of debit cards, better known internationally as point of sale (POS) transactions.[5] Paralleling this development has been the growth in automated teller machines (ATMs). The tremendous growth in this area is overshadowed by the expansion in functionality. Instead of being used simply as devices to obtain cash, ATMs are becoming virtual mini-branches, able to conduct almost all common banking-type transactions.

Increasingly, deposits, withdrawals and payments are completed electronically and 1999 marks the year when the large value transfer system (LVTS) was implemented by the Canadian Payments Association (CPA), the body responsible for clearings and settlements in Canada (Bank of Canada, 1999a).

Under the LVTS, members of the CPA will know with certainty, by the end of the day, the net outcome of their flows. Previously, payments would clear overnight and would be settled on a backdated basis. This system exists for financial transactions that are paper based (for example, cheques) so the LVTS is essentially meant for large transactions. The aim is to ensure that participants in the clearing system have a zero settlement balance each day. Surpluses earn 50 basis points below the bank rate – the rate at which the Bank of Canada lends to CPA members – while deficits would be financed at the bank rate, equal to 50 basis points above the overnight rate. Two other developments are worthy of mention. Shortly after the announcement by the government and the Bank of Canada of inflation targets, inflation rates fell considerably and both inflation and nominal interest rates are the lowest they have been in years. Partly as a result of these developments, individuals began to search for higher yields than could be obtained from conventional savings deposits. Paralleling a much earlier development in the US, money market mutual funds have become an increasingly important source of liquidity in the Canadian economy (see Atta-Mensah and Nott (1999) for additional details). The upshot is that technological change, also emphasized by Freedman and Goodlet (1998), is perhaps the main driving force behind financial innovation.

Historically, there has always been a concern in Canada about the degree of market concentration (that is, the extent to which a small number of firms in an industry account for a large proportion of its output, employment, profits and/or assets). Hence, while the typically large Canadian bank is small by international standards, the six largest domestic Canadian banks book a substantial majority of all deposits. In 1997, 63 per cent of total assets were booked at the six largest banks while 86 per cent of domestic assets resided with the same banks.[6] Despite this apparent high level of concentration, at least in this narrow dimension, there is little evidence that the Canadian banking industry is uncompetitive, at least by international standards. As noted earlier, the view that Canadian banks are not sufficiently competitive partly stems from the rigid ownership rules that prevent the flexibility necessary to react rapidly to changing market opportunities. Combined with the high cost of entry into the banking industry, this implies an absence of contestability. Contestability refers to the likely success of potential competitors to enter a particular industry. Evidence on this score is mixed (for example, see Nathan and Neave, 1989; McFetridge, 1998), but the issue does raise the question of what impact mergers and acquisitions in the financial sector have had on the economy. After all, one could argue that if banks need not worry about the threat of a takeover, they may be less efficient than possible. The discussion so far leads us to the dominant issue in the Canadian financial sector in 1998 and 1999, namely whether large existing domestic banks should be permitted to merge.

In January 1998, the Royal Bank and the Bank of Montreal announced plans to merge. In April, the Canadian Imperial Bank of Commerce (CIBC) and the Toronto Dominion Bank announced similar merger plans. The plans were announced despite ongoing activities at the federal government level which was involved in a mid-term review of the 1991 Bank Act.

In December 1996 the minister of finance commissioned a Task Force on the Future of the Canadian Financial Services Sector, since known as the MacKay Task Force report (1998). Following analysis by the Competition Bureau and the Office of the Superintendent of Financial Institutions, the minister of finance rejected the bank merger proposals in a press release at the end of 1998 (Department of Finance, 1998). Although the rejection was based on purely economic grounds, there are more than a few hints that the ultimate decision had distinct political overtones. Nevertheless, the decision to block the mergers was based on the following criteria:

1. mergers would lead to an 'unacceptable' increase in market concentration;
2. mergers would produce a 'significant reduction of competition'; and
3. mergers would affect the federal government's ability to 'address future prudential concerns'.

As noted earlier, the banks argued that financial sector consolidation was a worldwide trend most notably in the US, and equated the need for maintaining efficiency, and presumably bank profitability, in the global financial world, with the need to increase in size. As the CEO of the CIBC wrote, following the rejection of the merger proposals, 'a merger would have been in the best long-term interests of Canadians and of shareholders' (Baillie, 1998). Smith (1999) argues that, based on a cross-country comparison of return on equity (ROE), there appears to be no empirical connection between size (as measured by bank capital) and profitability. The same study finds that cost efficiencies and diverse income sources are the driving force behind the relatively high profitability of Canadian banks, which were ranked among the top three most profitable in a survey of 16 industrial countries (only Spain and the US have more profitable banks). Mathewson and Quigley (1998) argue that the pressure for mergers is driven by the need to maintain cost economies in a market that is experiencing excess capacity. This can only be addressed via a reduction in the size of the branch banking network which is a politically sensitive option. Consequently, mergers would enhance competition *vis-à-vis* other banks operating in a global environment. Indeed, McKinsey & Co. (1998, Exhibit 2–52) conclude that efficiency gains in Canada have largely been tapped.[7] In any event, regardless of the pros and cons of mergers, the MacKay Task Force (1998) pointed out the need for a process by which merger proposals can be addressed and, as discussed in the next subsection, the minister of finance seems to agree. Part of the difficulty, also noted by Mathewson and Quigley (1997), and further underlined by the MacKay Task Force, is the tension between a regulatory model which is industry- or form-specific versus one that is based on the functions of the firm. At present, the conflicts arising from such tensions have yet to be resolved. The tension between industry specific and functional regulation is critical since corporate debt, for example, is increasingly financed via non-bank sources (for example, bankers' acceptances, corporate bonds).[8] Consequently, regulations aimed specifically at banks may unduly impose additional costs which are avoided by non-traditional sources of credit.[9]

A recurring theme in recent policy discussions surrounding chartered bank behaviour and performance has been the perception that chartered banks deliberately avoid making loans to small and medium-sized businesses. The MacKay Task Force essentially confirmed the view that this group receives subpar service (also see McKinsey & Co., 1998, Exhibit 2–24; and Siklos, 2001, pp. 360–61), largely because of above-average service charges and fewer product choices than their US counterparts have.[10] Not surprisingly then there is considerable interest in skewing reforms (see next subsection) towards increasing financial and regulatory incentives (and/or penalties for ignoring) to induce banks to satisfy the credit needs of small to medium-sized businesses.

Table 3.2 provides summary information about the principal assets and liabilities of chartered banks, at December 1998.

Table 3.2 Chartered bank assets and liabilities (December 1998 average)

Assets	CDN$ (millions)	Liabilities	CDN$ (millions)
Liquid			
Notes and coins	3,747	Personal savings deposits[9]	287,889
Deposits at the Bank of Canada	415	Non-personal term and notice deposits[9]	142,507
Treasury bills[1]	14,820	Demand deposits[10]	57,713
Government of Canada bonds[2]	58,182		
Short-term assets[3]	30,298		
Total	107,462	Total	488,109
Less Liquid			
Personal loans[4]	96,571	Government of Canada	2,931
Government	2,080		
Businesses[5]	169,544		
Non-residents[6]	15,124	Bankers' acceptances	48,744
Mortgages[7]	251,484	Subordinated debt	15,105
Securities[8]	50,637	Foreign currency	103,170
Total	692,902	Total[11]	794,624
Total (Canadian dollar assets)	794,624		
Net foreign currency assets	−32,850		

Notes:

1. Amortized value.
2. All maturities.
3. Call and short loans, short-term paper and other.
4. Personal loans, credit cards, lines of credit and other.
5. Reverse repos, business loans and lending receivables.
6. Reverse repos and business loans.
7. Residential and non-residential.
8. Provincial, municipal and corporate.
9. Chequable, non-chequable, fixed term.
10. Less private sector float.
11. Not all items shown, so total does not add up.

Source: *Bank of Canada Review*, Spring 1999, Tables C1 and C2.

Future

The timing of this publication is fortuitous in so far as a discussion of future directions for the Canadian financial system is concerned. At the end of June 1999, the minister of finance outlined a 'framework' which, after consultation, would provide a basis for the next Bank Act (Department of Finance, 1999b).

The proposed framework is intended to accomplish the following objectives:

1. provide all financial institutions with 'flexibility' to enter into new lines of business subject, however, to some overarching constraints. In particular, chartered banks would continue to be barred from automobile leasing and the sale of life insurance at the retail level, and ownership limitations will persist;[11]
2. lighten, 'whenever possible', the regulatory burden on all institutions;
3. increased consumer protection via the creation of a new agency to ensure financial institutions comply with government-mandated consumer protection policies; and
4. improve the monitoring of financial institutions' policies towards lending to small and medium-sized businesses.

The vision outlined by the minister of finance is intended to enhance competitiveness. For example, trust companies would be permitted to diversify their balance sheets through access to investment vehicles they were previously prevented from being engaged in; credit unions would be allowed to form national alliances or networks, presumably to take advantage of economies of scale; access to the CPA will be available to life insurers; and, finally, through an easing of entry costs into the financial sector.

Interestingly, a formal merger review process will be enacted and the creation of holding companies will be permitted, perhaps along the lines of the US model which emerged as a result of federal and state regulations that strictly limited the growth of commercial banks across states.[12] Presumably, the holding company concept may be interpreted as a half-way house of sorts between the existing regime and one which would permit mergers in an unfettered environment.

Interestingly, there is relatively little recognition in the proposals about global pressures for reform, or change in the financial sector which is consistent with the view that the largest banks should remain in domestic hands.[13] Yet, it is precisely such pressures that are vital to the growth of the largest banks, as noted earlier. Moreover, the proposals strike one as attempting to patch up existing problems or deal with current competing interests. As Neave and Milne (1998) point out, the ideal financial legislation should provide equality of opportunity, not equality of outcome. Yet, policy makers must also be mindful that functional regulation does not protect depositors from insolvency or undue risk-taking activities. These are problems at the institutional level. Perhaps for this reason, the proposals for reform emphasize the need for consumer protection and institutional transparency.

4 DEPOSIT INSURANCE AND BANKING SUPERVISION

Past

Deposit insurance was introduced in Canada in 1967. Insurance is provided through a Crown corporation known as the Canada Deposit Insurance Corporation or CDIC. Coverage is per account not institution. Hence, since each account is insured for CDN$60,000 – the amount has not changed in several years – the insured can enjoy protection which is effectively many multiples of the notional CDN$60,000 maximum. Unlike several other countries (see Siklos, 2001, p. 300), not all financial instruments booked with a financial institution are protected against loss. Eligible deposits typically include cheque and savings type deposits, so with the significant change in the investment portfolio of households, effective protection has been decreasing.

In the early 1990s the activities of the CDIC were extensively re-examined. This followed on the heels of devastating losses throughout the decade of the 1980s and into the early 1990s. The oil boom of the 1980s in western Canada created the desire to shift away some of the banking and financial power concentrated in Toronto. As a result, several western banks were formed but lax banking supervision or diligence led to some of the most spectacular banking failures in Canadian history. The Estey Commission (1986) made clear that the existing Bank Act and poor supervision by the then Inspector General of Banks were primarily responsible.[14] Together with the still larger failures of several trust companies in Ontario, this led the CDIC to effectively become insolvent. A patchwork of reforms was put into place, mainly relying on tougher supervision by the various regulatory authorities (see next subsection) and, despite a flurry of discussion and policy proposals (for example, Carr et al., 1994), there were few fundamental reforms of the system until recently.

Present

One can subdivide the regulatory structure of financial services in Canada into roughly three categories, in addition to the role played by the Bank of Canada. The pattern is similar in most industrialized countries. They are:

1. *Prudential regulation* The relevant regulations are meant to ensure the safety and soundness of banks via, for example, the specification of minimum capital requirements. OSFI is the agency primarily responsible for this area of regulation although it should also be noted that informational institutions, such as the Bank for International Settlements (BIS), are playing an increasingly important role in such areas. Finally, note should also be taken of attempts, largely spearheaded by Canada, to set up early-warning mechanisms to mitigate the likelihood of currency and banking crises of the kind which affected international financial markets in 1998.
2. *Regulation of competition* The Competition Bureau is generally responsible for ensuring proper conduct in the marketplace. However, as noted in the previous section, there are gaps in this area as far as the financial sector is concerned since merger and acquisition policies are not yet clearly spelled out, for example.
3. *Protection of the consumer* At present this role is primarily filled by the CDIC although the Bank Act also stipulates some disclosure rules and the reporting of financial information. Again, there are thought to be gaps in this area since current proposals for reform are intended to enhance consumer protection rules.

As in the discussion of the forces affecting the banks, technological change remains the most potent force facing regulators today. For example, innovations which permit non-financial firms to store money electronically are essentially outside the purview of regulators like the CDIC, as are certain financial transactions over the internet. Again, consumer protection issues also loom large and policy makers have found it difficult to keep pace with technological developments.[15]

As noted earlier, the experience of the 1980s and early 1990s placed pressure on policy-makers to change the deposit insurance structure with an emphasis on early-warning systems and reforms to the premium structure, which was essentially a flat-rate structure and did little or nothing to mitigate the twin well-known problems of moral hazard and adverse selection in the provision of insurance services.[16]

In 1999, the CDIC introduced a new premium structure by reducing existing premiums and introducing risk-based rates. Legislative changes passed in 1996 permitted such changes and the new premium structure came into force at the end of March 1999. Four premium categories were introduced, with premium rates ranging from 1/24th of 1 per cent of insurable deposits for the safest banks to one-third of 1 per cent for the least safe financial institutions. Other than the least safe banks, the current regime implies that virtually all institutions will pay the same or lower premiums than under the previous system. Moreover, even the least safe institutions are given a two-year transition to improve their risk standing. 'Criteria for determining the classification . . . include capital adequacy, profitability and asset concentration' (CDIC, 1999b). The ratings are to be kept confidential which, unfortunately, reduces the transparency of the regime.

Future

As noted earlier, the current regulatory structure in Canada is subdivided along three lines. It is tempting to argue that the regulatory system should be centralized. The idea was considered but rejected by the MacKay Task Force (1998), and it is unlikely to be seriously reconsidered. First, there is always the danger of allocating too much control or influence to one agency which, after all, must regulate an industry which is constantly evolving and where entry by non-traditional firms further complicates the regulators' tasks.

What is likely to be more feasible is a comprehensive review of the functions and authority of existing agencies to ensure not only a minimal amount of overlap but also that there is sufficient flexibility built in to permit the regulators to adapt to changing circumstances.

Other than the addition of a new agency which extends consumer protection rules to dealings with banks and other financial intermediaries, the recent proposals by the minister of finance, discussed in Section 3 of this chapter, put relatively little emphasis on a philosophy of regulation of the financial sector.

Moreover, there continue to be tensions between the federal and provincial governments over certain aspects of legislation dealing with the financial sector. For example, there is reluctance to allow a national body to handle securities regulation, which remains in provincial control. As many have pointed out (for example, Neave and Milne, 1998) this approach seems archaic given that firms in this industry operate at the national and international levels.

Finally, and importantly, just as central banks have felt the winds of change in recent years, leading them to operate in a far more transparent fashion, the same developments would be welcome in the rest of the financial sector. Yet, there continue to be fairly strict limits over disclosure, and the CDIC's rationale for not making available to the public the rating of banks, namely that it matches practice in other countries, is at variance with the notion of transparency. After all, firms, including banks, are always assessed by the marketplace, whether it be through stock-price behaviour, profits or bond ratings. There is little reason then to retain the confidentiality of such ratings. In addition, the current policy may lead consumers, and others, to second-guess the adequacy of the model used to generate such ratings.

5 CONCLUSIONS

Canada, it can be fairly said, has an enviable record of financial stability. Moreover, the Bank of Canada remains at the forefront of central bank policies with its inflation targeting experiment. International comparisons, such as those featured in the extensive study by McKinsey and Co. (1998), and in the work of Freedman (1998), and Neufeld and Hassanwalia (1997), also paint the Canadian system in a favourable light. Yet, there remains an overall impression that financial innovation occurs relatively more slowly in Canada than elsewhere, in part because of restrictive ownership rules for the largest domestic banks. Unfortunately, the minister of finance, in the reforms described above, fails to provide a convincing justification for the strict ownership rules beyond the need to retain some 'domestic' control. However, the independent value of domestically owned financial assets is no longer clear in a global financial world. Just as the Bank of Canada cannot ignore developments in the US or elsewhere, and Canada cannot control commodity prices, which are dictated in world markets but are believed to greatly influence the exchange rate, there is little reason to believe that substantial foreign ownership is, by itself, harmful to the domestic economy or would materially affect government's ability to intervene on behalf of the public. They would, after all, retain supervisory and regulatory control. Consolidation need not, therefore, be feared (as Mishkin, 1999 also points out for much the same reason). Unlike other countries, the last wave of consolidation in the banking sector in Canada took place in the early decades of this century and, if we exclude Schedule II banks, the number of banks has remained remarkably stable since the 1930s. The trend internationally, however, has been towards more not less consolidation.[17]

An equally pressing issue is whether Canadian financial institutions will eventually be permitted to become like the universal banks which they seem to want to be. If so, the moral hazard problem alluded to earlier becomes all the more important and policy-makers will have a difficult time tackling that problem (for example, see Boyd, 1999).

Finally, the present study also makes it clear that the next few years will witness a number of substantial reforms to the Canadian financial system. Since it is difficult to predict what type of financial system will emerge from these reforms, the appendix lists some key websites that readers may wish to consult from time to time for updates.

NOTES

* Support from the Social Sciences and Humanities Research Council is gratefully acknowledged, as is the research assistance of Darren Jolley.

1. See the relevant references in Rymes (1994).
2. For details about how monetary policy is conducted in a system of zero reserve requirements, see Clinton (1997).
3. Another recent study which covers some of the aspects discussed below can be found in Freedman (1998).
4. Life insurance companies tend to be mutually owned which means that they are owned by policy holders. In 1998, these same companies asked the government for permission to 'demutualize'. Legislation permitting such a move, which allows life insurers to raise money in capital markets and thus level the playing field with banks and other financial institutions, was passed in 1999.
5. The number of POS terminals grew by over 60 per cent a year between 1992 and 1997, the number of transactions by over 100 per cent over the same period, the number of telephone banking transactions by 150 per cent annually, again since 1992, while the number of ATMs grew by about 40 per cent a year in the decade spanned by the years 1988–98. Based on data in Siklos (2001, ch. 19), Canadian Bankers Association (1999) and McKinsey & Co. (1998).
6. Namely, the Royal Bank of Canada, the Canadian Imperial Bank of Commerce, the Bank of Montreal, the Bank of Nova Scotia, the Toronto Dominion Bank and the National Bank of Canada.
7. Measured in terms of the ratio of non-interest expenses to total income. Also see Peters and Donner (1998) who cover much the same issues and provide an overview of the pros and cons of bank mergers in the Canadian context.
8. McKinsey & Co. (1998, Exhibit 4–1) reports that bank loans as a share of total corporate debt fell from 44 per cent to 34 per cent in the 1986–96 period.
9. For example, while the Bank Act might restrict certain financial activities of the chartered banks it cannot prevent or regulate a retailer from effectively providing credit, say, via a store-owned credit card. Indeed, this type of non-traditional banking activity has grown over the past few years.
10. Nevertheless, McKinsey & Co. (1998, Exhibits 6–25, 6–26 and 6–29) found that average monthly fees paid to banks in Canada were slightly higher than in nine other countries sampled (Canada ranked sixth) and, despite lower costs of delivery of new types of banking services, most notably ATM, telephone, internet and personal computer banking, fees are comparable for the most part to those paid via banking directly at a bank branch.
11. Under the proposed amendments to the Bank Act, ownership restrictions would be greatly liberalized for small to medium-sized banks (the latter are defined as having capital of between 1 billion and 5 billion Canadian dollars).
12. Hence, certain lines of business could be moved out of the regulated sector into some joint venture with another bank or group of banks.
13. The fear of American domination of the Canadian financial sector is an old one. See Siklos (2001).

14. The name of this office was subsequently changed to the Office of the Superintendent of Financial Institutions (OSFI).
15. Indeed, the CDIC in its Corporate Plan (1999a) highlighted the 'challenge' for regulators in this area.
16. The initial reaction of policy makers to the failures of the 1980s and early 1990s was to raise premiums for *all* members.
17. See, for example, Saunders and Wilson (1999) who exclude Schedule II banks from their discussion without explanation.

REFERENCES

Atta-Mensah, J. and L. Nott (1999), 'Recent developments in the monetary aggregates and their implications', *Bank of Canada Review* (Spring): 5–20.

Baillie, A.C. (1998), 'TD says merger decision disappointing', *Canada News Wire*, December, available at http://www.newswire.ca.

Bank of Canada (1998a), 'Monetary conditions', Backgrounder, July.

Bank of Canada (1998b), *Price Stability, Inflation Targets, and Monetary Policy*, Proceedings of a Conference held at the Bank of Canada, May 1997, Ottawa: Bank of Canada.

Bank of Canada (1999a), 'The framework for the implementation of monetary policy in a large value transfer system environment', 31 March.

Bernanke, B. and F.S. Mishkin (1992), 'Central bank behavior and the strategy of monetary policy: observations from six industrialized countries', NBER, in O.J. Blanchard and S. Fischer (eds), *Macroeconomics Annual 1992*, Cambridge, MA: MIT Press, pp. 183–227.

Bordo, M. and A. Redish (1987), 'Why did the Bank of Canada emerge in 1935?', *Journal of Economic History*, **47** (June): 405–17.

Bordo, M., H. Rockoff and A. Redish (1994), 'The U.S. banking system from a northern exposure: Stability versus efficiency', *Journal of Economic History*, **54** (June): 325–41.

Boyd, J.H. (1999), 'Expansion of commercial banking powers . . . or, universal banking is the cart, not the horse', *Journal of Banking and Finance*, **23**, 655–62.

Canada Deposit Insurance Corporation (CDIC) (1999a), *Corporate Plan 1999/2000 to 2003/2004*, available at http://www.cdic.ca.

Canada Deposit Insurance Corporation (CDIC) (1999b), 'New premium structure and rates for CDIC member institutions', *News Release*, available at http://www.cdic.ca.

Canadian Bankers Association (1999), *Canadian Bank Facts*, Pickering, ON: Canadian Bankers Association.

Carr, J.L., G.F. Mathewson and N. Quigley (1994), *Ensuring Failure: Financial System Stability and Deposit Insurance in Canada*, Toronto: C.D. Howe Institute.

Clinton, K. (1997), 'Implementation of monetary policy in a regime with zero reserve requirements', Bank of Canada Working Paper 97–8, April.

Courchene, T.J. (1981) *Money, Inflation, and the Bank of Canada: An Analysis of Monetary Gradualism, 1975–1980*, Toronto: C.D. Howe Institute.

Courchene, T.J. and R.G. Harris (1999), 'From fixing to monetary union: options for North American currency integration', CD Howe Institute Commentary, 22 June.

Crow, J.W. (1988), 'The work of Canadian monetary policy', *Bank of Canada Review*, February.

Department of Finance (1998), 'Minister of Finance announces decision on bank merger proposals', *News Release*, 98–123, 14 December, available at http://www.fin.gc.ca.

Department of Finance (1999a), 'Foreign bank branching legislation comes into force', *News Release*, 99–060, 28 June, available at http://www.fin.gc.ca.

Department of Finance (1999b), 'Finance minister welcomes G-7's progress on promoting stability in the international financial system', *News Release*, 99–020, available at http://www.fin.gc.ca.

Freedman, C. (1998), 'The banking system', Bank of Canada, March.

Freedman, C. and C. Goodlet (1998), 'The financial services sector: past changes and future prospects', Bank of Canada Commentary, March.

Grant, J. (1997), 'The Bank of Canada's operating framework', in Laidler (ed.), pp. 207–24.

Howitt, P. (1986), *Monetary Policy in Transition: A Study of Bank of Canada Policy, 1982–95*, Toronto: C.D. Howe Institute.

Laidler, D.E.W. (ed.) (1997), *Where We Go From Here: Inflation Targets in Canada's Monetary Policy Regime*, Toronto: C.D. Howe Institute.

Laidler, D.E.W. (1999), 'The exchange rate regime and Canada's monetary order', Bank of Canada Working Paper 99–7.

Laidler, D.E.W. and W.B.P. Robson (1993), *The Great Canadian Disinflation: The Economics and Politics of Monetary Policy in Canada, 1988–93*, Toronto: C.D. Howe Institute.

Mathewson, G.F. and N.C. Quigley (1997), 'Reforming the Bank Act: regulation, public policy and the market', *Canadian Business Law Journal*, **29** (September): 1–16.

Mathewson, G.F. and N.C. Quigley (1998), 'Canadian bank mergers: efficiency and consumer gain versus market power', C.D. Howe Institute Commentary.

McFetridge, D.G. (1998), 'Competition policy issues', Research Paper prepared for the Task Force on the Future of the Canadian Financial Services Sector, September.

McKinsey & Co. (1998), 'The changing landscape for Canadian financial services: new forces, new competitors, new choices', Research Paper prepared for the Task Force on the Future of the Canadian Financial Services Sector, September.

Mishkin, F.S. (1999), 'Financial consolidation: dangers and opportunities', *Journal of Banking and Finance*, **23**, 675–91.

Muirhead, B. (1999), *Against the Odds: The Public Life and Times of Louis Rasminsky*, Toronto: University of Toronto Press.

Nathan, A. and E. Neave (1989), 'Competition and contestability in Canada's financial system: Empirical results', *Canadian Journal of Economics*, **22** (August): 576–94.

Neave, E.H. and F. Milne (1998), 'Revising Canada's financial regulation: analysis and recommendations', C.D. Howe Institute Commentary.

Neufeld, E.P. and H. Hassanwalia (1997), 'Challenge for the further restructuring of the financial-services industry in Canada', in G.F. von Funstenberg (ed.), *The Banking and Financial Structure in NAFTA Countries and Chile*, Boston: Kluwer: pp. 44–106.

Peters, D.D. and A.W. Donner (1998), 'Bank mergers: the public policy challenge', paper presented at the Sixth Annual Policy Conference, Laurentian University, September.

Rymes, T.K. (1994), 'On the Coyne–Rasminsky Directive and responsibility for monetary policy in Canada', in P.L. Siklos (ed.), *Varieties of Monetary Reforms: Lessons and Experiences on the Road to Monetary Union*, Boston: Kluwer, pp. 351–66.

Saunders, A. and B. Wilson (1999), 'The impact of consolidation and safety-net support on Canadian, US and UK Bonds: 1893–1992', *Journal of Banking and Finance*, **23**, 537–71.

Siklos, P.L. (1997), 'Charting a future for the Bank of Canada: inflation targets and the balance between autonomy and accountability', in Laidler (ed.), pp. 101–84.

Siklos, P.L. (1999), 'Inflation target design, persistence and inflation performance in industrial countries', *Review of the Federal Reserve Bank of St. Louis*, **81** (March/April): 47–58.

Siklos, P.L. (2000a), 'Is the MCI a useful signal of monetary policy conditions? An empirical investigation', *International Finance*, **3** (November): 413–38.

Siklos, P.L. (2000b), 'Understanding the Great Depression in the United States versus Canada', in Theo Balderston (ed.), *World Economy and National Economies in the Interwar Slump*, London: Macmillan, forthcoming.

Siklos, P.L. (2001), *Money, Banking, and Financial Institutions: Canada in the Global Environment*, Toronto: McGraw-Hill Ryerson, third edition.

Smith, R.T. (1999), 'Money in the bank: comparing bank profits in Canada and abroad', C.D. Howe Institute Commentary.

Task Force on the Future of the Canadian Financial Services Sector (1998), 'Report of the Task Force' (MacKay Task Force report), Ottawa: Supply and Services Canada, September.

APPENDIX 3A SELECTED SOURCE OF INFORMATION ON THE INTERNET ABOUT THE CANADIAN FINANCIAL SECTOR

Bank of Canada	http://www.bankofcanada.ca
Canadian Bankers Association	http://www.cba.ca
Department of Finance, Canada	http://www.fin.gc.ca/fin-eng.html
Canada Deposit Insurance Corporation	http://www.cdic.ca
C.D. Howe Institute	http://www.cdhowe.org
Canada's Credit Unions	http://www.cucentral.ca
Conference Board of Canada	http://www.conferenceboard.ca

4. Financial system reform in China

Margot Schueller

1 INTRODUCTION

The reform of the financial system is of crucial importance for China's successful transition to a market economy. Despite the progress made in restructuring banks and non-bank institutions and introducing new financial instruments over the last ten years, China does not yet have a well-functioning financial market.

2 CENTRAL BANK REFORM

Over the last 20 years, China's central banking system underwent some major changes. Among the most important reform steps were: (i) the establishment of a two-tier banking system; (ii) the introduction of laws and regulations as well as instruments to enable the central bank to supervise and regulate the financial market better; and (iii) the restructuring of the central bank's administrative structure in order to become more independent from the interference of local governments.

Before China began to reform its economic system in 1979, a Soviet-style mono-banking system existed in which the People's Bank of China (PBC) handled most financial transactions and was responsible for currency issuance and foreign exchange management. Within the PBC, two specialized banks, the Bank of China (BOC) and the People's Construction Bank of China (PCBC), operated as special departments of the PBC. The banks were restricted to facilitating the financing of the economic plan, and thus became 'treasuries for local governments' (Bowles and White, 1993, p. 70). There was no need for separate commercial banks as the centrally planned economy only required an accounting system to balance the books of state-owned enterprises (SOEs). Besides the settlement of enterprises' transactions, the intermediation function of the PBC was limited to the administration of working capital, short-term investment and the collection of household savings.

During the first period of the reform of the financial system reform, from

1979 to 1984, the transformation of the PBC into a central bank took place. In its directive for the reform of the financial system of 1979, the State Council announced the gradual commercialization of banks, and a transformation of budgetary grants into bank loans, and also authorized the PBC and the specialized banks to allocate medium- and long-term loans to SOEs. By 1982, the composition of funds allocated to SOEs already accounted for 80 per cent of bank loans compared to 70 per cent of budgetary grants in 1978. Most of the PBC's commercial business was taken over by the PCBC, which granted loans to the construction sector, and by the BOC, specialized in foreign currency transactions. Two other specialized banks were established as well: the Agricultural Bank of China (ABC) was founded in 1979 and took over the rural banking business and the supervision of the network of 60,000 rural credit cooperatives (RCCs) from the PBC; and the Industrial and Commercial Bank of China (ICBC), established in 1984, took over the urban commercial banking activities of the PBC. The formal restructuring of the PBC into a central bank followed a September 1983 directive by the State Council, effective from 1 January 1984, and ended the transformation into a two-tier banking system (Mehran et al., 1996, pp. 10–12).

According to provisional regulations on banking from 1986, the PBC was explicitly made responsible for monetary policy and the supervision of the financial system, including the money and capital markets. Although the PBC received a mandate for fulfilling the traditional function of a central bank, it did not have adequate authority over interest rates and money supply to carry out its new tasks. The PBC's ability to perform its regulatory function was also reduced by the allocation of loans according to the credit plan, the predominance of policy lending and the interference of local governments in the decision making of local PBC branches. Equivalent to a line ministry under the State Council, the PBC was not an autonomous regulatory body, but dependent on the approval of its economic and financial decisions by the State Council. As a consequence of the political weakness of the PBC, monetary policy was practically dictated by the central government and subject to the influence of local governments. The political weakness of the central bank was accompanied by a declining effectiveness of monetary control through the credit plan system. With the emergence of new regional and local banks and non-bank financial institutions (NBFIs) operating outside the credit plan, the central bank's control over lending diminished rapidly. By the middle of 1996, about 40 per cent of loans were created outside the credit plan and thus were not subject to the PBC's supervision.

During the economic overheating in 1993 it became obvious that the central bank needed greater autonomy and that the regulatory regime of the banking system showed great weaknesses. Large outflows of funds from the banking system using a black interbank market at very high interest rates supported a wave of speculation in real estate and the stock market. As a consequence, the treasury market was negatively affected, the growth of new bank deposits fell significantly and banks suffered a liquidity squeeze. To restore financial stability, the central government introduced a reform package in which the PBC's organizational restructuring and an increase of its autonomy were the cornerstones. The head office of the PBC was strengthened by recentralizing the lending authority of its regional branches, which were no longer allowed to grant loans to the head offices of the specialized banks (Pei, 1998, pp. 330–43).

The People's Bank Law of 1995 further enhanced the legal status of the central bank's authority. According to this law, the PBC is under the leadership of the State Council, but should not be subject to intervention by local governments, other administrative organs or individuals. The law explicitly bans the PBC from financing government budget deficits and from making loans to central and local government agencies. Before 1995, the PBC was expected to pursue multiple objectives, such as promoting economic growth, full employment and price stability. In contrast, the central bank law defines monetary stability as the primary objective, which should facilitate economic growth. The central bank law also defines two other functions of the PBC, that is, the supervisory function over financial institutions and the whole financial system as well as the regulatory function for monetary policy. For a transitory period, the law allowed the credit quota system to remain in place as a means of direct control, but required indirect instruments to be introduced gradually, such as open market operations, discounting and rediscounting activities and so on (People's Bank Law). By January 1998, the PBC replaced the credit plan system (for both working capital loans and fixed investment loans) by an indicative non-binding target and required banks to achieve specific asset/liability ratios. The reform allowed the banks to lend according to commercial considerations as long as their total lending was in line with the given ratios and the policy targets of the PBC (Mo, 1999, p. 99).

As a reaction to the Asian financial crisis, the Chinese government introduced new reforms to the financial system. Among other reform steps, the PBC's organizational structure was changed at the end of the 1990s from 31 provincial-level branches into nine national branches crossing several administrative units. The nine branches were established in the cities of Tianjin and Shanghai and in the provincial capitals Shenyang, Nanjing, Jinan, Wuhan, Guangzhou, Chengdu and Xian. The new branch structure aims at reducing intervention from local governments and improving the effectiveness of monetary policy (Lee, 2000, p. 174; Lardy, 1998, p. 202–9).

3 INSTITUTIONAL REFORM

The establishment of new banks and other financial institutions played an important role in the transformation of China's financial system. New financial institutions were supposed to create competition among banks, enlarge the scope of banking business, improve the financing system, diversify the ownership structure and support the commercialization of the four specialized state banks. To enable them to compete with the newly established banks, restrictions on their lending activities outside their traditional domain were lifted. The Law on Commercial Banks, enacted in May 1995, further enhanced the transition to a diversified market-oriented and independent banking system. Although state banks remained the predominant players in the banking system by the end of the 1990s, a monopolistic structure of the banking system no longer existed. Besides diversification, the separation of banking and non-banking activities was another crucial step in the institutional reform of the banking system. (Figure 4.1.)

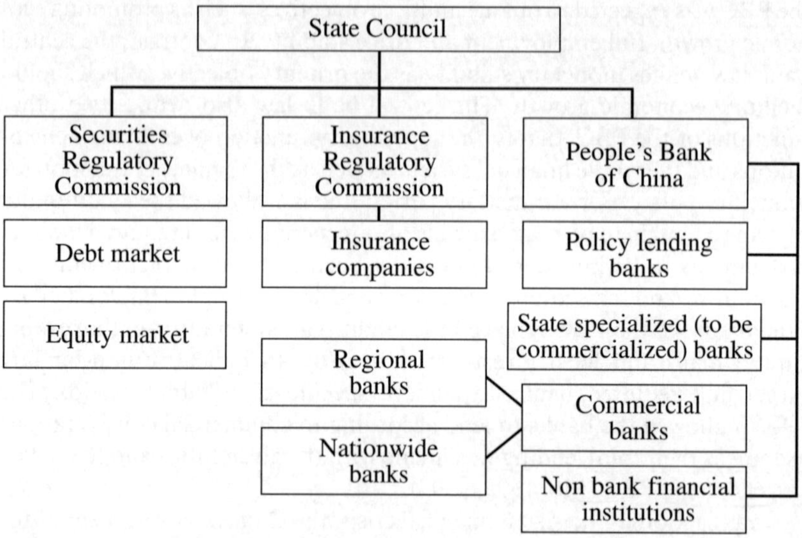

Figure 4.1 Structure of China's financial sector, 1999

Institutional diversification in the banking sector began with the foundation of the state-owned China Investment Bank (established 1981), the joint-stock Bank of Communications (1986) and the CITIC Industrial Bank (1987), owned by China Investment and Trust Corporation. More joint-stock banks owned by large state-owned conglomerates were allowed to compete in the market at the beginning of the 1990s, among them the China Merchant Bank, the Hua Xia Bank and the Everbright Bank. The first private bank, the Minsheng Bank, was founded in 1995. Additionally, regional commercial banks, such as the Guangdong Development Bank, the Shanghai Development Bank and the Shenzhen Development Bank, and local banks, such as the Fujian Industrial Bank, the Yantai Housing Saving Bank and the Bengbu Housing Saving Bank, emerged. NBFIs, comprising trust and investment corporations (TICs), rural and urban credit cooperatives, finance and leasing firms, insurance companies and securities firms began to appear in the 1980s as well. As a consequence of more competition among financial institutions, the market share of the newly founded banks and non-bank intermediaries increased at the expense of the market share of the four large state-owned banks.

In 1994, three state policy lending banks were established which were allowed to grant loans at subsidized interest rates. These banks were the State Development Bank of China, responsible for financing key construction and infrastructure projects, the Agricultural Development Bank of China, supposed to finance the state's procurement of agricultural products and agricultural development projects, and the Export–Import Bank of China, designed to support export and import activities by supplying loans to sellers and buyers. These state banks were founded to take over the policy loans from the four specialized state banks and thus support their commercialization. Policy lending can be defined as 'part of bank lending that is made at the request of (or strongly encouraged by) the government to promote its economic, industrial, and sectoral policies and to assure funding for priority activities' (Mehran et al., 1996, p. 14). While the creation of policy-lending banks and the separation between policy lending and commercial lending had a positive impact on the structure of the four large state banks' loan portfolios, the problem of policy lending to poorly performing SOEs by these banks has not yet been solved. On the one hand, there is a large stock of non-performing loans (NPLs), which is the result of past policy lending policy, and on the other hand, state banks are still not able to grant loans according to purely commercial consideration. (Table 4.1.)

Additionally, foreign banking institutions were allowed to enter the Chinese market, but their business scope and their choice of location remained strongly restricted. At the end of October 2000, foreign banks had established 234 representative offices, the number of foreign bank branches had increased to 157, and their total assets amounted to US$34.3 billion. Their market share, however, was still rather small in 1999. Foreign banks' share of total foreign currency loans was 12.8 per cent, and their share of total assets of all financial institutions was only 1.53 per cent (*China Nachrichten*, 2000, p. 51). With China's accession to the World

Table 4.1 Asset quality at the four state-owned commercial banks, end of 1996

	Capital adequacy rate (%)	Interest recovering rate (%)	Net profit–asset ratio (%)	NPLs as % of total loans
Total	4.37	60	5.55	24.4
Industrial and Commercial Bank of China	4.35	–	6.17	–
Agricultural Bank of China	3.49	–	1.44	–
Bank of China	4.84	–	10.29	10.29 (1998)
China Construction Bank	4.81	–	5.70	–

Source: Li Xinxin (1998).

Trade Organization (WTO) in 2001, restrictions on foreign banking institutions will be lifted gradually, and thus, competition will be intensified.

With regard to the relationship between banks and NBFIs, another important institutional change took place during the 1990s. The TICs and International Trust and Investment Corporations (ITICs) became increasingly important as sources of revenues for state banks, local branches of the PBC as well as for the central government and the local governments, which owned and operated them. In contrast to Western countries, Chinese TICs and ITICs basically performed the role of commercial banks but without much regulation and restriction (Hong and Yan, 2000, p. 290). Strong incentives to set up these NBFIs led to a surge in their numbers to about 620 at the end of 1982. Despite the government's attempt to regulate their performance and restructure them, their numbers increased to more than 1,000 by 1988, contributing to financial disorder and inflation. Although their number was cut back by more than half in the following years, their close relationship with banks continued. As a consequence, they became involved in large-scale speculation in the real estate and stock markets during the period of economic overheating in 1993. The law on commercial banks from 1995 finally required cutting off the ownership ties between banks and TICs. In 1997, the PBC even prohibited banks from operating or engaging in trust and investment activities (Pei, 1998, pp. 329–44). Due to excessive domestic and foreign debt and mismanagement, some TICs and ITICs became insolvent and were merged or closed down at the end of the 1990s. CADTIC (China Agricultural Development Trust and Investment Corporation), one of China's largest TICs and under the direct control of the central government, was taken over by the China

Construction Bank in January 1997. CADTIC had not only been involved in high-risk activities, but was engaged in international shipping, travelling, manufacturing, food production and so on (Hong and Yan, 2000, pp. 290–91). Other examples were the closure of China Venturetech Investment Corporation in 1998 and of GITIC (Guangdong International Investment and Trust Corporation) (Cai, 1999, p. 170).

4 SUPERVISORY REFORM

The Asian crisis has demonstrated that a strong supervisory system is of crucial importance for the stability of the whole financial sector. To enhance supervision, China introduced some important reform steps in the 1990s such as: (i) business segregation in the financial industry and introduction of new regulatory agencies; and (ii) the supervision of commercial banks on the basis of the Basel Core Principles.

Unified supervision of the whole financial system was exercised by the PBC until the end of the 1990s. In the course of the reform of the financial system, it became clear that business segregation was necessary in order to avoid the spread of risks within the banking sector. As banks were either the owner of securities houses, TICs and insurance companies or their largest investors, the close relationship between banks and NBFIs had negative impacts on the key function of banks and on the competition from smaller financial institutions. According to the principle of business segregation and on the basis of the relevant laws on securities, insurance and commercial banks, an involvement of banks in trust, insurance and securities business became strictly forbidden. At the end of 1998, the PBC's duty to supervise the insurance industry was transferred to the newly founded Insurance Regulatory Commission of China. The Securities Regulatory Commission of China was established as a third supervisory authority for the supervision of the securities industry. Additionally, new regulations were introduced aiming at a supervision of commercial banks on the basis of the requirements of the Basel Capital Accord.

The Basel Core Principles comprise a set of guidelines which provide a framework for effective banking supervision. Since the Asian crisis, China has made some progress in the adaptation of the Basel Core Principles to its financial system. Among the most important measures were:

1. Strengthening of the capital base of state-owned banks in order to increase the minimum capital adequacy ratio. Estimates about the scope of NPLs vary quite substantially. At the end of 1997, the PBC disclosed an official estimate of NPLs amounting to 20–25 per cent of

total bank loans. However, only 5–6 per cent were defined as irrecoverable. Independent analysts presented alternative estimates of NPLs ranging from 30–60 per cent (Watanabe, 2000, p. 39). New capital was injected into the banks in August 1998 through the issuance of 270 billion renminbi (RMB) (US$32.5 billion) in special government bonds. The PBC recalled part of the loans by lowering the legal reserve requirements from 13 per cent to 8 per cent, enabling the banks to purchase bonds issued by the ministry of finance (MoF) which transferred the proceeds to the state-owned banks. Through this double-swap transaction, on the one hand an asset swap of bonds for reserve deposits between state-owned banks and the MoF and on the other hand a liability swap of equity for central bank borrowing between the state-owned banks and the PBC, the capital of state-owned banks was doubled. However, minimum capital adequacy ratios required by the Bank for International Settlements (BIS) were still not achieved. In addition to replenishing the banks' capital, four asset management companies connected to the four large state-owned banks were established to repackage and sell the problem loans of the SOEs.

2. Introduction of a new system of classification of loans, and closer monitoring of risks in financial institutions. Under the 'old' system of loan classification, loans were classified according to the overdue period as 'overdue' (up to three months), 'doubtful' (less than 24 months) and 'bad' (more than 24 months). Banks were not required to make provisions against overdue loans. In contrast, the new four-category risk-based loan classification system demands that banks pursue a capital risk management approach by making provision according to the defined risk category of the loan (Mo, 1999, pp. 90–97).
3. Introduction of standard procedures for the exit of problem financial institutions. During 1997 and 1998, the PBC closed down 42 problem depository institutions, namely one commercial bank (Hainan Development Bank), 23 urban and 18 rural credit cooperatives, as well as three TICs (China Agricultural Trust and Investment Corporation, China Venture Investment Corporation, and Guangdong International Trust and Investment Corporation). A set of standard procedures for closure, liquidation and management takeover was also established by the PBC (Liu, 1999, pp. 298–301).

5. FINANCIAL DEREGULATION

Deregulation of the markets for money and capital and liberalization of the foreign exchange system followed a gradualist reform approach, typical for

China's whole transition to a market economy. The approach comprised small-scale experimentations, gradual liberalization and decentralization of decision making.

The *money market*, which includes all financial instruments with a maturity of one year or less, can be characterized by: (i) a slow development in terms of scope and diversification; (ii) a predominance of interbank loans; and (iii) an underdeveloped market for repurchase agreements, commercial bills, treasury bills and other short-term government bonds.

Although the money market transaction volume has expanded gradually since the end of the 1980s, the ratio of the transaction volumes of interbank loans, repurchase agreements and commercial paper to GDP was only 79 per cent by 1996. Compared to other countries this ratio was still very small and pointed to the underdeveloped function of the money market in China (Chang et al., 2000, p. 179). The interbank market started on an experimental basis in the 1980s in the coastal city of Wenzhou, allowing branches and sub-branches of the Agricultural Bank of China to lend and to borrow from one another. By the middle of the 1980s, large cities such as Beijing, Shanghai and Guangzhou opened interbank markets (so-called financing centres) as well. However, under the condition of state-fixed interest rates and a segmented financial market, these rudimentary markets were not able to balance the inter-regional liquidity flow, and most of its transactions were unsecured. When the first problems occurred in 1990, such as the borrowing of short-term funds to finance long-term lending, the PBC started to regulate the market by setting a reference rate for the interbank market rate and introducing some provisional regulations.

Over the following years, the numbers of financing centres increased substantially (44 by 1994), and the volume of lending and borrowing in the interbank market grew manifold. Excess liquidity of the interbank market went into fixed asset investment and contributed to the strong wave of stock and real estate speculation in 1993 (Mehran et al., 1996, pp. 24–7). To unify and better regulate the fragmented market, a nationwide interbank market was created in January 1996. Within a system of two trading levels, participants of the primary network include 15 headquarters of commercial banks, 35 financing centres, four urban credit cooperatives and several TICs. Transactions are conducted through the computerized central trading system. The secondary network comprises 35 financing centres in provinces, municipal cities and autonomous regions; participants are commercial bank branches at the prefecture and municipal levels, local TICs and urban and rural credit cooperatives. The interest rate in the national interbank market became basically market determined, but influenced by the PBC's monetary policy (Chang et al., 2000, pp. 175–80).

Compared to the transaction volume of the interbank market, other short-term debt instruments are of minor importance in China's financial market. Repurchase agreements (repo), as an acquisition of funds through the sale of securities, appeared in China's financial market in 1991, when the Shanghai Stock Exchange and the Securities Trading Automatic Quotation (STAQS) system were established. However, there has been no unified repo market with a centralized clearance system: thus, efficient allocation of capital and enforcement of government regulations remains difficult. Although the commercial paper market began in the early 1980s and promulgation of the 'Commercial Paper Law' stabilized its legal basis, the market transaction volume remained much smaller compared to the interbank market. Among the reasons for the slow market development were the lack of reliable risk assessments by rating agencies and a lack of enforcement of market regulations (Chang et al., 2000, pp. 182–8).

Starting at the beginning of the 1980s, the *capital market* saw a fast development. Characteristic features of the market were: (i) the predominance of government bonds; (ii) a gradual diversification of securities; and (iii) a strengthening of the regulatory framework of the market.

The *primary securities market* opened as early as 1981 with the first issuance of government treasury bonds. In the initial period, these treasury bonds were used by local governments as instruments to tap financial resources complementary to the credit plan and to borrowing from the PBC. They were issued by the MoF and sold on a compulsory basis to lower-level governments at administrated rates and through the same channels used to implement the credit plan. Local governments then allocated these bonds to SOEs under their jurisdiction, which allocated them to their workers as part of their salary. In the course of the 1980s, the government securities market adopted more market-oriented techniques. Instead of administrative sales of treasury bonds, underwriting syndications was introduced, the maturity period shortened and the interest rate raised to make these investments more attractive to households. Starting in 1988, government bonds were indexed during periods of high inflation (Burdekin and Hu, 2000, pp. 261–8). By the end of the 1980s, new government debt instruments were introduced, such as key construction bonds for financing specific projects of the State Planning Commission as well as treasury bills and savings bonds with comparatively short maturity periods of six months to two years. The government securities market was complemented by the issuance of non-government securities, such as financial bonds by the specialized banks, enterprise shares and corporate bonds. However, in the initial period, enterprise shares were more bond-like as they had a fixed base return and no voting rights were connected to share holding (Xu, 1998, p. 38).

The new-issue and offering process of enterprise shares possessed some specific characteristics:

1. The State Planning Commission, the PBC and the China Securities Regulatory Committee (CSRC) decided on the aggregate amount of new shares issued each year and allocated a certain quota to individual provinces.
2. To list on the stock exchange, enterprises were chosen on the basis of good performance and according to additional criteria, such as sector development objectives.
3. Various share categories were introduced such as non-tradable shares (held only by the government or employees), legal entity shares called C-shares (held by other SOEs), domestic individual A-shares (held only by private Chinese citizens), foreign individual B-shares, Hong Kong issued H-shares and shares issued at the New York Stock Exchange, called N-shares. Different requirements exist for these various types of shares. Companies issuing B-Shares denominated in foreign currency not only have to satisfy the securities regulations, but also have to demonstrate a need for foreign exchange and a stable source of foreign exchange income. The approval process for the issuance of B-shares is much stricter compared to A-shares, especially in terms of disclosure of accounting and auditing documents. B-shares and shares listed on overseas stock exchanges are not issued according to fixed quotas but on a case-by-case approval basis.
4. Government control over most companies is maintained through the partial sales of stocks to other SOEs and government organizations.
5. Shares are allocated to retail investors through a lottery mechanism at basically fixed IPO prices for all investors (Zhang and Thomas, 1999, pp. 51–6; Su and Fleisher, 2000, pp. 244–6).

The *secondary market* for shares has the following features: (i) dominance of retail investors amounting to around 60 million private households compared to only a small number of institutional investors; (ii) lack of transparency leading to high volatility and speculation; and (iii) two national stock exchanges, competing with each other, one in Shanghai and the other one in Shenzhen. Technically, the secondary market for securities is well developed, comprising an electronic network for securities trading (STAQS). The network provides onscreen price information and a centralized clearing and settlement facility not only for stocks but also for government securities. To limit speculation and high volatility, margin trading and short selling are forbidden. Additionally, various laws and regulations strengthened the legal basis of the stock market in the 1990s, especially the promulgation of the Securities Law at the end of 1998. However, enforcement of existing regulations remained weak, leading to various problems such as price manipulation and insider trading.

In February 2001, new steps in the restructuring of the primary and secondary market for enterprise shares were made. The CSRC announced the integration of the markets for B-shares and A-shares. Domestic investors with a foreign currency account were officially allowed to buy B-shares. The move was designed to invigorate the B-share market. At the end of 2000, the B-share market realized a market capitalization of only US$7 billion for its 114 registered companies compared to a market capitalization of US$560 billion in the A-share market which comprises around 1,200 registered companies. In addition, the quota system for the allocation of stocks will be abolished in the future and enterprises will be allowed to issue stocks according to market demand. The CSRC is also preparing to de-list companies running at a loss for several years in a row, and announced they would integrate the two national stock exchanges in the near future. According to the CSRC vision, the Shenzhen stock exchange should concentrate on the issue of high-tech companies' stocks.

China's *foreign exchange regime* underwent a transformation from a highly centralized system at the end of the 1970s to a semi-open system with current account convertibility at the end of the 1990s. The major reforms included: (i) deregulation and devaluation of the exchange rate; (ii) establishment of swap centres and retention quotas; (iii) integration of regional markets and unification of exchange rates; and (iv) introduction of current account convertibility.

Foreign trade began to play a new role with the opening of the Chinese economy, and thus the foreign exchange rate started to become important as well. To compensate for increasing export prices, the exchange rate was devaluated six times between 1981 and 1993 with a range from 9.6 per cent to 44.9 per cent. In the initial years of economic reform, an internal settlement rate existed, but this was abolished in 1985. Thereafter, all transactions were conducted at the official rate decided on the basis of a system of managed floating by the State Administration of Exchange Control (SAEC), responsible for implementing and enforcing exchange regulations on behalf of the PBC. The exchange rate was split up again into two different rates at the end of 1996 when foreign trade companies were allowed to retain a certain proportion of their foreign exchange earnings as incentives to expand their export activities. The recently founded foreign exchange adjustment centres (FEACs) allowed companies to buy and sell retention quotas and foreign currency at a basic market-determined swap rate. While the official exchange rate for tourism or other currency transactions remained fixed, the FEACs' exchange rates gradually depreciated. In 1994, the 24 swap centres with an electronic trading system, comprising 90 per cent of the total swap market, were integrated into a national centre (China Foreign Exchange Trade System: CFETS) in Shanghai. At the end of the 1990s, 37 foreign exchange trading centres located in major cities were linked electronically to the national CFETS. The retention quota system was abolished and the two exchange rates were unified at the swap-market exchange rate of RMB8.7 per US dollar in 1994. Until the beginning of 2001, the RMB exchange rate against major currencies remained basically the same.

The last reform step took place at the end of 1996 when China announced that it had fulfilled the International Monetary Fund (IMF) requirements for current account convertibility. Foreign-funded enterprises were allowed to maintain a foreign exchange settlement bank account at authorized domestic banks for current account transactions. Since October 1997, domestic companies in need of foreign exchange can convert Chinese currency into foreign exchange at authorized banks by presenting a valid proof of need and commercial bills. Based on the weighted average price of foreign exchange transactions during the previous day's trading at the interbank foreign exchange market, the PBC publishes a daily reference rate for the RMB against the US dollar, the Hong Kong dollar and the Japanese yen. The PBC has defined certain limits within which the buying and selling rates of the RMB against foreign currencies may deviate (Mehran et al., 1996, pp. 55–63; Wong and Wong, 1998, pp. 205–54; IMF, 1998, p. 211).

During the process of economic transformation, *interest rates* became more flexible but they are not yet fully liberalized. The PBC is responsible for formulating interest rate policy and defines benchmark interest rates and floating limits for lending rates. The interest rate structure comprises: (i) rates for deposits and loans between the PBC and financial institutions, including basic rates for required reserves and re-lending; (ii) rates for deposits and lending between banks and customers, which are decided by the PBC as well but allowed to vary around 20 per cent of the given rate; and (iii) rates for the bond and interbank markets (Xu, 1998, pp. 148–53). In view of China's accession to the WTO, the PBC announced in July 2000 that interest rates would be liberalized within the following three years. Starting with the relaxation of rates that banks pay on foreign deposits, the interbank rates and securities market rates would then be allowed to fluctuate more freely. Flexible interests rates on loans would be first introduced into rural and later into urban areas (*International Herald Tribune*, 20 July 2000).

The Asian crisis demonstrated that a sound financial system comprises safety-net arrangements that both prevent bank runs and enhance *consumer protection.* Deposit insurance systems protect depositors who have placed funds with a bank from suffering losses (Ketcha, 1999, pp. 221–39). In China, the Commercial Bank Law of 1995 requires the banks to make provisions for guaranteeing their solvency. Prudential supervision by the PBC has been strengthened through guidelines on asset-liability management, introduction of a loan classification system and through gradual increases in provisions for loan losses. Between 1995 and 1998 the provision for loan losses grew from an annual average level of 0.6 per cent to 1 per cent (Mehran et al., 1996, p. 69).

REFERENCES

Bowles, Paul and Gordon White (1993), *The Political Economy of China's Financial Reforms*, Boulder, San Francisco, New York: Westview Press.

Burdekin, Richard C.K. and Xiaojin Hu (2000), 'China's experience with Indexed Government Bonds, 1988–1996', in Chen et al. (eds), pp. 261–84.

Cai, E-Sheng (1999), 'Financial supervision in China: Framework, methods and current issues', in Bank of International Settlements (ed.), pp. 169–73.

Chang, Hong, Baizhu Chen and Yang Li (2000), 'Money market in China', in Chen et al. (eds), pp. 179–95.

Chen, Beizhu, J. Kimball Dietrich and Yi Fang (eds) (2000), *Financial Market Reform in China. Progress, Problems and Prospects*, Boulder, CO: Westview Press..

China Nachrichten, (2000), Wirtschaftskammer Österreich, Beijing, No. 4.

Hong, Zhaohui and Ellen Y. Yan (2000, 'Trust and Investment Corporations in China', in Chen et al. (eds), pp. 285–98.

International Monetary Fund (IMF) (1998), *Exchange Arrangements and Exchange Restrictions, Annual Report 1998*, Washington, DC: IMF.

Karmel, Solomon M. (1994), 'Emerging securities markets in China: capitalism with Chinese characteristics', *China Quarterly*, pp. 1105–20.

Ketcha, Nicholas, J. Jr (1999), 'Deposit insurance system design and considerations', in Bank of International Settlements, *Strengthening the Banking System in China: Issues and Experience*, Basel, Policy Papers No. 7, October, pp. 221–39.

Lardy, Nichlos R. (1998), *China's Unfinished Economic Revolution*, Washington, DC: Brookings Institution Press..

Lee, John Wai Sing (2000, 'Banking reform in China (1978–1998) – A review and appraisal', *Asian Profile*, **28** (3), pp. 169–86.

Li Xinxin (1998), 'China's financial difficulties with reference to the East Asian crises – analysis of asset quality of state-owned commercial banks', *Gaige Reform* (in Chinese), No. 3, pp. 31–9.

Liu, Shiyu (1999), 'China's experience in small and medium financial institution resolution', in Bank for International Settlements (ed.), *Strengthening the Banking System in China: Issues and Experience*, Basel, Policy Papers No. 7, October, pp. 298–303.

Mehran, Hassanali, Marc Quintyn, Tom Nordman and Bernard Laurens (1996), *Monetary and Exchange System Reforms in China. An Experiment in Gradualism*, International Monetary Fund, Occasional Paper No. 141, Washington, DC, September.

Mo, Y.K. (1999), 'A review of recent banking reforms in China', in Bank of International Settlements, *Strengthening the Banking System in China: Issues and Experience*, Basel, Policy Papers No. 7, October, pp. 90–109.

Pei, Minxin (1998), 'The political economy of banking reforms in China, 1993–1997', *Journal of Contemporary China*, **7** (18), pp. 321–50.

Su, Dongwei and Belton M. Fleisher (2000), 'Explaining IPO underpricing in China', in Chen et al. (eds), pp. 243–60.

Watanabe, Mariko (ed.) (2000), *China's Non-Performing Loan Problem*, Tokyo: Institute of Developing Economies, March.

Wong, Richard Y.C. and M.L. Sonia Wong (1998), 'Liberalizing China's Foreign Exchange Regime', in Dorn, James A. (ed.), *China in the New Millennium*, Washington, DC: CATO Institute, pp. 205–24.

Xu, Xiaoping (1998), *China's Financial System Under Transition*, New York: Mcmillan Press.

Zhang, Yilei and W.A. Thomas (1999), 'Operational mechanism and characteristics of China's primary and secondary stock markets', *Journal of Asian Business*, **15** (1), pp. 49–64.

5. Financial reform in Germany

Beate Reszat

1 INTRODUCTION

Germany, with the most powerful economy in Europe and, until the introduction of the euro, a currency ranking second in the world, has long been notorious for its financial market backwardness. Outdated structures, high costs and a high degree of bureaucracy deterred investment, venture capital was hardly available and the stock market played a far smaller role in relation to the size of the economy than in other leading industrial countries. All this is gradually changing with the dramatic rise in government funding needs in the wake of German unification on the one hand and the growing competition German financial institutions face with the introduction of the euro on the other. New laws make the markets more flexible and attractive to both investors and issuers and privatizations such as Deutsche Telekom gave a new impetus to equity awareness, not to speak of the dotcom mania that seized Germany like many other countries. One result of this process is that the traditional lending role of German banks is being steadily eroded. This is the main reason why the banks have broadened their international activities with their attention focusing increasingly on the opportunities of the single currency on the one hand and on developments in eastern Europe and emerging markets in Asia and Latin America on the other. Their renewed strength in world financial markets in turn adds to the strength of their home market, further improving Frankfurt's international competitiveness.

It has been a long haul from the reopening of the regional stock exchanges, the establishment of a central bank system along the lines of the US Federal Reserve system and the currency reform in the second half of the 1940s to the *Finanzplatz Deutschland* of the 1990s. The post-war years were characterized by the challenge of financing reconstruction and economic growth – a challenge met, above all, by the German universal banks. In the 1960s, the internationalization process of German industry became a crucial driving force for banks to widen their activities abroad. In the 1970s and 1980s, the rise of the euromarkets, the transition to floating exchange rates, the revolution of computer and information technologies and the development of new financial instruments and techniques meant new opportunities as well as new risks. The 1990s marked a period of high turbulence for the banks. Plagued by scandals, such as Schneider, Balsam and Metallgesellschaft, high losses in the emerging markets of Asia and eastern Europe and a growing competition from outside, the banks struggled to cope with the financial challenges of unification, prepare themselves for the introduction of the euro and, at the same time, prop up Frankfurt as a European financial centre in order to catch up with London, Paris and other places.

The following will trace the major financial reforms and developments in Germany leading to the *Finanzplatz Deutschland*, a process which is far from completed. Over the years, despite all its financial backwardness, the country had two major advantages in international comparison: the strength of its economy and the strength of its currency. The latter had its roots in the vigour and independence of the German central bank.

2 CREATING A MYTH: THE BUNDESBANK

Historically, the German Bundesbank is widely considered the most independent of all central banks (Goodhart, 1994). Its predecessor was the Bank Deutscher Länder, a joint subsidiary to coordinate the decisions of the legally independent central banks of the German federal states or *Länder*, which were established by the western Allied powers in 1946/47 along the lines of the US Federal Reserve system to carry out joint tasks in the currency area of the newborn German mark (Born, 1977). In 1957, this two-tier central banking system was replaced by the Deutsche Bundesbank and the state central banks lost their autonomy. However, a certain federalist element was maintained with the right of the *Länder* governments to propose the president of the state central banks who in turn were members of the Bundesbank council or *Zentralbankrat*.

Initially, the strength of the Bundesbank was rooted in its legally guaranteed independence. According to the Bundesbank Law of 1957 its primary goal was the safeguarding of the currency which was widely understood as protecting both the internal value of the D-mark against inflationary pressures and its external value against exchange-rate instability or loss of purchasing power. The law also stated that the Bundesbank was bound to support the government's overall economic policy although it always made clear that the protection of the currency had first priority and that it would exercise its discretion in this respect in case of conflicts (Jarchow, 1992). However, it was less its legal status than its *factual* independence grounded in the broad support the Bundesbank had from wide parts of the population that mattered. In general, this was explained by the 'abhorrence of Germans for inflation' (Goodhart, 1994: 67) recalling the country's experience with the hyperinflation in the 1920s.

Monetary Targeting

Following Briault et al. (1996) a distinction can be made between goal independence and instrument independence with the former defined as a central bank's ability to set its own targets – or at least to determine how these targets are specified – and the latter referring to its ability to choose its own instrument setting. With respect to *instrument independence*, before the European Central Bank (ECB) took over, there was not much difference between the Bundesbank and other G-7 central banks as, for example, most of them were free to set interest rates or intervene in the foreign exchange market. However, in addition, the Bundesbank was found to have the highest *goal independence* among central banks of major developed countries in that, in contrast, for example, to the Bank of England or the Bank of Japan, it could set its own monetary or inflation targets.

With respect to those targets, there had been three decisive breaks in the history of the Bundesbank policy. The first came in December 1974 when in reaction to the transition to floating exchange rates the Bundesbank announced an annual *money supply target* taking the monetary base both as an indicator and intermediate target of monetary policy. This strategy was revised several times. While in the beginning it was formulated as a fixed number for the money growth, later on it consisted of a band or 'target corridor'. From 1988 onwards the monetary base was replaced by the broad monetary aggregate M3 in order to account for an expansion in cashless payments and shifts between deposits of different maturities.

The Bundesbank was the first among the leading economies' central banks to introduce a monetarist concept and it became the last to stick to it. However, the Bank has never taken a pure monetarist line as is demonstrated by the on average poor hit rate for its monetary target which during the first 20 years was met only half the time. Nevertheless, the Bank always managed to keep up appearances of being a rule-based central bank. Its seemingly uncompromising attitude gained it an unrivalled reputation and credibility, which is one reason why the statutes of the ECB are closely modelled on those of the Bundesbank.

Challenges of Unification

The second break in the history of the Bundesbank came with *German unification* which proved far more complex – and more expensive – than widely expected. On 1 July 1990, monetary union started with the D-mark becoming legal tender in East Germany and the monetary competence of the Bundesbank being extended, respectively. On 3 October, political unification followed. Both meant a radical change of the environment of monetary policy in Germany. The exchange rate for currency union was set at one D-mark for two Ostmarks or East German marks, the GDR currency, despite the fact that suggestions ranged between 1:3 and 1:10 and East German companies engaged in foreign trade worked at a rate of 1:4.4. The reason was political: there were fears that a lower rate would cause turmoil and further mass migration to the west leading to a dramatic loss of skilled labour in the east.

At first, above all, monetary unification was a logistic task. With the assistance of West German banks a functioning financial system was built in the eastern states. In addition, in 1990, the banks took over credit assets from East German institutions before the newly founded privatization agency, the *Treuhandanstalt*, was established. In November 1992, an amendment of the Bundesbank Law brought a restructuring of the Bundesbank organization. The maximum number of seats on the *Zentralbankrat* was reduced. The five new states did not acquire a new central bank each adding to the 11 in the west. Instead, the state central banks were cut to nine and at the same time, the maximum number of Bundesbank directorate members on the council was cut to eight from a previous ten. State bank representation was to account as far as possible for land area, population and economic size with the larger western *Länder* retaining single representation.

Monetary targeting became a big challenge. With unification, the German money supply rose by about DM180 billion or 15 per cent. Even with initially comparably favourable estimates of a real growth potential of about 10 per cent – which later on turned out to be overoptimistic – this number bore a high inflationary potential. The stable and highly predictable behaviour patterns which had formed in the western states could not be assumed to hold in the east where the population faced a stable convertible currency for the first time. In addition, there was only a vague impression of the growth of real production potential in the east. Nevertheless, in December 1990, the *Zentralbankrat* decided to stick to monetary targeting despite all foreseeable hindrances. In contrast to all reservations the pace of inflation remained moderate. It accelerated from 2.7 per cent in 1990 to 4.0 per cent in 1992 and slowed down thereafter to a moderate 1.7 per cent in 1995.

One of the immediate results of unification was a massive flow of payments to the east. Financial transfers from west to east totalled DM132 billion in 1991, DM156 billion in 1992 and DM170 billion in 1993 with a still rising tendency during the next few years. In addition, there was the cost of privatizing east German companies. When the *Treuhand* was closed down at the end of 1994, its debt had risen to about DM205 billion. Up to October 1995 alone, the German Kreditanstalt für Wiederaufbau (KfW) lent DM91 billion to east Germany, and the Deutsche Ausgleichsbank, another development bank, lent DM37 billion (Shirreff, 1996). One effect of the unification was a sharp rise in government funding needs. This should prove one of the strongest motives for financial reform in Germany in the years to come.

European Monetary Union

The 1990s also marked the third and most radical break in the history of the Bundesbank. It started with the 1992 Maastricht Treaty which established a timetable for the completion of European Monetary Union (EMU). On 1 January 1999, the Bank became just one of many organs of the new European quasi-federal financial system with its functions largely taken over by the ECB. In late January, it published its last-ever money supply data for Germany. The diminution of the Bundesbank's decision-making role raised many questions concerning its organizational structure. For example, the justification of a large policy advisory committee in the form of the existing Bundesbank Council was much debated, and the total number of 16,000 employees in the Bundesbank system dealing with only one of the EU member countries appeared excessive considering that, in March 1999, at the ECB just over 600 employees formulated and coordinated monetary policy for 11 countries (Saunderson, 1999).

At the end of January 2001, the German government announced plans to reform the Bundesbank. Since 30 April 2002, an eight-person Board of Directors, replacing the Central Bank Council, the Directorate and the Executive Boards of the *Länder* Central Banks is running the Bank. It consists of the President, the Vice-President and six other members. President, Vice-President and two other members of the Board are nominated by the Federal Government while the other four members are nominated by the Bundesrat in agreement with the Federal Government. Excluding the *Länder* representatives considerably strengthens the president, who represents Germany in the ECB's policy-making governing council, putting an end to long-complained interference from regional Bundesbank officials. The Bundesbank maintains nine Regional Offices in the German federal states.

3 FINANCIAL DEREGULATION, INNOVATION AND STRUCTURAL CHANGE

The 1990s brought a downgrading of the Bundesbank, but an upgrading of the *Finanzplatz Deutschland*. Beside unification, EMU was the second major event giving an impetus to raise Frankfurt's competitiveness as a financial centre and to break open encrusted market structures. Up to the early 1990s, financial liberalization in Germany had proceeded very slowly. Despite the fact that the German Banking Act, the *Kreditwesengesetz* (KWG), which is generally considered as the basic law for German banks and bank regulation (Büschgen, 1997), had been amended several times – for instance, a crucial revision was the liberalization of interest rates in 1967 – the country's financial system was widely regarded as backward with respect to the establishment of new markets and the introduction of new financial instruments. One example is the creation of functioning forward markets. Opportunities to take, or hedge against, risks by means of forwards, futures and options were strongly limited in Germany before the 1980s. Forward transactions in securities had been forbidden since 1931 as a reaction to the worldwide stock market crash in 1929. It was only in 1970 that options trading was allowed again, but only in stocks and only in those stocks which were admitted to options trading on an exchange. In addition, from 1986, trading in options on fixed-income instruments was allowed but volumes in both market segments remained low and in 1987 trading on stock exchanges in both was ended officially.

New Financial Instruments

The first real change came with the establishment of the *Deutsche Terminbörse* (DTB), a screen-based futures and options exchange, in July 1988. Trading started in January 1990 with a future on long-term bonds, a future on the DAX index and options on 15 leading equities. Trade in DAX options and options on the long-term bond future began in summer the same year. Other instruments followed. The DTB became an instant success: only four months after its inception it traded a daily average of 24,000 contracts, compared with cautious advance estimates of 15,000. In 1997, annual trading volume had risen to 112,164,106 contracts, of which the *bund* future alone accounted for 31,337,633 contracts.

From the beginning, there had been fierce competition between the DTB and the then leading financial futures exchange in Europe, the London International Financial Futures and Options Exchange (Liffe), which for a long while dominated trading in German interest rate products. Competition includes the *Bobl*, a future on five-year German government bonds and, above all, the German 10-year *bund* future. When the DTB launched the latter an almost identical product had already traded highly successfully on Liffe for two years and had become a kind of flagship of the exchange. It was only in 1998 that Liffe lost the *bund* contract to its chief rival.

Competition with Liffe was also a driving force behind the cooperation between the DTB and other European exchanges. In 1993, the DTB and the French Matif agreed to link operations so that traders in each market would gain access to the other in an effort to improve liquidity and cut costs to investors. In October 1998, the DTB and the Swiss Options and Financial Futures Exchange (Soffex) merged into one market, Eurex, developing a single set of futures and options contracts in preparation for the euro. With the introduction of the common currency, Eurex strongly benefited from the 10-year *bund* future being the benchmark for government bonds in the eurozone. Meanwhile, it has become the world's leading derivatives market with 429 participants from 16 countries and a trading volume of 454 million contracts at the beginning of the new millennium.

What were the implications of these developments for the German banks? In some respect, the exchange's success was seen as a mixed blessing. Since the advent of the DTB, equity commissions in Germany have halved and clients were observed to opt for a cheaper and often more flexible exposure to the market via derivatives. On the other hand, banks as owners of the *Deutsche Börse*, the holding society of the DTB, profited directly from this development. Banks hold 81 per cent of Deutsche Börse AG: 88 per cent of them are German and 12 per cent are foreign institutes. This explains the big interest German banks have in the functioning of the exchange, contradicting all impressions of rivalry between the stock market and the banks derived from the German universal banking system.

Another example of financial innovation widening the range of financial products in Germany is *money market instruments*. Commercial paper had long been facing two obstacles. First, there were two paragraphs of the Civil Code requiring cumbersome registration procedures and finance ministry approval to new securities issues. Second, there was a turnover tax on securities transactions requiring the purchaser to pay between 0.1 and 0.25 per cent of the value of securities changing hands which would easily have eaten up spreads. Both were abolished in January 1991. Another hindrance was attitudes. German banks were said to have long opposed what they saw as a tendency towards disintermediation with corporate borrowers selling short-term debt more or less directly to institutional investors. Although German companies had been active in the US commercial paper market and in markets of other currencies before, the first D-mark commercial paper programme arranged for Daimler Benz by Deutsche Bank was considered to be breaking a taboo in this field (Campbell, 1991a). Other money market instruments such as certificates of deposit did not become attractive because of the minimum reserve requirements enforced by the Bundesbank.

Bank opposition also arose to German-registered money market funds which were only introduced with the Second Financial Market Promotion Law (*Zweites Finanzmarktförderungsgesetz*) coming into effect on 1 August 1994. Although most large German banks had been offering D-mark cash funds via their Luxembourg subsidiaries before, they feared the increasing competition on their home ground (*The Banker, 1994*). However, the largest resistance in this case came from the Bundesbank. The Bank generally opposed shortening of maturities in fear of its destabilizing effect on the German capital markets, and saw the funds as threatening its monetary steering ability. Thus, it did not come as a surprise when 17 days after the law came into effect the Bank cancelled regular issues of its own short-term paper, the *Bulis*, announcing that they had not been successful in the intended promotion of D-mark liquidity in the hands of domestic non-banks, despite the fact that since 1 March 1993 around DM25 billion *Bulis* of three- and six-month maturities had been in circulation. The general impression was that the Bank simply did not like the idea of offering investment possibilities to money market funds itself, thereby contributing to a general trend towards shorter maturities in financial markets.

Structural Changes

Deregulation and innovation in Germany not only comprises new products such as derivatives and money market instruments but the whole range of financial activities over both regions and sectors. In recent years, the landscape of German banking has undergone some structural changes with far-reaching consequences for banks' domestic and foreign business. Domestically, the most obvious change is an ongoing process of *concentration and restructuring*. Examples among the top German private banks are the acquisition of a 5.21 per cent stake in Bayerische Vereinsbank by Deutsche Bank in July 1996 and the merger of Bayerische Vereinsbank and Bayerische Hypotheken- und Wechselbank to become Bayerische Hypo- & Vereinsbank, Germany's second-largest bank in 1997. One example involving a foreign bank is the takeover of BHF-Bank, announced by the Dutch financial services group ING in August 1999 – the largest foreign purchase of a German financial institution so far. But, consolidation is also under way among the 3,000 or so public savings banks and cooperative banks. The most spectacular case here was the merger between the Südwestdeutsche Landesbank, the Landeskreditanstalt Baden-Württemberg and the Landesgirokasse in January 1999, creating Landesbank Baden-Württemberg, Germany's eighth-largest bank.

Another sector facing increased pressure for consolidation is German mortgage banks or *Hypothekenbanken*. Mortgage banks raise funds by issuing *Pfandbriefe*, bonds backed by mortgages or public sector loans. They suffer from two developments: mounting risk provisions and sinking margins. On the one hand, every bank in Germany, and even some insurance companies, can do mortgage banking but mortgage banks are largely restricted to financing real estate and public sector projects. This makes their margins shrink under growing competition in the domestic market. On the other hand, mortgage banks are engaged in markets which after the first euphoria of reunification suffered a sharp slowdown when eurozone interest rates rose, central and local government borrowing declined and public promotion measures for residential housing were withdrawn leading to a steep decline in construction. The reactions of the banks differed. While smaller groups considered closer cooperation with parent groups such as the big German commercial banks, the larger ones responded by extending lending activities throughout the rest of the European Union and even lobbying for access to North America. The outstanding example is DePfa (Deutsche Pfandbrief Bank), a former not-for-profit state agency and meanwhile one of Germany's biggest banks with $140bn in assets. In 2002, twelve years after its privatization, DePfa split its operations into two independent units with a Dublin-based company specializing in public sector financing, benefitting from a favourable tax and accounting environment for its advisory services for public sector clients, and a Wiesbaden-based one focused on real estate lending. Generally, the overall international prospects for *Pfandbriefe* are regarded as highly promising since eurozone budget deficits in decline are expected to leave a strong demand for large, liquid bond substitutes.

Despite these developments, consolidation progress in general is slow and, on the whole, Germany must still be considered overbanked. In order to cut costs and improve service and efficiency banks have been streamlining their branch networks, concentrating back office activities and shedding staff. Cash dispensers have become more and more common. In addition, banks entered into new activities such as electronic banking and opened up new markets (Wandel, 1998). Under increasing competition for private customers, in 1995, the big banks established so-called *Direktbanken* (direct banks), subsidiaries offering interest on current accounts, a 24-hour service seven days a week, discounts on brokerage and other advantages. There is a growing tendency of big institutions to engage in all areas of financial business becoming an *Allfinanzkonzern* or all-finance group bringing together universal banks, investment funds, mortgage banks, building societies and insurance companies under one roof (Naßmacher et al., 1998). Further impetus for progress came with the *internet* when banks started to establish their own online units. By the end of 1999, more than 10 million Germans had access to the internet, a number which is expected to nearly triple by 2002. Offering online financial products is one of the strongest-growing market segments. In 2000, the number of domestic clients of Comdirect, the market leader, rose from over 226,000 to nearly 537,000. Also, the firm's operations are not restricted to Germany: there are efforts to establish a pan-European network with activities in Austria, France, Great Britain and Italy.

German banks have generally expanded their foreign business in recent years. Part of the reason is the fragmented nature of the domestic market and, in particular for the private banks, a dominance of public sector banks limiting their possibilities of generating sufficient profits domestically. On the other hand, institutions are driven by the desire to seize the opportunities offered by the emergence of new markets and businesses resulting from monetary union in Western Europe as well as political and economic developments in Eastern Europe and the emerging markets in Asia and Latin America. A further motive, in particular for the biggest banks, is to become a global player and show a presence in all world financial centres. The same motive makes them join the legislators in their efforts to enhance the attractiveness of the *Finanzplatz Deutschland.*

4 FROM MYTH TO REALITY: *FINANZPLATZ DEUTSCHLAND*

As already noted, for many years, the German financial system was notorious for its backwardness. With regard to its stock market there were – and still are – two characteristics which made critics in and outside Germany call for a drastic change: the dominance of the German banks and the deficiencies of the country's pension system. Both are in a state of transition.

Bank Dominance in Decline

Universal banks are the primary source of corporate finance in Germany. But, in general, they are not especially profitable compared to foreign financial institutes. In addition, until very recently, Germany was one of the largest importers of financial services, indicating a poor performance of the domestic banking system (Lascelles, 1990). The banks' dominance raised suspicions about the functioning of corporate governance and control. In order to fully understand the role of German banks in corporate governance, beside their lending activities some aspects which are not reflected in banks' balance sheets must be considered, such as securities and safe custody business (Edwards and Fischer, 1994). The first is the control of equity voting rights by banks which allows them to exert a significant influence at shareholders' meetings. This influence is not only derived from banks' direct holdings of equities, but from proxy votes whose permission to use is obtained annually from client shareholders. Second, there is the banks' substantial representation on firms' supervisory boards. Third, the underwriting of new share issues, and in particular the leadership of syndicates for new share issues by large listed *Aktiengesellschaften* or AGs (literally: stock corporations), is largely concentrated in the hands of the big banks.

It is not each single component, but the interplay of these factors, which critics consider a major threat to efficiency. Banks lend directly to firms and, at the same time, take equity stakes, provide underwriting services and send their representatives to the firms' supervisory board. As a result, corporate governance and control is largely exerted behind closed doors and changes of control rarely occur through a stock-market takeover as in Anglo-Saxon countries. There are rare counterexamples: the bid by the Flick brothers and then Veba AG for Feldmühle Nobel AG in 1988 and 1989, respectively, by Pirelli for Continental AG in 1990 and 1991, by Krupp AG for Hoesch AG in 1991 and 1992 (Franks and Mayer, 2000), and the spectacular takeover bid for Mannesmann by Vodafone in 2000.

However, attempts to meet the criticisms, and to adjust both domestically and internationally to a changed environment, brought some changes in this respect. Between 1986 and 1994, banks' equity stakes in traded firms have clearly fallen – although the total number of firms in which banks hold equity positions has risen over that decade – and the banks have increasingly become minority shareholders. Shareholder representation at annual meetings of large firms is in decline as well and representation of private banks on the supervisory boards of the 100 largest German firms has shrunk from 114 board seats or 8 per cent in 1986 to 99 or 6 per cent in 1994 (Emmons and Schmid, 1998). New impetus for the banks to wind down their industrial holdings was given in the second half of the 1990s by a growing awareness of the importance of shareholder value and stock-market developments. This holds in particular for Deutsche and Dresdner Bank, which planned to list their shares in the United States. But, in the past, there had been limits to those kinds of activities. One reason is taxes: stakes on the banks' books are often at low historical values and the gains from selling them at higher market values were taxed at more than 50 per cent. In 2002 this was changed by a tax reform. After that, there has been some progress. Deutsche Bank has cut its holdings in insurers

Allianz and Munich Re. Allianz itself – one of Germany's most influential shareholders, with stakes in companies such as BASF, BMW and KarstadtQuelle – has issued more than $10bn of exchangeable bonds in various holdings. In addition, buying Dresdner Bank before the changes had taken effect in 2001, in using complex financial instruments it made sure to take advantage of the reform. But, none of the big banks appears really prepared to let go of profitable holdings or wholly refrain from the relationship banking of the past. Deutsche and Dresdner, for example, established new subsidiaries for their industrial assets which at the end of 1998 had a combined worth of DM70 billion. Those subsidiaries are assumed to manage the assets more actively at arm's length. For instance, Deutsche's DB Investor whose estimated industrial portfolio at the end of 1998 was around DM45 billion ($27 billion) is working closely with existing holdings to boost their value and is even involved in the restructuring of whole industries. But, at the same time, in the search for adding value it is also making new investments, further widening the web of stakes and relations (*The Economist*, 1999).

Pensions

The universal banking system is one reason for the historically limited scope of the German stock market. The country's *pension system* is another one. The current pension system is a pay-as-you-go system relying on the contributions of employers and employees. Based on the insurance principle and on an implicit social contract between generations, today's employees finance today's pensioners. This is not only impossible to achieve with an ever-growing share of old people – like other industrial countries Germany is facing the ageing of a large part of the population – it also reduces the importance of the markets of long-term financial assets.

The *state pension*, which is currently in a process of reform, is the most important component of the German system. *Private pension payments* typically represent only a supplement which accounts for 10 to 30 per cent of total payments. Those rest on two pillars. One is *personal provision* by saving in the form of contributions to life insurance firms and private pension funds. Their importance has increased steadily over the years. But, as analysts emphasize, due to the life insurers' investment policy this has not led to an increase in the significance of those firms as a source of funds for private enterprises. Mainly because of legal restrictions, life insurers invest to a large extent in the banking, government and housing sectors. Only a small portion of their funds goes to producing enterprises (Edwards and Fischer, 1994). In summer 2001, the German government introduced a pension reform. Since January 2002, Germans can put up to 4 per cent of their eligible pay into private retirement accounts through state-subsidised individual retirement schemes, the so-called 'Riester-Rente', named after the minister who piloted them through parliament. But, the system is complicated and demands intensive counselling and the number of offered schemes is huge. In the first 12 months German savings and co-operative banks alone offered more than 3,200 plans. This helps explain why up to June 2002 a mere 1.9m of 35m eligible citizens have opted to buy any of those products.

The second pillar of private pension payments is *enterprise pension schemes*. Here, the most important one takes the form of a direct commitment by firms to their employees. Under this scheme, the firms make pension provisions not by paying contributions for employees' pensions into a separate pension fund but merely by making provisions on their balance sheets. As a result, 'only current pension obligations require current expenditures. . . . accrual of future pension liabilities provides a source of financing (cash flow) for current corporate activities' (Emmons and Schmid, 1998: 32). This contributes in two ways to the weakness of the German capital market. On the one hand, it reduces the demand for long-term financial assets to fund pension-holders' accounts. On the other, to the extent that they finance current operations by increasing pension liabilities, firms need not supply long-term financial assets to the market. This means that, compared to countries with a different private pension scheme such as a defined-contribution scheme, Germany has a comparably small capitalization of stock and bond markets and lower trading volumes (Emmons and Schmid, 1998). But, the pension reform of 2001 also started to modify this system allowing Germans to invest part of their pay in 'Eichel schemes' offered via the employer. Again, there are major drawbacks. The banks issuing those products must set up insurance-related frameworks to work out the complicated actuarial arithmetic for estimating incoming and outgoing payments based on death rates and supervising large amounts of customer files, and corporations were not prepared for the costs to administer the plans and to issue the capital guarantees.

The *reform of the state pension* which is under way will bring some changes for the capital market in that, in the long run, the share of state payments will be reduced and the importance of private schemes, promoted by a generous public state programme, will necessarily rise. But, whether this will stimulate the growth of independently managed pension funds along Anglo-Saxon lines expanding the equity market and thus making it easier, in particular for smaller companies, to raise money, as some enthusiasts expect, must be doubted. On the one hand, in principle, the reform still does not touch the existing system of enterprise pension schemes. On the other, the strict controls on approved private pension schemes restrict them largely to insurance-type products. A third hindrance is that overall incentives to invest in private funds will remain low as long as the comparably comfortable pay-as-you-go state pension system is not altered fundamentally. Whether, in the long run, reforms like this will result in major improvements for the German capital market will also depend on attitudes – of the employees towards putting their money spent for pension provision at risk and of German financial institutes and public authorities towards breaking up existing structures to enhance the market's attractiveness and competitiveness.

Promoting the *Finanzplatz*

In order to raise the appeal of the German market, since the 1980s, four Financial Market Promotion Laws have been passed. The first one came under the heading *Restliberalisierung* (rest liberalization) of the German capital market and brought among other things the admission of financial innovations such as floating rate notes, zero bonds, dual-currency issues and certificates of deposits. The reforms of the second included the outlawing of insider trading, tightening of share disclosure requirements and the establishment of a centralized regulatory body for Germany's securities markets, the German Federal Securities Supervisory Office, BAWe (Bundesaufsichtsamt für den Wertpapierhandel). The BAWe became the fourth agency responsible for financial supervision in Germany, beside the Bundesbank, the Federal Banking Supervisory Office, BAKred (Bundesaufsichtsamt für das Kreditwesen) and the agency responsible for insurance supervision, BAV (Bundesaufsichtsamt für das Versicherungswesen). In January 2001, the German government announced plans to amalgamate BAKred, BAWe and BAV into a single independent body, taking the UK's Financial Services Authority as an example, which is overseeing everything from consumer banking and home loans to building societies and financial advisers to stockbrokers and investment banks. The aim was twofold: to further strengthen the *Finanzplatz Deutschland* and to act as a catalyst for a Europe-wide regulatory system. In May 2002, the new unified financial regulatory body, the Bundesanstalt für Finanzdienstleistungsaufsicht (BAFin), was formally launched. It has a three-pillar structure reflecting the three main sectors it covers.

Until the Second Financial Market Promotion Law, *insider trading* was one topic that had long been hotly debated by the German public . Despite the fact that European Community-wide insider trading rules had existed since 1989, and would have had to be implemented by June 1992, German legislation did not come up with a respective law before 1994 – to be applied from 1995 onwards – and even then only reluctantly. Traditionally, in contrast to many other countries, in Germany insider trading was not a crime. There only existed a voluntary agreement barring traders from making use of inside information. Only the DTB had insider rules with legal force from the start and could pursue traders involved through the prosecutor's office. Observers agreed that there were frequent abuses. Occasionally, those were brought to light in the wake of criminal investigations, for example, focusing on suspected tax evasion. The turn in public opinion came in 1993 when the head of IG Metall at that time, Germany's most powerful union, was suspected of speculating in Daimler Benz AG shares, while serving on the supervisory board. In particular, there were concerns that the incident could damage Germany's international reputation as a financial centre. As Karl Otto Pöhl, the former Bundesbank president, put it, American investors in particular found it hard enough to understand why leading trade unionists were on the supervisory boards of German companies (*The Financial Times*, 1993).

Although the rules of the Second Financial Market Promotion Law were widely considered as remarkable improvements, in particular foreign banks in Germany called for further changes on the regulatory and tax side – above all, those related to the relaxation of rules affecting asset-backed securities, minimum reserve requirements on time deposits, indexation of capital market instruments and the accounting treatment of branch offices (Fisher, 1995). The Third Financial Market Promotion Law passed in February 1998 was not a direct reaction to these criticisms. It had above all three aims: to increase access to venture capital for small and medium-sized unlisted firms, to facilitate raising capital for listed companies and to widen the range of investment instruments for private savings. The law incorporated over 100 separate provisions to promote liberalization and regulation. Transaction costs in the stock exchange and securities sector were reduced, investment funds were made more attractive by the introduction of new types of funds and the admission of additional financial market products and there was an amendment of the law on equity investment companies and the improvement of tax treatment of those companies aimed at enlarging the supply of capital to small and medium-sized firms.

In July 2002, the *Fourth Financial Market Promotion Law* designed, above all, to improve investor protection, curb insider trading and tighten financial market regulations took effect. The law includes fines of up to $1.5m for market manipulation or late disclosure of information. It also increases the investigative powers of regulators regarding movements of German government bonds, in response to evidence of 'squeeze' operations on Germany's bonds and futures markets, as well as measures on money laundering and terrorism.

A New Equity Culture?

The *Third Financial Market Promotion Law* largely contributed to what is widely seen as a fundamental change in Germany's *equity culture*. Traditionally notorious for their reluctance to buy shares, recently, more and more Germans have switched from fixed income and real estate to stocks, mutual funds and other investments. One reason is the growing awareness that state pensions can no longer be regarded as guaranteed and other ways to secure retirement incomes must be found. Another is the impetus given by sales of state assets such as Veba, Lufthansa and, above all, Deutsche Telekom. A special phenomenon in this context is the euphoria which greeted the *Neuer Markt* (new market), a segment established in 1997 and operated by the *Deutsche Börse*. Essentially, the *Neuer Markt* is seen as Germany's stock market for young and high-growth companies, especially with a high-tech bias, which otherwise might have shun the bourse or opted for a listing on NASDAQ, the computerized US exchange.

For many years, reformers had tried to overcome liquidity constraints for small and medium-sized German firms which hampered growth and employment, especially in those sectors of the economy widely considered as typical growth industries. The 1987 established *Geregelter Markt*, a segment of the German stock exchange especially designed as a market for small and medium-sized firms, did not meet respective expectations (Hopt and Baum, 1997: 357). *Neuer Markt*, which is formally part of the unlisted securities market (*Freiverkehr*) and therefore less regulated than the former with respect to the firms' age and size (which, however, is compensated by strong listing and reporting requirements), proved particularly attractive for two kinds of companies: high-growth companies, which may still be losing money and therefore may have difficulties getting bank loans, and small and medium-sized *Mittelstand* firms which increasingly turn to initial public offerings to raise funds or solve family succession issues. The prospects of the latter are particularly promising: of the country's 1.6 million family-owned firms, around 320,000 are expected to seek a successor between 1999 and 2004 and an estimated third of these will end up being sold (Benoit, 2001).

Some of the early *Neuer Markt* floats had been hugely successful. For example, Mobilcom floated in March 1997 at DM62 and its shares soon traded up to DM550. But the biggest incentive were the strong first-day price gains of at least 40 per cent which attracted in particular younger first-time retail investors. There were spectacular debuts such as CE Computer Equipment which was floated in April 1998 at DM98 and immediately traded at DM400 (Lee, 1998). But, meanwhile, the high-flying spirit of the founding days is over. It made way for succesive bouts of pessimism over the future of new-economy and high-technology stocks. At the end of 2000, many shares were trading below their listing price and since then the market has followed a volatile and uncertain course. Companies' rush to issue was said to have led to great quantity but questionable quality. The resulting oversupply of equity, along with delayed and unsuccessful issues and falling share prices, has diminished Germans' appetite for stocks once again. In 2001, the number of IPOs at *Neuer Markt* was 11. In June 2002, the Nemax 50 index was below 1000, down from more than 9,600. In reaction to market failures and scandals and concerns about the market's reputation a series of reforms was introduced. The aim was to weed out non-performers (penny stocks) and to check the quality of new entrants even more rigorously. Eventually, in September 2002, Deutsche Börse announced its intention to close the market in 2003 and to replace it with a market segment called 'Prime Standard'.

A more lasting phenomenon is that, since the early 1990s, the German stock market has attracted more and more *foreign investors*. This is also showing up in the numbers: whereas in 1990 Germany had still exported DM66 billion of long-term capital, in 1992 the country imported a net DM47 billion. Foreigners began to hold large stakes in big companies: about 40 per cent at Siemens, more than 40 per cent at Deutsche Bank, nearly a third at Veba, nearly 40 per cent at Commerzbank and over 20 per cent at BASF (Waller, 1993). When the *Deutsche Börse* went public in February 2001 around 77 per cent of demand came from institutional investors from the UK, Italy, Spain, Switzerland and the US (Wassener, 2001). In addition, foreign banks and investment houses were catching up on or boosting a Frankfurt presence. In parts, this is the result of the described reforms and financial market liberalizations. However, location decisions were also influenced partly by the additional economic significance of Germany since unification. East German households brought with them savings in the bank of DM115 billion, adding to the country's already vast pool of private resources which could be channelled into securities.

Financial liberalization and reform considerably increased the international competitiveness of the *Finanzplatz Deutschland* and of German banks in world financial markets. On the other hand, it reinforced the risks associated with bank business. This, in turn, complicated the task of supervisors who in some areas were facing wholly new kinds of challenges.

5 FINANCIAL RISKS AND THE CHALLENGES TO SUPERVISION

Over the years, the internationalization of bank business, banks' switch from providers of capital for German firms both domestically and abroad to truly international players, the emergence of new financial markets and instruments and German reunification were all accompanied by special dangers imposing additional strains on the German financial system. In principle, three kinds of risks can be distinguished. One is the traditional *credit or default risk* which is the possibility that a financial institution will experience a loss when a counterpart fails to perform. The second is *market risk*, standing for the possibility of losses arising from adverse movements in market prices. The third is *operational risk* which, for general purposes, can be distinguished into two categories: operations risk and business event risk (Parsley, 1996). Operations risk comprises transaction risks such as execution, booking or settlement errors as well as situations of fraud and rogue trading, but also systems risks such as programming errors and IT systems failures. Business event risks are even harder to cope with, covering a broad range of events that may happen in day-to-day operations such as currency convertibility risk but also changes in reputation or shifts in credit rating, legal and institutional changes and even disasters and a collapse or suspension of markets. Behind all these is looming systemic risk: the danger that a sudden collapse of one or several market participants could trigger a chain reaction causing a financial crisis country- or worldwide.

Accumulation of Risks

Although, in principle, financial institutions in industrial countries all face the same kinds of risks, in the past, German banks often bore a more than proportionate share of them. There are outstanding examples of failures such as the case of Bankhaus I.D. Herstatt which occurred shortly after the transition to floating exchange rates in the 1970s. Herstatt was a relatively small bank, but one of the largest dealers in foreign exchange in Germany. When the 1973 oil shock increased price volatility and market risk, and disrupted capital flows, many banks suffered losses. The case of Herstatt became famous because of its handling by the German authorities. The Bundesaufsichtsamt für das Kreditwesen announced the bank's closure on 26 July 1974, in the early afternoon, German time, after settlement of same-day interbank systems in Germany had taken place, and several of the bank's counterparts from the United States and elsewhere had paid out D-marks to Herstatt to meet their obligations from D-mark/dollar trades. Payments for the transaction of the dollar legs had already been ordered by Herstatt's correspondent bank in New York as well, but there, it was still late morning. As it shut before the New York settlement system opened, the failure of the bank left over $620 million worth of foreign exchange trade outstanding. The markets were close to panic. Since then, a situation like this is known as 'cross-currency settlement risk' or 'Herstatt risk' (Gup, 1998).

Another incident attracting much attention was the case of the German conglomerate Metallgesellschaft, whose US subsidiary, M.G. Corporation, lost about $1.3 billion trading oil derivatives in 1993. Again, it was market risk by which the firm was caught trying to hedge long-term delivery contracts with short-term futures that were constantly rolled over. For the banks involved it was credit risk. They had to agree to an emergency line of credit, and in a widely disputed decision Deutsche Bank sent a 'firefighter' who liquidated many of the firm's positions. Academic critics, including Nobel laureate Merton Miller, claimed that the supervisory board and the supporting banks may not have understood the hedging strategy forcing the liquidation prematurely. But, observers in the world's trading rooms at that time opposed this view, pointing to the huge monthly losses of the strategy accumulating from margin calls due to sinking oil prices (Edwards and Canter, 1995).

Other spectacular incidents involving large German banks were two cases of operations risk in 1994, the collapse of the Jürgen Schneider property group, triggering a crisis in the property market, and the débâcle of Balsam, a manufacturer of flooring materials used in sports installations. For many years, Schneider had systematically deceived the banks before he suddenly disappeared in April 1994 owing DM5.4 billion to around 50 banks – DM1.2 billion to Deutsche Bank alone. Although within four years his debt had risen sevenfold his creditors never became suspicious. The Balsam case was significantly smaller, with direct and indirect credit risk spread between 40 banks and no individual bank owing more than DM100 million. Nevertheless, there were some worrying parallels between the two: both firms were led 'by charismatic entrepreneurs' (Waller, 1994), both were always punctual in meeting their payments to bankers before the breakdown, and in both cases their apparent wealth served to dampen bankers' fears about mounting debts and large German financial institutions appeared particularly involved.

The lessons from these cases still have to be learned, as the example of Philipp Holzmann, Germany's once second-biggest construction group, demonstrated some years later. The firm, founded in 1849, has become a symbol of the problems afflicting corporate Germany. In 1999, it announced potential losses of DM2.4 billion ($1.26 billion) on past property deals. Among the 20 core creditors, Deutsche Bank in many respects played a dominant role. Its relations to the group had a long tradition. Hermann Josef Abs, later Deutsche's chairman, had been chairman of Holzmann's supervisory board after 1939 for more than 30 years. In 1999, too, the head of the supervisory board was a member of the Deutsche Bank management board. The bank was the group's biggest creditor with loans totalling almost DM2.2 billion. At the same time, with a 15 per cent stake, it was also its second-biggest shareholder. In addition, it was widely regarded as the group's 'quasi-manager' (Major, 1999). In this role, in 1997, the bank had decided to instal a new management at Holzmann in an effort to stem heavy losses, a measure which, in retrospect, was widely criticized as inadequate by other creditors. In 1999, the group was rescued by political intervention from the newly-elected chancellor Schröder – only to go bust three years later.

While some observers regarded these and other examples as isolated cases, critics considered them as symptomatic of the system's informality and lack of transparency and control. Other risks the banks took were less spectacular. For example, in the 1990s, for the large banks promoting the *Finanzplatz Deutschland* on the one hand, and playing in the league of global players on the other, took its toll. Heavily engaged in foreign exchange and derivatives trading the banks became highly vulnerable to market risk. Losses must have been particularly high in the first years of the DTB when the banks were strongly interested in actively promoting the exchange's success – when, for example, Deutsche, Dresdner and Commerzbank together with JP Morgan allegedly agreed to commit themselves to trading a minimum daily volume of contracts, and foreign financial institutions boasted about the money they made from German banks' inexperience and mistakes. Other potential losses threatened from poorly performing foreign investments and acquisitions. In particular, the big banks' relatively aggressive expansion into international investment banking worsened earnings quality and increased their overall risk profile (Barber, 1999). Another source of risk was the building up of ever-larger positions to emerging economies, which made the banks highly vulnerable to systemic risk during the crises in Latin America, Asia and Russia. In all those cases, together with other European banks, German financial institutions appeared particularly exposed (JP Morgan, 1998). Still other dangers resulting from international activities were wholly unforeseen, raising questions about the overall quality of the banks' risk management and control. An example is the breakdown of Long-Term Capital Management (LTCM), the US hedge fund, in 1998 where two German banks were involved and even Deutsche Bank was among the 14 institutions participating in the rescue operation organized by the Federal Reserve Bank of New York.

An additiosnal source of risk was *reunification* which, as already noted, imposed huge extra burdens upon the banks. To a large extent, the banks underestimated the related dangers. This became apparent when the first euphoria about a booming east German property market evaporated. In 1997, large German banks' exposure to east German commercial property ranged from 36 per cent of shareholders' equity for Deutsche Bank up to 112 per cent for HypoVereinsbank (*The Economist*, 2000).

Inequalities

However, not all banks in Germany face the same risks, and the same costs of risk management. There are large discrepancies between private and public banks, which has long been debated both domestically and internationally. Mainly for historical reasons, the public sector plays an unusually prominent role in the German banking system. This is generally explained by the need to reconstruct the country after the Second World War and, according to its proponents, cannot be abandoned without putting at risk the financing of small and medium-sized German companies. In September 2000, the public banks accounted for about 35 per cent of German bank assets, with the *Landesbanks* alone commanding a share of 20 per cent, about the same as the big four commercial banks. In recent years, the public banks have come under increasing criticism from the European Commission which launched several investigations into the system of state support to these banks. The Commission's focus is on two guarantees, *Anstaltslast* and *Gewährträgerhaftung*. *Anstaltslast* makes sure that the banks cannot go bankrupt. Under *Gewährträgerhaftung* the guarantors are liable to pay creditors should a bank's assets prove insufficient. One result is that the public banks internationally get AAA ratings, enabling them to borrow at rates significantly lower than their private bank competitors. Some have used this advantage to become aggressive market players – a role hardly compatible with the original tasks the guarantees were intended for. In January 1997, among the 11 German banks with a Moody's Triple-A rating, ten were public banks (Brost, 1999).

The European Commission flatly rejects the bank guarantees as illegal state aid. Unlimited both in duration and amount, and provided for free, those guarantees give the banks the advantage of much lower capital costs. The resulting distortion prevents private banks from competing with state-owned banks on a level playing field. Early in 2001, the situation was moving when Westdeutsche Landesbank, the biggest of the public sector banks, in a meeting with the European Union's competition commissioner, formally presented a plan to restructure itself, splitting into two separate private and public institutions: a subsidiary without state guarantees taking over the bank's commercial business, and the parent which would continue to assume its traditional public functions. But, as critics stress, plans like this do not get far enough to remedy the 'ossifying effect' (*The Financial Times*, 1999) the system of state support has on the German financial sector. The Westdeutsch Landesbank approach even does not address the heart of the problem, because the private unit will still be 100 per cent publicly owned. As a next step, in 2002, the German government agreed with the European Commission to phase out state guarantees for the Landesbanks by 2005. This decision which is expected to raise banks' borrowing costs and force them to restructure themselves has already shown first effects: in March 2002, Landesbank Schleswig-Holstein announced its planned merger with Hamburgische Landesbank.

In general, the German authorities prefer an *informal approach to supervision* relying largely on the system's self-regulation. As the example of insider trading demonstrated, in principle, banks coming up with proposals of self-regulation and self-constraint in view of threatening official initiatives are not untypical for the system. Usually, laws and official rules are established only when strong indications of the insufficiency of the informal approach are found or international requirements have to be met. An example is the Herstatt case. The bank's failure led to an amendment of Principle I of the German Banking Act which restricted banks' loans and investments. In what became Principle Ia, the amount of risk that could be taken in forward foreign exchange and precious metals trading became limited, although there was as yet no obligation to back these risks with capital (Luz, 1998).

Regulation and Reregulation

In Germany, official bank regulation has existed since 1931, when it was first established in reaction to the banking crisis the same year (Wandel, 1998). The *Kreditwesengesetz* (KWG) dates back to 1934. Since then, it had been amended several times in ever shorter intervals. The first revision came in 1961, the next one 15 years later, while the fourth and fifth KWG amendments followed in January 1993 and December 1995. The sixth and so far latest revision was in October 1997. This development reflects the dynamics of a rapidly changing national and, above all, international environment. While the 1976 revision focused on granting the authorities a greater control over bank business, which up to that time was only possible under very special circumstances, the following ones served mainly to implement directives of the European Commission into German law.

In the early 1990s, promoting the *Finanzplatz Deutschland* meant not only the liberalization of market practices, but also coping with the urgent task of *reregulation* to close some of the gaps in Germany's supervisory capacities which had become more and more apparent (Campbell, 1991b). While the fourth and fifth KWG amendments laid the basis in Germany for a single European market in banking services, the sixth amendment widened financial supervision to investment firms and other enterprises providing financial services on a commercial basis. In addition, the list of banking business was extended to include electronic money.

The *capital adequacy rules* which were established in accordance with the Basle Accord of 1988 and/or the EC Solvency Ratio Directive and the EC Own Funds Directive of 1989 are not directly established in the KWG but in so-called 'Principles' which are formulated according to the law by the Federal Banking Supervisory Office in accordance with the German Bundesbank. When in October 1998 Principles I and Ia were replaced by the new Principle I, for the first time, financial institutions were required to back *market price risks* with capital. In order to calculate the capital needed for the respective positions, banks have the choice between standardized methods and internal risk models computing their 'value at risk' (VAR). The admission of internal models posed considerable challenges to both financial institutions and supervisors, and the old school of lawyers in the regulators' offices had to be supplemented by people with solid mathematical training. So far, there is no generally accepted method of VAR estimation and results for different kinds of instruments and portfolios differ widely. A particular problem is posed by derivatives, where the relation between the asset's market price and value is a non-linear one (Reszat, 1997). Among the German banks, Deutsche Bank was the first to publish a VAR number for its derivatives portfolio in 1995. The figures showed that the bank's money at risk at the end of 1994 was DM131 million ($93.5 million) compared to a nominal value for the derivatives portfolio of several trillion D-marks (*The Financial Times*, 1995).

The implementation of the Basle proposals to replace the rules of the 1988 Accord (Basle II) will add to the existing problems of both banks and supervisors. Among the banks, worries focus on the planned capital charge for interest-rate risk in the banking book and for hardly quantifiable operational risk exposures. They hint at the foreseeable lack of data and of criteria for risk management. In addition, there are still considerable differences in technical skills, computer equipment and availability of rating models between larger and smaller banks. And, although there is widespread agreement that a functioning supervision according to the Basle II rules will be an indispensable prerequisite for the further development of the *Finanzplatz Deutschland*, observers fear that, at least in transition, regulators will have neither the staff nor the expertise to deal adequately with banks' risk-management operations.

6 CONCLUSIONS

This overview of more than 50 years of financial reform in Germany necessarily allows only a small glimpse of the main strands of development.

Reform processes have often been much more painstaking and laborious than described and, of course, German financial institutions are a far less homogeneous group than assumed here. In particular, there are large differences between banks with respect to both profitability and risks, although, on average, profits seem low, and the rapidly accumulating risks increasingly high, in international comparison. Seen as a whole, reform has taken a rather modest pace. The remarkable progress made in recent years to develop the *Finanzplatz Deutschland* to a European financial centre cannot hide the fact that many of the old structures and relations still exist – and, at times, are functioning astonishingly well. But, the increasing frequency of crises and failures indicates that the system, in a sense, has become out dated. The banks' efforts to restructure and consolidate, as well as to exploit new markets and business opportunities both at home and abroad, and the authorities' moves to put the supervision of financial institutions and activities on a more reliable basis indicate that financial reform in Germany is still an ongoing project.

REFERENCES

Banker, The (1994): 'The banks bare their teeth', October, 58–60.

Barber, Tony (1999): 'Deutsche looks to widen its horizons', *The Financial Times*, 8 March.

Benoit, Bertrand (2001): 'Equity culture boosts soaring German wealth', *The Financial Times*, 10/11 February.

Born, Karl Erich (1977): *Geld und Banken im 19. und 20. Jahrhundert*, Stuttgart: Kröner.

Briault, Clive, Haldane, Andrew and King, Mervin (1996): 'Central bank independence and accountability: theory and evidence', *Bank of England Quarterly Bulletin*, February, 63–8.

Brost, Marcus (1999): 'Typisch deutsch: Bankenlandschaft mit viel Staat', *Die Zeit*, 15 July.

Büschgen, Hans-E. (1997): *Das kleine Banklexikon*, Düsseldorf: Verlag Wirtschaft und Finanzen.

Campbell, Katherine (1991a): 'Risks and rewards of change in Frankfurt', *The Financial Times*, 7 January.

Campbell, Katherine (1991b): 'Roles are reversed for city of bankers', *The Financial Times*, 28 October.

Economist, The (1999): 'Untangling', 14 August.

Economist, The (2000): 'A Bavarian botch-up', 5 August.

Edwards, F.R. and Canter, M.S. (1995): 'The collapse of Metallgesellschaft: unhedgeable risk, poor hedging strategy, or just bad luck?', *Journal of Futures Markets*, No. 3, 211–64.

Edwards, Jeremy and Fischer, Klaus (1994): *Banks, Finance and Investment in Germany*, Cambridge: Cambridge University Press.

Emmons, William R. and Schmid, Frank A. (1998): 'Universal banking, control rights and corporate finance in Germany', *Federal Reserve Bank of St. Louis Review*, July/August, 19–42.

Financial Times, The (1993): 'An insider speaks out', 24 May.
Financial Times, The (1995): 'Timing the turn', 10 April.
Financial Times, The (1999): 'Taming the *landesbanks*', 8 July.
Fisher, Andrew (1995): 'Bankers call for further change in German markets', *The Financial Times*, 1 February.
Franks, Julian and Mayer, Colin (2000): 'Ownership and control of German corporations', mimeo, revised 15 August.
Goodhart, Charles A.E. (1994): 'Central bank independence', *Journal of International and Comparative Economics*, No. 3, reprinted in Goodhart, Charles A.E. (1995): *The Central Bank and the Financial System*, Chatham: Macmillan, 60–71.
Gup, Benton E. (1998): *Bank Failures in the Major Trading Countries of the World – Causes and Remedies*, Westport, CT: Quorum Books.
Hopt, Klaus J. and Baum, Harald (1997): 'Börsenrechtsreform in Deutschland', in Hopt, Klaus J., Rudolph, Bernd and Baum Harald (eds): *Börsenreform – Eine ökonomische, rechtsvergleichende und rechtspolitische Untersuchung*, Stuttgart: Schäffer-Poeschel Verlag, 287–467.
Jarchow, Hans-Joachim (1992): *Theorie und Politik des Geldes, Vol. 2: Geldmarkt, Bundesbank und geldpolitsches Instrumentarium*, Göttingen: Vandenhoeck & Ruprecht.
JP Morgan (1998): 'Battling global banking sector head winds', *World Financial Markets*, 7 October, 11–16.
Lascelles, David (1990): 'Universal banks may not be exportable', *The Financial Times*, 19 March.
Lee, Peter (1998): 'Surfers' paradise – for now', *Online: Euromoney Magazine*, December.
Luz, Günther (1998): 'Bankenaufsicht vor neuen Herausforderungen', in Naßmacher et al. (eds), 106–19.
Major, Tony (1999): 'Holzmann lenders query role of bank', *The Financial Times*, 22 November.
Naßmacher, Karl-Heinz, von Stein, Heinrich and Büschgen, Hans-E. (eds) (1998): *Banken in Deutschland*, Opladen: Leske & Budrich.
Parsley, M. (1996): 'Risk management's final frontier', *Euromoney*, September, 74–9.
Reszat, Beate (1997): 'Sources of increasing systemic risk in international financial markets', *Intereconomics*, September/October, 211–19.
Saunderson, Alan (1999): 'The central question', *The Banker*, March, 32.
Shirreff, David (1996): 'The Achilles' Heel of Europe', *Euromoney*, April, online version.
Waller, David (1993): 'A shine on its financial face', *The Financial Times*, 14 July.
Waller, David (1994): 'Light escape likely for Balsam bankers', *The Financial Times*, 9 June.
Wandel, Eckhard (1998): *Banken und Versicherungen im 19. und 20. Jahrhundert*, Munich: R. Oldenbourg Verlag.
Wassener, Bettina (2001): 'Deutsche Börse starts at 335 on strong demand', *The Financial Times*, 5 February.

6. Financial reform in Hong Kong

Y.C. Jao

1 INTRODUCTION

Financial reform has been an ongoing feature of the financial sector of Hong Kong during the past 50 years, both under the British administration and since the territory's reversion to China on 1 July 1997. This chapter reviews the essential facts and characteristics of the reform process, and discusses their implications.

2 CENTRAL BANK REFORM

There is no formal central bank in Hong Kong, but this does not mean that central bank functions are unknown to the territory. Before the establishment of the Hong Kong Monetary Authority (HKMA) in 1993, such functions were shared by a number of public and private agencies. Thus, the issue of legal tender was handled by two British banks (the Hongkong and Shanghai Banking Corporation, now called HSBC, and Standard Chartered Bank), the supervisory function and the conduct of monetary policy were undertaken by the Monetary Affairs Branch of the Hong Kong government, the maintenance of exchange rate stability was the responsibility of the Exchange Fund, the lender of last resort was performed jointly by the Exchange Fund and the two note-issuing banks and so on. The Monetary Affairs Branch itself was created in 1976, which marked the first attempt of the government to streamline certain central banking functions. The Exchange Fund, set up in 1935 when Hong Kong left the silver standard and opted for the sterling exchange standard, was steadily enlarged to include not only foreign exchange reserves as backing for the note issue, but also the government's fiscal surplus.

In 1993, the HKMA was established by combining the Exchange Fund Office with the Commissioner of Banking Office. This new statutory body was justified on the grounds that central banking functions needed to be further streamlined and strengthened in order to ensure exchange rate and banking stability in preparation for the transition to Chinese sovereignty in

1997. The remaining part of the former Monetary Affairs Branch was reorganized into a new Financial Services Bureau, which is mainly responsible for the supervision of non-bank financial institutions, and securities markets.

The HKMA is widely regarded as the de facto central bank of Hong Kong. Certainly it performs an impressive array of traditional central bank functions, such as the conduct of monetary policy, maintenance of exchange rate stability, prudential supervision of banks, custody and management of foreign exchange reserves, provision of clearing, discount window and lender of last resort facilities (Yam, 1994). However, it is important to note that in several important respects, the HKMA differs from the fully-fledged central bank. First, it does not issue legal tender notes. Under Hong Kong's present currency system, which is a variant of the Currency Board Arrangement (CBA), the Exchange Fund issues on demand Certificates of Indebtedness (CIs) to the note-issuing banks on payment of US dollars at the fixed exchange rate of US$1 = HK$7.8, which has remained unchanged since 17 October 1983. The CIs form the legal backing for the notes, and can be redeemed in US dollars at the same exchange rate. In 1994, the Bank of China joined the two British banks as the third note-issuing bank. Second, the HKMA does not require commercial banks and other depository institutions to keep with it non-interest-bearing reserves, other than a positive balance in their clearing accounts. Third, under the present linked exchange rate system, the HKMA cannot conduct monetary policy independently of the Federal Reserve System of the United States (Jao, 1990, 1998a).

The chief executive of the HKMA (equivalent to the governor of a central bank elsewhere) reports to the financial secretary of the government, who is in charge of all economic, fiscal and financial policies. Otherwise, the HKMA enjoys a very high degree of autonomy in day-to-day operations. Legally, it is a statutory body outside the civil service, and has full powers over its staffing and financing. The HKMA is advised on policy matters by five committees: the Exchange Fund Advisory Committee, the Sub-committee on Currency Board Operations, the Land Fund Advisory Committee, the Banking Advisory Committee and the Deposit-taking Advisory Committee.

China has adopted a sensible policy towards Hong Kong's monetary independence. Both the Sino-British Joint Declaration of 1984 and the Basic Law of 1990 stipulate that the Hong Kong dollar is to continue circulating as a convertible and separate currency after 1 July 1997. In 1996, Chen Yuan, then deputy governor of the People's Bank of China (PBC), the central bank of China, enunciated to an international audience seven principles that should govern the financial relationship between Mainland

China and Hong Kong after reunification. First, the currencies and monetary systems of Mainland China and Hong Kong will be mutually independent of each other. Second, the two monetary authorities, the PBC and HKMA, will also be mutually independent, but will cooperate closely with each other. The PBC will not set up any office in Hong Kong. Third, financial institutions in Mainland China and Hong Kong setting up branches of offices in each other's territory will be regulated by the host authorities, and treated respectively as foreign entities. Fourth, the PBC will support currency stability in Hong Kong. Fifth, financial transactions between Mainland China and Hong Kong will be conducted in accordance with international rules and practices. Sixth, mainland financial institutions in Hong Kong must abide by the laws of Hong Kong, and will be supervised by the HKMA. Seventh, Shanghai and Hong Kong will have complementary and mutually reinforcing relationships as financial centres (Chen, 1996). Since the handover, China has faithfully observed these principles.

Since its inception, the HKMA has steadily expanded its central banking functions, while simultaneously carrying out important reforms. To meet international standards and minimize settlement risks, real time gross settlement (RTGS) was introduced on 9 December 1996 for large-value interbank payments. All licensed banks were required to keep a clearing account direct with the HKMA, rather than with the HSBC as before. No daylight overdraft was allowed, though liquidity assistance could be obtained through the HKMA's liquidity adjustment facility (LAF). Thus, the HKMA effectively took over the central-clearing function from the HSBC, the largest bank in Hong Kong, whose role in the past had attracted some adverse comment (Jao, 1988). Earlier, in 1990, the government also set up a Central Moneymarkets Unit (CMU) which serves as a central custodian and clearing agent for Hong Kong dollar debt instruments issued by the private sector. As a result, there is now a seamless interface between the funds transfer system and the book-entry debt securities clearing system, worthy of a world-class financial centre (Monetary Policy and Markets Department, 1997). A US dollar clearing system was also launched in August 2000.

As the manager of the Exchange Fund, the HKMA has taken over from the two British banks the role of the lender of last resort (LOLR). Moreover, in order to prevent moral hazard, the HKMA has also spelt out the conditions for last resort lending: the applying bank must be locally incorporated, solvent, and have a risk-based capital adequacy ratio (*à la* Basle) of not less than 6 per cent; it must provide acceptable collateral, and must have already exhausted other means of liquidity assistance and so on. The Exchange Fund, which now incorporates the former Land Fund, is the sole repository of the government's foreign and local currency assets. As at the end of June 2000, its assets totalled HK$956 billion (US$123 billion), of which US$97 billion were in foreign currencies. Though a small territory, Hong Kong has a foreign exchange reserve that ranks fourth in the world (or second in the world on a per capita basis).

As early as 1996, the HKMA began preparations for dealing with the Y2K problem. In June 1999, the HKMA was able to announce that Hong Kong's payments system had successfully solved the problem, one of the earliest in the world to do so. In the same month, the payments system also passed with flying colours a test administered by the New York Clearing House.

Another significant reform has been greater openness and transparency. Prior to 1993, the balance sheet of the Exchange Fund had been kept secret and unpublished since 1940. Soon after its establishment, the HKMA decided to publish all financial accounts of the Exchange Fund, initially on an annual basis, subsequently on a monthly basis. The compilation and release of monetary statistics have also greatly improved, in accordance with the International Monetary Fund's Special Data Dissemination Standard (SDDS). The HKMA now regularly publishes a *Monthly Statistical Bulletin* and a *Quarterly Bulletin* containing articles on important monetary and banking issues. It also publishes occasional papers and booklets on various aspects of monetary and banking policy measures, and daily forecasts of the banking system's clearing balance.

Still another useful role is the promotion of the local debt market. The absence of a risk-free benchmark rate was often blamed in the past for the rudimentary state of Hong Kong's bond market. This has now been remedied by the issue of Exchange Fund bills and notes. The bills have maturities of 91, 182 and 364 days, while the notes have maturities ranging from two to ten years. These bills and notes are not issued for covering the fiscal deficit, but solely for monetary policy purposes. As at the end of June 2000, the total outstanding amount of such obligations stood at HK$105.6 billion (US$13.6 billion).

Since the onset of the Asian financial crisis, the HKMA has successfully repulsed at least three massive attacks on the Hong Kong dollar. But the stability has been achieved at the cost of the high level and volatility of interest rates, causing great damage to the real economy. To increase confidence in the currency and to reduce interest rate volatility, the HKMA unveiled in September 1998 seven 'technical measures' as follows:

1. The HKMA provides a clear undertaking to all licensed banks to convert Hong Kong dollars in their clearing accounts into US dollars at the fixed exchange rate of HK$7.75 to US$1.
2. The bid rate of the LAF is abolished.

3. A discount window replaces the LAF with the base rate (formerly known as the LAF offer rate) to be determined from time to time by the HKMA.
4. The HKMA removes the restriction on repeated borrowing in respect of the provision of overnight Hong Kong dollar liquidity through repo transactions using Exchange Fund bills and notes.
5. New Exchange Fund paper will be issued only when there is an inflow of funds.
6. A schedule of discount rates is applicable for different percentage thresholds of holdings of Exchange Fund paper by the licensed banks for the purpose of accessing the discount window.
7. The restriction on repeated borrowing in respect of repo transactions involving debt securities other than Exchange Fund paper is retained.

The first measure clearly demonstrates the government's commitment to the linked exchange rate system. The second measure is designed to prevent some banks from deliberately placing funds with the HKMA rather than lending them to the interbank market. The third and fourth measures allow freer access to day-end liquidity through the use of the Exchange Fund paper, which is fully backed by foreign currency. This will make the monetary system less susceptible to manipulation and dampen excessive interest rate volatility without departing from CBA discipline. The fifth measure will ensure that all new Exchange Fund paper will be fully backed by foreign exchange reserves. The sixth and seventh measures ensure that the interest rate adjustment mechanism is fully operational when the Hong Kong dollar is under significant pressure.

Events since then have vindicated these measures. Confidence in the currency has increased, and both the level and volatility of the term structure have eased across the board. One reliable and sensitive indicator of confidence is the yield differential between the two-year Hong Kong Exchange Fund note and US treasury notes. This narrowed from 566.5 basis points on 31 August 1998 to 22.2 basis points on 31 August 2000, or a fall of 544.3 basis points in two years. Another is the premium on the 12-month US dollar forward contract, which fell from 6,450 to −200 decimal points during the same period.

It will be noted that the convertibility undertaking rate was initially fixed at 7.75, not 7.8, the official rate. This was so because, when the Mexican peso crisis spread to Asia in early 1995, the HKMA chose to intervene whenever the exchange rose to 7.75. This practice was repeated when the Asian crisis broke out in July 1997. In time, the market came to regard 7.75 as the de facto official rate. The HKMA's strategy had been severely criticized as a violation of the automatic adjustment mechanism inherent in the CBA. The HKMA's response was that allowing the exchange rate to rise above 7.75 might well precipitate a *sauve qui peut* due to the public's 'herd instinct'. It is difficult to either support or reject this claim, because of the impossibility of conducting controlled experiments. But there are two undesirable side-effects which the HKMA implicitly acknowledges: overvaluation of the domestic currency and excessive interest rate volatility. Accordingly, shortly after the seven 'technical measures' were implemented, the HKMA also announced that effective from 1 April 1999, the exchange rate would be raised by HK$0.0001 every day, so that by the end of 500 days, the convertibility undertaking rate would coincide with the official rate. On 12 August 2000, the convertibility undertaking rate converged to the official rate as planned. Since then, the actual market rate has remained very close to, though slightly below, the official rate of 7.8.

3 INSTITUTIONAL REFORM

Prior to 1970, Hong Kong's banking structure was monolithic in the sense that no specialist banks or near-banks other than the traditional commercial banks (called 'licensed banks') were in existence. In 1970, the appearance of a number of merchant banks with international backgrounds spawned a host of smaller finance companies, which exploited a legal loophole in taking only time deposits. At first, there was no regulation at all of these new intermediaries, whose number soon escalated to over 2,000. In 1976, a Deposit-taking Companies Ordinance was passed, under which all depository institutions other than licensed banks were required to register with the government, and to observe a minimum paid-up capital requirement (then HK$2.5 million). Officially known as deposit-taking companies (DTCs), these intermediaries were allowed to take time deposits of any maturity of an amount not less than HK$50,000 for each account, but were barred from taking demand and savings deposits. Not being members of the interest rate cartel of the licensed banks, the DTCs grew very rapidly in the 1970s, causing some erosion of the deposit base of the licensed banks. In retaliation, the licensed banks formed DTC subsidiaries of their own, and simultaneously put pressure on the government to tighten its regulation of their rivals. The result was the three-tier system inaugurated in 1981, which can be divided into two phases: the first phase from 1981 to 1989, and the second phase from 1990. Institutional details of this banking structure are summarized in Table 6.1.

All depository institutions under the three–tier system are officially known as 'authorized institutions' (AIs). The rationale of this system is that the scope of banking business should vary directly with the degree of prudential supervision. Thus licensed banks, which are the most strictly

Table 6.1 The three-tier system in Hong Kong

	Old three-tier system (1981–89)	New three-tier system (from 1990)
1. First Tier		
Name	Licensed banks	Licensed banks
Minimum paid-up capital	HK$100 million	HK$150 million
Scope of deposit taking	All types of deposits	All types of deposits
Minimum denomination and term to maturity of deposits	No restriction	No restriction
Minimum liquidity ratio	25%	25%
Minimum capital adequacy ratio	5% after 1 September 1988, but banking commissioner may order a bank to raise it to 8%	8%, but banking commissioner/HKMA may order a bank to raise it to 12%
2. Second Tier		
Name	Licensed Deposit-taking Company (LDTC)	Restricted Licence Bank (RLB)
Minimum paid-up capital	HK$75 million	HK$100 million
Scope of deposit taking	Time deposits only	Time deposits only
Minimum denomination and term to maturity of deposits	HK$500,000, no restriction on maturity	HK$500,000, no restriction on maturity
Minimum liquidity ratio	25% after 1 September 1986	25%
Minimum capital adequacy ratio	5% after 1 September 1988, but banking commissioner may order an LDTC to raise it to 10%	8%, but banking commissioner/HKMA may order an RLB to raise it to 16%

Table 6.1 (*continued*)

	Old three-tier system (1981–89)	New three-tier system (from 1990)
3. Third Tier		
Name	Registered Deposit-taking Company (RDTC)	Deposit-taking Company (DTC)
Minimum paid-up capital	HK$10 million	HK$25 million
Scope of deposit taking	Time deposits only	Time deposits only
Minimum denomination and term to maturity of deposits	HK$100,000, not less than 3 months	HK$100,000, not less than 3 months
Minimum liquidity ratio	25% after 1 September 1986	25%
Minimum capital adequacy ratio	5% after 1 September 1988, but banking commissioner may order an RDTC to raise it to 10%	8%, but banking commissioner/HKMA may order a DTC to raise it to 16%

Notes: Liquidity ratio is defined as the ratio of liquefiable assets to total one-month liabilities. Capital adequacy ratio is defined as the ratio of the sum of paid-up capital, reserves and undistributed profits to total risk assets.

regulated, can take all types of deposits. For the two other tiers, for which regulation is less demanding, deposit taking is confined to time deposits. Note that the second tier 'restricted licence banks' since 1990 comprise mostly merchant banks/investment banks, which can call themselves 'banks' provided this is qualified by a description such as 'restricted licence', 'merchant', 'investment' or 'wholesale'. The change in terminology is motivated by the desire to promote Hong Kong as an international financial centre. Since 1981 it has also been the policy of the authorities to weed out undercapitalized DTCs. No new DTCs will be permitted to commence business unless they are majority owned by licensed banks.

The transition to the post-colonial era having taken place much more smoothly than expected, a longer-term planning for the banking industry becomes necessary in view of the globalization of financial markets, proliferation of new financial products, rapid progress in information technology and growing competition from other financial centres. Therefore, in March 1998, the HKMA commissioned a consultant firm, KPMG Barents, to conduct an in-depth review of Hong Kong's banking sector for the next five years. The report of the consultants was completed and released at the end of 1998, the main recommendations of which are summarized in Table 6.2 (KMPG Barents, 1998).

At the time of writing (May 2001), the government has accepted most of the recommendations on deregulation (see the section on financial deregulation below), and on the clarification of the role of the LOLR, but is still considering other recommendations. The recommendation on simplification of the three-tier system would probably mean the eventual phasing out of the third tier, namely, the DTCs.

Institutional reform is also being implemented for the securities markets. Under government prodding, the Stock Exchange of Hong Kong (SEHK) and the Hong Kong Futures Exchange (HKFE) announced in August 1999 that they had agreed in principle to demutualize and to merge. In 2000, the enabling legislation was completed, and the two were formally merged to form the Hong Kong Exchanges and Clearing Ltd (HKEC). In November 1999, a second board, called Growth Enterprise Market (GEM), was launched, to encourage innovative, especially high-tech companies without a record of profitability to list on the stock exchange. Its rationale is therefore roughly equal to that of NASDAQ in the United States.

4 SUPERVISORY REFORM

Before 1964, Hong Kong's banking sector was conspicuous by the absence of any prudential supervision. This state of affairs has been variously

Table 6.2 Proposed banking reform

Phases	Regulatory recommendations	Supervisory recommendations
Phase 1: enhanced risk-based supervision	*To enhance safety and stability:* • Introduce financial disclosure by foreign branch banks (limited disclosure introduction in progress) • Clarify the HKMA's role as lender of last resort *To enhance competitiveness:* • Relax the one-building condition to allow three branches for foreign banks • Begin monitoring process prior to start of deregulation of IRRs	• Develop a formal strategic planning process • Develop a formalized risk-assessment framework and quality assurance programme • Integrate risk-management principles into off-site surveillance activities • Revise on-site surveillance activities to more explicitly evaluate institutions' risk-management capabilities • Develop guidelines as to types and degrees of supervisory responses • Define core capabilities, revise job descriptions and the performance management process, develop a formalized career development programme, perform a training needs assessment and expand the current training curriculum • Create additional specialist teams • Enhance the supervisory database and management information systems • Assess risks associated with longer-term economic integration with Mainland China

Phase 2: market restructuring	*To enhance safety and stability:* • Raise minimum capital requirements for local authorized institutions • Study of alternatives to enhance explicit depositor protection *To enhance competitiveness:* • Simplify the three-tier system • Reassess access criteria for RTGSs • Stage 1 of deregulation of the IRRs (time deposits up to 6 days) • Stage 2 of deregulation of the IRRs (current accounts)	• Assess supervisory gaps and/or overlaps and options to address
Phase 3: market liberalization	*To enhance safety and stability:* • Implementation of enhanced explicit depositor protection scheme *To enhance competitiveness:* • Stage 3 of deregulation of the IRRs (remove all remaining interest rate caps) • Reduce the time period and relax the association with Hong Kong entry criteria	

Note: IRRs = Interest rate rules, RTGS = Real time gross settlement.

Source: KPMG Barents.

described as 'free banking' or 'wildcat banking', depending on the point of view of the observer. The first Banking Ordinance of 1948 was derisively rudimentary by present-day standards. It provided only for the licensing of banks, examination of bank books, publication of bank statements and the appointment of an advisory committee. No mention was made of a supervisory body, or prudential measures such as minimum capital and liquidity ratio. Following a bank run in 1961, the government invited a senior official from the Bank of England to advise on a new ordinance. The result was the revised Banking Ordinance of 1964, which provided for the appointment of a banking commissioner, laid down minimum paid-up capital (then HK$5 million) and a liquidity ratio of 25 per cent, and limitations on loans and investments and so on (Jao, 1974). Ironically, this ordinance was followed almost immediately by a severe banking crisis. Between 1964 and 1982, there had been relatively minor amendments to the ordinance. Then another banking crisis engulfed Hong Kong in 1982–86. The confidence crisis at that time over Hong Kong's future after 1997, resulting in a collapse of the asset markets, was undoubtedly a contributory factor, but imprudence and mismanagement (especially overexposure to the property market), or even fraud, remained the principal causes. The government had had to use the Exchange Fund to bail out several banks in distress (Jao, 1987b). An overhaul of the whole regulatory regime therefore became urgent. Again, a team from the Bank of England was commissioned in 1984 to study the issue, whose report laid the groundwork for the new Banking Ordinance which came into force on 1 September 1986 (Hall, 1985; Jao, 1988; Ho, 1991). The main points of this new ordinance can be summarized as follows:

1. Additional discretionary powers given to the banking commissioner, such as revoking and suspending licences, vetting the backgrounds of owners, directors and managers, issuing guidelines and so on.
2. Tightening of the auditing process by a tripartite – management, commissioner, auditor – review, appointment of a second auditor, disciplinary action against negligence or misconduct of the auditor(s).
3. A 'fit and proper' test for and tougher vetting of owners, directors and managers of a bank before their appointment.
4. Stricter limitations on loans to a group of companies, directors and advances to a company against its securities.
5. A minimum capital adequacy ratio of 5 per cent, which the commissioner might at his discretion raise to 8 per cent for banks and 10 per cent for DTCs.
6. Redefinition of the 'liquidity ratio' as the ratio of 'liquefiable assets' to 'qualifying liabilities' and so on, liabilities maturing or callable within one month.

The 1986 Ordinance marks a significant shift in the focus and orientation of prudential supervision. The regulatory authorities are no longer satisfied merely with the *pro forma* observance of ratios or quantitative indicators, but will look more closely into the quality of management of the supervised institution, by on-site and off-site examinations, as well as by more rigorous auditing. For the first time, a minimum capital adequacy ratio (CAR) was imposed, two years ahead of the Basle Accord.

Since 1986, the ordinance has been regularly reviewed and updated in the light of developments in the banking industry, but so far most amendments have been of a technical nature. For instance, after 1993, the term 'Monetary Authority' (MA), the abbreviation for HKMA, replaces 'Commissioner'. The ordinance was amended in 1995 to establish the MA as the licensing authority responsible for the authorization, suspension and revocation of all three types of AIs. It was further amended in 1997 for the purpose of regulating the issue of multipurpose stored value cards, and money brokers operating in the interbank forex market. A Code of Banking Practice has also been issued and in 1998, two surveys were made to assess the compliance by AIs. It was reported that the compliance rate was 90 per cent (HKMA, *Annual Report*, 1998).

When the 8 per cent CAR was announced under the Basle Accord, Hong Kong was well-positioned to meet it. Indeed, Hong Kong met the 8 per cent criterion in 1990, two years ahead of the target date of 1992. More remarkably, at the end of 1998, when Hong Kong was in a deep recession because of the Asian crisis, the average CAR of the banking system was still as high as 18.6 per cent despite huge provisions for non-performing loans (HKMA *Annual Report*, 1998). Hong Kong also fully and conscientiously observes the Basle Concordat of 1975 and the Basle Committee's 'Core Principles for Effective Banking Supervision' issued in 1997 (HKMA, 1997).

Like banking, Hong Kong's securities markets were at first totally unregulated. During the stock market boom in the early 1970s before the first oil crisis, there were no less than four stock exchanges. It was not until 1986 that the four exchanges were combined, under intense government pressure, into one single entity, the Stock Exchange of Hong Kong (SEHK). During the worldwide stock market crash commencing on 19 October 1987 led by Wall Street, the Hong Kong Futures Exchange (HKFE) was unable to fulfil its obligations. Both the SEHK and the HKFE suspended trading for four days. When trading resumed on 26 October stock prices and futures prices fell by 33 per cent and 44 per cent, respectively, in one single day, forcing the government to organize hastily a HK$4 billion package to bail out the HKFE.

Stung by this scandal, the government appointed a special committee to review the operations of the two exchanges and their regulatory bodies. The report of this committee (Securities Review Committee, 1988) strongly criticized not only the two exchanges for poor management, but also the two regulatory bodies, the Securities Commission and the Commodities Trading Commission, for ineffective supervision. The committee therefore recommended a reconstitution of the two exchanges, and the establishment of a new independent supervisory body outside the civil service to regulate the securities market. The government accepted these recommendations, and thus the Securities and Futures Commission (SFC) came into being in 1989, replacing the previous two commissions (Wong, 1991). It supervises the securities, financial investment and futures industries, and administers a host of ordinances relating to protection of investors, securities, commodities trading, insider dealing, leveraged forex trading and so on. The SFC also registers or licenses securities, forex and commodities dealers.

In the summer of 1998, taking advantage of the deep recession in Hong Kong and Japan, and the marked economic slowdown and devastating floods in China, hedge funds and other speculators launched simultaneous attacks on the Hong Kong dollar and the stock market. Although the Hong Kong dollar held firm, the stock and futures markets fell sharply, with the Hang Seng Index (HSI) of stock prices falling to 6,660, some 60 per cent off its peak at 16,673 on 7 August 1997. At that point, the government, using the resources of the Exchange Fund, intervened massively in the stock and futures markets, buying up some US$15 billion worth of shares to thwart the speculators. This unexpected intervention was widely condemned, especially abroad, for violating free market principles, and for vainly trying to prop up stock prices. However, Mr Joseph Yam, Chief Executive of the HKMA, argued forcefully that speculators were engaged in a vicious 'double market play', and the free fall of the stock market, if unchecked, could lead to a collapse of the banking system and the currency (Yam, 1998a and b). Whatever the rights and wrongs of the intervention, the authorities have succeeded in their double objective of punishing the speculators and stabilizing the securities markets. An independent company, the Exchange Fund Investment Ltd (EFI), has been formed to manage the government's huge portfolio. From November 1999, the EFI has gradually been disposing of its portfolio through a unit trust called Tracker Fund. By the end of March 2001, a total of HK$119 billion had been sold to the public, more than recouping the original costs of acquisition. The government, however, still retained a portfolio worth some HK$110 billion. The government also unveiled in early September 1998 a 30-point programme for tightening supervision and enhancing transparency of the securities market, including measures against illegal short-selling, and strict enforcement of the 'T+2' (settlement two days after transaction) rule, to prevent manipulation by speculators (Jao, 1999).

Last but not least, all types of insurance business, as well as private occupational retirement schemes, are supervised by the Insurance Authority under the Insurance Companies Ordinance.

Thus, compared to the situation before 1964, when there was no prudential supervision of any kind in the whole financial sector, Hong Kong during the past 35 years has built up a comprehensive and sound, though by no means perfect, prudential framework covering virtually all financial institutions, markets, services and instruments. While some of the prudential reforms are the direct result of market failures or even crises, others are the natural concomitants of Hong Kong's rise as a major international financial centre.

5 FINANCIAL DEREGULATION

Hong Kong has always been recognized internationally as one of the most financially liberalized economies in the world (Williamson and Mahar, 1998). Our review so far seems to suggest Hong Kong's financial sector has evolved from a regime of pure *laissez faire* to one of extensive prudential regulations. The real story is more complex, however. Some regulations, seemingly appropriate at the time of their imposition, may with the passage of time outlive their usefulness, and may even become obstructive of progress and welfare. There are two major examples in the banking sphere.

Soon after the banking crisis of 1965, the government, arguing that Hong Kong was overbanked, imposed a moratorium on new banking licences. Foreign banks that wished to enter the local banking market could only do so by acquiring equity interests in existing banks, or, after 1970, by buying into existing DTCs, or by setting up their own DTC subsidiaries. In the late 1970s, however, multinational banks became increasingly frustrated by their inability to open full service branches in Hong Kong. Confronted with growing pressure from such banks, and competition from Singapore, the government announced in March 1978 that it would resume licensing foreign banks provided they met three regulatory requirements and accepted one condition. The three requirements were: incorporation in jurisdictions with effective supervision, total assets net of contra items of over US$3 billion (subsequently raised to US$16 billion in several steps), and some reciprocity to Hong Kong banks. The one condition was that newly licensed banks could only operate one branch in one building. The response from foreign banks was dramatic: the number of foreign banks increased from 40 to 154 between 1978 and 1995 (Jao, 1997). The influx of foreign banks was also encouraged by the abolition of withholding interest tax on foreign currency deposits in 1982.

The one-branch restriction was partly motivated by the desire to protect small local banks which operated mainly in the retail banking market. Most foreign banks licensed after 1978 did not seem to mind this restriction very much at that time, since they were interested primarily in the wholesale banking market. However, with Hong Kong's population having grown from 4.6 million to nearly 7 million in the ensuing 21 years, the retail market has suddenly loomed large, and foreign banks licensed after 1978 have become increasingly irritated by their exclusion from it. To maintain Hong Kong's position as an international financial centre, the government-appointed consultants have therefore recommended allowing such foreign banks to operate up to three branches, as shown in Table 6.2. Moreover, after 21 years, the local banks' case for continued protection has weakened considerably.

The other example is the interest rate cartel officially known as 'Interest Rate Rules' (IRRs). This cartel was formed in the early 1960s in order to stop the 'interest rate war' during the era of 'wildcat banking'. Under this arrangement, banks were classified into several categories, so that the largest international banks offered the lowest rates, while the smallest local banks offered the highest rates on time deposits. The rate on savings deposits was uniform for all banks, while that on demand deposits was identically zero (Jao, 1974). At that time, the IRRs were hailed as a stabilizing device for preventing cut-throat competition.

With the passage of time, however, the stabilizing function of this cartel has come to be more than offset by its allocative inefficiency and distributive injustice. The rise of consumerism has further increased public consciousness of the cartel's defects. In a commissioned study, the Consumer Council strongly attacked the cartel for exploiting depositors, and extracting abnormal profits for the banks (Consumer Council, 1994). Rising public anger and pressure eventually forced the Hong Kong Association of Banks (HKAB) to agree to a partial deregulation of interest rates on time deposits of more than seven days during 1994–95. Further deregulation was postponed in early 1995 due to the Mexican crisis and the impending change of sovereignty. The consultancy report now considers that the time is ripe for removing the remaining part of the IRRs. The HKMA has accepted this recommendation, and the IRRs will be phased out within two years from 1 July 1999.

These two measures of deregulation will increase competition in the retail banking sector, whose full impact is likely to be borne mainly by smaller local banks. Since the crisis of 1965, most small local banks have already allowed larger and stronger foreign and Mainland China banks to acquire minority or majority equity interests in them, but the two measures will further accelerate the process of consolidation. Even the larger local banks may be compelled to consider mergers or strategic alliances to strengthen their competitive capabilities. Note that the IRRs are confined to Hong Kong dollar time deposits of 15 months or more and savings and demand deposits only. Other local currency time deposits and foreign currency deposits are not covered by the cartel. Moreover, restricted licence banks (RLBs) and DTCs, not being members of the HKAB, are also not bound by the IRRs. In other words, there has always been strong competition for large denomination time deposits and foreign currency deposits. At this juncture, it is difficult to determine the net gain to depositors, because banks are very likely to increase their service charges once the IRRs are phased out.

Exchange rate liberalization has not been a problem, since the Hong Kong dollar has always been a freely convertible currency. However, as a member of the Sterling Area from 1935 to 1972, Hong Kong was obliged to observe exchange control, administered from London, on sterling transactions (Jao, 1974). After the United Kingdom removed all exchange control in 1979, even transactions in sterling have become totally free. As to the Chinese currency, the renminbi, it has always been treated as a foreign currency, even after 1 July 1997, as already mentioned above. China still retains a panoply of exchange controls on capital account, but this is administered by the Chinese, not the Hong Kong government. In Hong Kong, such controls are administered by Mainland China banks acting as agents of the Chinese government. Thus the position of the renminbi is not unlike that of sterling under British administration.

6 ENHANCED CONSUMER PROTECTION

The gradual abolition of the interest rate cartel has already been discussed. One major remaining issue of consumer protection is deposit insurance. Previous proposals of deposit insurance have come to nothing due to the strong opposition of large banks, such as the HSBC. Asserting that they enjoy the full confidence of their depositors, these banks argue that their payment of a premium will be tantamount to a subsidy of their rivals. The serious problems of moral hazard and adverse selection in non-risk-based deposit insurance schemes in many countries have also cast doubt on the feasibility and desirability of deposit insurance for Hong Kong. The general feeling seems to be that a more vigilant prudential system, and better bank management and risk control, provide better consumer protection in the long run (Jao, 1992).

As mentioned earlier, the government had bailed out a number of institutions during the 1980s to protect depositors. But this protection was only implicit and on a case-by-case basis. In 1991, for example, the government refused to rescue the Hong Kong subsidiary of the BCCI, causing considerable loss to its depositors. The only explicit protection is provided in the Companies Ordinance, under which depositors are entitled to priority payment for their deposits up to a maximum of HK$100,000. But even this is contingent on the availability of sufficient assets.

Perhaps cognizant of these considerations, the consultancy report only vaguely recommends that 'an enhanced form of explicit depositor protection would be beneficial', and that the HKMA 'consider the alternatives available by way of a more detailed study on the various forms of explicit depositor protection' (KPMG Barents, 1998, p. 42).

Consumer protection is, however, available in other implicit forms. Thus, the Code of Banking Practice requests all banks to provide the terms and conditions of their services to customers in both Chinese and English, and to include fees and charges in the calculation of their annualized percentage rate. The HKMA also engages in a very active anti-money-laundering programme, which has been positively assessed by an international body, the Financial Action Task Force (FATF). It has taken part in the Asia Pacific Group on Money Laundering. The Y2K problem has been successfully tackled, as already mentioned earlier. In late 1997, the HKMA conducted a study of the security issues arising from banking transactions over the internet. It considered that an effective way of addressing these issues would be to encourage the development of a proper public key infrastructure, and to enhance legal certainty in the conduct of electronic transactions. This view has been accepted by the government (HKMA, *Annual Report*, 1998).

The amended Banking Ordinance also provides for much tougher sanctions against fraud. For example, any director, manager, trustee or agent of any AI that commits a fraudulent act is liable on conviction to a fine of HK$500,000 and to imprisonment for five years (Art. 123).

There is a United Exchange Compensation Fund (UECF) to compensate investors in the event of the default or failure of their brokers. In the summer of 1998, following the collapse of two securities firms, the Peregrine Group and the C.A. Pacific Group, the SFC conducted a review of the existing compensation arrangements. Its report proposes to change the current UECF from a lump-sum fund to one that also includes reinsurance as its second-tier financing source for compensation.

Insider trading used to be notoriously prevalent in the absence of proper supervision. The Insider Dealing Tribunal, established under the Securities (Insider Dealing) Ordinance of 1991, did not commence operations until 1994. Since then, the tribunal has successfully concluded eight cases, three of them in 1998. While insider dealing is not a criminal offence, a person identified as an inside dealer can be barred from office, and heavily fined up to three times the profit made or the loss avoided.

7 FINANCIAL INNOVATIONS DUE TO FINANCIAL REFORM

As an international financial centre in the Asia Pacific region, Hong Kong plays host to more than 400 banks and depository institutions, 200 insurance companies and 1,000 mutual funds or unit trusts. Furthermore, more than 800 multinational corporations use Hong Kong as their regional headquarters for Asia Pacific or Greater China (Jao, 1997). A large congregation of these financial institutions and multinational corporations provides a fertile ground for financial innovations, as both suppliers of and demanders for innovations interact in close proximity.

Such innovations are a function of financial reform. Thus, the liberalization of foreign bank entry and the abolition of withholding tax directly triggered an influx of foreign banks, which introduced many banking-related innovations, such as certificates of deposits (CDs), syndicated loans, interest and currency swaps, loan securitization, note-issuing facilities (NIFs), multi-option financing facilities (MOFFs) and so on. The influx of banks, in turn, spawned a similar influx of non-bank intermediaries, which together with the banks, are responsible for many securities-related innovations, such as futures, options, warrants and other derivatives. A healthy development of financial innovation also requires better investor information and protection. Here, prudential reform and enhanced consumer protection again help. A study (Jao, 1987a) shows that, by the mid-1980s, over 80 per cent of financial innovations originating in the United States or the euro-currency market were 'significantly present in Hong Kong'.

New products introduced by the HKFE in 1998 included the Taiwan Index, one-month HIBOR (Hong Kong Inter-bank Offered Rate), and Hang Seng 100 Index futures and options contracts.

Mortgage securitization began relatively late, being introduced by some American banks in the early 1990s, but it received a strong boost with the establishment of the government-owned Hong Kong Mortgage Corporation (HKMC) in 1997. Modelled on the US Federal National Mortgage Association ('Fannie Mae'), the HKMC purchases mortgage loans from the banks, and repackages and resells them as marketable securities to investors. As such, it can enhance liquidity and correct 'maturity mismatch' in the banking sector, encourage securitization and promote the development of capital markets. It plans to issue bonds of about HK$20 billion to fund its operations.

The HKMC, together with the Central Moneymarkets Unit (CMU), real time gross settlement (RTGS), and the Mandatory Provident Fund (MPF), which began operations at the end of 2000, can be regarded as government-sponsored innovations as part of the overall financial reform process.

8 CONCLUDING REMARKS

During the past 50 years, Hong Kong has transformed itself from a small entrepôt into a world-class financial and business centre. Financial reform has been an integral part of this metamorphosis.

However, in the course of its remarkable transformation, Hong Kong has also suffered many setbacks and crises. And some of its policy measures have been quite controversial. Hong Kong must now face squarely the challenge of how to constantly upgrade its prudential framework without throttling the dynamism of its financial sector, and equally important, without damaging its well-deserved reputation as a non-interventionist market economy.

REFERENCES

Chen, Y. (1996), 'Prospects for the financial relationship between Mainland China and Hong Kong after 1997', *Hong Kong Monetary Authority Quarterly Bulletin*, February, pp. 38–43.

Consumer Council (1994). *Are Hong Kong Depositors Fairly Treated*?, Hong Kong: Consumer Council Steering Group on Financial Services.

Hall, M.J.B. (1985), 'The reform of banking supervision in Hong Kong', *Hong Kong Economic Papers*, No. 16, pp. 74–96.

Ho, R.Y.K. (1991), 'The regulatory framework of the banking sector', in R.Y.K. Ho, R.H. Scott and K.A. Wong (eds), *The Hong Kong Financial System*, Hong Kong: Oxford University Press, Chapter 5.

Hong Kong Monetary Authority (HKMA) (1993–98), *Annual Report*, various years.

Hong Kong Monetary Authority (HKMA) (1997), *Prudential Supervision in Hong Kong*, Hong Kong: Hong Kong Monetary Authority.

Jao, Y.C. (1974), *Banking and Currency in Hong Kong: A Study of Postwar Financial Developments*, London: Macmillan.

Jao, Y.C. (1987a), 'Theories and policy implications of financial innovations', *Journal of Economics and International Relations*, Vol. 1, No. 1, Spring, pp. 61–92.

Jao, Y.C. (1987b), 'A comparative analysis of banking crises in Hong Kong and Taiwan', *Journal of Economics and International Relations*, Vol. 1, No. 4, Winter, pp. 299–322.

Jao, Y.C. (1988) (ed.), *Hong Kong's Banking System in Transition*, Hong Kong: Chinese Banks Association.

Jao, Y.C. (1990), 'From sterling exchange standard to dollar exchange standard: the evolution of Hong Kong's contemporary monetary system', in Y.C. Jao and F.H.H. King, *Money in Hong Kong: Historical Perspective and Contemporary Analysis*, Hong Kong: Centre of Asian Studies, University of Hong Kong, pp. 51–169.

Jao, Y.C. (1992) (ed.), *Deposit Insurance: Issues and Evaluation,* Hong Kong: Chartered Institute of Bankers.

Jao, Y.C. (1997), *Hong Kong as an International Financial Centre: Evolution, Prospects and Policies*, Hong Kong: City University Press.

Jao, Y.C. (1998a), 'The working of the Currency Board: the experience of Hong Kong, 1935–97', *Pacific Economic Review*, Vol. 3, No. 3, October, pp. 219–42.

Jao, Y.C. (1998b), *Money and Finance in Hong Kong: Retrospect and Prospect*, Singapore: Singapore University Press.

Jao, Y.C. (1999), 'The financial sector in the wake of the Asian economic crisis', in Wang Gungwu and John Wong (eds), *Hong Kong in China: The Challenges of Transition*, Singapore: Times Academic Press, Chapter 6.

KPMG Barents (1998), *Hong Kong Banking into the New Millennium: Hong Kong Banking Sector Consultancy Study – Detailed Recommendations*, Hong Kong.

Monetary Policy and Markets Department (1997), 'Hong Kong's real time gross settlement system', in *Money and Banking in Hong Kong*, Vol. 2, Hong Kong: Hong Kong Monetary Authority, pp. 159–68.

Securities Review Committee (1988), *Report on the Operations and Regulation of the Hong Kong Securities Industry*, Hong Kong: Government Printer.

Williamson, J. and M. Mahar (1998), *A Survey of Financial Liberalization*, Essays in International Finance, No. 211, Princeton, NJ: Princeton University Press.

Wong, K.A. (1991), 'The Hong Kong Stock Market', in R.Y.K. Ho, R.H. Scott and K.A. Wong (eds) *The Hong Kong Financial System*, Hong Kong: Oxford University Press, Chapter 10.

Yam, J. (1994), 'Central banking and monetary policy in Hong Kong', in *The Practice of Central Banking in Hong Kong*, Hong Kong: Hong Kong Monetary Authority, pp. 2–23.

Yam, J. (1998a), 'Why we intervened', *Hong Kong Monetary Authority Quarterly Bulletin*, November, No. 17, pp. 1–4.

Yam, J. (1998b), 'Defending Hong Kong's monetary stability', *Hong Kong Monetary Authority Quarterly Bulletin*, November, No. 17, pp. 75–9.

7. Financial reform in Italy

Marco Onado

1 INTRODUCTION

Financial reform in Italy has meant a complete reshaping of the regulations formulated in the 1930s. As a matter of fact, the Italian Banking Act (1936) survived longer than any of the laws that in all European countries were prompted by the Great Depression, the most serious 'market failure' that ever occurred. For the first time, banking became a regulated industry and financial stability was given a top priority on the political agenda.

The pressure to change the banking laws of the 1930s began to be felt as soon as the post-war economic growth made it clear that the overwhelming weight given to stability had kept backstage the other objectives of financial regulation: efficiency; competition; and disclosure in financial markets. Italy has lagged behind other countries in this process; the reasons for the delay are to be found in the specific conditions that made the country particularly ill-suited to tackle the external shocks of the mid-1970s.

This chapter charts the recent evolution of Italian financial reform. The next section reviews the theoretical framework for the analysis of financial regulation. Section 3 gives an overview of the main changes in Italian financial regulation and its main characteristics, particularly as regards the division of responsibilities among regulators. The following sections sketch the main lines of reform for each final objective of regulation: price stability (Section 4); financial stability (Section 5); disclosure (Section 6); and competition (Section 7). Section 8 concludes.

2 THE RATIONALE OF FINANCIAL REGULATION

The *raison d'être* of financial regulation, as in any form of economic activity is to correct market failures. Both economic theory and historical experience show that financial intermediation is particularly prone to market failures, due to the information asymmetries that dominate the relationship between borrowers and lenders. These asymmetries can destroy the fiduciary relationship that lies at the heart of both using money and lending. In other words, the question of whether financial intermediation needs to be regulated is equivalent to the question, 'Why do financial intermediaries exist?' (Onado, 2000).

From both a practical and a theoretical point of view, the debate on financial regulation started well before the Great Depression. Since the nineteenth century, it was pointed out that banks' liabilities were redeemable at sight and circulated as a means of payment, while their cash reserves were a fraction of the deposits; on the other hand, the interest-bearing assets had a longer duration than deposits and were to a great extent represented by risky loans, subject to imperfections we now call information asymmetries. As a consequence, the liquidation value of bank assets is lower than the face value of its liabilities; this entails a risk of runs, contagion and eventually the systemic consequences which were a characteristic of the frequent bank crises that exploded even at the dawn of the modern banking era.

This was sufficient to support, even in a *laissez-faire* world, the idea that banking had to be somehow 'regulated', which in those times meant in the UK giving the Bank of England a special status and a special responsibility as regards the level of exchange rates (and the level of prices), and the liquidity of commercial banks. In other words, the first two objectives of financial regulation were identified as:

1. to control the money supply and, via price stability, the fiduciary nature of bank-created money (hence monetary policy and the macroeconomic function of central banks); and
2. to control the liquidity and solvency of banks to protect depositors (hence, supervisory powers).

Credit of last resort granted by the central bank has traditionally been the link between the two objectives, as was immediately stressed by authors such as Thornton (1802) and Bagehot (1873). Even in modern times, this link has led many scholars (Goodhart, 1985) to assert that the financial stability function of central banks preceded the monetary policy function, not vice versa.

Although the stability of banks (and generally speaking, of financial intermediaries) has been historically the first economic need that regulation was meant to satisfy, there are other motives for regulating financial activity. All financial contracts are dominated by information asymmetries and are required to protect investors against insufficient information, fraud, negligence, conflicts of interest, mismanagement and unfairness of the mechanism that translates information into prices. These asymmetries can undermine the operations of the markets, by making it impossible for investors to assess the 'real' quality of securities. Other objectives of regulation are therefore to ensure comparable, transparent and reliable information, as well as the correctness of behaviour of financial agents towards their clients (Llewellyn, 1999).

The need for a specific regulation aimed at disclosure (broadly defined) is theoretically rooted in the information asymmetries that dominate financial contracts and the ensuing problems of adverse selection and moral hazard. The growing importance of securities markets coupled with a few significant cases of heavy damage to investors led gradually to the creation of specific regulation to protect investors. Following the example of the American Securities and Exchange Commission (SEC) (established in 1934), in Europe, France (1967) and Italy (1974) took the lead; other countries followed suit. Disclosure and rules of conduct were given an outstanding position as regulatory objectives. *Ad hoc* regulators, more or less modelled on the American SEC, were established.

Finally, there is another reason why economic activity, and financial markets in particular, need to be regulated, that is, to remove obstacles to competition, which is essential for productive and allocative efficiency. Financial markets may be unable to reach autonomously a sufficient competitive condition, due to the specific nature of some services (in the payments system there are natural monopolies, such as information networks; demand mobility is geographically bound; and so on) or to information asymmetries that make retail banking markets contestable only to a limited extent. It is important to stress that the objective of competition refers to all the components of the financial system: intermediaries, instruments and markets. In particular, present technology now also allows for a full contestability of services offered by exchanges and other trading systems which have traditionally been viewed as natural monopolies.

Table 7.1 identifies the four main objectives of financial regulation, their typical areas of intervention and the main instruments used to secure them. The last column points to the main steps of the Italian reform for each objective. It is important to stress that the balance among the four objectives varies over time. In the climate of opinion prevailing in the 1930s, particularly in the European countries, regulators looked on competition with a suspicious eye. As a matter of fact, while it is true that many banking crises were characterized by overbanking and cut-throat competition, it is also true that in those times there was no specific instrument to monitor bank risks. Therefore, in many respects, the regulators of the 1930s were inclined and to some extent forced to think that restraining competition would help to keep bank rates to levels favourable to bank profitability. If oligopolistic conditions followed, it seemed a fair price to pay for soundness and stability of the banking system as a whole.

Table 7.1 Financial regulation: a taxonomy

Final objectives	Broad areas	Instruments	Main reform
Price stability (macro)	Monetary policy	Open market operations Refinancing	Transposition of Maastricht Treaty and creation of the European System of Central Banks (ESCB)
Financial intermediaries stability (micro)	Lending of last resort	Secured credit (repos) Emergency credit	Transposition of Maastricht Treaty and creation of the ESCB
	Refunding of losses	Deposit insurance compensation schemes	Deposit Insurance Scheme
	Prudential supervision	• Structural controls (bank chartering and controls on entry) • Restrictions on asset holdings and activities • Separation of the banking and other financial industries, such as securities, insurance, real estate; capital requirements • Special reporting to the supervisory authorities • On-site inspections	1993 Banking Act (*Testo Unico Bancario*)

Table 7.1 (*continued*)

Final objectives	Broad areas	Instruments	Main reform
Disclosure and fairness • Issuers • Intermediaries • Markets	Disclosure	• Financial information • Prospectus • Price-sensitive information (insider trading and market abuse)	1993 Securities Act (*Testo Unico della Finanza*)
	Company and shareholders' rights	• Company law • Bankruptcy law	
	Corporate governance rules	• Company law • Self-regulation	
	Rules of conduct	• Specific regulation (brokers; mutual funds)	
	Orderly and efficient functioning of the markets	Regulation of exchanges	
Competition	Rules to prevent • Cartels • Abuses of dominant positions	• Approval of mergers • Measures against restrictive business practices	1990 Act on Competition

This is why bank regulation was characterized by heavy structural controls: barriers to entry; restraints on assets and liabilities; and a tangled web of limits requiring specific authorizations. The whole fabric of financial regulation was designed to ensure that institutions remained profitable most of the time. The 'uniqueness' of banks from a theoretical point of view was the justification for the special regulation and the extent of structural controls.

In most European countries, there was a further motive giving strength to this kind of regulation: the myths of economic planning and public ownership of banks in those times went hand in hand, giving strength to the idea that banking was a very special sector, where the principles of market freedom had somehow to bow to 'superior' interests of controlling the economy and the private sector.

The net result was a drastic stifling of competitive impulses, both in the market for financial services and in the market for corporate control. The suspicion against competition and the penchant for the control of credit by the state, explain why in most European countries, bank legislation gave a powerful control on the banking system both to the bank regulator (normally the central bank) and to the government (normally, the ministry of finance).

At the same time, the growing role of monetary policy as an anti-inflation and countercyclical weapon, gave new life to the role of central banks, giving them a key role in the making of economic policy as a whole. Although always important, central banks became policy makers only after the reforms following the Great Depression. Price stability and bank stability became the two cornerstones of financial regulation, both from the political point of view (as is demonstrated by the growing importance of central banking as a constitutional subject) and the theoretical point of view. Objectives, instruments and the *modus operandi* of monetary policy soon became one of the main themes of academic research and political debate.

Only since the 1960s has the objective of bank stability been pursued through specific instruments instead of through restricting competition and raising, *ceteris paribus*, bank profits. Structural controls were gradually phased out in favour of prudential, non-discretionary measures. Gradually, since the late 1960s, competition in banking was more and more seen as an independent objective, as it became clear that the excess weight given to stability came at the expense of efficiency and the benefits to consumers which are the typical outcomes of competitive conditions. Slowly (and in some countries very slowly), the public policy objectives were achieved by relying upon competition and market forces rather than upon structural controls (OECD, 1998).

Particularly important has been the gradual shift from structural controls to prudential controls as a means to achieve financial stability. The real watershed has been the international agreement on minimum capital requirements (Basle Agreement). Since then, the objective of micro stability can rely on instruments aiming at assuring a cushion of capital related to the risks taken by each institution. For the first time regulators were in the position of using *specific* instruments of prudential, *ex ante* supervision to control the riskiness of bank portfolios. From this point of view, this achievement marks the end of the Bagehot era.

At the same time (but also as a consequence of the adoption of capital adequacy measures) this change enhanced the role of market forces in achieving bank efficiency. The adoption of capital ratios strengthened for each bank the relationship between profitability, growth and equity. Banks had to follow the same behaviour as other firms and had to compete in the market for products and financial resources. Competition and stability were no longer seen (at least officially) as mutually exclusive (Ciocca, 2000).

An important driver of the financial reform has been European integration, encouraged by the European directives. It is important to remember that the directives find their basis in the Treaty of Rome (arts 85 and 86), although their full application to the banking sector has been questioned, at least until 1981, when a Court of Justice decision explicitly stated that those articles could also be applied to banks (Ghezzi and Magnani, 1998). This means that the idea of the 'uniqueness' of banks was well rooted in the European regulators' minds. Both in the Commission and in most countries this was a major cause of tiresome discussion on whether and how to design and implement banking directives. This is the main reason why it took more than 20 years after the Treaty of Rome to issue the First Banking Directive (1979) and another 12 years to implement it in the country (Italy) which chose the longest possible period of implementation.

The EC legislative framework for financial markets is grounded in a concept known as 'competition among rules', which takes the reality of separate and distinct national legal and regulatory systems as given, but states that member states must recognize the validity of one another's laws, regulations and standards. The mutual recognition was meant to facilitate free trade in goods and services without the need for prior harmonization. The objective of this period was to remove the obstacles to the free circulation of financial services among EU members and, in particular, to lift any barriers to the free provision of services, both with a physical presence or on a cross-border basis.

Directly derived from this principle is the Second Banking Directive (1989) provision for a *single passport*, under which credit institutions incorporated in any member state are permitted to carry out a full range of 'passported services', detailed in the directive's annex, throughout the Community. Similar guidelines are laid down for the provision of investment services in the Investment Services Directive (1993).

Mutual recognition was built, in turn, on two pillars; harmonization of minimum standards of supervision, and home-country control. The former was meant to provide a common denominator for prudential controls; in other words, to restrain the scope for competition among rules above this bottom line. Home-country control seemed from the practical point of view the only criterion compatible with internationalization of financial activity on the one hand and the need for supervision on a consolidated basis on the other.

The European convergence made it easier to remove another important component of structural controls; restraints on classes of assets and liabilities that were a major factor behind segmentation in each market. Albeit slowly, thanks to the Second Banking Directive and the Investment Services Directive, the universal banking model was allowed in each European country. A major obstacle to competition *within* national markets and *among* national markets was therefore removed. Those principles were applied to all financial activities (although insurance companies succeeded in remaining partially unaffected) so the net result was – at least theoretically – a competition *à tout azimut*: among intermediaries, among markets and among financial systems. It is worth remembering that the idea of mutual recognition and the European passport was worked out when monetary union was still a long-term objective for most Europeans (scholars, practitioners and authorities), something that still inhabited the realm of Utopia. In other words, this philosophy was prior to (and independent from) monetary union and the consequences that this can create *per se* on the achievement of a single market.

Therefore, during this second stage of harmonization, every effort of harmonization in the field of financial regulation was confined to the objective of working out the necessary conditions for mutual recognition, that is, the necessary and sufficient conditions of prudential supervision for each country to host safely banks from other EU members, supervised by other authorities.

The third stage begins with the achievement of monetary union. From the point of view of the architecture of financial regulations it meant the transfer of the objective of monetary stability from national central banks to the European System of Central Banks (ESCB), that is, the European Central Bank (ECB) plus 11 (now 12) national central banks. For the first time, the responsibility of price stability was assigned to a 'federal' system made up of a supranational body directed by two boards, one where national central banks are the majority and one, the executive board, comprising members directly appointed by the European Council.

3 AN OVERVIEW OF THE ITALIAN FINANCIAL REFORM

Table 7.2 highlights the main steps in Italian financial reform. As can be seen, the pace of reform has accelerated dramatically in the last 20 years and did not originate only from the European integration. The point worth stressing is that the process started a few years later than in major European countries. Two reasons explain the lag: on the one hand, the difficulty of overcoming the opposing forces to any change is an important component of the economic and political apparatus which had ruled Italy since the end the Second World War; and, on the other hand, even those favouring the change were induced to prudence by the fragility of the Italian economy after the first oil shock. Inflation and the explosion of the public debt (since the return to positive real interest rates in the early 1980s) were the main emergencies to cope with.

It has been shown (Ciocca, 2000) that the longevity of the 1936 Banking Law or, alternatively stated, the reluctance to change, faded away only when it became clear to everyone that the political and economic mechanism based on public ownership (both in banking and industry) and state intervention, which has supported the Italian economic development at least since the end of the Second World War, were no longer compatible with the international competitiveness of the country and, particularly, with financial equilibrium. This explains the acceleration of the reform in the last two decades and the unreserved adhesion of Italy to the principles of international competition and European integration.

A further important characteristic of the Italian reform which is worth stressing is that the process of change was mainly conceived within and backed by the Bank of Italy. Both the mainstream theoretical research in the field of economics and law and (more comprehensibly) the banking profession strengthened the reasons in favour of the status quo: the special legal status of banks, seen as firms that had to pursue a public interest before (instead of?) the maximization of profit and wealth; the dangers to stability coming from excessive competition; and the superior model of banking intermediation for a country which was a latecomer to the industrial and financial revolution.

The impulses towards financial reform were also throttled by the emergency conditions of the 1980s. The structural weaknesses of the Italian economy, the explosion of fiscal deficits and the high inflation were all good

Table 7.2 Main steps in Italian financial reform

Year(s)	Financial reform
1974	Establishment of the securities regulator, Consob, and first reform (albeit minor) of the Company Law
1979–87	Reform of the government securities market, both in the primary segment (competitive issuing techniques; financial innovation and so on) and in the secondary segment (a new screen-based, efficient market: MTS, *Mercato Secondario dei Titoli di Stato*)
1982–87	Gradual phasing out of structural controls and implementation of the free-entry principle (First Banking Directive: CEE 77/780)
1983	Introduction and regulation of mutual funds
1986–96	Deposit insurance schemes are first introduced and then enhanced as a consequence of the European directive
1989–92	Public banks adopt a 'private' company status, through the separation of the public bodies (a foundation) and the bank (joint-stock company). The private legal status is a precondition to the privatization of the industry
1989–92	Implementation of the Second Banking Directive (CEE89/646), based on the principles of mutual recognition, minimum harmonization of prudential regulation and home-country control
1990	Antitrust Law. The Bank of Italy is given the main responsibility in the banking field
1991	First comprehensive Securities Act
1991–92	Implementation of directives in the securities field: public bids; insider trading etc.
1993	Banking Act (*Testo Unico Bancario*)
1993–	Privatization of banks
1996–98	Implementation of the Investment Services Directive and new Company Law
1998	Securities and Investment Act (*Testo Unico della Finanza*)

reasons not only to postpone major changes, but even to further reduce competition within the financial system.

Monetary policy and the whole financial regulatory policy had to cope with emergency conditions that prevented any major reform. As a matter of fact, until the mid-1980s, monetary policy had to be pursued with administrative controls (credit ceilings) that stifled competitive impulses within the banking sector. At the same time, the public ownership of banks (which accounted for some 80 per cent of total deposits) prevented competition in the market for corporate control.

The reform called for radical changes in the very fabric of the Italian financial system: in other words it required a clear-cut separation of the four objectives of regulation, among which competition (*lato sensu*) was up to then almost neglected. The following part of this section reviews the main components of the structural side of the reform.

In Italy, financial reform had at least two prerequisites; the construction of an efficient financial market and a clear-cut identification of the final objectives of financial regulation. From the first point of view, the phasing out of administrative controls as the main tool of monetary policy required the building of a monetary market based on the sensitive issues of treasury bills, new and more competitive techniques for central bank financing, an enhanced payment system and a proper interbank market. This process of change began only in the late 1970s. At the same time, the Treasury and the Bank of Italy switched the financing of the government's borrowing requirement from the banks to the securities market. Securitization and financial innovation became the two keywords for the public debt. Treasury bills and government bonds (most of them indexed to short-term rates) became common components of the Italian financial system. Treasury bonds, not bank deposits, became the main item of Italian households' portfolios.

The primary market underwent a continuous process of innovation aiming at efficiency and competitive conditions. In 1987, a new feature was added with the creation of an efficient secondary market for government bonds (MTS), which is still a leader in the European Union. From this point of view, the explosion of fiscal deficits had a beneficial effect on the financial system, thanks – it is worth repeating – to the decision to use market instruments which must be credited to the Bank of Italy and to the Treasury.

The second prerequisite of financial reform was a clear-cut identification of the final objectives of financial regulation. As has been said, only stability of financial institutions mattered under the 1936 Banking Law. In 1974, the securities regulator (Commissione Nazionale per le Società e la Borsa: Consob) was established together with a first overhaul of the Company Law.

It was not until 1990 that an anti-trust legislation established an *ad hoc* authority (Autorità Garante per la Concorrenza e il Mercato). In the meantime (1979), a new authority for insurance companies (Istituto Vigilanza sulle Assicurazioni: Isvap) had been established. Although the architecture of financial regulation still leaves something to be desired, as there is overlapping among authorities, it can be said that with the establishment of four regulatory authorities the scene was set for an efficient and complete financial regulation.

4 PRICE STABILITY: THE BANK OF ITALY AND THE EUROPEAN SYSTEM OF CENTRAL BANKS

Since the launch of the single monetary policy for the 11 countries of the euro area, the Bank of Italy has been a component of the ESCB.

Most countries participating in the European Monetary Union had to reform their central banks to give them the independence required by the Maastricht Treaty. Italy had to make only minor changes (related to the overdraft credit to the Treasury and the fixing of official discount rates) as the independence of the Bank of Italy has been one of the cornerstones of the Italian economic and political scenario. No 'constitutional' change was needed, as the Bank of Italy has traditionally been totally independent from government. Powers are completely separated: the government is responsible for the appointment of the governor (and members of the *Direttorio*) but the process begins with a designation by a special body of the bank (*Consiglio Superiore*). Moreover, the mandate of the governor has no maturity, the only example in all industrialized countries.

The Bank of Italy has always been well separated from the Treasury and the government. Well before the Maastricht Treaty, at the beginning of the 1980s, the pillars of orthodoxy of central banking were reinforced. First, it is important to remember the firm request from the Bank of Italy for a parliamentary vote to grant a 'special overdraft credit' to the Treasury. It was a signal (in the difficult period we have just recalled) that the bank, although conscious of the emergency conditions, was not prone to obeying any request coming from the government. Second, the 'divorce' freed the central bank from the obligation to absorb any excess of offer in the treasury bill auctions. In other words, while fiscal policy was losing control of public deficits, which skyrocketed under the joint effect of rising real interest rates and growing total expenditure, the Bank of Italy and the Treasury (particularly thanks to the Ministry Beniamino Andreatta) tightened the barriers of monetary orthodoxy. The main channels of monetary financing of the public debt were cut off, making easier the return to normality which began after the lira crisis of September 1992.

5 FINANCIAL STABILITY REGULATION

Financial stability has traditionally been assigned to the Bank of Italy. From this point of view it is important to stress that Italy has never felt the need to separate the conduct of monetary policy from the prudential supervision of banks. This choice differs from the majority of other European countries, not only as regards regulatory powers (most European central banks are in charge of prudential controls, see BCE, 2000) but also as regards independence.

It has been said that, initially, the separation approach was dictated by the desire to avoid excessive concentration of powers (Wymeersch, 1998). It was also dictated by the propensity of some European governments to have a foothold in supervisory bodies (witness the case of France and Germany). As a matter of fact, after the Maastricht Treaty, while the institutional safeguards of central bank independence were reinforced, there was mounting pressure to widen the distance between monetary policy and bank supervision. This point is particularly important as the Italian reform did not sever the link between monetary policy and supervisory functions, which is the essence of central banking.

This solution makes it easier, in a monetary union based on a federated model of central banking, to keep the supervisory function at the local level while at the same time keeping the necessary link with the lending of last resort. As has been said (Fazio, 2001)

> [F]und-raising and lending are still centred on national markets, even in the case of larger intermediaries. Risks of instability transmitted from international markets must be countered and circumscribed through adequate supervision. Effective supervisory action and the prevention of instability require the direct and timely supply of detailed information, closeness to the institutions supervised and knowledge of the environment in which they operate. Supervision is necessarily rooted in national legal systems owing to the close relationships between its tasks and public and private normative institutions, the system of deposit insurance and the possible repercussions of insolvencies on the public finances. It is linked with other institutional bodies and participates in more and more advanced forms of worldwide cooperation.

In sum, the Italian architecture, as amended by the reform of the 1990s, could be an example for all European countries.

In Italy, the reform had to be directed not at the responsibility of the central bank, but at the kind and extent of instruments provided to achieve bank stability. Structural controls were the main (one can say, the only) weapon given to the Bank of Italy for achieving financial stability. But it was given in heavy doses coupled with maximum discretion. Authorizations were necessary for establishing a bank, for opening new branches (and were granted following an 'economic need' criterion), for acquiring participations and new buildings, and for granting loans exceeding a given percentage of the bank's capital.

When in the mid-1970s the oil crisis and the following inflation hit the industrialized countries, the government (one should say: the many governments of that political era) and the regulator judged that the structural financial fragility of the Italian economy prevented any major deregulatory process, and made it expedient to use the banking sector as the instrument for special administrative controls which were meant to achieve the fundamental economic objectives.

Given the poor performance of the economy as a whole in terms of inflation (and exchange rates) and public debt, the best we can say about that period is that given the political and social constraints that determined the real level of wages and public expenditure, monetary policy had to minimize the damage for the economy at large.

The intermediate objectives of monetary policy were defined in terms of aggregate quantities (*credito totale interno*), and the instruments were credit ceilings that each bank could not exceed without incurring heavy penalties.

The net result was that the market shares in the loan and deposit markets were frozen, competition minimized and reforms regarded as a threat to the fragile financial scaffolding erected around the fragile building of the Italian economy. Just to recall one example, the first European Directive (1979), which established the principle of free entry, was implemented in Italy only in the early 1990s.

As we have seen in Section 3, the objective of financial stability was clearly divided from disclosure, first by the 1991 Act and then by the 1998 Securities Act.

The principle has, however, major exceptions. The most important (also common to most European countries) is the responsibility of Isvap for insurance companies as regards both stability and disclosure. It is a clear remnant of a regulation 'by subject' which reflects a segmentation of the markets which does not exist any more. By the same token, the newborn Italian regulator on pension funds (Covip), responsible for pension funds, overlaps with the Bank of Italy and Consob.

The main results of the reform related to financial stability regulation can thus be summarized:

1. The 1993 Act identifies the ultimate goal of banking in the '*sana e prudente gestione*' (sound and prudent management) which means that stability rests first on the shoulders of each bank. This calls for a clear identification of the top management responsibilities and an efficient mechanism of corporate governance, including internal controls. In particular, Article 14 of the Banking Act (*Testo Unico Bancario*) states that the authorization by the Bank of Italy is subject to the following conditions:

a. the legal form can be only that of a joint-stock company or cooperative bank (with limited liability). Only three legal categories are therefore left: banks; *banche popolari*; and *casse di credito cooperativo* for the smallest segment of the market (credit unions);
b. the legal capital cannot be lower than the limit fixed by the Bank of Italy (in accordance with EU directives);
c. the managers must present a strategic programme of activity; and
d. directors, internal auditors and managers have to meet the professional and eligibility standards determined by the Bank of Italy (always in accordance with EU directives).

The law explicitly states that the Bank of Italy refuses authorization if, from the analysis of the above points, it judges that sound and prudent management is not guaranteed.

2. The instruments to achieve financial stability are now basically capital requirements, on both an individual and a consolidated basis, according to the reform prompted by the Basle Agreement and European Union directives. All major structural controls which were responsible for the high degree of geographical and operational segmentation have been removed.
3. The reform has finally adopted the 'universal banking' model allowed by the Second European Directive and the Investment Services Directive. Stability is no longer sought through specialization rules that were the (weak) theoretical argument underpinning the 1936 Banking Act.
4. 'Separateness', that is, the separation between banks and industry, is still judged to be an important topic in the Italian legislation. Rules are stricter than in other countries. In particular:

4(i). Participation in banks. The Banking Act (art. 35) states that:
   a. a participation in a bank, greater than 5 per cent of capital, must be authorized by the Bank of Italy;
   b. authorizations are required when thresholds of 10, 15, 20, 33 and 50 per cent are breached;
   c. authorization is required for acquiring control, whatever the percentage;
   d. non-financial companies cannot hold a participation in a bank greater than 15 per cent.

4(ii). Participation of banks is always subject to specific authorization, according to the following criteria:
   a. Participation in other banks. Authorizations are required for stakes greater than: 5 or 10 per cent of the acquiring bank; 10 per cent (of the regulatory capital) of the controlled bank.

b. Participation in insurance companies. As above, but the participation cannot exceed 40 per cent of the regulatory capital of the insurance company.
c. Participation in operating companies functional to the banking activity. Authorizations are needed only in the case of control.
d. Participation in non-financial companies. The stake cannot, in any case, exceed 15 per cent. Each participation cannot exceed 3 per cent of the regulatory capital of the bank, and overall they cannot exceed 15 per cent.

As can be seen, the grid of authorization is very narrow and gives the Bank of Italy a firm control at the very heart of banks' strategic decisions. It is important to remember that these powers have been used in at least two cases to block (in 1999) hostile bids on Italian banks: on Banca di Roma (by San Paolo-Imi) and on Banca Commerciale Italiana (by Unicredito Italiano).

5. Another important aspect which bears on stability is bank ownership. Until the late 1980s, some 80 per cent of the Italian banking system was public, either directly owned by the Treasury (BNL, IMI and the banks owned by IRI, such as Banca Commerciale Italiana, Credito Italiano, Banca di Roma) or public institutions with no owner at all (Banca di Napoli, Banca di Sicilia, Banco di Sardegna, all savings banks).

The 1990 reform (Amato-Carli Act) identified the conditions for a radical change separating the bank, which was given a joint-stock structure, from the foundation which initially owned 100 per cent of the banks' shares. The foundation has to pursue general interests, particularly linked to the local community: culture, research, health and so on. To this end it had an incentive to sell bank shares in order to diversify its portfolio. The incentive became an obligation in 2000.

This reform has radically changed the Italian banking system and has favoured a steady process of concentration. The market share of banks controlled by either the Treasury or foundations fell dramatically from 68 per cent in 1992 to 17 per cent in 1999 (Fazio, 2000). A side-effect has been the increase in the number of banks listed on the stock market. The total assets of the banking groups listed on the stock exchange rose from 30 to more than 70 per cent (ibid.).

6. As already mentioned, the reform has favoured mergers and acquisitions within the banking sector and led to a significant increase in foreign banks investment in Italian banks' capital.

From the first point of view, between 1990 and October 2000 there were 508 concentrations and the number of banks fell from 1,167 to

862. The concentration ratio, as measured by the market shares of the five largest groups, rose to 51 per cent, in line with France and higher than Germany, but lower than the UK and Spain.

From the second point of view, foreign intermediaries are now 'substantial shareholders in Italy's leading banks and hold sizeable interests in the five largest banking groups' (Fazio, 2000, p. 21).

7. Such a radical change in all components of the financial stability regulation was, not surprisingly, accompanied by a period of recurrent bank crises, as in many other European countries. In the last decade Italy, like many other developed countries, has met with a major financial crisis. For many years, Italian banks have been sheltered from instability by three factors: regulation; public ownership; and the huge public deficit. Structural controls have kept competition at low levels, at least until the mid-1980s, while a restrictive monetary policy based on credit ceilings lowered the level of competition in the loan market. At the same time, the public ownership of most banks stifled the contestability of the market for corporate control, at least until the beginning of the 1990s. In a few years, the new Banking Act and the Amato-Carli Act and finally straightforward privatizations, changed the Italian financial landscape.

Unlike other European countries, the episodes of crisis have been concentrated in a specific region: the Mezzogiorno. At the end of the 1980s, research from the Bank of Italy (Banca d'Italia, 1990) had demonstrated that southern banks were less capitalized, less efficient, and had more bad loans than their northern competitors. The spark to this explosive combination was given by the economic slowdown of the early 1990s.

Not surprisingly, the disappearance of so much protection had made the points of inefficiency no longer sustainable. Given the structural weaknesses of the Italian economy, the crisis immediately hit the southern banks. In a few years, practically all of them experienced a dramatic increase of bad loans which wiped out their already thin capital bases. In all cases, other banks from northern regions stepped in – under the auspices of the Bank of Italy – and acquired the majority or even the whole control of the ailing bank. Only in one case (Banco di Napoli) did the bailing out involve a cost to the taxpayer. The intervention of the deposit insurance scheme was limited to a few marginal cases. The net result has been a major change in the ownership of the Italian banking system and in its concentration ratio.

So Italy, like any other European country, has paid its toll to the 'tough' period of the early 1990s which ended with the devaluation of the lira and the suspension from the exchange rate agreements. Unlike other European countries, the burden to the taxpayer has been quite small (particularly if one spreads the cost over the entire credit cycle) because failing banks were bailed out by other banks which were better capitalized and more efficient. In other words, higher bank profits (the endowment of the period when competition took a back seat as a regulatory objective) have been the internal shock absorber of the wave of instability of the 1990s.

It must, however, be stressed that the system has proved to be very resilient; such a serious crisis has been met internally, that is using resources coming from within the banking system, while all indicators of profitability and capitalization continue to rank fairly high in the international comparison (Landi et al., 2000).

6 DISCLOSURE REGULATION

The most important piece of reform in this field has been the 1998 Securities Act, which:

1. confirmed the division of responsibilities between the Bank of Italy and Consob;
2. completed the privatization of the exchanges which had begun in 1996;
3. gave an impulse to the asset management industry allowing the unification of collective and individual management in the hands of the same intermediary (*società di gestione del risparmio*);
4. modified the law on public bids, so as to increase the contestability of listed companies. As a result, a group of private entrepreneurs led by Colaninno could take over a newly privatized company, Telecom Italia; and
5. significantly increased the level of protection of minority shareholders. In particular (Bianchi and Enriques, 2001), the quorums for legal actions were lowered; the powers and responsibilities of internal auditors (*collegio sindacale*) were enhanced; and proxy fights, which were previously banned, were allowed.

An important exception to the general principle set by the 1998 Securities Act has been the partial exemption of bank bonds from disclosure requirements. The underlying hypothesis is that banks, being subject to prudential supervision, are less risky than any other issuer. Needless to say, this hypothesis is not consistent with financial theory and the prevailing attitude of regulators which ask for more 'market discipline', which should apply to all uninsured bank liabilities.

The securities regulator, Consob, has been particularly vocal in criticizing this choice and in stressing the damage to the final investor. As has been said, the new Italian legislation is clearly based on the idea that disclosure of bank conditions does not endanger their stability. In a world where most financial intermediaries are listed, market discipline can be pursued only through complete disclosure, which means reducing the area of privileged information that supervisors traditionally have.

Another weak point of the 1998 reform concerns the regulation of insider trading. On this point, the assessment of Consob (1998, pp. 8–10) was unequivocal and is worth citing in full:

> Here, unfortunately, the *Testo Unico* has missed an opportunity. It does not strengthen the existing system, and may even weaken it . . . The effectiveness of the fight against insider trading is based on the deterrent effect of the regulations, and hence on the speed and impact of their enforcement. The principle is also affirmed in the Community directive, which requires member states to impose sufficiently dissuasive penalties, leaving countries free to impose more severe or additional sanctions, provided they are general in scope. Consob had hoped for the institution of a system of fines that were both rapidly applicable and sufficiently heavy to serve as a deterrent for those who exploit privileged information in their dealings. In order to avoid any overlapping of spheres, the criminal nature of an action could have been linked to the existence of a financial gain for the insider. The *Testo Unico* did not create an effective system of enforcement. The investigative powers assigned to Consob have been extended, but without any coercive powers, so their effectiveness depends on the goodwill of those being investigated. The weapons for the fight against insider trading thus remain less efficient than those available to authorities in other countries.

7 COMPETITION REGULATION

It has already been mentioned that the peculiar characteristics of the Italian framework give the Bank of Italy the responsibility for both stability and competition in the banking field. This is an exception to the rule adopted in other countries (in the United States, where the Fed has the first decision, appeals go to the 'natural' jurisdiction). This solution has been justified on the grounds of the complementary relationship between concentration and competition (Ciocca, 2000) and the superior information that supervisors have (Fazio, 2000).

It must, however, be pointed out that the authority in charge of competition has no *ex post* powers, as it intervenes only when there is a threat to competition coming from specific facts (an agreement among producers; any other practice against other producers) or from a planned merger. There is also an *ex ante* component of competitive forces which is always under the control of the bank supervisors, for example, structural controls, controls on entry, authorizations to acquire significant or control stakes in other firms (financial or not) and authorizations to acquire an (even minority) participation in a bank.

As a matter of fact the reason why in 1990 this responsibility was given to the Bank of Italy lies in the fact that in these very years the bank was beginning to lift its structural controls and to unleash new competitive impulses. The underlying idea was that the competitive action of the prudential regulator was so important and even politically fragile that it had to avoid any possible overlapping or even conflict with a newborn authority.

As a consequence, the choice was made to give the regulator on bank stability the *ex post* powers on competition (that is, interventions in the case of mergers or allegedly collusive behaviour). On the other hand, the Bank of Italy keeps, like any other bank regulator, strong *ex ante* powers in terms of authorizations to important banks' strategic decisions that eventually impact on competitive conditions, perhaps even stronger than in other countries.

Given the strong powers of the Bank of Italy, one can wonder whether in this field lies the real Italian exception (see, for example, the narrow grid of authorization required for acquiring participations, both by banks and in banks). It is important to remember that the decision to block the two hostile bids already mentioned, was formally based on this kind of power.

8 CONCLUSIONS

The Italian market came of age in the 1990s and now compares quite satisfactorily with other European countries in terms of size, liquidity and efficiency. This has been a real breakthrough in the race to efficiency and competition, not only because it has opened up new alternatives for external financing, but also because it has prompted important changes in the general regulatory environment. In particular, it has increased – at least in principle – the importance of the objectives of disclosure and competition.

One point that strikes non-Italian observers is the huge gap between the intensity of regulatory changes, at least in the last 20 years, and the dismal results in terms of maximizing growth and minimizing internal duality conditions. On the one hand, the Italian growth rate is systematically lower than the European average and on the other hand, the gap between the North and South is the widest among European countries and is still widening.

Does that mean that the Italian financial system is less efficient than others? A recent interpretation (Ciocca, 2000) reverses the argument; the new financial framework is in fact the only success in a landscape of unsatisfactory or aborted reforms of economic institutions and legal frameworks. Italy has simply failed to adapt its institutions to the economic needs of the last decades of the twentieth century. As a consequence, she has seen her competitiveness fade away and her rate of growth slow down. There is therefore no direct link (or a very tenuous link) between the performance of the Italian economy and the efficiency of the Italian financial system. Alternatively stated, a hostile environment (the rigidity of the labour markets, the inefficiency of the general legal system and the diffusion of the 'black economy') had a negative effect on economic performance which more than offset the positive impulses coming from financial reform.

REFERENCES

Bagehot, W. (1873), *Lombard Street. A Description of the Money Market*, London: H.S. King

Banca Centrale Europea (BCE) (2000), 'L'UEM e la vigilanza bancaria' in *Bollettino mensile della BCE*, Frankfurt: BCE, April, p. 21.

Banca d'Italia (1990), *Il sistema finanziario del Mezzogiorno* (edited by G.P. Galli and M. Onado), Rome: Banca d'Italia.

Bianchi, Marcello and Enriques, Luca (2001), 'Corporate governance in Italy after the 1998 reform: what role for institutional investors?' in *Consob Quaderni di Finanza*, no. 43, January, p. 31.

Ciocca, Pierluigi (2000), *La nuova finanza in Italia. Una difficile metamorfosi (1980–2000)*, Turin: Bollati Boringhieri.

Commissione Nazionale per le Società e la Borsa (Consob) (1998), *Relazione Annuale per l'anno 1997*, Rome: Consob.

Fazio, Antonio (2000), 'Competition, growth and the banking system', Address at the Conference, 'Competition and the Antitrust Authority. A review of the first ten years of the law', Rome, October, mimeo.

Fazio, Antonio (2001), 'Finance, stability and growth', Address at the Conference, 'International Banking and Financial Systems: evolution and stability', Rome, 9 March.

Ghezzi, Federico and Magnani, Paola (1998), 'L'applicazione della disciplina antitrust comunitaria al settore bancario', Rome, Ente Einaudi, mimeo.

Goodhart, Charles (1985), The Evolution of Central Banks, London: London School of Economics and Political Science.

Landi, A., Lusignani, G. and Onado, M. (2000), 'Redditività e ristrutturazione nei sistemi bancari europei. Un'analisi di lungo periodo', *L'Industria*, December, pp. 239–40.

Llewellyn, David (1999), The economic rationale for financial regulation', Financial Services Association Occasional Paper, London, April.

Onado, Marco (2000), *Mercati e Intermediari finanziari. Economia e regolamentazione*, Bologna: Il Mulino.

Organization for Economic Cooperation and Development (OECD) (1998), *Enhancing the Role of Competition in the Regulation of Banks*, Paris: OECD.

Thornton, H. (1802), *An Enquiry into the Nature and Effects of the Paper Credit of Great Britain*, London: Hatchard.

Wymeersch, E. (1998), 'The implementation of the ISD and CAD in national legal systems', in Ferrarini, G. (ed.), *European Securities Markets. The Investment Services Directive and Beyond*, London: Kluwer Law International, p. 30.

8. Financial reform in Japan

Akio Kuroda

1 INTRODUCTION

The purpose of this chapter is to briefly review recent financial reform in Japan. The problems that the Japanese financial system has been facing are twofold. First, Japan has to solve the problem of huge bad loans that major financial institutions have been experiencing as a result of the bursting of the so-called 'Bubble Economy'. Second, Japan has to drastically reform the Japanese financial system through the so-called 'Japanese Big Bang' so that it can recover competitive strength in the globalized financial markets. It is certainly not an easy task to solve these two problems simultaneously. Nevertheless, wide-ranging financial reform in Japan has been going on now for some time and we should pay close attention to its outcome.

Section 2 will discuss central bank reform with particular attention being paid to the revision of the Bank of Japan Law of June 1997. I show how the Bank of Japan has acquired its independence from the government and how its conduct of monetary policy has been changed. Section 3 will present a brief review of the process of financial deregulation in Japan since the late 1970s, focusing on such once-regulated areas as the separation of financial institutions, interest rate ceilings, and capital movements to and from overseas. It will also analyse the causes and consequences of the 'Bubble Economy' and its eventual bursting. Section 4 will discuss the implications of the 'Japanese Big Bang' for the Japanese financial system. I show how the regulatory and supervisory agencies have been changed in Japan, reviewing the shift of power from the Ministry of Finance to the newly established Financial Supervisory Agency (the present Financial Services Agency), and how prudential policy in Japan should be changed.

2 CENTRAL BANK REFORM IN JAPAN

The Revision of the Bank of Japan Law

The new Bank of Japan Law was promulgated in June 1997 and came into force in April 1998. The old Bank of Japan Law, which was enacted in

February 1947, was revised after the Ministry of Finance (MOF) was criticized for the self-righteous way it administered the financial system, it itself being reorganized in June 1998. Rather ironically, it was not really the efforts of the Bank of Japan (BOJ), but the struggles between the MOF and political parties (particularly, the Liberal Democratic Party) that actually gave birth to the new Bank of Japan Law. Nevertheless, the BOJ now enjoys a more independent legal status under the new law than under the old one.

Because the old law was enacted during the Second World War, the government characterized it with a strong regulatory tone. Article 1 of the old law determined the purposes of the BOJ as follows:

> The Bank of Japan has as its objective the regulation of the currency, the control and facilitation of credit and finance, and the maintenance and fostering of the credit system, pursuant to the national policy, in order that the general economic activities of the nation might be enhanced adequately.

Under the old Law, the BOJ was put under the strict control of the MOF and was not allowed to be independent from the government at all. For example, the prime minister could dismiss the governor and the deputy governor of the BOJ when deemed necessary. The minister of finance could dismiss the executive directors of the BOJ in the same manner. Furthermore, the MOF could issue directives to the BOJ concerning its overall functions, thereby controlling monetary policy as well as prudential policy of the BOJ.

The new law clearly states that 'the BOJ's independence regarding currency and monetary control shall be respected' (Article 3). In accordance with that philosophy, the new law guarantees the status to the governor, the deputy governor, and the other members of the Policy Board of the BOJ in the sense that they shall not be dismissed against their will during their five-year terms (Article 25). Moreover, the MOF cannot issue any directives concerning the business operations of the BOJ, although it may request a report or relevant documents from the BOJ when deemed necessary (Article 58). It should be noted, however, that the BOJ is urged to maintain close contact with the government and to exchange views sufficiently so that its monetary policy and the government's economic policy should be mutually harmonious (Article 4).

The new law determines that 'the objectives of the BOJ are to issue banknotes, to carry out currency and monetary control, and to ensure smooth settlement of funds among banks and other financial institutions, thereby contributing to the maintenance of an orderly financial system' (Article 1). In addition to those objectives, the new law states that 'the principle of currency and monetary control of the BOJ shall be aimed at, through the pursuit of price stability, contributing to the sound development of the national economy' (Article 2). Those statements concerning the objectives of the BOJ are not at all clear since they include not only the objectives, but also the functions of the BOJ such as banknote issue and funds settlement. Besides, it is hard to distinguish the 'objectives' stated in Article 1 from the 'principle' stated in Article 2. The question arises whether or not the pursuit of price stability is more important for the BOJ than the maintenance of an orderly financial system.

The official view of the BOJ, after the promulgation of the new law, is that the missions of the bank are to maintain price stability and the stability of the financial system, thereby laying the foundations for sound economic conditions. The BOJ claims that those two objectives are like 'both wheels of a rickshaw' and should be pursued simultaneously. However, we should have in mind that conflicts between those two objectives could sometimes occur and the BOJ might have to make a tough choice between them. Besides, since the MOF and the Financial Supervisory Agency (FSA) (the present Financial Services Agency), which was newly established in 2000, are primarily responsible for maintaining the stability of the financial system, they might urge the BOJ to treat the stability of the financial system as a top priority. We should reiterate that, as the nation's central bank, the BOJ should stick to the maintenance of price stability and, accordingly, the final objective of the BOJ should be focused on it more than the new law has stated.

Organizational Change at the BOJ

The organizational structure of the BOJ was changed several times, even under the old BOJ Law. In particular, the Policy Board was established in 1949 as the supreme decision-making body of the BOJ under the direction of the General Headquarters (GHQ) of the allied forces. Then, the Policy Board consisted of seven members: the governor of the BOJ, two representatives of the government and four members appointed by the cabinet. The purpose of establishing the Policy Board was to democratize the decision-making process of the BOJ, but, in fact, it became dormant under bureaucratic manoeuvring by BOJ staff and soon it was metaphorically called 'the Sleeping Board'. Instead, the Executive Board, which consisted of the governor, the deputy governor and the executive directors, acted as the de facto decision-making body of the BOJ.

In May 1990, drastic organizational restructuring of the BOJ, involving all its departments, was implemented so that the BOJ would be able to cope with a rapidly changing financial environment; namely, financial deregulation and the globalization of financial markets. For example, the Credit and

Market Management Department was reorganized so as to integrate the monitoring functions *vis-à-vis* financial institutions with respect to international finance as well as domestic finance. Meanwhile, a new Financial and Payment System Department was set up in order to assume major responsibility for the prudential supervision of financial institutions as well as the maintenance of an efficient and stable payment system. Furthermore, consolidating all operations-related departments, a new Operations Department was set up so that the BOJ could deal more efficiently with various aspects of funds and securities settlement.

After the passage of the new BOJ Law through the Diet in 1997, the BOJ studied how its organization should be changed in accordance with its philosophy of independence from the government and accountability towards the Diet and the general public. In April 1998, the new Policy Board, which comprised the governor, two deputy governors and six deliberative members, was established as the sole decision-making body of the BOJ. (Accordingly, the Executive Board was abolished.) At the same time, further organizational reform took effect, as shown in Figure 8.1. The 13 departments, two offices (Secretariat of the Policy Board and the Governor's Office), and one institute (Institute for Monetary and Economic Studies) were reorganized into ten departments, five offices and one institute. First, the Secretariat of the Policy Board was strengthened by incorporating the Governor's Office and by absorbing the functions of the media relations section, which had been part of the Policy Planning Department until then. Second, in order to streamline the decision-making process, the Policy Planning Department, the Financial and Payment System Department and the Budget and Management Department were changed to become 'offices' and their staff were placed under the direct orders of the respective executive director in charge. Third, functions performed by the Credit and Market Management Department were transferred to the newly created Financial Markets Department, which was put in charge of monetary control, and to the Bank Supervision Department, which was put in charge of the surveillance of financial institutions. (Accordingly, the Credit and Market Management Department, which had been the most powerful department in the BOJ for a long time, was abolished.)

Furthermore, in May 2000, operations related to foreign exchange were transferred from the International Department to the Financial Markets Department so as to strengthen monetary control of the BOJ.

Changes of Functions Performed by the BOJ

The functions of the BOJ do not differ much from those performed by other central banks. Namely, the BOJ performs three major functions: (a)

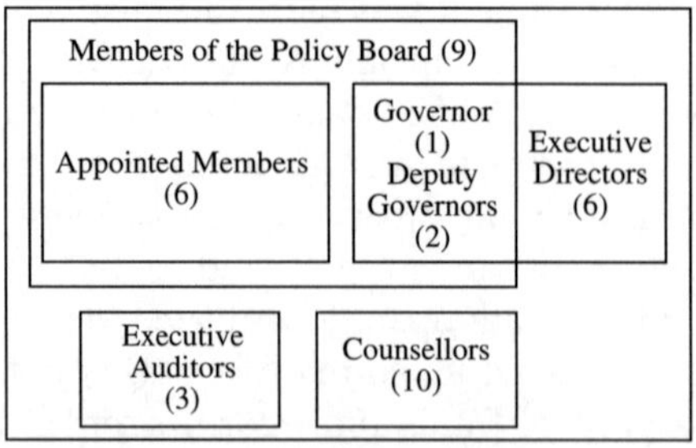

Department/office	Functions
Secretariat of the Policy Board • Coordination Division • Secretaries' Division • Diet Liaison Division • Press Division	Arranges proceedings for Policy Board meetings; with the Diet, the media and industry associations; reviews the content and wording of draft proposals for decision at Policy Board meetings and of other important documents from the legal perspective: handles legal matters regarding the Bank of Japan Law and other laws and ordinances; handles particular matters as directed by executives: supports the executive auditors in auditing; provides administrative services for executives; is responsible for the safekeeping of official stamps of the bank and executives
Internal Auditors' Office	Audits the bank's operations
Policy Planning Office • Planning Division I • Planning Division II • Policy Research Division	Plans and formulates monetary policy measures and handles related matters
Financial,Markets Department • Money and Capital Markets Division • Open Market Operations Division • Foreign Exchange Division	Determines the specifics of daily market operations; monitors and analyses developments in financial markets in Japan as well as overseas, including foreign exchange markets, and activities of financial institutions in these markets; deals with issues relating to improvement of the functioning of the Japanese financial markets including the foreign exchange market; intervenes in the foreign exchange markets for the purpose of stabilizing the' exchange rates as the agent of the minister of finance and/or on behalf of other countries' monetary authorities; conducts purchases/sales of foreign currencies on behalf of overseas central banks and international organizations for the purpose of, assisting investment of their assets
Research and Statistics Department • Economic Research Division • Economic Statistics Division • Price Statistics Division	Conducts research on the domestic economic and fiscal situation; compiles statistics
Financial and Payment System Office • Financial. System Division • Payment System Division	Plans and formulates measures that contribute to the maintenance of an orderly financial and payment system
Bank Examination, and Surveillance Department • Planning Division • Examination Division • Surveillance and Monitoring Division	Conducts on-site examinations and off-site monitoring of client financial institutions that have current accounts with the bank; judges financial institutions' eligibility to hold current accounts with the bank and to have access to its lending facilities; determines the specifics of credit extension by the bank to maintain an orderly financial system; liaises with financial industry associations
International Department • Planning and Coordination Division • Global Economic Research Division • Balance of Payments Division	Manages external assets held by the bank; makes arrangements for investment in yen assets by overseas central banks and international organizations; conducts operations for international financial support; liaises with overseas central banks and international organizations; conducts research on global economic and financial conditions; conducts business entrusted to it by the Ministry of Finance related to the Foreign Exchange and Foreign Trade Law and Foreign Exchange Fund Special Account Law

Currency Issue Department • Planning and Management Division • Cash and Custody Division • Currency Verification Division	Conducts planning and operations relating to banknotes; conducts payment/receipt of coins, and examines and takes custody of them; exchanges banknotes and coins unfit for further circulation; conducts business related to clearing of bills and cheques; manages securities and other items entrusted to the bank for safekeeping
Operations Department • Planning and Coordination Division • Operations Control Division • Agency Supervision Division • Money Markets Division • Settlement Service Division • Treasury Fund Business Division • Treasury Accounting Division • Government Bond Certificate Division	Conducts banking operations including the following: (1) discounting of bills; (2) loan extension; (3) purchasing/selling of bills (including those drawn by the bank) and securities; (4), borrowing/lending of securities with cash collateral; (5) accepting deposits; (6) domestic funds transfer; (7) taking custody of bills and securities as collateral; (8) purchasing/selling of gold and silver bullion; (9) bidding and underwriting Japanese government securities; (10) operations relating to treasury funds; (11) handling of government affairs related to currency and finance; (12) business operations of policy measures to maintain an orderly financial system; and (13) conducting other banking business of the bank not listed above and operations relating to the bank's agents
Information System Services Department • Systems Planning Division • Systems Development Division • Systems Operation Division	Manages the design and development of the bank's computer systems as required in order to automate the bank's business procedures; operates the bank's computer systems
Public Relations Department • Public Information Division • Documents and Library Division • Savings Information Division	Is responsible for public relations; disseminates information on financial services; administers the bank's library
Budget and Management Office • Planning and Coordination Division • Budget Division	Plans and formulates measures relating to the organization and resources of the bank; is responsible for the bank's budgeting
Human Resources Management Department • Planning and Administration Division • Personnel Division • Human Resources Development Division	Handles personnel policy issues relating to recruitment, assessment of job performance, career planning and training, wages and salaries, the bank's ethical discipline code, and other aspects of personnel administration
Administration Department • Planning and Coordination Division • Premises Management Division • General Supplies Division • Welfare Division • Security and General Services Division	Conducts administrative operations relating to the following: real estate holdings, supplies, staff welfare, security, transportation, payment of expenses, subscription certificates of the bank's capital, mailing and safekeeping of slips
Institute for Monetary and Economic Studies • Research Division I • Research Division II • Research Division III	Studies theoretical, institutional, technological and historical aspects of monetary and economic issues; collects, preserves and exhibits historical materials and documents related to monetary and economic issues; exchanges views on monetary and economic issues with academics
Branches	The 33 branches mainly conduct operations relating to currency issue and banking operations, and research on the economic and financial situation in each area
Local offices in Japan	The Fuchu computer centre operates the bank's systems. The other 12 local offices handle some of the operations of the head office or branches
Overseas Representative Offices	The 6 overseas representative offices perform a liaison function, gather information, and conduct research

Source: Bank of Japan Homepage (http://www.boj.or.jp).

Figure 8.1 Organization of the Bank of Japan

issue for the currency, (b) banker to banks (more precisely, banker to financial institutions) and (c) banker to government. We should, however, point out some changes in those functions in relation to the implementation of the new BOJ Law.

First, the BOJ is the sole note issuer in Japan. The banknotes issued by the BOJ are legal tender and have an unlimited circulation for all transactions, both public and private. The Issue Department of the BOJ, as well as its 32 branches all over the country, takes care of the banknotes so that they can be put back into circulation in good condition. Also, it employs a wide range of measures such as watermarks and micro-lettering in order to prevent counterfeiting.

As for the amount of issue of BOJ notes, the old BOJ Law stated that the minister of finance should determine its maximum. It also stated that BOJ notes must be fully backed up by eligible assets, such as commercial bills, loans, government bonds, foreign exchange and gold and silver bullion. The new BOJ Law, however, has neither the provision concerning the maximum amount of issue of BOJ notes nor the provision concerning back-up assets. This is a reflection of the fact that the maximum amount of issue has been repeatedly changed in parallel with the increasing demand for BOJ notes. It is also a reflection of the widely supported recognition that the value of BOJ notes is not necessarily related to what the BOJ has as its assets. Consequently, under the new law, the BOJ has been given the discretionary power of controlling the issue of BOJ notes. This means, in turn, that it is the responsibility of the BOJ's monetary policy to adequately control the amount of BOJ notes, thereby maintaining the value of the currency (that is, price stability).

Second, as banker to financial institutions, the BOJ accepts current deposits from financial institutions and extends credit to them. The scope of financial institutions that it extends credit to is somewhat narrower than the one that it accepts current deposits from. BOJ deposits are used as the means of settlement for various transactions among financial transactions, for example, call and bills transactions. They are also used for the final net settlement of obligations among financial institutions under the Bill and Clearing System, the Domestic Fund Transfer System (the *Zengin* System), and the Foreign Exchange Yen Settlement System. Since October 1988, the BOJ has operated an electronic funds transfer system, the Bank of Japan Financial Network System (BOJ-NET), in order to facilitate fund transfers among financial institutions, thereby maintaining an efficient settlements system. Under the new law, the BOJ is expected to make contributions to the smooth functioning of the settlement system among financial institutions (Article 39). For example, the BOJ has recently restructured the BOJ-NET so as to introduce real time gross settlement (RTGS) for fund transfers as well as settlement for government bonds, thereby reducing settlement risk.

BOJ lending has been a traditional means of providing credit to financial institutions. The former Credit and Market Management Department frequently utilized loans against collateral (in the form of bills or government bonds) as a means of daily reserve adjustments in the money markets. Meanwhile, it was advantageous for financial institutions to receive the BOJ loans because the official lending rate was usually maintained below money market rates. Since July 1995, however, the relationship between the official lending rate and money market rates was reversed and the BOJ (the present Financial Markets Department) nearly stopped using its loans as a means of daily reserve adjustment. However, BOJ lending to troubled financial institutions increased significantly in the late 1990s.

As for the 'lender of last resort' function performed by the BOJ, the new BOJ Law states that the BOJ may provide uncollateralized loans to financial institutions when they unexpectedly experience a temporary shortage of funds due to accidental causes, including computer system troubles (Article 37). Accordingly, the BOJ can independently cope with cases of liquidity shortage at its own judgement. The new law also states that the minister of finance may request the BOJ to provide loans to troubled financial institutions 'when deemed necessary for the maintenance of an orderly financial system' (Article 38). In fact, the MOF (and the FSA) frequently requested the BOJ to provide emergency loans to financial institutions which fell into distress in the late 1990s. And most of the BOJ loans outstanding at end-year 1997 (4.9 trillion yen) were provided in accordance with Article 38 of the new BOJ Law. Such a situation is certainly rather problematic in the sense that easy access to the BOJ loans might have caused 'moral-hazard' problems for troubled financial institutions, and that concern for maintaining an orderly financial system might have weakened the independence of the BOJ.[1]

It should be noted that, starting from March 2001, the BOJ introduced a 'Lombard-type lending facility', through which the BOJ extends loans at the request of financial institutions at the official discounts rate. Thanks to this facility, financial institutions can now flexibly borrow funds from the BOJ as long as they have eligible collateral, even when there is turmoil in the market.

Third, the BOJ plays a role as the bank of the government in the fields of treasury funds and government securities. Namely, it handles receipts and disbursements of treasury funds (for example, tax collection and payment of public works, social welfare and so on) and conducts accounting and bookkeeping for the government. It also deals with the whole business related to government securities (mostly, government bonds), that is, issuance, registration, coupon payments and redemption. The Operations Department of the BOJ is responsible for those businesses related to the government. Meanwhile, the Financial Markets Department of the BOJ closely monitors developments in the foreign exchange markets and sometimes makes intervention in the markets as an agent of the minister of finance when deemed necessary. The MOF, however, continues to keep the power of intervention in the foreign exchange markets and even under the new BOJ Law the BOJ needs the authorization from the minister of finance in order to intervene in the markets (Article 39).

As for BOJ credit to the government, the new BOJ Law states that the BOJ may make loans, without collateral, to the government, and subscribe or underwrite government bonds as prescribed in the exceptional clause of Article 5 of the Fiscal Law (Article 34). It also states that the BOJ may subscribe or underwrite financial bills or other bills issued by the government for temporary borrowing. This is certainly an undesirable amendment to the BOJ law because the financing of public deficits by central bank credit will loosen fiscal discipline, thereby bringing about the problem of inflation afterwards. It should be noted, however, that the MOF started issuing financing bills (FBs) through public competitive-price auctions in April 1999, switching from the traditional way of issuing them through underwriting by the BOJ.

Policy Reform of the BOJ

The BOJ's top priority in implementing monetary policy is to ensure price stability, although it is also concerned with several other objectives, such as economic growth, stability of the foreign exchange rate and equilibrium of the balance of payments. Such a traditional policy stance of the BOJ has been confirmed by Article 2 of the new BOJ Law. Meanwhile, the major instruments of monetary policy for the BOJ are (a) changes in the official discount rate, (b) market operations in various bills and securities, and (c) changes in reserve requirement ratios. All of these three instruments involve financial transactions between the BOJ and financial institutions. They have a direct impact upon various financial markets, through which real economic activities as well as price levels would be gradually affected. In relation to such a transmission mechanism, I would like to consider how the operating and intermediate variables of the BOJ's monetary policy have been changed, or otherwise.

First, the operating variables of the BOJ had always been call rates, ever since Japan's high-growth period in the 1960s, until March 2001 when the BOJ started its 'quantitatively easing policy'. Call rates, which are representative interest rates in interbank money markets, are determined through the reserve management of the BOJ. More precisely, under the Law Concerning the Reserve Requirement System of 1957, most financial institutions in Japan are subject to the reserve requirement system and are obligated to place legal reserve deposits (namely, current deposits) with the BOJ. The required reserves of financial institutions are calculated as the product of the required reserve ratio and the average outstanding balance of deposits, debentures and so on during one calendar month. A reserve maintenance period begins from the 16th of that month and ends on the 15th of the next. Several factors cause fluctuations in reserve deposits of financial institutions as a whole and they can be summarized in the following equation called 'Demand and Supply of Funds in Money Markets', which is equivalent to the equilibrium equation relating the demand for and the supply of high-powered money:

Increase (decrease) in reserve deposits = Inflows (outflows) of banknotes
+ Payments (receipts) of the government
+ Provision (withdrawal) of credit by the BOJ

The market operations of the BOJ in conducting the reserve management in this equation and in controlling call rates were characterized as being 'defensive' until September 1998. That is, they were 'defensive' in the sense that the BOJ neutralized fluctuations in the market factor (the first two items on the right-hand side) by its credit provisions or withdrawals on a daily or seasonal basis. Moreover, the BOJ controlled the amount of total credit to financial institutions so as to ensure that an average outstanding balance of reserve deposits held by financial institutions through a maintenance period eventually became equal to the average amount of legal reserve requirement, ignoring the negligible statistical errors. Accordingly, Japanese financial institutions maintained excess reserves almost at zero and minimized the opportunity cost of holding such non-interest-bearing deposits. Under such 'defensive' reserve management, the BOJ controlled call rates by adjusting the path of the 'progress ratio of reserve deposits'.[2] (The ratio was defined as the ratio of reserve deposits accumulated from the first day of a maintenance period against the total cumulative reserve deposits required for that period.) When the BOJ intended to put upward pressure on call rates, it reduced the 'ratio' relative to the standard path. On the other hand, when the BOJ intended to put downward pressure on call rates, it increased the 'ratio'. It should be added that the official discount rate played a critical role in determining call rates. That is, changes in the official discount rate directly influenced call rates through the announcement effects by revealing the changes in the BOJ's policy intent to the general public.

On 15 September 1998, the final day of a reserve maintenance period, the BOJ provided credit to financial institutions more than sufficient to meet their required reserves, thereby reducing call rates to around 0.25 per cent, which was lower than the official discount rate of 0.5 per cent at that time. Since then, the 'defensive' reserve management of the BOJ changed in such a way that financial institutions hold significant amounts of excess reserves through a reserve maintenance period. In other words, the BOJ started to influence call rates through the amount of excess reserves, not through the 'progress ratio of reserve deposits'. Furthermore, as the BOJ pursued a so-called 'zero-interest-rate policy' (by reducing the overnight call rate almost to zero per cent) from February 1999, the amount of excess reserves held by financial institutions as well as the BOJ deposits held by money market dealers increased significantly.

Second, in order to strengthen the transmission mechanism of monetary policy, the BOJ has liberalized call and bill markets and has encouraged arbitrage transactions among various money markets since the late 1970s. Types of transactions were significantly diversified in call and bill markets, while the restrictions that prohibited arbitrage between the interbank markets and open markets, such as the *Gensaki* market, were gradually abolished. Meanwhile, new open markets were established, such as the certificate of deposit (CD) markets in 1979, the treasury bill (TB) markets in 1986 and the commercial paper (CP) market in 1987. At the same time, the BOJ gradually included these new open-market instruments within its market operations, for example, CD operations in 1986, CP operations in 1989 and TB operations in 1991.

As a consequence, various short-term interest rates in the interbank and open markets in Japan now move almost in parallel with one another through the active arbitrage transactions among those markets. If the BOJ controls call and bill rates as its operating targets, it can also control the interest rates in the other money markets. In other words, the BOJ has secured the smooth transmission mechanism of monetary policy, at least within the boundary of various money markets. It should be noted that the markets for short-term government securities such as TBs and FBs, which have remained underdeveloped in Japan even in the 1990s, have at last become the core market for the BOJ's operations since 1999. This is because the MOF started issuing FBs through public competitive-price auction in April 1999.

Third, among the various financial variables that can be treated as intermediate targets of monetary policy, the BOJ has paid closest attention to the broadly defined money stock since the latter half of the 1970s. This is because the BOJ recognized the importance of controlling the money stock from its own experience of the great inflation in 1973–74. More precisely, in the third quarter of 1978, the BOJ began to announce quarterly forecasts for broad money (M2 at first and M2+CDs since the second quarter of 1979). The forecasts were made for the coming quarter in terms of the percentage change in the average outstanding balance over the corresponding period of the previous year.

The BOJ, however, did not adopt the monetary targeting policy in the same way as other central banks, such as the Federal Reserve System in the United States and the Bundesbank in Germany. In fact, the BOJ followed a rather pragmatic approach in the sense that it did not set any target zones for the money stock and treated it as one of a number of important economic indicators in reaching a so-called 'comprehensive judgement' about the state of the Japanese economy. Included among those indicators were various interest rates, foreign exchange rates, industrial production, investment/consumption expenditures and so on. None the less, under such a pragmatic approach, the BOJ succeeded in gradually lowering the growth rates of M2+CDs during the late 1970s and the early 1980s. Meanwhile, the rates of increase in nominal GDP and in the GDP deflator followed a declining trend almost in parallel with those of M2+CDs.

In contrast, the growth rates for M2+CDs accelerated into double digits during the period from the second quarter of 1987 to the first quarter of 1989 and stock prices continued to soar to their historically highest levels around the end of the 1980s. Also real estate prices rose sharply, almost in parallel with stock prices. Such sharp hikes in asset prices constituted the so-called 'Bubble Economy' in Japan. Then, as a result of monetary tightening by the BOJ from April 1989 to July 1991, the growth rate for M2+CDs indicated a sharp decline, to around 0 per cent, during 1992–93 (negative growth rates in the fourth quarter of 1992 and in the first quarter of 1993 were recorded). At the same time, stock prices as well as real estate prices declined sharply and Japan experienced the bursting of the Bubble Economy after 1990. I examine the causes and consequences of the Bubble Economy in more detail in Section 3.

After having experienced the Bubble Economy during the late 1980s and its subsequent bursting, the BOJ began to question the stability of the relationship between the rate of growth of M2+CDs and the rate of inflation, measured by general price indices. The BOJ argued that inflation, as measured by the consumer price index (CPI) and the wholesale price index (WPI), remained stable at a relatively low level despite abrupt changes in the growth rate of M2+CDs and that monetary policy should shift towards the 'comprehensive judgement' approach. In other words, the BOJ began to downgrade the importance of the money stock as the intermediate target of its monetary policy. However, we should remember that the double-digit growth of M2+CDs during the late 1980s was one of the major reasons for the Bubble Economy, and that the BOJ was obviously responsible for the mishandling of the money stock during that period.

Last, but not least, it should be pointed out that the most immediate task for the BOJ's monetary policy at the present moment is not to fight against the inflation problem, but to conquer the deflation problem as an aftermath of the bursting of the Bubble Economy. As the Japanese economy has been experiencing a prolonged recession since the middle of the 1990s, the BOJ has to fight, for the time being, against the deflation, as measured by the WPI and the CPI, as well as asset prices. Meanwhile, the growth rates for lending provided by financial institutions sharply decreased as the Japanese financial system fell into a crisis situation after the failures of the Hokkaido Takushoku Bank and Yamaichi Securities in November 1997. The burden of huge non-performing loans as well the capital constraint *à la* Basle Accord of 1988 have been the major causes of such a credit crunch.[3] Certainly the new BOJ Law has given independence to the BOJ so that it can fight, more than anything else, against the inflation problem. But, ironically, the BOJ was recently urged to pursue zero (or some positive) rate of inflation as its policy target. The BOJ pursued the so-called 'zero-interest-rate policy' (by reducing the overnight call rate almost to zero per cent) from February 1999 to August 2000. Even though the BOJ lifted the zero-interest-rate policy in August 2000, the Japanese economy was still experiencing a rather serious problem of deflation. It was natural that the BOJ adopted the 'quantitatively easing policy' (by increasing the average outstanding balance of current accounts held at the BOJ from some 4 trillion yen to 5 trillion yen) in March 2001. Accordingly, the BOJ has changed its operating target from call rates to the quantitative measures (namely, average outstanding balance of current accounts held at the BOJ) for the first time in its history.

3 FINANCIAL DEREGULATION AND THE BUBBLE ECONOMY

Categorization of Japanese Financial Institutions

Japanese financial institutions can be categorized as shown in Figure 8.2, based on the type of business conducted and the identity of their customers. The classification is done in the following three stages.

The first stage is whether a financial institution is private or public. The public financial system has quite a big share in the Japanese financial system. In particular, the Postal Saving System, which is operated by the Agency of Posts and Telecommunications, collects deposits from the public

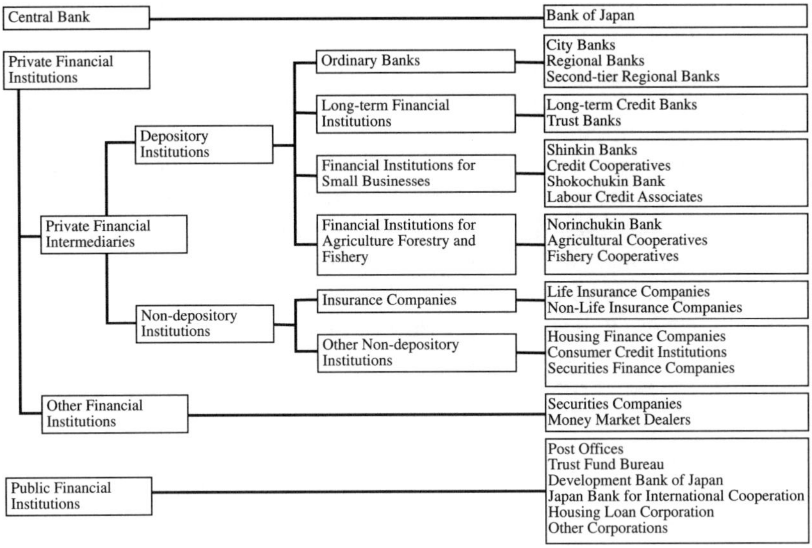

Figure 8.2 Categorization of Japanese financial institutions

through its extensive network of about 24,000 post offices nationwide. At the present moment it accounts for about one-third of total deposits held by the household sector in Japan. Before the fiscal year 2001, the Trust Fund Bureau of the MOF accepted funds from the Postal Saving System together with those from other sources and made loans and/or investments to public financial institutions as well as public corporations, public enterprises and local governments. Included among those public financial institutions were the Japan Policy Investment Bank, the International Cooperation Bank, the Housing Loan Corporation and so on.[4]

Starting from April 2001, however, the Postal Saving System has been allowed to manage its funds at its own discretion and not to deposit them in the Trust Fund Bureau. At the same time, some of the public financial institutions have begun to issue their own bonds (*Zaitokikan Sai*) in order to raise funds from the markets.

As the second stage of the classification, private financial institutions are divided into financial intermediaries and other financial institutions. The latter include securities companies (such as Nomura Securities). They play a key role in securities markets in Japan through their engagement in brokerage, dealing, selling and underwriting of stocks and bonds. They also deal in CDs and offer various investment funds, such as money market funds (MMFs). Also included among the latter are money market dealers, which engage in brokerage and dealing in short-term money market instruments in collaboration with the BOJ.

As the third stage of the classification, the private financial institutions are divided into depository institutions and non-depository institutions. Depository institutions consist of four types: ordinary banks (commercial banks), long-term financial institutions, financial institutions for small businesses and financial institutions for agriculture, forestry and fishery. First, ordinary banks consist of city banks, regional banks, and second-tier regional banks (once categorized as *Sogo* banks).[5] The city banks (such as the Tokyo-Mitsubishi Bank and the Sumitomo-Mitsui Bank) comprise the largest share among the ordinary banks and have been the most important institutions in the Japanese financial system as the so-called 'Main Banks' of large Japanese corporations. Second, long-term financial institutions consist of long-term credit banks (such as the Industrial Bank of Japan) and trust banks (such as the Sumitomo Trust Bank). However, it should be noted that long-term credit banks have actually vanished since the failures of the Long-Term Credit Bank of Japan and the Nippon Credit Bank in 1998. Besides, the Industrial Bank of Japan set up a financial holding company (Mizuho Holdings) together with two city banks in October 2000. Third, financial institutions for small businesses consist of *Shinkin* banks (and the Shinkin Central Bank as their central organization), credit cooperatives (and the National Federation of Credit Cooperatives as their central organization), the Shokochukin Bank and labour credit associates. Fourth, financial institutions for agriculture, forestry and fishery are organized at the national, prefecture and municipal levels. The Norinchukin Bank acts as a central organization in such a three-tier financial system for Japanese primary industries. It is the biggest institutional investor in Japan, holding the largest portfolio of Japanese government bonds.

Finally, included among non-depository financial institutions are insurance companies, which are divided into life insurance companies (such as Nihon Life Insurance) and non-life insurance companies (such as Tokyo Marine and Fire Insurance). Also included among this group of institutions are housing finance companies (*Jusens*), consumer credit institutions, securities finance companies and so on. It should be noted that most of the *Jusens* have already failed.

Deregulation of the Separation of Financial Institutions

The Japanese financial system has been characterized by rather strict functional separation among different categories of financial institutions. Such separation of functions has been observed between banks and securities companies, between long-term financial institutions and short-term financial institutions, between deposit banks and trust banks, and between insurance companies and the other financial institutions.

The separation of banking business from securities business existed even before the Second World War as an informal practice, although there were no legal provisions concerning such separation. In the post-war period, the separation was legally established by Article 65 of the Securities and Exchange Law of 1948, which was basically a Japanese version of the Glass–Steagall Act in the United States. The article prohibited banks from engaging in securities business except in cases where there was an investment purpose or a trust contract. Also allowed as exceptions were banks' businesses of government bonds, local government bonds and government-guaranteed bonds. However, in actual practice, banks engaged only in the underwriting of government bonds during Japan's high-growth period in the 1960s. The other bond businesses allowed by the law as exceptional cases were in fact prohibited by the administrative guidance (*Gyosei Shido*) of the MOF in order to restrict competition between banks and securities companies.

The separation of long-term finance from short-term finance has been based on the commercial banking philosophy similar to that of the United Kingdom. The philosophy is to make clear distinctions between commercial funds related to transactions of commodities and manufacturing funds related to production in various manufacturing sectors. After the Second World War, the Long-Term Credit Bank Law was enacted in 1952 and, accordingly, long-term credit banks, which specialized in long-term finance and could float financial debentures, were established. The maturity of financial debentures issued by long-term credit banks was set at five years. On the other hand, depository financial institutions (such as city banks) were not allowed to issue deposits with a maturity of longer than three years until 1998. Although there were no legal provisions regarding the maturity of funds raised by those depository financial institutions, the MOF exercised an administrative guidance over the maturity of deposits in order to restrict competition between financial debentures issued by long-term credit banks and deposits issued by depository financial institutions.

As for the separation between banks and trust banks, which are another long-term financial institution, banks were once permitted to conduct trust business as well as banking business when the former trust companies were converted into banks in 1948. In 1952, however, the MOF started to promote the separation between banks and trust banks through forcing trust departments of banks to merge with trust banks. Accordingly, quite a limited number of banks (such as the Daiwa Bank) continued to engage in trust business after then.

Finally, the separation between insurance companies and the other financial institutions was most strictly enforced by the MOF in the sense that only insurance companies could engage in insurance businesses. Furthermore, even among insurance companies, there was a clear separation between life insurance companies and non-life (marine and fire) insurance companies.

Regulations concerning the business areas of financial institutions have been liberalized starting from the late 1970s, and such deregulation has accelerated during the 1980s. For example, banks were allowed to handle many securities businesses, starting with the over-the-counter sale of public bonds (government bonds, local government bonds and government-guaranteed bonds) in 1983. They were also allowed to deal in public bonds in 1984. Meanwhile, securities companies developed, through tie-ups with *Shinkin* banks, a new financial instrument, which linked medium-term government bond funds with bank deposits, thereby entering the field of settlement business. As a result, the distinction between banks and securities companies gradually blurred. At the same time, the distinction between short-term finance and long-term finance gradually blurred as banks increased the share of de facto long-term lending (short-term lending with repeated maturity extension) to business corporations. Also an increasing number of banks, including foreign banks, started to engage in trust business.

In June 1991, the Financial System Research Council, an advisory body to the minister of finance, published a report entitled 'On a New Japanese Financial System' which recommended the restructuring of the Japanese financial system. It concluded that mutual cross-entries among individual financial categories in the form of separated subsidiaries would be the appropriate approach to take towards a new Japanese financial system. At the same time, the Securities and Exchange Council, another advisory body to the minister of finance, published a report on the revision of regulations concerning the separation between banking business and securities business. It concluded that the establishment of separated subsidiaries would be appropriate, too. Subsequently, the Law concerning the Reform of the Financial System was enacted in June 1992 and it became possible for ordinary banks, long-term credit banks, trust banks and securities companies to set up wholly-owned subsidiaries in the designated financial categories, starting from April 1993. Although there were still important restrictions in terms of the type of securities business which banks could engage in (for example, banks were not allowed to engage in stock-brokerage), the first securities subsidiaries formed by two long-term credit banks, two trust banks and the Norinchukin Bank started operation in July 1993. Similarly, subsidiary trust banks formed by four securities companies and the Bank of Tokyo (the current Tokyo-Mitsubishi Bank) started operation in

October 1993. Meanwhile, the big city banks had to wait for a while before setting up securities subsidiaries and/or trust subsidiaries since the MOF worried about the 'adverse' impact of those entries upon small securities companies and trust banks.

The timing of deregulation in insurance business was a little later than in the other financial businesses. In 1992, the Insurance Council, another advisory body to the minister of finance, published a report on the revision of the Insurance Business Law. Subsequently, the law was revised in June 1995 so that mutual cross-entries between life insurance companies and non-life (marine and fire) insurance companies were admitted in the form of separated subsidiaries.

Deregulation of Interest Rate Ceilings and Foreign Exchange Control

In addition to the separation of financial institutions, the regulation of interest rates and the control of foreign exchange transactions have characterized the Japanese financial system.

The agreement on regulating deposit interest rates had its origin in the pre-war experiences of repeated banking crises in Japan. There was a strong fear that interest rate competition in gathering deposits would weaken the soundness of depository financial institutions. In December 1947, the Temporary Interest Rate Adjustment Law was promulgated and implemented. The minister of finance determined whether or not interest rate regulation was necessary in the light of general economic conditions and then, if necessary, the Policy Board of the BOJ determined the upper limits on deposit interest rates after having consulted with the Interest Rate Adjustment Council. Since then, the regulation of deposit interest rates was strictly maintained for a long period of time and, in fact, was always binding.

Deposit interest rates were steadily liberalized after 1979 when banks started to issue negotiable CDs. Large-denomination time deposits bearing market interest rates as well as large-denomination money market certificates (MMCs) were first introduced in 1985. Restrictions on minimum amount and maturity of these new deposits with liberalized interest rates were gradually relaxed thereafter. Interest rates on time deposits became virtually free of any regulation in 1993 and interest rates on demand deposits were fully liberalized in 1994, except those on cheque accounts (*Touza-Yokin*) with zero per cent regulation.

Now, let us turn our attention to foreign exchange control. During the high-growth period in Japan, there was a clear segmentation between domestic and foreign financial markets because of rather strict control of foreign exchange. However, after Japan had shifted from a fixed exchange rate system to a flexible exchange rate system in 1973, such strict control of foreign exchange was gradually eased in line with the international trend of liberalizing capital movements across borders. The Foreign Exchange and Foreign Trade Control Law was fully revised in 1980 and the basic principles concerning international capital movements changed from one of 'prohibition' to one of 'freely allowed', though regulated in case of emergency.

In May 1984, the Joint Japan–US Ad Hoc Group on the Yen/Dollar Exchange Rate issued a report and suggested a number of measures to deregulate the raising and investing of funds by both Japanese and foreign financial institutions in order to promote the internationalization of the yen. Included among those measures were the removal of yen-conversion limits of banks, the liberalization of euroyen trading, and the elimination of the so-called 'real demand rule' for forward exchange transactions. (The rule stated that forward exchange transactions between banks and their customers should be based on 'real' transactions, such as commodity trade.) The lifting of yen-conversion limits contributed to expanding euroyen interbank transactions as well as interbank eurodollar transactions with foreign exchange swaps. Those transactions, in turn, contributed to increased arbitrage between domestic interbank and open markets. The elimination of the 'real demand rule' contributed to the smoother functioning of the Tokyo foreign exchange market than before, because it contributed to the increased arbitrage between spot and future markets.

It should be added that direct dealing and international brokerage were introduced in the Tokyo foreign exchange market in 1985 and that the Japan offshore market (JOM) was established in 1986.

The 'Bubble Economy' and its Bursting

In the late 1980s, there were significant changes in the environment surrounding financial institutions in Japan. Deregulation of the separation of financial institutions, interest rate ceilings and foreign exchange control all contributed to increased competition among financial institutions. The most conspicuous response from depository financial institutions, particularly ordinary banks, to the actual (or potential) loss of their franchise value was to expand loans to less traditional areas, such as the real estate industry and non-bank firms. Moreover, many of those non-banks were bank affiliates whose purpose was to lend to real estate companies and to make equity investments. Banks also expanded their equity portfolios, directly or indirectly through special trust funds (*Tokkin*). Similar behaviour was observed on the part of long-term credit banks, trust banks and many of the financial institutions for agriculture, forestry and fishery.

As has already been stated, the stock prices in Japan continued to soar during the late 1980s apart from a temporary fall on 'Black Monday' in October 1987. The Nikkei 225 stock price index rose from an average of 12,565 in 1985 to an average of 34,058 in 1989. Meanwhile, the increase in real estate prices in central Tokyo had already started in the early 1980s, but accelerated sharply around 1986–87. The rapid increase in land prices gradually spread to the suburbs of Tokyo and to other major cities in Japan. Several non-monetary factors could be cited as the background to the increase in land prices. That is, (a) the demand for offices increased in the metropolitan area as Tokyo became one of the world's financial centres, and (b) there were favourable tax treatments for investments in land with respect to inheritance tax and capital gains tax.

It was also true that the economic environment and macroeconomic policy contributed significantly to the increase in those asset prices. The Japanese economy, which had been in recession due mainly to the deflationary impact of the substantial appreciation of the yen after the Plaza Accord in September 1985, exhibited significant recovery in 1987 and 1988. However, the BOJ did not change its easy monetary policy until 1989, because the general price index, such as the CPI and the WPI, remained stable due to the appreciation of the yen, in stark contrast to the sharp rises in asset prices.

In May 1989, the BOJ tightened its monetary policy by raising its official discount rate from 2.5 to 3.25 per cent. (After that, it was raised another four times until it reached 6 per cent in August 1990.) Meanwhile, in March 1990, the MOF urged private banks to contain the growth in their loans related to real estate (that is, their loans to real estate companies, construction companies and non-banks) to less than that of their total lending. Asset prices continued to rise for a while even after these policy changes, but they stopped rising or started to decline around the end of 1989. The Nikkei 225 stock price index fell sharply from its peak of 38,917 in December 1989 to its nadir of 14,309 in August 1992. Since then, it recorded new peaks and troughs several times, recording a low of 9,504 in September 2001. Meanwhile, land prices showed a sharp downturn by the end of 1991, and they have been following a declining trend since then. The recent level of land prices in metropolitan commercial areas is at about one-fifth to one-quarter of their peak level.

Using the National Wealth Statistics published by the Economic Planning Agency in December 1998, we can statistically summarize the Bubble Economy in the late 1980s and its bursting after 1990 as follows. The market value of shares increased from 242 trillion yen at the end of 1985 to 890 trillion yen at the end of 1989, and then decreased to 335 trillion yen at the end of 1997. The market value of land increased from 1,004 trillion yen at the end of 1985 to 2,365 trillion yen at the end of 1990, and then decreased to 1,659 trillion yen at the end of 1997. That is, total capital losses associated with shares and land from their peaks to the end of 1997 amounted to more than 1,261 trillion yen, which was equivalent to 2.5 times the nominal GDP of 505 trillion yen in 1997. It should be noted that outstanding loans by private financial institutions increased from 395 trillion yen at the end of 1985 to 660 trillion yen at the end of 1990 and then further increased to 702 trillion yen at the end of 1997.

The quality of loans provided by those financial institutions deteriorated as asset prices fell rapidly. In particular, most of the loans to real estate companies, construction companies and non-banks turned out to be non-performing loans. In October 1992, the MOF published a report on current policy concerning the non-performing loan problem. The MOF admitted that the total amount of non-performing loans (bankrupt loans and loans with no interest payments for six months or more) held by city banks, long-term trust banks and trust banks reached 12.3 trillion yen at the end of September 1992. The problem continued to expand after then. At the end of September 1995, the total amount of non-performing loans (defined as the sum of bankrupt or past due loans and restructured loans) held by member banks of the Federation of Bankers Association of Japan (*Zenginkyo*) stood at 31 trillion yen. Included among those member banks are city banks, long-term credit banks, trust banks, regional banks and second-tier regional banks. It remained at nearly the same level of 32 trillion yen at the end of March 2001. Meanwhile, according to the self-assessments made by those member banks in March 2001, the total amount of credit that was included in risk categories II, III and IV (doubtful credits) stood at 66 trillion yen, which was 12.2 per cent of their total credit amounting to 536 trillion yen.[6]

The Changing Landscape of the Financial Services Industry

There were not many changes in the landscape of the Japanese financial industry during the high-growth period in the 1960s and through the stable-growth period in the late 1970s and the early 1980s. Regulatory bodies in Japan, primarily the MOF, strictly controlled new entries into each category of financial institution. Besides, the number of failures of financial institutions was quite limited due to the various regulations that restricted competitive forces. However, such a static landscape started to abruptly change as a result of the bursting of the Bubble Economy in the 1990s. Some financial institutions, including major banks (city banks, long-term credit banks and trust banks) went into bankruptcy because of the burden of non-performing loans, while other financial institutions were forced to merge under the more competitive environment than before.

At the end of March 1992, there were 11 city banks, three long-term credit banks, seven trust banks, 64 regional banks, 66 second-tier regional banks, 440 *Shinkin* banks and 397 credit cooperatives. Then, the total number of depository financial institutions that belonged to those seven categories was 988.[7] At the same time, there were also 210 securities companies, 27 life insurance companies, 25 non-life insurance companies, eight housing finance companies (*Jusen*) and so on. The following were the major changes that occurred subsequently in several categories of financial institution.

First, among the city banks, the long-term credit banks and the trust banks, four major financial groups have been formed. In August 1999, the Industrial Bank of Japan, the Daiichi-Kangyo Bank and the Fuji Bank agreed to merge by April 2002 and set up a financial holding company called Mizuho Holdings in September 2000. In April 2000, the Sumitomo Bank and the Sakura Bank agreed to merge and to establish a new bank called the Mitsui-Sumitomo Bank by April 2001. In April 2000, the Tokyo-Mitsubishi Bank and the Mitsubishi Trust Bank agreed to set up a financial holding company called the Mitsubishi-Tokyo Financial Group by April 2001. In October 2000, the Sanwa Bank, the Tokai Bank and the Toyo Trust Bank agreed to set up a financial holding company called the UFJ (United Financial Group of Japan). Meanwhile, the Hokkaido Takushoku Bank failed in November 1997. The Long-Term Credit Bank and the Nippon Credit Bank failed in October and November 1998, respectively.

Second, there occurred several failures of second-tier regional banks until 1996. For example, the Toho Sogo Bank failed in April 1992, then the Hyogo Bank in 1995, the Taiheiyo Bank in May 1995 and the Hanwa Bank in November 1996. Furthermore, there occurred five failures of second-tier regional banks in 1999, that is, the Kokumin Bank in April, the Kohuku Bank in May, the Tokyo Sowa Bank in June, the Namihaya Bank in August and the Niigata Chuo Bank in October. Also, many *Shinkin* banks as well as credit cooperatives failed. At the end of March 2000, the total number of *Shinkin* banks and credit cooperatives decreased to 386 and 292, respectively, as a result of those failures as well as mergers among them.

Third, among the so-called 'Big Four' of Japanese securities companies, Yamaichi Securities failed in November 1997. Also, among middle-sized securities companies, Sanyo Securities failed in November 1997. Meanwhile, there occurred several mergers among medium- and small-sized securities companies in line with the consolidation of the above-mentioned four major financial groups.

Fourth, there occurred several failures of life insurance companies as well as non-life insurance companies. Nissan Life Insurance and Toho Life Insurance failed in April 1997 and in June 1999, respectively. Then, in May

2000, Daiichi Fire & Marine Insurance and Daihyaku Life Insurance failed. Also, Taisho Life Insurance failed in August, as did Chiyoda Life Insurance and Kyowa Life Insurance in October of the same year. In March 2001, Tokyo Life Insurance failed. Meanwhile, several cases of mega mergers among major insurance companies have been proceeding rapidly since 2000.

Fifth, and last, seven out of the eight housing finance companies (*Jusens*) failed and the Housing Loan Administration Corporation took over their assets in August 1996.

4 THE 'JAPANESE BIG BANG' AND SUPERVISORY REFORM

The Japanese Big Bang

In November 1996, Prime Minister Hashimoto announced a financial deregulation package for drastically reforming the Japanese financial system. The aim of the package was to revitalize the Japanese (particularly Tokyo) financial market by transforming it to a 'free, fair, and global' market by the year 2001. The 'free' market meant a liberalized market under market principles; the 'fair' market meant transparent and reliable markets; and the 'global' market meant an international and advanced market. The financial deregulation package was called the 'Japanese Big Bang' after the 'Big Bang' of the London financial market in October 1986.

Such drastic reform of the Japanese financial system was proposed at that time because the Japanese financial market had been gradually 'hollowing out' in the 1990s. For example, transaction volume in the Tokyo stock exchange decreased sharply after 1990. And many Japanese companies continued to issue their corporate bonds in overseas markets, avoiding the cumbersome procedure of issuing in the domestic bond market. Meanwhile, in the 1990s, the growth rates of transaction volume in the Tokyo foreign exchange market became significantly lower than the growth rates in the New York and the London foreign exchange markets. Moreover, the use of the yen as an international currency was not advanced at all. Such hollowing-out phenomena observed in the 1990s were partly due to the bursting of the Bubble Economy, but they were also due to the insufficient infrastructure of the Japanese financial system, for example, outstanding financial regulations, unfavourable tax system for investors and opaque accounting system.[8] In fact, we should admit that the gradual process of financial deregulation in Japan since the late 1970s was too slow to catch up with the rapid developments in the other globalized financial markets (not only in New York and London, but also in Hong Kong and Singapore).

In response to the initiative of Prime Minister Hashimoto, the MOF acted quickly as a promoter of the Japanese Big Bang, realizing that its power of financial administration was at stake. In November 1996, Minister of Finance Mitsuzuka requested each of the five councils (the Securities and Exchange Council, the Business Accounting Council, the Financial System Research Council, the Insurance Council and the Foreign Exchange Council) to start deliberations on the reform proposals. Among those five councils, the Foreign Exchange Council was the first to have submitted a report, which called for abolition of almost all of the foreign exchange controls. Accordingly, in May 1997, the Diet passed a bill to amend the Foreign Exchange and Foreign Trade Control Law, which was renamed the Foreign Exchange and Foreign Trade Law and was enforced in April 1998. Under the new law, the purchase and sale of foreign currencies was liberalized, and the permission and prior notification requirement on capital transactions was abolished. That is, the liberalization of cross-border securities transactions and foreign deposits has greatly expanded the choice of investments for business companies as well as for individuals. Besides, many business companies have benefited from the liberalization of the foreign exchange netting scheme. Such drastic deregulation of foreign exchange control as well as capital movements to and from overseas has been called the 'front runner' of the Japanese Big Bang.

Subsequently, in June 1997, the Financial System Research Council, the Securities and Exchange Council and the Insurance Council submitted to the minister of finance reports on specific measures for financial reform in the areas of banking business, securities business and insurance business, respectively. All the reports included specific measures for financial reform and proposed target dates for the implementation of those measures, although the stance for financial reform varied significantly among them. On the one hand, the report by the Securities and Exchange Council took the most active stance for the implementation of a financial reform. On the other hand, the report by the Insurance Council took a rather defensive stance, trying to protect the vested interests of the insurance industry. Summing up the reports submitted by the individual councils, the MOF released a report entitled 'Financial System Reform' with the timetable and details of the reform attached. Then, in June 1998, the Diet passed the so-called 'Financial System Reform Law', which amended 22 related laws (Banking Law, Securities and Exchange Law, Insurance Law, and so on).

The contents of the Financial System Reform Law were too extensive to be covered item by item. Nevertheless, they can be summarized, with reference to the MOF's report in June 1997, from the following four perspectives. First, the law aimed to expand choice for investors and borrowers. More specifically, the ban on securities derivatives (for example, options on individual stocks) was completely lifted in December 1998. And, in order to promote the use of asset-backed securities (ABSs), special-purpose companies (SPCs) were approved in September 1998. Meanwhile, banks were allowed to engage in the direct sale of securities investment trusts, as well as over-the-counter (OTC) derivatives in December 1998. Furthermore, banks were allowed to sell insurance policies related to housing loans in April 2001.

Second, the law aimed to improve the quality of services provided by financial intermediaries by increasing competition among them. More specifically, the business scope of separate subsidiaries was expanded. (Remaining restrictions on securities subsidiaries and trust subsidiaries were fully lifted by October 1999.) Meanwhile, the licensing regime for securities companies was replaced by a registration regime in December 1998, and brokerage commission for stock trading was fully liberalized by October 1999. Furthermore, restrictions on borrowing instruments (bonds and CPs) of non-bank financial firms were abolished in May 1999. It should be noted that holding companies for financial institutions were allowed in December 1997.

Third, the law aimed to develop a more useful market. More specifically, the restriction of off-exchange market trading for exchange-listed stocks was abolished in December 1998. (The electronic-based private transaction system for stocks was liberalized.) And, the registered OTC stock market (JASDAQ) was improved so that it would function equally well as the Tokyo Stock Exchange. Meanwhile, in the short-term money markets, competitive price auctions of FBs were implemented for the first time in April 1999, as has already been stated in Section 2.

Fourth, but by no means least, the law aimed to establish a framework and rules for fair and transparent transactions. More specifically, the accounting system was improved to some extent in the sense that there was a shift towards the disclosures based on consolidated accounting, starting from April 1999. And, starting from April 2001, new accounting standards for financial instruments, such as securities and derivatives, were established so as to introduce extensively the use of market value accounting (MVA). Moreover, the law aimed to formulate rules which would govern the explanation of non-depository financial products to consumers. In July 1999, the Financial Council of the MOF published an interim report and pointed out that clear rules concerning the merchandising and solicitation of various new financial products (such as derivatives and investment trusts) were necessitated. Accordingly, the Financial Services Act, which sets rules for financial transactions and protects consumers, was promulgated in May

2000 and was enforced in April 2001. Meanwhile, 'prompt corrective action', based on capital ratios, was introduced in April 1999, as is mentioned later in this section, and new measures for preventing international money laundering were taken on enactment of the new Foreign Exchange and Foreign Trade Law in April 1998.[9]

Changing Supervisory Agencies and the Safety Net

Almost in parallel with the implementation of the Japanese Big Bang, the regulatory and supervisory regime of the Japanese financial system, including the MOF itself, has experienced rapid change in the late 1990s. Before assessing the implications of such changes for prudential policy in Japan, I shall briefly review how the regulatory and supervisory agencies, including the Deposit Insurance Corporation, have already been changed.

After the Second World War, the MOF continued to be the dominant power with respect to financial regulation and supervision. According to the Ministry of Finance Law of 1949, the MOF was responsible for the following seven areas of administration; (a) treasury, (b) currency, (c) finance, (d) foreign exchange, (e) securities transactions, (f) mint, and (g) printing. Before the drastic reorganization in 1998, the organization of the MOF consisted of the minister's Secretariat and seven bureaux: the Budget Bureau, the Tax Bureau, the Customs and Tariffs Bureau, the Financial Bureau, the Securities Bureau, the Banking Bureau and the International Finance Bureau.[10] Among these, the Banking Bureau, the Securities Bureau and the International Finance Bureau played an important role as regulatory and supervisory agencies for various types of financial institutions. First, the Banking Bureau was responsible for the regulation and supervision of most of the financial institutions, such as city banks, long-term credit banks, trust banks, regional banks, second-tier regional banks and *Shinkin* banks, under the Banking Law and other special laws. Also, its Insurance Department was responsible for the regulation and supervision of insurance companies. Second, the Securities Bureau was responsible for the regulation and supervision of the Stock Exchange and securities companies under the Securities and Exchange Law. Third, the International Finance Bureau was responsible for the regulation and supervision of capital movements to and from overseas under the Foreign Exchange and Foreign Trade Control Law. In addition to these three bureaux, the Inspection Department of the minister's Secretariat conducted on-site examinations of financial institutions, while the Securities and Exchange Surveillance Commission played a role as the guardian of securities transactions in general.

Although the MOF was the major regulatory and supervisory agency for most of all Japanese financial institutions, including public financial institutions, there were some exceptions. For example, credit unions were under the direction of prefecture governments. Meanwhile, the Shokochukin Bank was primarily under the direction of the Ministry of International Trade and Industry, and financial institutions for agriculture, forestry and fishery were primarily under the direction of the Ministry of Agriculture, Forestry and Fishery. As for the public financial institutions, the most notable exception was the Postal Saving System, which was managed solely by the Ministry of Post and Telecommunications.

In the late 1990s, the mighty MOF was sharply criticized by political parties (particularly, the Liberal Democratic Party) as well as the general public in relation to its mishandling of the *Jusen* failures. The MOF decided to inject public funds of 685 billion yen in order to offset the loss incurred by the *Jusen*, but did not give a clear explanation as to why public funds were necessary. To make matters worse, misconduct by MOF's senior bureaucrats was coincidentally disclosed to the general public. (They quite often received lavish entertainment from private financial institutions.)

In February 1996, the ruling coalition parties (that is, the Liberal Democratic Party, the Social Democratic Party and the New Party Sakigake) started a project for the thorough revision of the administration of the financial system, with particular attention being paid to the role played by the MOF.[11] In September 1996, the project team released a report which suggested that the MOF's departments related to financial administration should be streamlined. In December 1996, the ruling coalition parties reached an agreement such that the Financial Supervisory Agency (FSA) should be newly established as an agency of the Prime Minister's Office and that it should be in charge of inspection and supervision of private financial institutions. They also reached an agreement such that the Banking Bureau and the Securities Bureau of the MOF should be abolished.

The Diet passed a bill to establish the FSA in June 1997. Subsequently the FSA was established in June 1998 as the agency that is mainly responsible for the regulation and supervision of private financial institutions. At the same time, the MOF was drastically reorganized. The Securities and Exchange Surveillance Commission was transferred from the MOF to the FSA. The Banking Bureau and the Securities Bureau of the MOF were abolished, while the Financial Planning Bureau was newly set up within the MOF in order to be responsible for the planning of the financial system. The minister's Secretariat was reorganized to take charge of the supervision of public financial institutions, and the International Finance Bureau was reorganized to some extent and was renamed the International Bureau. (See Figure 8.3.)

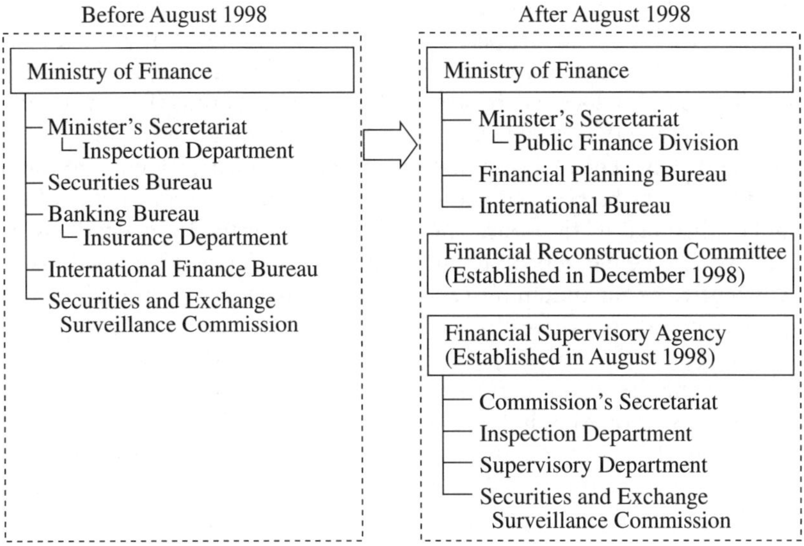

Figure 8.3 Regulatory and supervisory agencies in Japan, before and after August 1998

Furthermore, in December 1998, the Financial Reconstruction Commission (FRC), with the minister of state as its chairman, was newly established as a temporary agency that would take control of the FSA. The final report of the Administration Reform Council, led by the former Prime Minister Hashimoto, suggested that the FSA should evolve into the Financial Services Agency (the new FSA), which is to be totally responsible for prudential policy in Japan, around the start of 2001. In July 1999, the Diet passed a bill for the Reorganization of Ministries and Agencies of the Central Government. Accordingly, the FSA has become the Financial Services Agency (as an agency of the Prime Minister's Office) and has absorbed the Financial Planning Bureau of the MOF in July 2000. Then, in January 2001, the new FSA took over the job of the FRC and has become responsible for most of the administration of the financial system. Meanwhile, the MOF has been renamed the *Zaimu-sho* (the Ministry of Finance in English), which is responsible mainly for the budget, tax collection, treasury and international finances. However, it is expected that the *Zaimu-sho* will continue to be involved in prudential policy, particularly in the crisis management of failed financial institutions, together with the new FSA.

Now, let us briefly explain about the Deposit Insurance System in Japan, since it has played an important role in dealing with the Japanese financial crisis in the 1990s. The Deposit Insurance Corporation (DIC) was established under the Deposit Insurance Law, which was promulgated in April 1971. The current Deposit Insurance Law stipulates that the aim of the DIC is to protect depositors with a view to maintaining the stability of the financial system. The DIC can make insurance payments (that is, pay-offs) to depositors in the event of the suspension of deposit repayments of its member financial institutions. The DIC can also extend 'financial assistance' to facilitate mergers or acquisitions of failed financial institutions.

Currently the maximum *de jure* amount of payment is 10 million yen (plus its interest) per depositor of a failed financial institution. However, in June 1995, the MOF publicly announced in the report entitled 'Reorganizing the Japanese Financial System' that there would be no pay-off until the end of March 2001. In other words, the MOF guaranteed all the deposits of failed financial institutions until that date, as an emergency measure. Furthermore, in May 2000, the Deposit Insurance Law was revised so that all the deposits will be protected in full until the end of March 2002. Besides, demand deposits will be protected in full for another year.

Financial institutions that are legally obligated to participate in the Deposit Insurance System in Japan include all the following types: (a) banks (city banks, regional banks, second-tier regional banks, trust banks and long-term credit banks), (b) *Shinkin* banks, (c) credit cooperatives, and (d) labour credit associates. Member institutions must pay insurance premiums, which are calculated by multiplying the premium rate and the total amount of insured deposits and other liabilities. The insurance premium rate was raised from 0.012 per cent of eligible liabilities to 0.084 per cent in April 1996 and has been maintained at that level until now. (In March 1999, the MOF determined to maintain the premium rate at the same level until the end of March 2001.) Meanwhile, the deposits and other liabilities of member institutions that are legally insured under the system are as follows: (a) deposits, (b) instalment savings, and (c) money-in-trust, of which principal is guaranteed (such as loan trusts and jointly managed money trusts). However, in December 1997, the MOF announced that the other liabilities of failed financial institutions, such as debentures, foreign-currency denominated deposits and so on, which were not legally insured, would be protected, too, until the end of March 2001. That is, the safety net by the DIC has been temporarily expanded so as to protect most of the liabilities of failed financial institutions. Furthermore, in May 2000, the Deposit Insurance Law was revised so that debentures held by individuals as well as earned interest on deposits would be protected, too.

The Resolution and Collection Bank (RBC) and the Housing Loan

Administration Corporation (HLAC) have worked closely with the DIC in recent cases of failed financial institutions. The origin of the RBC was the Tokyo Kyodo Bank, which was established in order to take over the business of two failed credit cooperatives, that is, the Tokyo Kyowa Credit Cooperative and the Anzen Credit Cooperative, in March 1995. Then, in September 1996, the Tokyo Kyodo Bank was restructured to establish the RCB in order to facilitate the disposal of failed credit cooperatives. The DIC provided the RCB with a capital subscription of 12 billion yen and set up the 'Special Account for Credit Cooperatives' in accordance with the amendment of the Deposit Insurance Law. Meanwhile, the HLAC was established in order to take over the assets of the failed *Jusen* in July 1997. At the same time, the DIC set up the 'Financial Stabilization Contribution Fund' of about 1 trillion yen by collecting contributions from private financial institutions (city banks, long-term credit banks, trust banks and so on) related to the *Jusen*. In April 1999, the RBC and the HLAC merged to establish the Resolution and Collection Company (RCC), which has been playing an important role as a 'servicer' by collecting bad loans in collaboration with the DIC.

The 'Convoy'-type Administration and Capital Injection

The MOF's traditional way of administering the financial system was characterized by various kinds of regulations in order to restrict competitive forces in financial markets, thereby protecting individual financial institutions. It was metaphorically described as a 'convoyed fleet vessels' type (or simply 'convoy' type) of administration of the financial system in the sense that it protected even the weakest financial institution from falling into bankruptcy. However, under the circumstances of financial deregulation and internationalization since the late 1970s, the convoy-type administration by the MOF was forced to gradually change, as it became difficult to maintain regulations that restricted competitive forces. In fact, we can point out some cases where financial institutions fell into distress because of reckless management and for other reasons (for example, the failure of the Heiwa Sogo Bank in 1985). Therefore, the MOF could not maintain, literally speaking, the 'convoy'-type administration even before the bursting of the Bubble Economy.

In the case of troubled financial institutions, the Banking Bureau of the MOF tried to solve the problem by forcing them to be absorbed by much larger and/or healthier financial institutions that had close relationships with them. Also, the MOF requested the resignation of the managers of the former institutions so as to take responsibility for their failures. Consequently, the timing and the way of solving these cases were solely dependent on the discretion of the MOF's senior bureaucrats. In fact, they considered that those cases would offer challenging opportunities for showing their administrative skills and powers. Such a traditional way of dealing with troubled financial institutions was maintained even after the 'financial assistance' by the DIC was introduced as a legal procedure for dealing with troubled financial institutions. In April 1992, the DIC provided financial assistance, for the first time, to the Iyo Bank which acquired the failed Toho Sogo Bank. In June 1996, the DIC introduced the 'special financial assistance' that expanded the amount of the financial assistance beyond the pay-off costs. (The special financial assistance is to protect deposits and other liabilities in full until the end of March 2001.) In December 1997, the DIC temporarily expanded the range of recipients of the financial assistance to include financial institutions that would be established through a merger of two or more failed financial institutions.[12] Thus, the MOF tried to maintain its discretionary power of dealing with troubled financial institutions by utilizing those means provided by the DIC.

However, as the number of failed financial institutions increased, the amount of financial assistance as well as special financial assistance increased so rapidly that the outstanding balance of the Deposit Insurance Fund was nearly exhausted by the end of 1997.[13] The failure of Yamaichi Securities and the Hokkaido Takushoku Bank in November 1997 put the Japanese financial system into a serious financial crisis and the premium rate that Japanese financial institutions had to pay in raising funds in overseas markets (the so-called 'Japan premium') rose sharply. In responding to the worsening situation, in February 1998, two laws on emergency measures aimed at stabilizing the Japanese financial system (the so-called 'Financial System Stabilization Law') were promulgated and implemented. According to them, the DIC was provided with public funds totalling 30 trillion yen. More precisely, it was provided with funds totalling 17 trillion yen that would be available for use in the disposal of troubled financial institutions (the 'Special Business Account'). The fund was to be disbursed through the RCB, which was reorganized to deal with troubled cases of city banks, long-term credit banks, trust banks and so on, in addition to credit cooperatives. The DIC was also provided with funds totalling 13 trillion yen that would be available for recapitalization of viable private financial institutions for the sake of stabilizing the financial system (the 'Financial Crisis Management Account'). The Financial Crisis Management Examination Board, which was established within the DIC in order to implement the recapitalization, decided to inject a total of 1.8 trillion yen to 21 major banks (city banks, long-term credit banks, trust banks and regional banks) in March 1998, after having examined their restructuring plans. (The Long-Term Credit Bank and the Nippon Credit Bank, both of which failed later in the same year, were included among those 21 major banks.)

Furthermore, in October 1998, nine laws related to the soundness and reconstruction of the financial system were promulgated and implemented. Among those laws, the so-called 'Financial Reconstruction Law' provided a legal framework for the failure resolution of financial institutions, that is, (a) placement under the financial reorganization administrator, (b) temporary nationalization and (c) bridge bank. (It should be noted that the FSA assumed the role of implementing those laws from the MOF.) In addition, the public funds available for the DIC were enlarged to 60 trillion yen. More precisely, the DIC was provided with additional funds totalling 18 trillion yen that would be available for use in compensating costs required in those procedures. (Under this framework, the Long-Term Credit Bank of Japan and the Nippon Credit Bank were placed under state control.) At the same time, the so-called 'Financial Function Early Strengthening Law' provided a new framework for the recapitalization of viable financial institutions. The 'Financial Crisis Management Account' of the DIC was renamed the 'Financial Function Early Strengthening Account' whose total funds were increased to 25 trillion yen. Under this framework, public funds totalling 7.5 trillion yen were injected into 15 major banks in order to enhance their capital bases in March 1999. There were capital injections of public funds to some of the regional banks and the second-tier regional banks during the fiscal year 1999.

In summary, the current comprehensive safety net in Japan includes a framework for capital injection using public funds, the full protection of deposits and other liabilities of depository financial institutions, and a scheme to establish public bridge banks or temporarily nationalize banks. The total cost of such a safety net has already added up to about 70 trillion yen (about 14 per cent of Japanese GDP). Although these emergency measures have been necessary in order to cope with the financial crisis in Japan since the middle of the 1990s, we should be very much concerned about the moral hazard problems that the safety network has created for financial institutions as well as depositors.

Prudential Policy Based on Market Principles

In order to achieve the purpose of maintaining a sound and stable financial system, it is very important to set up a financial environment in which market discipline could prevail. Certainly, zero failures of financial institutions should not be considered as the final objective of prudential policy, because the soundness and efficiency of the financial system could probably not be achieved under such circumstances.

In contrast, the convoy-type administration by the MOF was basically one to restrict competitive forces and to protect all financial institutions. The MOF relied on measures such as detailed *ex ante* regulations and one-on-one guidance to individual financial institutions. Consequently, even those financial institutions that were inefficient and exposed to too many risks continued to survive. At the same time, however, financial institutions became indifferent to their risk management and their own responsibilities. Under such circumstances, it was quite natural that they were encouraged to adopt the 'do as-everyone-else-does' attitude. For example, during the Bubble Economy in the late 1980s, most Japanese financial institutions extended too much credit to the real estate-related industry without paying due attention to the concentration risk.

Another result of the convoy-type administration was the lack of incentives for Japanese financial institutions to develop new financial products. The cumbersome procedure for getting the permission of the MOF in order to introduce new financial products quite often prevented the innovative financial institutions from getting entrepreneurial profits. Consequently, Japanese financial institutions offered only very similar financial products, and the Japanese financial system was often called 'the system without innovations'. For example, those financial services that have recently been introduced by the Japanese Big Bang, such as options on individual stocks, wrap accounts of securities companies and defined contribution pension plans were developed a long time ago in the other major countries. That is, Japan has lagged far behind most major countries in this respect.

Therefore, first of all, both the regulatory and supervisory agencies and financial institutions in Japan must recognize philosophies concerning the importance of market mechanisms. This was one reason why the Japanese Big Bang was necessitated. The three catchphrases of the Japanese Big Bang, namely, a 'free, fair and global' market, means that the Japanese markets should be changed into one where market disciplines would prevail. It is expected that the wide-ranging liberalization measures proposed in the Japanese Big Bang would promote competition among various types of financial institutions (both domestic and foreign). The increased competition will surely urge those financial institutions to be more innovative in developing new financial instruments in order to survive. It will also urge them to be more skilful in the measurement, undertaking and management of various financial risks in their portfolios.

On the side of the regulatory and supervisory agencies, it is expected that the newly established FRC–FSA (and the new FSA) will not continue the convoy-type administration of the MOF, but instead will adopt prudential policy based on market discipline. In this regard, the capital ratio requirement *à la* Basle Accord of 1988 has important implications for prudential policy in Japan. That is, starting from April 1999, the FRC–FSA (and the new FSA) has adopted 'prompt corrective actions' against those financial institutions with low capital ratios. More precisely, financial institutions that engage in international finance business are now classified by their capital ratio (r) *à la* Basle Accord as follows: (a) being sound if $r \geqq 8\%$, (b) being undercapitalized if $8\% > r \geqq 4\%$, (c) being significantly undercapitalized if $4\% > r \geqq 2\%$, (d) being extremely undercapitalized if $2\% > r \geqq 0\%$ and (e) being bankrupt if r is negative. The cut-off ratios for financial institutions that engage only in domestic finance business are 4, 2, 1 and 0 per cent in cases (a), (b), (c) and (d), respectively. And, in fact, the FRC–FSA (and the new FSA) have already ordered 'prompt corrective actions', by applying those criteria to the Kohuku Bank and the Hokkaido Bank in April 1999, to the Tokyo Sowa Bank and the Niigata Chuo Bank in May 1999 and to the Namihaya Bank in June 1999. Of these, bankruptcy proceedings were initiated against the Kohuku Bank, the Tokyo Sowa Bank and the Namihaya Bank, as determined by the Financial Reconstruction Law.

The FRC–FSA (and the new FSA) is also expected to conduct on-site examination of financial institutions more rigorously than the MOF, which performed a role of not only regulating and supervising, but also protecting and promoting financial industries. In April 1999, they published the new manual of on-site examination of financial institutions so that the definitions of non-performing loans as well as the criteria for loan write-offs and loan provisions would be clarified. Now, they intend to conduct on-site examination of financial institutions more frequently than the MOF did. According to the new FSA plan, Japanese banks will be examined in principle once every year, while securities companies, insurance companies and foreign banks will be examined in principle once every three years. Since the staff of the new FSA is quite limited (about 400 in total), it should be noted that the BOJ conducts on-site examination of financial institutions, too. The new BOJ Law clearly determined that the BOJ might enter a contract with the corresponding financial institutions (with deposits and/or loan transactions) regarding on-site examination (Article 44). The BOJ has recently announced its supervision policy such that it will strictly check non-performing loans as well as the risk management of financial institutions. It is expected that the new FSA and the BOJ will cooperate closely with each other so that they can enhance the flexibility of their on-site examinations.

As I have already stated, the FRC–FSA (and the new FSA) has already been primarily responsible for prudential policy in Japan. However, there remain several questions concerning the role of the new FSA. First, what should be the division of work between the new FSA and the *Zaimu-sho* in financial crisis management? Second, should the public financial system, such as the Postal Savings System and public financial institutions, be regulated and supervised by the new FSA, too? Third, what should be the division (or the integration) of work between the new FSA and the BOJ in on-site examinations of financial institutions?

NOTES

1. In providing loans to troubled financial institutions, the BOJ has been insisting that the following four criteria should be strictly observed. First, there must be a real threat of systemic risk materializing. Second, there is no alternative to the provision of central bank funds. Third, appropriate measures must be taken to prevent moral hazard. And fourth, the financial soundness of the BOJ must not be impaired. However, these criteria have not been observed, strictly speaking, in several cases of failure that occurred in the 1990s.
2. See Suzuki et al. (1990) for more details about the traditional way of reserve management conducted by the BOJ.
3. In order to cope with the credit crunch, the government introduced an emergency policy package in October 1998. The package included 20 trillion yen credit insurance facilities available for small companies through the Credit Insurance Public Corporation. Meanwhile, the BOJ temporarily increased the amount of CP purchases and introduced a special scheme for providing BOJ loans to financial institutions that increased their lending to companies.
4. In order to streamline the public financial system, the Japan Development Bank and the Hokkaido and Tohoku Development Corporation were merged to become the Japan Policy Investment Bank in October 1999. Similarly, the Export and Import Bank of Japan and the Overseas Economic Cooperation Fund were merged to become the International Cooperation Bank in October 1999.
5. It should be noted that foreign banks are included in ordinary banks. As of end-March 2000, the number of foreign ordinary banks in Japan was 84.
6. The definitions of credit categories II, III and IV are as follows. Category II is the credit for which banks have judged that detailed management is needed. Category III is the credit on which banks doubt collection in full, but have difficulties with accurate estimation of losses. Category IV is the credit that banks have judged to be non-collectable or of no value.
7. At the end of March 1992, there were 47 labour credit associates. Besides this, there were 3,446 agricultural cooperatives and 1,661 fishery cooperatives. Although the number of agricultural and fishery cooperatives is large, it is not appropriate to consider them as being separate institutions since they are closely related to each other under the direction of the Ministry of Agriculture, Forestry and Fishery.
8. As for the unfavourable tax system for investors, the securities transaction tax as well as the exchange tax were abolished in April 1999, while the capital gains tax was reformed in April 2001.
9. According to the Foreign Trade and Foreign Exchange Law of 1998, banks and money exchangers are now legally required to verify the identity of counterparties for foreign remittance and, in cases involving the export or import of means of payments (such as cash), a reporting system involving the customs authorities has been introduced. Moreover, in August 1999, three laws related to the prevention of organized crimes were passed in the Diet. Among those laws, measures to prevent money laundering were included.
10. Moreover, the Mint Bureau, the Print Bureau and the Institute for Fiscal and Monetary Studies were special institutions of the MOF headquarters.

11. It should be noted that the Advisory Group on the Central Bank, the advisory council to Prime Minister Hashimoto, started deliberations on the revision of the BOJ Law in the same context and issued its report in November 1996.
12. The merger between the Fukutoku Bank and the Naniwa Bank, so as to establish a new bank called the Namihaya Bank in October 1998, was the only case to which such amendment of the DIC Law was applied. The amendment was abolished in March 1999 and, later that year, the Namihaya Bank failed (in August 1999).
13. There were about 30 cases of 'financial assistance', including 'special financial assistance', provided by the DIC until March 1998. Among them, notable cases of failure were the Hyogo Bank and the Kizu Credit Cooperative in August 1995, the Taiheiyo Bank in May 1996, the Hanwa Bank in November 1996, and the Hokkaido Takushoku Bank and the Tokuyo City Bank in November 1997.

REFERENCES

Kuroda, Akio (1994), 'Recent developments in the Japanese financial system: prudential supervision by the Bank of Japan', *Bulletin of the Institute of Social Sciences*, Meiji University, Vol. 17, No. 1, pp. 1–25.

Kuroda, Akio (1998), 'Prudential policy in Japan', in Craig Freedman (ed.), *Japanese Economic Policy Reconsidered*, Cheltenham, UK and Northampton, MA, USA: Edward Elgar, pp. 219–45.

Kuroda, Akio and Tomohiro Kinoshita (1993), 'Central banking in Japan: an overview', Macquarie University Working Paper Series No. 93-1, January.

Suzuki, Yoshio (1987), *The Japanese Financial System*, Oxford: Oxford University Press.

Suzuki, Yoshio, Akio Kuroda and Hiromichi Shirakawa (1990), 'Monetary control mechanisms in Japan', in Peter Hooper, Karen H. Johnson, Donald L. Kohn, David E. Lindsey, Richard D. Porter and Ralph Tryon, *Financial Sectors in Open Economies: Empirical Analysis and Policy Issues*, Washington, DC: Board of Governors of the Federal Reserve System.

9. Financial sector reforms in Singapore

Kee Jin Ngiam

1 INTRODUCTION

The financial sector has played a major role in Singapore's economic development. Before the onset of the Asian financial crisis, which began with the collapse of the Thai baht in July 1997, financial services in Singapore had consistently grown faster than the rest of the economy, and currently account for some 12 per cent of its GDP. To promote Singapore as a financial centre, the government started the process of gradually deregulating its financial system and opening up its financial markets to foreign players from the late 1960s. These measures have been fairly successful in transforming Singapore into a major financial centre, serving not only the domestic economy but also the region and beyond.

Despite the various steps taken by the authorities to deregulate and liberalize their financial markets, the financial sector in Singapore remained fairly tightly regulated until 1997. The approach to regulating and supervising the financial sector in Singapore before 1997 had been to set high standards, establish strict rules and take minimum risks. This approach protected not only the financial system as a whole but also individual institutions from failing. The trade-off was that Singapore was traditionally slower than other financial centres, like Hong Kong, in introducing innovative financial products and new markets.

Recognizing the financial sector as a crucial engine for growth in the next millennium and the challenges posed by the global trends in banking and finance, the Monetary Authority of Singapore (MAS) made a fundamental policy shift in 1997. The new approach emphasizes the 'need to regulate the financial centre with a lighter touch, accept more calculated risks, and give the industry more room to innovate and stretch the envelope'.[1] Since then, MAS has carried out a comprehensive range of bold reforms at the regulatory and supervisory levels and in individual markets. The reforms are aimed at creating a more conducive regulatory environment and make Singapore into one of the key financial centres in the East Asian time zone.

Against the above background, this chapter surveys the actual development of financial reforms in Singapore from 1997 onwards, assesses why these reforms were pursued despite the ongoing Asian financial crisis, and asks what lessons can be drawn by Asian economies. The chapter is organized as follows: Section 2 analyses the major developments in the Singapore financial scene before 1997, that is, in the years when it was highly regulated; Section 3 examines the financial reforms and strategic policy changes since 1997 to meet the new challenges facing Singapore as a financial centre; Section 4 discusses the benefits and risks to Singapore from liberalizing the Singapore financial sector; Section 5 contains the lessons that can be drawn for Asian economies that are contemplating deregulating and liberalizing their financial systems; and Section 6 provides the conclusions.

2 AN ERA OF TIGHT REGULATION: THE FINANCIAL SCENE PRIOR TO 1997

The government has identified financial services, along with manufacturing, as the two most important engines of growth for Singapore. Towards this end, the government has constantly reviewed its strategies and approaches on regulating and promoting the financial sector. MAS, which was formed in 1971 to perform various central banking functions, has been the driving force behind the reforms to transform the financial landscape of Singapore.[2]

Some of the concrete steps towards deregulation and liberalization taken before 1997 are chronicled in Table 9.1. Three kinds of financial sector reforms can be observed. The first was the domestic financial deregulation which began in 1975 with the abolition of the cartel system for fixing interest rates. The second involved the capital account liberalization which took place in 1978 when the last vestiges of exchange controls were lifted. The third was the internationalization of financial services which occurred when the domestic market was opened up to more foreign banks in 1970 and to more foreign broking firms in 1987.

However, these reforms have been implemented rather cautiously and were aimed primarily at opening up the Singapore financial market to foreign participants in a gradual and orderly fashion. Prior to 1997, certain regulations were considered sacrosanct by the authorities even though they hindered the development of Singapore as a financial centre. Two of the most controversial regulations were the tight control of the banking sector and the restrictions imposed on the use of the Singapore dollar.[3]

Stringent Controls on the Banking Sector

Before 1971, there was only one type of commercial bank in Singapore. All banks were permitted to conduct the whole range of banking services,

Table 9.1 Chronology of financial sector reforms in Singapore before 1997

Date	Financial sector reform
September 1970	Policy towards admission of foreign banks is liberalized
July 1972	Cartel system for fixing exchange rates is abolished
May 1973	Stock Exchange of Singapore (SES) was set up after the split of the joint Stock Exchange of Malaysia and Singapore
July 1973	Floating of the Singapore dollar is instituted
August 1973	Dealings in the gold market are completely liberalized
July 1975	Cartel system for fixing interest rates is abolished
June 1978	Exchange control is completely liberalized
December 1983	A derivatives exchange known as the Singapore International Monetary Exchange (SIMEX) is formed
February 1987	SES set up a second board known as SESDAQ to allow small companies to raise funds in the equity market
March 1987	The stock-broking industry is opened to local banks and foreign financial institutions
March 1989	An over-the-counter market known as Clob International is established to trade in Malaysian shares after Malaysia delisted Malaysian companies from the SES
March 1992	Seven foreign broking houses are allowed to trade directly on the SES
September 1996	Foreign companies with substantial business in Singapore can list and trade their shares in Singapore dollars on the SES

regardless of their country of incorporation. These included the operation of different kinds of accounts (current, savings and fixed deposit), the financing of imports and exports, the transfer of funds, commercial letters of credit, trust receipts, travellers' cheques and currency transactions. To attract international banks to Singapore and to avoid excessive competition in domestic banking, MAS began to issue other types of licences for specialized banking services. Restricted licences were issued in 1971, and offshore licences in 1973.[4]

Currently, only 'full-licence' banks are authorized to transact the whole range of domestic banking business under the Banking Act. By 1988, 25 of the 36 full-licence banks had been granted Asian currency unit (ACU) licences to engage in the Asian dollar market.[5] An ACU is a separate section within a bank and deals only with claims denominated in non-Singapore currencies. It does not need to maintain minimum cash and liquidity reserve requirements. In contrast, the domestic banking business has to maintain a minimum cash balance and a liquid assets ratio of 3 and 18 per cent, respectively, of the bank's liabilities base.[6]

All restricted licence banks and offshore licence banks had approval to operate in the Asian dollar market. Their operation in the domestic banking business is tightly controlled. For example, restricted licence banks are permitted to accept deposits in Singapore dollars from non-bank customers only if they amount to S$250,000 or more. They are allowed to lend Singapore dollars only to resident non-bank customers. Offshore licence banks cannot accept deposits in Singapore dollars from resident non-bank customers and can only lend Singapore dollars to resident non-bank customers up to a total of S$500 million.[7] As a result, such banks have to obtain their Singapore dollar funding from the interbank market or from engaging in Singapore dollar swaps.

Until 1997, the banking sector in Singapore had been regulated rather stringently. MAS gave the highest priority to protecting the soundness and resilience of Singapore's financial system and the interests of depositors and investors. Hence, every effort was taken to minimize risks, banking failures and financial scandals so as not to undermine Singapore's market credibility. As a result, it was commonly said that in Hong Kong anything not expressly forbidden is permitted, whereas in Singapore anything not expressly permitted is forbidden.

Restrictions on the Singapore Dollar

Singapore has traditionally imposed various kinds of restrictions on the use of the Singapore dollar. These controls can be broadly classified into two categories: (a) controls on bank lending in Singapore dollars, and (b) controls on Singapore dollar-denominated instruments and derivatives.

Controls on bank lending in Singapore dollars

The control on bank lending in Singapore dollars was probably one of the most controversial financial regulations in Singapore. The most definitive statement on MAS's policy on bank lending in Singapore dollars, conveyed to banks on 1 November 1983 (popularly known as MAS Regulation 621), read as follows:

> Banks should observe the Authority's policy of discouraging the internationalization of the Singapore dollar. Specifically, banks should consult the Authority before considering Singapore dollar credit facilities exceeding S$5 million to non-residents, or to residents where the Singapore dollars are to be used outside Singapore. Banks managing syndicated loans, bond issues, or other financial papers exceeding S$5 million should do likewise. The terms 'residents' or

> 'non-residents' include bank and non-bank customers. Details of such proposals should be submitted in writing to the Manager, Banking and Financial Institutions Department.

The problem with the above policy statement was that it was too general and had been subject to different interpretations by the financial community. For example, some banks preferred to obtain clearance from MAS even if the amount to be lent to a non-resident was less than S$5 million. Others preferred to avoid prior consultations with MAS by structuring the loan amount to below the S$5 million limit. As Singapore dollar loans can also be obtained through the issuance of Singapore dollar securities, banks managing such securities were asked to observe MAS's ruling as well.

In July 1992, MAS Regulation 621 was revised. The revised regulation specified clearly those activities which banks could finance, for whatever amount in Singapore dollars, without seeking MAS approval (the 'approved' category) and those which banks were banned from financing in Singapore dollars (the 'banned' category). The approved activities were: (i) direct exports from and imports into Singapore; (ii) hedging by forward sales of Singapore dollar receipts from exports to Singapore; (iii) issue of performance bonds for economic activities in Singapore in favour of Singapore parties; and (iv) guarantee of payments arising from construction or other activities in Singapore. The banned activities were: (i) direct or portfolio investments outside Singapore by non-residents; (ii) third-country trade by non-resident-controlled companies; (iii) non-resident subscription to equity in a Singapore company where the proceeds are used for takeovers or financial investments; and (iv) speculation in the local financial and property markets by non-residents. For those activities which were not specifically mentioned in this revised regulation, banks were reminded that they should continue to consult MAS. One such activity was direct investment abroad by residents.

This regulation has been defended on the ground that internationalization of the Singapore dollar would render the conduct of monetary policy more difficult. However, the cost of maintaining such a policy is that the money and capital markets in Singapore would not be fully developed. Realizing that the cost is high, MAS has since 1988 embarked on a policy of gradually liberalizing the use of the Singapore dollar. This issue will be discussed in the next section.

Controls on Singapore dollar-denominated financial instruments and derivatives

The government also kept a tight grip on the growth of Singapore dollar-denominated financial instruments and derivatives until September 1998.

While some controls were imposed to discourage the internationalization of the Singapore dollar, others were simply the direct consequences of MAS's policy on bank lending in Singapore. Because of MAS restrictions on bank lending in Singapore dollars to non-residents, the local currency and interest rate derivatives had not been fully developed. To ensure that the restrictions were not being circumvented through financial derivatives, MAS had defined Singapore dollar credit facilities to cover a wide range of financial instruments, including foreign exchange swaps, currency swaps, interest rate swaps and facilities incorporating options and forward rate agreements in Singapore dollars. This was because market players could always use these financial instruments to get around MAS restrictions. For example, a firm or individual could attempt to borrow Singapore dollars indirectly by first borrowing US dollars and then doing a foreign exchange swap (which involves the buying of Singapore dollars spot using US dollars with the simultaneous selling of Singapore dollars forward). This would replicate, or synthesize, a Singapore dollar money market loan with a 'lock-in' Singapore dollar interest rate. In order to abide by the letter and spirit of MAS regulations, banks would normally scrutinize forward sales of Singapore dollars by clients to ensure that they were not part of a swap.

The stock market in Singapore was another victim of MAS's policy on the non-internationalization of the Singapore dollar. Until recently, all secondary listings of foreign stocks other than Malaysian stocks on the Stock Exchange of Singapore (SES) were denominated in non-Singapore currencies because the government was determined to keep a tight control on the flow of funds in Singapore dollars. Malaysian stocks traded on the SES (which ceased trading after Malaysia declared exchange controls effective on 1 September 1998) had all along been denominated in Singapore dollars. Probably because of their listing in Singapore dollars and their familiarity to Singapore investors, Malaysian stocks were much more heavily traded than other foreign stocks listed on the SES.

The development of derivatives markets involving Singapore dollar instruments also suffered because of a fear by the authorities that they might cause instability in the domestic financial markets. The Singapore International Monetary Exchange (SIMEX) had been reluctant, until recently, to introduce derivatives on Singapore-dollar instruments such as the Singapore stock index and Singapore-dollar interest rates. It seemed to be content with futures and options on non-Singapore dollar financial instruments such as the eurodollar, the euroyen, and the Nikkei stock index.

3 FINANCIAL SECTOR REFORMS, 1997–2000

The year 1997 could be considered a watershed year in the development of Singapore as a financial centre. In that year, MAS announced a new approach to financial-sector management in an effort to boost Singapore's status as a financial centre. The new approach emphasized the need for a 'lighter touch', with the emphasis changing from regulation to supervision. Financial institutions were given more scope to innovate and take calculated risks. The motivation for the sea-change in policy was the realization by MAS that the rapid growth of Singapore as a financial centre could not be taken for granted. This was particularly so given the rapid changes in the financial industry worldwide. Falling regulatory barriers, advances in information technology, financial innovations and a wave of mergers among financial institutions have moved the world closer to a global financial marketplace. A radical change in approach was deemed essential to quicken the pace of market development and innovation.

The sweeping financial reforms undertaken by MAS over the period from 1997 to 2000 encompassed: (a) supervisory and regulatory changes; (b) liberalizing commercial banking; (c) redefining the prudential standards of local banks; (d) liberalizing the Singapore dollar; (e) developing the equity and derivatives markets; (f) developing the fund management industry; and (g) developing the insurance industry.

Supervisory and Regulatory Changes

The main thrusts of the financial reforms in Singapore were to create a more conducive regulatory environment and to actively promote the financial sector. On the regulatory front, MAS shifted from a 'one-size-fits-all' regulation to a risk-focused supervisory approach. The focus of supervision is on systematic risks rather than the risks of individual institutions or transactions. The tasks of MAS are now devoted to monitoring and examining financial institutions for compliance with guidelines, and ensuring that they maintain adequate internal controls and risk-management systems. This move towards performance-based regulation will provide greater leeway for stronger and better managed institutions.

MAS is also shifting away from relying on extensive regulation to protect investors and customers. The new rule of the game is *caveat emptor* (or 'let the buyer beware'). In return, MAS will help investors make informed decisions by promoting adequate disclosure and greater transparency in the market. Among other things, banks are required to disclose details relating to their principal sources of income, loan loss provisions and off-balance sheet activities. They also need to disclose the aggregate amount of their non-performing loans as well as the market value of their investments and properties. Local banks are required to provide additional information on their exposures by geographical areas, industry groups and maturity bands. Better disclosure and market scrutiny should spur banks to operate more efficiently.

To further enhance corporate governance, all local banks were instructed in May 1999 to appoint nominating committees within their boards. The purpose of the five-member nominating committee is to ensure that the most competent individuals are appointed to the board and key management positions. In addition, the committee must ensure that the board comprises a majority of Singapore citizens or permanent residents. MAS retained its existing powers under the Banking Act to approve appointments to the board and key positions, and vet all reappointments. Local banks are also required to dispose of their non-core businesses (such as property development and hotel management) over a three-year period beginning mid-2001. By concentrating on their core business rather than operating as conglomerates, local banks are expected to build up the necessary expertise to compete globally and grow more rapidly as true financial institutions. Moreover, banking crises resulting from shocks in the non-core business of the banking sector can be averted.

MAS has also taken on an additional task as promoter of the financial sector by setting up the Financial Sector Promotion Department (FPD) in April 1998. The aim of the FPD is to attract reputable financial market participants to Singapore, and to encourage existing players to expand their range of financial services conducted in Singapore. As the primary mission of MAS is regulation, it is questionable whether it should also be in charge of promotion. The concern is that MAS may be too cautious in promotion, especially when conflicts between these two functions arise.

Liberalizing Commercial Banking

In May 1999, MAS introduced a programme to open up Singapore's commercial banking sector in response to the consolidation in the banking industry worldwide. The programme struck a delicate balance between acting on the imperatives of change and building up local banks. To achieve these two objectives, MAS has embarked on a controlled pace of liberalization over a period of five years.

The liberalization programme began in October 1999 with the creation of a new category of full-licence bank known as qualifying full banks (QFBs), to distinguish them from the existing class of full licence foreign banks. Incumbent full-licence foreign banks that were not awarded QFB status would retain their existing privileges. For a start, QFB licences were issued to four foreign banks – ABN Amro Bank NV, Banque Nationale de Paris, Citibank NA and Standard Chartered Bank.[8] Each QFB was allowed to expand in up to ten locations (branches and off-premise automated teller machines: ATMs), of which up to five could be branches. QFBs which already had more than five branches were capped at their present number, but were allowed up to five off-premise ATMs. MAS also allowed QFBs to share ATMs among themselves. Table 9.2 shows the number of branches and ATMs operated by the local banks, while Table 9.3 shows the potential number of branches and ATMs available to QFBs. It can be seen that the network of branches and ATMs of local banks continues to dwarf that of foreign banks even with the liberalization of the domestic banking sector.

Table 9.2 Local bank branches and ATMs

Local banks	No. of branches	No. of ATMs
Development Bank of Singapore	149	901
Overseas-Chinese Banking Corporation	44	326
United Overseas Bank	74	299
Overseas Union Bank	40	151
Keppel Capital Holdings	39	111
Total	346	1,788

Source: *The Business Times*, 27 May 1999, p. 54.

Table 9.3 Qualifying full banks' potential shared ATM network

Qualifying full bank (QFB)	No. of branches	No. of ATMs	Potential no of branches	Potential no. of ATMs
Standard Chartered	20	27	20	32
Citibank	3	19	5	26
ABN Amro	2	2	5	10
Banque Nationale de Paris	1	0	5	10
Total	26	48	35	78

Source: *The Straits Times*, 20 January 2000, p. 98.

Other measures taken by MAS to ease the entry barrier include increasing the number of restricted banks and lifting the 40 per cent limit on foreign investors' total shareholding in local banks. This latter measure would make it easier for local banks to forge strategic partnerships with foreign banks, and to pay for overseas acquisitions with shares. The requirement to have a majority of Singapore citizens and permanent residents on the board should ensure that the control of local banks rests with individuals or groups who will act in a manner consistent with the national interest.

Redefining the Prudential Standards of Local Banks

Since 1992, Singapore banks have been required to maintain a risk-based capital adequacy ratio (CAR) of 12 per cent. This is much higher than the 8 per cent recommended by the Bank for International Settlements (BIS). Moreover, MAS has also insisted that the entire 12 per cent of CAR be Tier 1 capital (or equity). In contrast, the BIS recommends that only 4 per cent of the 8 per cent CAR needs to be Tier 1. The remainder can consist of lower-quality Tier 2 capital.

To reduce the costs of funds for local banks, MAS refined the CAR in November 1998. The CAR of 12 per cent for Tier 1 capital was reduced to at least 10 per cent for Tier 1 capital, while the remaining 2 per cent may consist of Tier 2 capital. The definition of Tier 1 capital was also widened to include equity-like capital instruments. Tier 2 capital may comprise instruments such as perpetual cumulative preference shares and subordinated shares. According to MAS, the adjustments are in line with international norms and do not represent a lowering of prudential standards.[9]

Liberalizing the Singapore Dollar

In August 1998, MAS further liberalized the use of the Singapore dollar by announcing that MAS Regulation 621 would be replaced by a new notice, MAS Regulation 757. This new regulation contained three key features. First, Singapore-run companies, even if they were majority foreign owned, could borrow Singapore dollars from local banks for bona fide overseas projects provided that the proceeds were converted into foreign currencies for use outside Singapore. Second, foreign companies would face less stringent requirements for listing their shares in the Singapore dollar on the local bourse (this issue will be taken up in the next subsection). Third, foreign entities could borrow Singapore dollars by issuing Singapore dollar bonds where the proceeds were to be used offshore. However, they must swap the local dollar proceeds into foreign currencies for use outside Singapore. Through the swap, Singapore dollar liabilities of the foreign entities would be transformed into foreign currency liabilities. The MAS ruling was aimed at controlling the size of local currency loans held by foreigners, and the development of an offshore market in the Singapore dollar.

Within two months of the easing of controls on the use of the Singapore dollar, the International Finance Corporation (IFC), the investment arm of the World Bank, obtained permission from MAS to issue S$300 million worth of Singapore dollar-denominated bonds. This was shortly followed by local statutory boards, well-established foreign multinational corporations and other supranationals which quickly made their debut in the Singapore dollar bond market.

Despite the sudden flurry of issuance by both local and foreign borrowers, the Singapore dollar debt market remains in its infancy. Two major problems must be resolved before Singapore can become a regional hub for the issuing, arranging and trading of fixed income securities. First, Singapore has to develop a more liquid swaps market. Second, Singapore has to find ways to make the secondary market for trading bonds more liquid. Without a liquid swap market, foreign issuers of Singapore dollar debt securities would have to incur a high cost when swapping the proceeds, as is obligatory under MAS Regulation 757. To develop this market, MAS has allowed offshore banks to engage in Singapore dollar swaps in respect of proceeds arising from the issue of Singapore dollar bonds managed or arranged by them.[10] It has also exempted banks from setting aside reserves for Singapore dollars received from swaps with non-bank financial institutions and corporations. To further develop secondary market liquidity, MAS launched a five-year Singapore government futures contract in June 2001.

Developing the Equity and Derivatives Markets

Although SES and SIMEX have done well in catering for the financing needs of different segments of the market, they are finding themselves in an increasingly globalized and competitive environment. To meet the new challenges, the two exchanges were forced to work together to become more competitive and offer a wider range of products, including Singapore dollar instruments.

Working together, the authorities decided to demutualize and merge the two exchanges into a single integrated and privately-held company known as the Singapore Exchange (SGX). The SGX was launched in December 1999 with two trading arms, SGX-ST (SGX-Securities Trading) and SGX-DT (SGX-Derivatives Trading). Demutualization would reduce the potential conflict of interests between members, who are owners, and other users of the exchange. The merger should also benefit SES and SIMEX by aligning cash and derivatives business strategies, and increasing the financial capability to make heavy capital investments. To enhance the competitiveness of Singapore's capital markets, the SGX accelerated the freeing up of brokerage commissions. From 1 January 2000, brokerage commissions for large trades (above S$150,000) were fully negotiable, while the commissions on retail trades (below S$150,000) were lowered from 100 to 75 basis points. By October 2000, commissions became fully negotiable for all trades.

As for the offering of a wider range of products, MAS Regulation 757 of August 1998 had made it easier for foreign companies to list their shares in Singapore dollars on the local bourse. Under this new regulation, foreign firms with only 20 per cent of their revenues, profits or expenses attributable to Singapore could have such a listing. Previously, MAS allowed such firms to list Singapore dollar-denominated shares only if they had operational headquarters status, with at least 35 per cent of their revenues, profits and expenses generated in Singapore. Because of these stringent requirements, only two of the 40 foreign companies listed on the SES were able to convert their foreign currency floats into Singapore dollar listings.[11] With the easing of the rules on the Singapore dollar, SIMEX quickly introduced the Singapore stock index futures contract in September 1998, followed by the three-month Singapore dollar interest rate futures contract a year later. Financial institutions in Singapore also began to participate freely in Singapore dollar interest rate derivatives in the over-the-counter market.

Developing the Fund Management Industry

To encourage the growth of the fund management industry in Singapore, the authorities made a concerted effort to enlarge the pool of domestic funds available for fund management in Singapore. In February 1998, the Government of Singapore Investment Corporation (GIC) announced that it would place an additional S$25 billion over the following three years with fund managers who have offices in Singapore. In November 1998, MAS made a similar announcement although the sum promised was only S$10 billion. The Central Provident Fund (CPF), which operates a compulsory savings scheme for all workers, also liberalized its rules to allow more funds to flow into CPF-approved unit trusts. These efforts helped the fund management industry in Singapore to grow from S$150.6 billion in 1998 to S$276 billion in 2000, a phenomenal increase of some 84 per cent over a two-year period.

Developing the Insurance Industry

Singapore's insurance industry, which has lagged behind international developments for many years, was not spared the 'wind of liberalization' in Singapore. In March 2000, MAS liberalized entry into the direct life and general insurance industries (effectively closed since 1990 and 1984, respectively) and adopted an open entry policy for insurance brokers. To encourage more 'captive' insurers to come to Singapore, it has reduced the paid-up capital for such insurers from $1 million to S$400,000.[12] It also abolished the 49 per cent limit on foreign shareholdings of locally-owned direct insurers to enable local insurance companies to merge and form strategic alliances with foreign players. While promoting greater competition in the insurance industry, MAS, at the same time, raised the standards of corporate governance and market conduct to protect policyholders.

Going forward, the insurance industry in Singapore will be facing several new challenges. One is the development of new distribution channels in addition to the traditional, but costly, means of using insurance agents. The other is the development of new products to cater for the needs of an ageing population. Last, but not least, the industry has to ensure that the asset management capability, systems and reporting framework meet the highest international standards. By overcoming these challenges, it will be able not only to meet policyholders' expectations, but also to compete with unit trusts and other financial products. This will also have a bearing on the future of Singapore as the premier insurance hub in Asia.

4 BENEFITS AND RISKS OF LIBERALIZATION

Any modern society would desire a financial system that is both stable and efficient. Financial system stability means establishing and maintaining a structure of financial institutions and markets having a reasonable level of risk. Efficiency means that the services provided to the public are at the least cost for a given level of quality. The explicit and implicit costs of regulation imply that liberalization to improve system efficiency is also likely to reduce system stability. The two objectives are often inconsistent, and compromises are frequently necessary in the undertaking of financial reforms.

Benefits

The potential benefits to Singapore from the liberalization of its financial sector, particularly the opening up of its banking sector and the liberalization of the Singapore dollar, include (a) a more efficient financial sector, (b) a deepening and widening of the Singapore financial markets, (c) the development of more complete markets, and (d) the reduction in transaction costs and gains in seigniorage.

A more efficient financial sector

Opening up the financial sector to foreign competition should allow consumers to obtain better and more appropriate services more cheaply, and put pressure on domestic financial firms to improve their productivity and services. It would also encourage financial firms to access new technologies and ideas to help them raise efficiency. The effects of greater competition have already been felt in Singapore's banking sector. One clear example is the recent mortgage rate war among the full licence banks in the home loan market.[13]

Being a small island-state, Singapore's comparative advantage lies with financial and business services rather than with manufacturing. Manufacturing is generally more land intensive than financial and business services which tend to be more knowledge based. Hence, the active promotion of the financial services by MAS should make this sector grow much faster than the manufacturing sector. The latest policy changes clearly are part of a long-term, strategic move to transform Singapore into an important financial centre in Asia.

Deepening and widening of Singapore's financial markets

The liberalization of the Singapore dollar should lead to a 'deepening' of Singapore's financial markets because of the increasing flow of Singapore dollar funds. This should, in turn, stimulate the trading of Singapore dollars against other currencies. Although Singapore is the fourth largest foreign exchange trading centre in the world, with an average daily turnover of about US$140 billion, the share of Singapore–US dollar transactions constitutes only about 7 per cent.[14] The widening of Singapore's financial markets would arise when a broader range of Singapore dollar instruments, including swaps and other derivatives, are traded without too much restriction.

Development of more complete markets

The availability of a wider range of financial instruments in Singapore should provide investors with accessible hedges against market risk, broaden the information available to market participants, and contribute to the development of more complete markets. A complete market exists when the supply of instruments available is sufficient to satisfy the desires of investors. In contrast, an incomplete market implies an unfulfilled desire for a particular type of instrument by an investor. The liberalization of the Singapore dollar would thus allow financial institutions or SGX to introduce Singapore dollar instruments to meet the unfulfilled desires of investors, whether those desires have to do with longer maturity Singapore dollar bonds or derivatives based on Singapore dollar instruments.

Reduction in transaction costs and gains in seigniorage

Liberalization of the Singapore dollar should make the local unit more attractive as a medium of exchange. If the Singapore dollar were to become more widely used as a medium of exchange, Singapore traders would have greater scope for settling their accounts in the domestic currency. Thus, they would gain from a reduction in exchange rate risks and transaction costs because the need to hold working balances or to trade in a multitude of foreign currencies is diminished.

The Singapore dollar has the potential to play a more important role in regional trade. Figures from Malaysia and Thailand (in Table 9.4) show that the use of the Singapore dollar for trade settlement is only 4.4 per cent of Malaysia's trade even though Singapore accounts for about 16.2 per cent of Malaysia's trade. This suggests that only one-quarter of Malaysia's trade with Singapore is invoiced in the Singapore dollar. The use of the Singapore dollar in Thailand's trade with Singapore is much less as it is used to settle only 0.7 per cent of Thailand's trade. As Singapore accounts for some 9.2 per cent of Thailand's trade, it implies that the Singapore dollar is only used for 10 per cent of Thailand's trade with Singapore. Data are not available for Indonesia but anecdotal evidence suggests that the role of the Singapore dollar in Indonesia's trade with Singapore could be very large. This is not surprising as a substantial amount of Singapore's outward investment is in the Indonesian islands of Batam and Bintan. If the Singapore dollar can also play a role as a store of value (or as a reserve currency), Singapore would reap the seigniorage gains from issuing domestic money to non-residents.

Table 9.4 Malaysia and Thailand: currency of settlement of foreign trade, 1995–1996 (as per cent of total settlement of foreign trade in goods)

	Malaysia		Thailand	
	1995	1996	1995	1996
US dollar	61.7	66.0	84.9	83.9
Japanese yen	8.2	6.8	7.2	8.2
German mark	3.2	2.8	2.2	2.4
Singapore dollar	4.4	3.5	0.7	0.7
Home currency	18.7	17.8	1.5	1.0
Pound sterling	1.2	1.0	0.8	0.9
Others	2.6	2.1	2.7	2.8

Source: Senivongs (1997).

Risks

While Singapore can gain by liberalizing and deregulating its financial sector, there are also costs and risks involved. In Singapore, the main concerns are over the liberalization in two areas: the banking industry and the Singapore dollar. There is less concern over the liberalization in other areas, such as the insurance and fund management industries, probably because these industries have fewer linkages to monetary policy. For these industries, rules to ensure consumer protection rather than prudential regulation are probably more important. The remainder of this section examines the concerns about foreign bank entry into domestic banking and the liberalization of the Singapore dollar.

Concerns about foreign bank entry

The fears about foreign banks range from concerns that they will service only select segments of the market to concerns that foreign banks will dominate the domestic market. Some (for example, Vittas, 1991) have even argued that foreign banks lack the local commitment and contribute to capital flight. However, recent works by Levine (1996) and Claessens and Glaessner (1998) have suggested that many of these claims are unsubstantiated or not directly linked to foreign bank entry. The pertinent question is: are these concerns justified in the case of Singapore?

There is some truth in the argument that full-licence foreign banks in Singapore have served mainly wealthy clients and well-established corporations. A market-based business strategy suggests that foreign banks will attempt to carve out areas of comparative advantage. Without the extensive branch and ATM network of the local banks, full-licence foreign banks may have no choice but to rely on more sophisticated financial products and services to make themselves attractive. It just happens that clients using such products and services are usually households and firms which are sophisticated and wealthy. This is not a surprising or negative implication of foreign bank entry. Businesses attempt to find niche markets, and this manifestation of market-based competition will promote improvements in the provision of financial services to domestic clients.

However, foreign banks do not and will not dominate the domestic banking sector of Singapore. Currently, the local banks have 62 per cent of total resident deposits (which include the ACU). MAS has stated publicly that it will maintain the local banks' share at no less than 50 per cent of total resident deposits.[15] With the local banks still enjoying a comfortable margin of 12 per cent above the floor level, foreign bank entry could be further liberalized. This floor of 50 per cent would ameliorate the fear of domination while still permitting the benefits of foreign banks to flow into the domestic financial system.

There is no opportunity to test whether foreign banks will quickly retreat when faced with problems in the Singapore market or when faced with problems in their home market. Similarly, whether foreign banks contribute to capital flight has also not been tested in Singapore. This is probably due to two factors. One is that Singapore has enjoyed strong economic growth since 1973, interrupted only by the 1985 recession and the 1997 Asian financial crisis. The other is the adoption of sound and consistent macroeconomic policies in Singapore which ensure that its investment climate remains attractive. At any rate, all banks in Singapore are so well supervised by MAS that it would be rather difficult for them to facilitate capital outflow from Singapore.

Concerns about liberalization of the Singapore dollar

While substantial benefits can be reaped from liberalizing the use of the Singapore dollar, the build-up of a sizeable stock of Singapore dollar-denominated assets in portfolios of international investors entails the potential for a destabilization of the exchange rate. Attempts to offload these holdings can put pressure on the exchange rate. Moreover, the accessibility of derivatives on Singapore dollar-denominated instruments like the local stock index futures could provide speculators with the extra ammunition to speculate on, or cause instability in, the local financial markets.

Three pertinent questions that arise are: how serious would be the increase in financial instability from further liberalization; is Singapore able to cope with such instability, and will the benefits from a more liberal use of the Singapore dollar outweigh the costs in terms of greater financial instability and a loss of policy autonomy?

Singapore cannot really control the international use of the Singapore dollar. The Singapore dollar will be used by non-residents as long as it can serve as a unit of account, a medium of exchange and a store of value. However, it is absolutely out of the question that the Singapore dollar could ever assume an international role beyond the Southeast Asian region. Singapore does not possess the economic weight and a well-developed domestic financial market to make its currency attractive enough to be used internationally, even though there is confidence in its political stability and the value of its currency. With only a limited role for the Singapore dollar, the costs (and hence the benefits) of liberalization appear to be quite limited, with probably only a minimal rise in its exchange rate volatility. Even if liberalizing the use of Singapore dollars were to increase exchange rate volatility, traders and investors would quickly learn to hedge their positions and would have a wide range of instruments with which to do so.

Although MAS attempts to minimize Singapore dollar loans to non-residents through the control of bank lending to non-residents and the mandatory swaps imposed on foreign issuers of Singapore dollar bonds, it does not discourage them from accumulating Singapore dollar assets.[16] As Singapore is an important financial and trading centre as well as a host country for many multinational companies, the amount of Singapore dollar deposits accumulated by non-residents is substantial. In December 2000, non-residents had amassed some S$91.9 billion worth of Singapore dollar deposits (or about one-quarter of total liabilities) in local banks.[17] The unobstructed inflows and outflows of the non-residents' funds in Singapore dollar deposits could have qualitatively similar consequences for the exchange rate as increases or decreases in Singapore dollar loans. Despite the substantial holdings of Singapore dollar deposits by non-residents, Singapore was able to fend off speculative attacks on its currency in September 1985 and during the recent Asian currency crisis. Whether the Singapore dollar would yield to currency speculators had there been no control on bank lending to non-residents and no Plaza Accord in September 1985 to bring down the US dollar is an open question.[18]

The other important issue is whether a liberal use of the Singapore dollar would pose problems for exchange rate management in Singapore. The answer depends partly on whether currency attacks are associated with weak economic fundamentals (Krugman, 1979) or self-fulfilling speculation (Obstfeld, 1986). Those who believe that speculation is self-fulfilling view the exchange rate as intrinsically unstable and vulnerable to speculative attacks even if the authorities do all the right things. They tend to resist any liberalization measures which might make it harder for the authorities to manage the exchange rate. On the other hand, those who hold the view that currency attacks are due to weak fundamentals tend to take a positive view of speculation. According to them, the way to avoid currency crises is to adopt sound fiscal and monetary policies which make the commitment to the exchange rate objective credible. With Singapore's sound macroeconomic management, high savings and strong reserve position, MAS should be well placed to minimize exchange rate volatility. In an apparent support of sound fundamentals, the IMF chief, Michel Camdessus, made the famous remark: 'I have never seen a speculative attack when a macroeconomy is strong and government policies are sound'.[19] Indeed, what the Asian financial crisis has shown is that the relative stability of the Singapore dollar was due to Singapore's strong economic fundamentals.

Another interesting debate is over the effects on the domestic financial markets from the introduction of Singapore dollar-denominated derivatives. From a theoretical standpoint, there are no sound arguments evidencing a destabilizing effect of derivatives on the spot market, provided the futures and options markets are sufficiently liquid and efficient. The arguments attributing a destabilizing effect on the spot market to derivatives highlight the role of speculators who are attracted to the low costs and high leverage trading available in the derivatives markets. But rational speculators who buy undervalued assets and sell overvalued assets will draw prices towards levels consistent with fundamentals, thereby reducing volatility (Friedman, 1953). The misinformed speculators looking for easy profits and moving prices away from levels consistent with fundamentals will generally incur losses and will eventually leave the market. Whether derivatives are stabilizing or not is an empirical issue. Indeed, numerous empirical papers have addressed the issue for a wide range of futures and options contracts. However, these studies do not generally support the proposition that the introduction of futures and options has increased volatility on the related spot market (see Table 9.5).

Table 9.5 Empirical research on the effect of derivatives on spot market volatility

	Period analysed	Spot instrument analysed	Effect in terms of volatility
Figlewski (1981)	1975–79	GNMA (USA)	Increase
Bortz (1984)	1975–82	T-bond (USA)	Moderate decrease
Moriati and Tosini (1985)	1975–83	GNMA (USA)	No effect
Simpson and Ireland (1985)	1973–85	T-bills (USA)	Initial decrease, subsequent increase
Edwards (1988)	1973–87	S&P Index	Decrease
		Value Index	Decrease
		T-bills (USA)	Decrease
		Eurodollar deposit	Decrease
Baldauf and Santoni (1991)	1975–89	S&P Index	No effect
Hodgson and Nicholls (1991)	1981–87	Australian Stock Index	No effect
Lee and Ohk (1992)	1979–85	NYSE Index	No effect
	1983–89	Tokyo Stock Index	No effect
	1981–87	FT-SE 100 Index	No effect
	1983–89	Hang Seng Index	No effect
Robinson (1993)	1980–93	FT-SE All Index	Decrease
Ayuso and Nunez (1995)	1990–94	T-Bonds (Spain)	Decrease

Obviously, it would be useful to show how the purported benefits of liberalization stack up against the costs of exchange rate instability and possible loss of monetary control from a wider use of the Singapore dollar. Such a cost–benefit analysis is, however, beyond the scope of this chapter.

In their concept paper, Chan and Ngiam (1996) have shown that there are both costs and benefits from the liberalization of bank lending in Singapore dollars to non-residents. According to their study, Singapore should weigh the costs against the benefits, and not forgo the latter just because it fears instability. They concluded that the optimal approach is a partial liberalization of MAS policy. This conclusion is broadly consistent with the current government's policy of allowing a gradual and controlled internationalization of the Singapore dollar.

5 LESSONS FROM SINGAPORE

Despite the ongoing Asian financial crisis, MAS has undertaken major financial reforms with a series of strategic changes. Financial reforms, especially those relating to the liberalization of the banking sector and the Singapore dollar, are especially sensitive. Despite the consternation in certain segments of the financial community, MAS has remained steadfast in its belief that Singapore must press ahead with the necessary changes in order to become one of the major financial centres in the world. While it is too early to judge whether the reforms undertaken in the past few years have been successful, nothing so far has occurred that would support the fear that local financial institutions would lose their market shares to foreign competitors or that Singapore would lose control of its exchange rate management. Hence, the experience of Singapore may offer some useful lessons for other Asian economies that are in the process of deregulating their financial systems.

The first lesson is that financial sector reforms should be brought in voluntarily. Singapore could have rested on its laurels as its financial sector was in good shape even after the Asian financial crisis. Nevertheless, strategic changes were necessary if Singapore wanted to exploit the full potential of its financial sector and make it into the world league. In contrast, the crises-hit Asian economies of Indonesia, Thailand and South Korea took to reforms unwillingly under compulsions by the IMF. The experiences of these countries have demonstrated that it is much harder to undertake financial reforms under adverse economic conditions. They are still struggling with the much-needed financial reforms despite several years having elapsed since they were hit by the crises.

The second lesson is that Asian economies should undertake financial reforms quickly and decisively. Obviously, special interest groups and rent seeking can prevent reforms from being adopted. Singapore is no exception as its local banks have all along resisted opening up the banking sector. If reforms must be carried out because they are widely recognized as useful and positive, the authorities might as well act fast and early. Another reason why the authorities should not procrastinate is that it takes a long time to implement reforms and see the full results of their efforts. Despite the aggressive efforts by Singapore to develop a wider range of financial instruments, the Singapore dollar bond and derivative markets are still small and illiquid.

The third lesson is that a 'gradualist' (adopted by Singapore) rather than a 'big bang' approach (pioneered by London in the mid-1980s) towards financial liberalization may be the optimal approach for many Asian economies. This would allow their nascent financial institutions and markets to adjust and for their regulators to slow down or accelerate the pace of liberalization as needed. Recognizing that too fast a pace of banking liberalization could cause disruptions to some local banks, MAS decided to progressively open up the banking sector to foreign competition over a five-year period. Similarly, the Singapore dollar has been liberalized gradually to minimize the exchange rate instability.

Last, but not least, Singapore has shown that financial reforms undertaken in close collaboration between government and the industry produce highly effective results. In the formulation and implementation of financial reforms, MAS has actively consulted the industry. Market practitioners are in the best position to help regulators keep abreast of latest developments in the industry. Constructive dialogues are essential to help regulators fine tune their policies and avoid costly mistakes. However, the relationship between the regulator and the regulated should be at arm's length and not adversarial.

6 CONCLUSIONS

With Asian currencies in turmoil, the issue of financial sector reforms is especially delicate. While liberalizing the financial sector may be painful to some market players, especially those who are relatively weak, it also confers substantial benefits on Singapore as a whole. After weighing the costs and benefits, MAS has recently liberalized the financial sector in the hope of transforming Singapore into one of the major financial centres of the world. However, financial sector reforms undertaken by Singapore are incremental and evolutionary, rather than dramatic or spectacular.

In the longer term, liberalizing the financial sector should not only help Singapore to boost its financial stature, but also enable it to play a pivotal role in the economic reconstruction and rehabilitation of the region. A concern that has been frequently articulated in the aftermath of the Asian financial crisis is the excessive reliance of companies in the region on bank financing, as domestic bond markets are not well developed. An important component of the reform package suggested by multilateral agencies, such as the World Bank, the Asian Development Bank and the IMF, is the development of the domestic bond market. Because of the smallness of its domestic market, Singapore should strive to develop as the centre not only for Singapore dollar bonds, but also for the issue and trading of regional currency bonds. Developing a strong Singapore dollar bond is the crucial first step that should set the ball rolling. Despite the substantial progress that has been made, Singapore has a long way to go as its dollar bond market is still small and inactive.

There is tremendous scope for Singapore to develop not only the bond market but also the derivatives market. Over the next decade or so, Asian governments will need to borrow huge sums of money to finance fiscal deficits to rebuild their ravaged economies as well as to restructure and recapitalize their hard-hit financial institutions. Private companies in the region will demand a massive amount of funds to build their productive capacities which have been neglected during the Asian financial crisis. Having learned the hard way from the crisis, these borrowers will increasingly turn to longer-term sources like the bond markets in order to better match longer-term investment outlays with longer-term capital market instruments. They are also expected to rely on financial derivatives to hedge their interest rate and exchange rate risks. Singapore should be well poised to meet their needs provided that it is able to compete with other financial centres like Hong Kong and Tokyo. The gradual liberalization of Singapore's financial sector is a step in the right direction and may be viewed as part of a longer-term strategic goal to make Singapore into the premier capital and derivatives market of the region.

NOTES

1. See 'New approach to regulating and developing Singapore's financial sector', a Speech delivered by the Chairman of MAS, B.G. Lee Hsien Loong on 4 November 1997, SESDAQ 10th Anniversary Dinner, Singapore.
2. Only the issue of currency is entrusted to a separate body, the Board of Commissioners of Currency of Singapore (BCCS).
3. MAS has acknowledged, albeit belatedly, that its rules to discourage the internationalization of the Singapore dollar have constrained the growth of the bond market. See the Speech 'Financial sector liberalization: going global' by B.G. Lee Hsien Loong, 3 April 2000, MAS Work Plan Seminar, Singapore.
4. Currently, there are 140 commercial banks of which eight are local banks. All local banks have a full licence. Among the 132 foreign banks, 23 have full licences, 16 have restricted licences and 93 have offshore licences.
5. The first ACU licence was granted to Bank of America as far back as 1968.
6. In addition, profits from the domestic banking business are taxed at the corporate tax rate, currently at 26 per cent, while profits from the ACU are taxed at only 10 per cent.

7. Qualifying offshore banks approved by MAS may extend their Singapore dollar loans up to S$1 billion.
8. Before the introduction of QFBs, Citibank, NA and Standard Chartered Bank were full-licence foreign banks, while ABN Amro Bank NV and Banque Nationale de Paris had only offshore licences.
9. See the Speech 'Financial sector review: a round-up and next steps', by B.G. Lee Hsien Loong, 27 November 1998, Financial Sector Review Group Appreciation Dinner, Singapore.
10. Qualifying offshore banks will also be allowed to engage in Singapore dollar swaps, without any restriction on the purpose of the swaps.
11. After foreign company listing rules were liberalized, US dollar-denominated Osprey Maritime and GP Batteries managed to convert to local currency shares. See 'More S$ listings with new MAS rules', in *The Straits Times*, 14 August 1998, p. 1.
12. Captive insurers are set up by multinational corporations to underwrite in-house insurance for their affiliated companies.
13. See, for example, 'Why banks offer home loans at "suicide" rates', in *The Business Times*, 19 April 2001, p. 3.
14. See 'Singapore poised to be world's third-largest forex centre', in *The Straits Times*, 25 May 2001, p. 17.
15. See the MAS's statement 'Liberalizing commercial banking and upgrading local banks', 17 May 1999.
16. These include Singapore dollar bank deposits, Singapore dollar bonds, as well as Singapore shares and properties.
17. Monetary Authority of Singapore, *Monthly Statistical Bulletin*, February 2001, Vol. 22, No. 2, p. 16.
18. See Chan and Ngiam (1998) for a discussion on how Singapore coped with currency crises.
19. See *The Straits Times*, 17 March 1998, p. 7.

REFERENCES

Ayuso, Juan and Soledad Nunez (1995), 'Do financial derivatives destabilise the spot market? The Spanish experience in the government debt market', *Economic Bulletin*, Banco de Espana, April, pp. 71–77.

Baldauf, B. and G.J. Santoni (1991), 'Stock price volatility: some evidence from an arch model', *Journal of Futures Markets*, **11**, pp. 191–200.

Bank for International Settlements (1995), *Central Bank Survey of Foreign Exchange Market Activity*, Basle: B15.

Bortz, G.A. (1984), 'Does the treasury bond futures market destabilize the treasury bond cash market', *Journal of Futures Markets*, **4**, pp. 25–38.

Cassard, Marcel (1994), 'The role of offshore centers in international financial intermediation', IMF Working Paper, No. WP/94/107.

Chan, Kenneth S. and Kee-Jin Ngiam (1996), 'Currency speculation and the optimum control of bank lending in Singapore dollars: a case for partial liberalization', IMF Working Paper, No. WP/96/95.

Chan, Kenneth S. and Kee-Jin Ngiam (1998), 'Currency crises and the modified currency board system', *Pacific Economic Review*, **3** (3), pp. 243–63.

Claessens, S. and T. Glaessner (1998), 'Internationalization of financial services in Asia', mimeo, World Bank.

Edwards, F. (1988), 'Does futures trading increase stock market volatility?', *Financial Analysts Journal*, **44**, pp. 63–70.

Figlewski, S. (1981), 'GNMA passthrough securities futures trading and volatility in the GNMA market', *Journal of Finance*, **36**, pp. 445–56.
Friedman, Milton (1953), 'The case for flexible exchange rates', in *Essays in Positive Economics*, Chicago: University of Chicago Press, pp. 157–203.
Hodgson, A. and D. Nicholls (1991), 'The impact of index futures trading on Australian sharemarket volatility', *Journal of Business and Financial Accounting*, **18**, pp. 27–51.
Krugman, Paul (1979), 'A model of balance of payments crises', *Journal of Money, Credit and Banking*, **11**, pp. 311–32.
Lee, S.B. and K.Y. Ohk (1992), 'Does futures trading increase stock market volatility?', the US, Japan, the UK and Hong Kong', *Review of Futures Markets*, **5**, pp. 727–53.
Levine, R. (1996), 'Foreign banks, financial development and economic growth', in Barfield, C.E. (ed.), *International Financial Markets*, Washington, DC: American Enterprise Institute, pp. 224–54.
Monetary Authority of Singapore, *Annual Reports*, various issues.
Moriati, E.J. and P.A. Tosini (1985), 'Futures trading and the price volatility of GNMA certificates: further evidence', *Journal of Futures Markets*, **5**, pp. 633–41.
Ngiam, Kee Jin (1996), 'Singapore as a financial center: new developments, challenges, and prospects', in Ito, Takatoshi and Anne O. Krueger (eds), *Financial Deregulation and Integration in East Asia*, University of Chicago Press, pp. 359–83.
Ngiam, Kee Jin (1998), 'Liberalising the Singapore dollar during the Asian currency crisis: a sound move?', *Malaysian Journal of Economic Studies*, **35**, pp. 15–28.
Obstfeld, Maurice (1986), 'Rational and self-fulfilling balance of payments crises', *American Economic Review*, **76**, pp. 72–81.
Robinson, G. (1993), The effect of futures trading on cash market volatility: evidence from the London Stock Exchange', Working Paper Series No. 19, Bank of England.
Ross, S. (1976), 'Options and Efficiency', *Quarterly Journal of Economics*, **90**, pp. 75–89.
Senivongs, Chirathep (1997), 'Currency internationalisation in selected ASEAN countries', unpublished Monograph.
Simpson, W.G. and T.C. Ireland (1985), 'The impact of financial futures on the cash market for treasury bills', *Journal of Financial and Quantitative Analysis*, **20**, pp. 371–9.
The Straits Times, various issues.
Vittas, D. (1991), 'Measuring commercial bank efficiency: use and misuse of bank operating ratios', Policy Research Working Paper No. 806, World Bank.

10. Financial reform in Thailand

Andy Mullineux, Victor Murinde and Adisorn Pinijkulviwat*

1 INTRODUCTION

The Bank of Thailand (BoT) was founded on 10 December 1942 to serve as the central bank of the Thai Kingdom. It was entrusted with a broad range of functions: to issue currency; to safeguard the value of money; to promote monetary stability and a sound financial structure; to promote economic growth; to act as the bankers' bank and provide lender of last resort facilities; and to act as banker and financial adviser to the government.[1] During most of its history, the BoT played an important role in promoting the development of financial markets in Thailand. However, following the Asian financial crisis which broke out in 1997, the BoT became vulnerable as Thailand started to experience a severe economic crisis. The crisis derailed all ongoing financial reforms and directly crippled the banking sector, the stock exchange and the foreign exchange market (McKinnon and Pill, 1998). Regarding the banking sector, the major problems associated with the crisis included: failure of financial institutions; insufficient bank liquidity and inadequate capital; high non-performing loans; and loss of momentum in rebuilding confidence among international investors, depositors and economic development organizations, potentially limiting future capital flows into Thailand. In this context, it is interesting to examine how a traditional central bank, like the BoT, is able to cope with a financial crisis of a magnitude far beyond its stipulated role.

Within the broader context of financial reforms and central bank regulation, this chapter examines the role played by the BoT in trying to cope with the financial crisis that hit Thailand in the summer of 1997. The emphasis is on the banking sector rather than the financial markets.

In what follows, the chapter is structured into six sections. Section 2 describes financial liberalization attempts and consequences in Thailand, especially with respect to interest rate and exchange rate liberalization. Section 3 focuses on extensions of the scope of banking and financial institution operations. The financial sector masterplan, which was conceived before the financial crisis, is discussed in Section 4. Section 5 examines the 1997 financial crisis and its impact on financial reforms. Restructuring and regulatory reform after the crisis are discussed in Section 6. Section 7 concludes.

2 FINANCIAL LIBERALIZATION

The Reregulation of Commercial Banking

Commercial banks dominate the financial system in Thailand, with a 73 per cent share of both household savings and credits extended by all financial institutions.[2] Local commercial banks and branches of foreign banks are governed by the Commercial Banking Act of 1962 together with the amendments made in 1979, 1985 and 1992. The first two amendments were designed to improve and revise the 1962 Act in order to make it more efficient and suitable to changing circumstances so that public interest could be protected. The main aim of the 1992 amendment was to introduce the capital adequacy standards of the Basle Committee (Laurisden, 1998).

Prior to the 1962 Act, foreign banks were allowed to open sub-branches; however, after 1962, the banks were not allowed to extend sub-branches in the Thai Kingdom.[3] In addition, the BoT became very restrictive in terms of granting licences to new local banks. Hence, domestic banks and branches of foreign banks remained low in number; for example, by the end of December 1993, only 15 local banks and 13 branches of foreign banks were operating in the Kingdom.

The major shareholders of domestic commercial banks mostly belonged to a group of families. For example, Bangkok Bank, the largest bank in the country with a market share of 21 per cent, belonged to the Sophonpanich family. The third largest bank with a market share of 13 per cent, the Thai Farmers Bank, belonged to the Lumsum family. The Bank of Ayuthaya, the fifth largest bank with a market share of 8 per cent, belonged to the Ruthanaruk family. There was only one state-owned bank, the Krung Thai Bank, which was the second largest bank in the Kingdom and held a market share of 15 per cent. The fourth largest bank, the Siam Commercial Bank, had a market share of 9 per cent; it was owned by the crown property. Family-owned banks were generally managed by a group of family members and mainly extended loans to the businesses of their executives and related persons. However, by 1979 commercial banks had gradually become public companies, although the family group still remained the major shareholders of banks indirectly. By 1994, the local commercial banks had expanded branches to the whole Kingdom with a network of 1,709 branches in 1983 to 2,838 branches in 1994, operating 2,320 ATMs throughout the country (Bank of Thailand, 1999).

It is useful to compare the scenario in 1994 with that in 1998. While, at the end of 1994, Thai commercial banks held a market share in deposits of 98 per cent, by 1998 the figure was 96 per cent. The market share for creditors was 88 per cent in 1994 but had fallen to 85 per cent by 1998; the branches of foreign banks, however, increased their market share from 12 per cent by 1994 to 15 per cent by 1998, as the confidence in local banks fell. In general, as shown in Table 10.1, commercial bank lending for personal consumption fell; there was also a decline in lending to real estate business, exports, agriculture, other financial services and wholesale and retail trade. However, the share of total lending to manufacturing, construction, imports and public utilities increased in 1998 compared to the 1994 base level.[4] Moreover, in 1998 commercial banks introduced electronic banking by providing deposit and withdrawal services through an on-line system to branches in almost all provinces, with over 2,320 ATMs (automated teller machines) in two pools namely, BANKNET and SIAMNET; these were used to provide out-of-hours deposit and withdrawal facilities nationwide. Swift, used for the transfer of funds among banks throughout the world, was introduced in 1985.

Table 10.1 Bills, loans and overdrafts of commercial banks, classified by sector

Sector	Year 1994	Share %	Year 1998	Share %
1. Agriculture	152.3	4	146.6	3
2. Mining	15.7	1	32.2	1
3. Manufacturing	836.2	24	1,606.3	30
4. Construction	142.0	4	264.8	5
5. Real estate business	364.2	11	506.1	10
6. Imports	115.7	3	192.5	4
7. Exports	166.5	5	174.0	3
8. Wholesale and retail trade	672.7	18	867.5	16
9. Public utilities	86.3	2	189.7	4
10. Other financial business	245.2	7	263.4	5
11. Services	268.4	8	418.6	8
12. Personal consumption	437.5	13	595.0	11
13. Others	–	–	–	–
14. Total	3,502.7	100	5,256.7	100

Note: Loan values are in billions of baht; shares are in sectoral percentages of the total.

Source: Bank of Thailand (1999).

Reforming the Exchange Rate System

The main reform of the Thai exchange rate system can be traced back to immediately after the Second World War when, due to economic difficulties and a serious shortage of foreign exchange, Thailand was forced to adopt a multiple exchange rate system. However, in 1963 the economic situation improved and the exchange rate regime was switched to a par value system such that the value of the baht was fixed in terms of gold. In order to maintain the baht parity, the Exchange Equalization Fund (EEF) was established with the aim of stabilizing exchange rate movements within prescribed margins. The successful operation of the EEF enabled full parity of the baht to be maintained for 15 years or so.

However, in 1978 the volatility of major world currencies forced the BoT to adjust the exchange rate, and the par value system was abolished. A system of pegging the baht to a basket of major currencies (in which the US dollar weight was 0.85) was introduced. The new system allowed greater flexibility in exchange rate adjustments to reflect more accurately economic and monetary conditions. It also facilitated the stability of the baht since the currency was no longer tied to any particular currencies. The system operated smoothly until 1981 when signs of trouble began to emerge due to the strong appreciation of the US dollar relative to other currencies. The baht depreciated rapidly, and although the government devalued the currency twice in mid-1981, public confidence could not be restored. However, in July 1981, a decision on the daily fixing was made, and the EEF fixed the exchange rate of the US dollar at 23 baht. This rate was held fixed until 1984 when the government announced a replacement of the dollar-pegging system by pegging the baht to a basket of currencies.

But it was not until 21 May 1990 that the BoT took the most important step in the process of exchange rate deregulation by accepting the obligations under Article VIII of the Articles of Agreement of the International Monetary Fund (IMF), and implementing the first phase of exchange control relaxation. The aim was to liberalize the foreign exchange system in line with the globalization of the economic and financial systems, and allow freedom of international capital movements. Specifically, exchange rate deregulation was implemented in three main phases.

- Phase I of the exchange control deregulation began on 21 May 1990 by allowing commercial banks to process customers' applications for the purchase of foreign currency for trade-related transactions, that is, imports and exports without prior approval from the BoT.[5]
- Phase II of the exchange rate deregulation began on 1 April 1991 by allowing greater flexibility to private businesses and the general

public in the purchase or sale of foreign exchange. All exchange controls were abolished and new forms were introduced for reporting purposes only. A limit of US$10 million was allowed for an annual investment for one person and for the acquisition of real estate and stocks overseas. Foreign funds, on the other hand, were allowed to move in and out of the country freely.

- Phase III began on 30 April 1992 to further provide more convenience for the public, and exporters in particular. Exporters were allowed to receive and make payment in baht in addition to foreign currencies, and to transfer foreign currency deposits for overseas debt payment.[6]

Capital flows responded in stylized fashion (Fry and Murinde, 1998). After the flotation of the baht currency in July 1997, net capital outflows peaked in the third quarter of 1997 and the baht currency kept on depreciating against the US dollar until it reached 55 baht per US dollar in January 1998. It then stabilized at around 36–40 baht per US dollar from the fourth quarter of 1998 onward. Although short-term nominal interest rates climbed to more than 20 per cent during the crisis, low confidence and exchange rate uncertainties led to huge capital outflows through non-renewal and repayment of short-term loans towards the end of 1997 through to 1998. The net outflows of private capital at the end of 1997 accounted for US$8.4 billion and continued to increase to more than US$16.0 billion in 1998. The banking sector, including the Bangkok International Banking Facilities (BIBFs), shouldered the biggest impact of the financial crisis. The commercial banks recorded a net outflow of US$4.7 billion in 1997, but this dropped in 1998 to US$4.3 billion. The BIBFs followed with net outflows of US$1.7 billion in 1997, peaking in 1998 at US$9.6 billion. Table 10.2 reports the private financial net flow position in Thailand during 1994–98.

By the end of 1999, the surging volume of foreign exchange activities and derivatives trading made it necessary to strengthen prudential supervision in this area. The BoT imposed net foreign exchange position limits and provided guidelines to reinforce existing internal control procedures and practices widely utilized by commercial banks in monitoring and controlling their foreign exchange activities. In 1999, the required ratio for commercial banks was limited within the range of 15 per cent of the net overbought (asset) position to 15 per cent for the net oversold (liability) position.

Financial liberalization through the BIBF considerably increased short-term debts since most of the credits were on a short-term basis and continually rolled over for long-term use. The deterioration of investor confidence and deceleration of economic growth made foreign creditors unwilling to

Table 10.2 Net private financial flows into Thailand (billions of US$)

	1994	1995	1996	1997	1998
1. Banks	13.9	11.2	5.0	−6.4	13.9
Commercial banks	3.8	3.1	0.4	−4.7	−4.2
BIBF	10.1	8.1	4.6	−1.7	−9.6
2. Non-banks	−1.9	9.6	13.2	−1.9	−2.0
Direct investment	0.9	1.2	1.5	3.2	4.7
Other loans	−5.6	1.5	5.5	−3.7	−4.3
Portfolio investment	1.1	3.3	3.5	4.5	0.5
Non-resident baht A/C	2.0	3.4	2.9	−5.9	−2.7
Trade credits	0.5	0.3	−0.1	−0.2	−0.5
Others	−0.6	−0.1	0.02	0.3	0.02
Net private capital inflow	12.0	20.8	18.2	−8.4	−16.0

Source: Bank of Thailand (1999).

roll over BIBF credits. The volatile exchange rates motivated borrowers to repay loans, resulting in high net capital outflows throughout the second half of 1997 and 1998.

Interest Rate Liberalization

As Lensink et al. (1998) have shown, interest rate liberalization is the key policy instrument used by many developing countries that wish to embark on financial liberalization. In Thailand, the liberalization of interest rates was conceived and implemented as a three-year plan (1990–93) aimed at enabling the banking system to adjust to changing demand and supply, both domestically and externally. With continuous economic expansion since 1987, there was apparent need to mobilize long-term and stable funds for national development. When it was evident that long-term deposits had not expanded in line with borrowing needs, the BoT deemed it appropriate to lift the ceiling rate on term deposits exceeding one-year maturity from the previous ceiling of 9.5 per cent to 10.5–11.0 per cent per annum in June 1989 in order to accelerate the process of savings mobilization. The gradual process of deregulation was aimed at allowing time for financial institutions and the public to make the necessary adjustments without major disruption.

With regard to the ceilings on other types of deposits, the BoT continued the interest rate liberalization policy. Ceilings on deposits for all maturity periods were abolished on 16 March 1990. On 8 January 1992, the BoT announced the removal of the ceiling on savings deposit rates. In June 1992, the BoT fixed the ceiling rate on promissory notes issued by finance companies and *credit foncier* (land banks). Competition for deposit mobilization in the form of attractive offer rates followed as a result of the liberalization process. This factor increased pressure for the ceiling on lending rates to be freely determined according to the prevailing liquidity positions while also minimizing adverse impacts on borrowers. After 1992, interest rates followed a downward trend and the timing was right to remove the lending rate ceilings for commercial banks, finance companies and *credit foncier* companies.

The lifting of the lending rate ceiling became effective on 1 June 1992, allowing domestic interest rates to fully adjust in accordance with demand and supply conditions. From January 1993, the BoT began to implement measures to encourage commercial banks to reduce their lending rates for general customers in response to changes in the cost of deposits. It managed to do so by requesting cooperation from commercial banks and cutting the bank rate twice, in June and September. As a result, commercial banks responded by reducing both their deposit rates and their lending rates and thus, narrowing the differential between the lending rate for general customers and the one-year time deposit rate to 6.75 per cent in September 1993. However, the BoT did not wish to lead or intervene in the operation of commercial banks every time, but wanted to establish an adjustment mechanism for the lending rate for retail customers to automatically adjust to the actual cost of funds, as determined by the market mechanism. The BoT and the Thai Bankers' Association set up a working group to study and determine the benchmark for the lending rate for retail customers. Finally, the working group agreed to introduce the minimum retail rate (MRR) as a reference lending rate for retail customers.[7] The commercial banks and branches of the foreign banks began to announce the MRR from the end of October, and the MRR was adopted by all banks in mid-November 1993. During the month when the MRR became effective, the interest margin between the lending rate for retail customers and the one-year deposit rate rose to 7.5 per cent, as commercial banks cut the deposit rate by more than the lending rate. Nevertheless, since the profit margin for retail customers was set at not more than 2 per cent, banks were forced to adjust by lowering the rates on both loans and deposits. Moreover, the lending at lower interest rates by the BIBF in the domestic market enhanced the stiff competition among banks and enabled borrowers to acquire cheaper loans.

In May 1997 the MLR (minimum loan rate) and the MRR were allowed to move freely according to the market mechanism in order to help stimulate the economy. The BoT asked the commercial banks to set the MLR limit in line with market conditions and the MRR, as well as the cost of funds, to reflect the risk differentials between the wholesale and retail customers. However, as the competition among financial institutions increased and customers were offered higher rates on both deposits and loans, difficulties arose in liquidity management because of the high cost of funds to the banks. In June–July 1997, the BoT temporarily limited the ceiling on time deposits to 12–14 per cent to reduce the high lending and deposit rates in order to maintain stability in the financial system.

Interest rates started to go up by late 1996, when the weakness in economic indicators, especially in the current account deficit, began to appear (see Table 10.3). The BoT was forced to maintain high interest rates to help support the baht currency, and to raise funds to bail out ailing finance companies through the Financial Institutions Development Fund (FIDF). The policy continued until the flotation of the baht in July 1997. Thailand then sought assistance from the IMF and had to follow the advice that high interest rates were necessary to help reverse the outflow of capital and stabilize the currency. As shown in Table 10.3, the interbank rate peaked in the third quarter of 1997 through the second quarter of 1998 at between 18 and 20 per cent, and began to fall to only 3.8 per cent at the end of the fourth quarter of 1998. The interbank rate bottomed out at around 1–2 per cent at the end of 1999.

Table 10.3 Movements in interest rates and exchange rates during the reform period

Year	Interbank interest rate (%)	Exchange rate (baht per US$)
1994	6.41	24.99
1995	10.17	25.12
1996Q1	7.30	25.23
1996Q2	7.24	25.28
1996Q3	11.41	25.30
1996Q4	10.97	25.46
1997Q1	11.31	25.84
1997Q2	11.99	25.87
1997Q3	19.32	32.95
1997Q4	20.15	40.71
1998Q1	20.64	47.11
1998Q2	18.03	40.33
1998Q3	9.52	41.06
1998Q4	3.84	36.05

Source: IMF (2000), Thailand, country pages.

Nevertheless, in July 1998, when the economy started to cool down, the BoT allowed commercial banks to adjust interest rates more freely by using the reference rate.[8] Interest payable on saving deposits was made subject to the reference rate plus not more than a 2 per cent mark-up, while time deposits of over 3 months were made subject to the reference rate plus not more than a 3 per cent mark-up. All the rates had to be disclosed, and the new rules applied to the head office and all branches. In addition, the central bank issued a new long-term government bond to refinance the liabilities of the FIDF. This helped to support the downward trend of short-term money market rates. Market liquidity improved markedly throughout 1999, allowing market interest rates to decline further. Deposit interest rates peaked at 14–15 per cent in 1998, but fell from 6–7 per cent in early 1999 to 3–4 per cent at the end of 1999 (Vatikiotis and Keenan, 1999).

3 EXTENSIONS OF THE SCOPE OF BANKING AND FINANCIAL INSTITUTION OPERATIONS

Encouraging Banks to Open Branches or Participate in Joint Ventures Abroad

In order to support Bangkok as the financial centre in the region, the BoT allowed the commercial banks to open branches in Laos, Kampuchea, Vietnam and Burma, as well as Mainland China. These branches could provide banking services not only to the local community, but also to Thai investors or foreign investors who use Thailand as a gateway or springboard to the region. Also, they would gather or collect prime information or data for new investors in Thailand.

On the other hand, in regions where branches are not permitted or where it was quite risky to open them due to the unfamiliar economic systems or the differences in language, joint ventures in banking businesses were encouraged to facilitate entry. In addition, local commercial banks were also allowed to open branches or set up wholly-owned subsidiaries in financial centres such as Singapore and the Cayman Islands. These could be used to tap cheap funds for their BIBF offices in Bangkok, which would enable the Thai BIBF offices to compete efficiently with foreign BIBFs.

Relaxation of Constraints on Financial Institution Portfolio Management

Since 1970, financial institutions have been required to contribute to rural development and overall development of the economy. Commercial banks, including branches of foreign banks, were required to fulfil the agricultural credit target, and branch opening requirements were imposed on domestic banks. Rural branches of domestic banks were required to extend at least 60 per cent of their deposits as credit to local people, and of this amount not less then 20 per cent must be lent to the agricultural sector. However, from 1990 the structure and economic environment of the country has changed tremendously. Consequently, the BoT deemed it appropriate to diminish its role of intervening in the decision-making process of financial institutions. In retrospect, the intervention policy could be perceived as unfair to the financial institutions concerned as well as to customers and other economic sectors.

During the 1990–93 three-year plan, the BoT streamlined and eliminated certain requirements imposed on financial institutions while retaining only those needed to maintain the stability and solvency of the financial system. This was intended to provide greater flexibility in the management of financial institutions and thereby to reduce their costs of operation, increase the quality of their assets and engender greater competition.

Streamlining the Rural Credit Policy

In the past, the BoT set targets for commercial banks, including the branches of foreign banks, to allocate credits in proportion to total deposits for agricultural enterprises. In 1987, however, a new definition and a new set of ratios were imposed on the so-called 'rural credit' policy. After 1987, the structure of the country's agricultural production shifted towards small-scale industries and the services sector. To give commercial banks greater flexibility in asset management and in responding to the government's policy to support regional small-scale industries, the BoT modified the rural credit policy to cover a wider scope of activities than the narrowly defined agricultural activities. Moreover, in January 1991, the BoT broadened the coverage of rural credits to include credits for wholesale trading of agricultural produce and regional industrial estates. In 1992, the definition was further broadened to include credits for the secondary occupation of farmers, and the export of farm products.

The Change in the Computation of Reserve Requirements

With effect from 23 June 1991, the BoT relaxed the constraints on commercial banks' portfolio management by replacing the reserve requirement ratio with the liquidity ratio.[9] This provided greater flexibility in relation to investment options and asset management. It should be noted, however, that since the BoT had not made full use of the reserve ratio as an instrument of monetary policy (as distinct from prudential control), the change, in effect, had no significant monetary policy implication.

Widening the Scope of Operation of Financial Institutions

In the 1990s, the BoT formulated policies to permit financial institutions to broaden their range of activities and to fully utilize their resources and expertise. Consumers of financial services stand to benefit from the greater variety of financial services as well as greater competition among financial institutions. Under existing conditions, where financial institutions compete on the basis of deposit as well as lending rates, the margin between the lending and deposit rates has narrowed from about 6 per cent in 1990 to 4 per cent in 1994, while the cost for administration is not less than 2 per cent. Financial institutions, therefore, had to seek revenue from fee-based income. Hence, broadening the scope of operation of financial institutions will benefit both the public and the financial institutions themselves. Nevertheless, the policy to broaden the scope of operation of financial institutions was undertaken in gradual steps, with due regard being paid to the efficiency and readiness as well as available expertise of financial institutions. The solvency and stability of the financial system, along with improved procedures for supervision and examination, will also be taken into account, along with customer protection.

In terms of widening the scope of banking business, it is useful to note that financial institutions' supervision in Thailand had always placed great emphasis on prudential control. Commercial banks were therefore not permitted to engage in businesses that were considered highly risky, or in those that required specialized skills. However, the financial liberalization policy increased competition among commercial banks. The new environment forced commercial banks to change their business perspectives and to seek fee-based income to boost their profits. From 1987, the BoT deemed it necessary to allow commercial banks to conduct business related to banking business.[10] Moreover, in 1992, commercial banks were permitted to jointly establish mutual funds management companies with local finance companies and foreign analysts with expertise in managing mutual funds. In the 1992–98 period they were allowed to conduct more businesses: for example, to act as agents to sell the government's and state enterprises' debt instruments such as bonds, debenture and commercial papers; to provide economic, financial and investment information services; to provide financial and advisory services; arranging, selling and trading debt instruments; to act as agents for secured and unsecured debenture holders; to act as trustees to mutual funds, securities registrars and as selling agents of unit trusts; to purchase and sell certificates of deposit; to receive orders to purchase or sell unit trusts to be delivered to the security companies or finance and security companies; to allow foreign branches of domestic banks to manage mutual funds for investment or international development; to manage provident funds and personal funds; to act as agents for collecting loans; to manage the project for securitization to be submitted to the Security Exchange Commission; and to purchase or transfer loan debtors. In addition, in June 1999, the BoT granted permission for commercial banks to act as agents to operate securities borrowing and lending business. Furthermore, in 1999, as a result of debt restructuring, the commercial banks were allowed to engage in the hire-purchase and leasing business for a trial period of three years.

In terms of widening the scope of financial conglomerates, it should be noted that in the past, banks' holdings in other companies were strictly limited to 10 per cent of the companies' shares sold. Thai commercial banks have, for various reasons, found it necessary to set up subsidiaries or affiliates to perform non-banking businesses. This has led some banks to shield their stake in the form of holding companies or nominees. In May 1994, the BoT recognized the need for transparency and consolidated supervision and announced that banks could seek the approval to hold shares exceeding the 10 per cent limit in the following cases. (In addition, the BoT has long imposed the maximum limit on portfolio investment to prevent excessive risk and concentration.) A commercial bank was allowed to hold an aggregate share value of up to 20 per cent of its first-tier capital. Once the BoT relaxed the 10 per cent limit on holding shares as well, so as to allow banks wider business opportunities, it became necessary to review this limitation. The BoT therefore allowed banks to hold an aggregate share value of up to 20 per cent of their total capital (instead of tier one capital). In addition, after the financial crisis of 1997, the proportion of non-performing loans in the financial system grew as a result of the economic deterioration and more stringent regulation on the classification of loans (Doukas et al., 1998). Debt restructuring helped contain the problem. As a result of debt restructuring, in November 1998, the BoT permitted financial institutions to hold shares exceeding 10 per cent of shares sold and 20 per cent of the aggregate share value on the condition that they reduce the shareholding to the legal limit within three years.

4 THE FINANCIAL SYSTEM MASTER PLAN (1995–2000)

The Background

The aim of the Financial System Master Plan was to guide the development of the financial system, facilitate policy coordination, and support the national economic development plans. The plan was set to run for five years, from 1 March 1995 to 29 February 2000. It was divided into two phases. Phase I, which included short-term plans, covered the period from March 1995 to February 1997. Phase II covered the medium- and long-term plan up to 2000.

The content of the Financial System Master Plan covered seven major areas.

- The first area was the expansion in the scope of operation of financial institutions. The idea was to enable private financial institutions, namely commercial banks, BIBFs, finance companies, *credit foncier* companies, securities companies and mutual fund management companies, to operate business in line with international best practice and to strengthen their competitiveness.
- The second area was the improvement of financial system structure. The aim was to ensure proper functioning of the money market as well as the capital market, in order to support the mobilization of savings, fund allocation and economic growth. It was also planned to establish three institutions, namely a Securities Finance Corporation (SFC), for extending credits to securities companies; a Special Purpose Vehicle (SPV) for paving the way of issuance of collateralized or asset-backed securities; and a municipal Bond Credit Guarantee Corporation for encouraging the issuance of municipal bonds instead of direct borrowings from banks.
- The third area related to enhancing competition and financial liberalization. The idea was to end oligopolistic practices and encourage competition in the financial system, paving the way for adhering to Thailand's agreed commitments under the General Agreement for Trade in Services (GATS). Consequently, by 1997, seven of the existing BIBFs had been upgraded to full branches.
- The fourth area included measures to support the government's provincial and rural development policy. Specialized financial institutions (SFIs) and private financial institutions (PFIs) were required to play important roles. SFIs were to set up a Rural Development Fund to provide new types of services, such as financing projects in the rural areas, particularly for infrastructure and educational projects, while PFIs (including commercial banks, finance and securities companies) were encouraged to open branches, sub-branches, credit extension offices and securities brokerage offices to facilitate the provision of services in the rural areas.
- The fifth area was the improvement of the efficiency of supervision of financial institutions. The idea was to take measures to enhance the efficiency of supervision, both in terms of regulatory guidelines

and techniques of supervision, in tandem with the process of financial liberalization and administrative expediency.

- The sixth area related to human resource development and promotion of business ethics in the financial industry. To alleviate the human resource constraint and elevate the quality of personnel in the financial services industry to meet the demands of the market, the authorities supported the work of private institutes in training and promoting business ethics among their employees, such as those run by the Thai Bankers' Association, the Association of Securities Companies, and the Securities Analysts Association.
- Finally, in order to achieve the goal of transforming Thailand into a regional financial centre, efforts were made to promote the BIBFs. It was also planned to introduce an electronic payments system as well as establish futures and options markets. However, the BIBFs later became the major contributors to the 1997 crisis.

Facilitation of New Entry (BIBFs and PIBFs)

Licensing of the BIBFs

Of all the financial liberalization measures, the development of offshore banking facilities, known as the BIBFs, was the most important for developing Bangkok as a regional financial centre. BIBFs were introduced in 1993 when the BoT perceived that the Thai financial system should be developed as a regional financial centre, given its stable economic conditions, liberal exchange rates and interest rates, as well as high international borrowing transactions. The BoT proposed the establishment of BIBFs in order to facilitate and reduce the cost of international borrowing, while encouraging foreign capital inflows to finance domestic investment as well as investment throughout the Indo-Chinese region. Initially, 46 BIBF licences were granted. Licensed banks could use foreign funds raised overseas to lend to their domestic customers (known as 'out–in' operations), or to overseas customers (known as 'out–out' operations). Apart from out–in and out–out operations, which were considered to be the core businesses, BIBFs were also allowed to provide other international banking services, such as cross-currency trading, trade financing on a strictly out–out operational basis, loan syndication arrangements, arranging the issue of debt instruments, and engaging in underwriting in foreign currencies. Regarding tax concessions, there were both reductions in tax rates and exemptions to help promote BIBFs. Corporate income tax was reduced from 30 to 10 per cent and stamp duties were exempted. Though BIBFs were required to maintain capital funds of not less than 100 million baht they were free to maintain the funds in any form of assets. Also, they were subject to setting provisions of not less than 0.25 per cent of outstanding loans, and were required to maintain the liquidity ratio on short-term borrowings of less than one year at not less than 6 per cent. However, they were allowed greater flexibility in their operations. The BoT relaxed all prudential regulations for commercial banks (including the branches of foreign banks), such as the capital adequacy ratio and the single lending limit. The relaxation was consistent with a view that BIBFs were supervised by the authorities of the country where the parent banks of BIBFs were located. In the early stages, the BIBFs' main operations consisted of out–in corporate finance. This indeed helped to alleviate the negative investment–savings gap, which stood at 7 per cent of GDP during the rapid growth of the economy.

At the end of November 1994, total BIBF loans outstanding stood at 481.8 billion baht (approximately US$19.3 billion), about 14.5 per cent of total loans including commercial banks. Of that amount, 417.5 billion baht (or about 86.6 per cent) was in out–in activities. The BIBFs of local banks accounted for 39.6 per cent, followed by 20.5 per cent of the BIBFs of foreign banks' branch, and 39.9 per cent of BIBFs previously without branches in Thailand. Among other businesses, the cross-currency business was the most active, followed by the loan arrangement business. At the end of 1996, BIBF lending amounted to 1,289 billion baht, an increase of 80 per cent from the previous year. Out–out lending demonstrated a substantial increase from 165 billion baht in 1995 to 482 billion baht in 1996, while out–in lending increased moderately from 541 billion baht in 1995 to 807 billion baht in 1996, accounting for 17 per cent of overall domestic credits. After the financial crisis in 1997, the out–in lending slowed down and tended to decline due to the cessation of lending to local borrowers (see Table 10.4).

As of 1998, the overall lending of BIBFs had fallen dramatically from 1,289 billion baht in 1996 to 914.0 billion baht and it further decreased to 600.0 billion baht by the end of November 1999. Out–out lending dropped sharply from 482.3 billion baht in 1996 to only 72.9 billion baht (a decrease of 85 per cent). Out–in lending also declined to a large extent, from 807.4 billion baht to only 527.1 billion baht (a decrease of 35 per cent), over the same period.

The financial crisis in 1997 was caused, in part, by the operation of BIBFs and could be attributed to the moral hazard induced by the fixed exchange rate system, in the sense that domestic borrowers did not find it necessary to hedge against foreign exchange risk (Abdalla and Murinde, 1997). In addition, the BIBFs were not restricted from lending to domestic borrowers in dollars. Thus, 'out–in' lending exposure grew very fast from 456.3 billion baht in 1994 to 1.4 trillion baht in 1997, much of it in

Table 10.4 Credit granted by BIBFs (including Thai banks, foreign branches and new BIBFs) (billion baht)

	1996	1997	1998	Nov. 99
Thai banks	330.2	513.2	211.9	108.4
Foreign branches	222.7	691.5	431.9	328.0
New BIBFs	254.5	206.9	121.7	90.7
out–in	807.4	1,411.6	765.5	527.1
Thai banks	16.3	35.4	28.9	21.7
Foreign branches	9.4	264.3	89.2	38.8
New BIBFs	456.6	171.1	30.4	12.4
out–out	482.3	470.8	148.5	72.9
Total	1,289.7	1,882.4	914.0	600.0

Source: Bank of Thailand (1999).

dollars. Shackled by the bad debts and with the economy moving into mild recession, banks sought to consolidate their balance sheets, restrict new lending and shore up their capital bases. The deepening economic recession caused the asset quality of all financial institutions to deteriorate further. Sharp declines in credit quality and falling earnings negatively impacted upon the efforts of all financial institutions to recapitalize. Given that most of the lending exposure of financial institutions in Thailand was collateral based, the banking system was badly exposed to the risk of asset price deflation.

Licensing the provincial international banking facilities (PIBFs)

Apart from promoting Bangkok to become a regional financial centre, it was also hoped that IBFs could be used as a tool in rural development, especially in terms of increasing competition in banking and in meeting the increasingly sophisticated needs of international trade and investment of domestic businesses. With this in mind, the Ministry of Finance and the BoT issued the notification relating to the operation of PIBFs in 1994. All existing BIBFs were eligible to apply for a licence.

In October 1996, seven BIBFs received approval to upgrade to banks: Banque National de Paris; Bank of Nova Scotia; Dresdner Bank AG; Industrial Bank of Japan; Dai-ichi Kangyo Bank; Sumitomo Bank; and the Bank of China.

5 THE 1997 FINANCIAL CRISIS AND ITS IMPACT ON FINANCIAL REFORMS

There is plenty of literature on the causes and symptoms of the Asian financial crisis in general, and the experience of Thailand in particular; see, for example, McKinnon and Pill (1998). Specifically, the poor supervision of commercial banks and finance companies by the BoT is widely seen as a key reason for the Thai economy's rapid collapse after the baht was floated in July 1997 (Vatikiotis, 1998), along with the aforementioned build-up of private international debt through the BIBFs. Shackled by the bad debts and with the economy moving into mild recession, banks sought to consolidate their balance sheets, restrict new lending and shore up their capital bases. The deepening economic recession caused the asset quality of all financial institutions to deteriorate further. Sharp declines in credit quality and falling earnings due to the economic downturn negatively impacted upon the efforts of all financial institutions to recapitalize. When the property and stock price boom were in full swing, financial institutions did not spend resources on valuing the underlying collateral because they believed that the gains would be substantial should the need for foreclosure arise.

Moreover, in 1998 the BoT tightened the asset classification and provisioning rules, aiming to further strengthen financial supervision and bring supervisory regulations in line with the international standards. The classification criteria would include on- and off-balance sheet items and would adopt 'three months past due loans' as the definition for non-performing loans (Doukas et al. 1998). The provisioning requirement was made such that banks had to set aside provisions of at least 20 per cent in each accounting period, and fully maintain these provisions by 2000. Recognition of accrued interest income was shortened from 12 months to conform with the new definition of non-performing loans. To facilitate the foreign inflow of funds for recapitalization, the restriction on foreign ownership in Thai financial institutions was relaxed, thereby allowing foreign entities to acquire up to 100 per cent ownership for ten years, after which they would be 'grandfathered' with respect to the absolute amount of their equity holding.

The economic downturn, together with the stringent regulations, made things even worse for the banking system. Heavy losses directly affected the ability to extend credits. Most financial institutions had to recapitalize to cover the increasing amount of non-performing loans. In connection with this, four banks which were financially vulnerable and could not recapitalize on their own, had to be nationalized; while the banks' management was replaced, and the existing shareholders' equity written off, to preserve the integrity of the financial system.

In solving the problem of non-performing loans in the financial system, which were continuously rising to an average of over 40 per cent at the end of 1998 due to the new loan classification system and the further economic downturn, new regulations for debt restructuring and collateral appraisal were issued as guidelines for banks. As part of an attempt to monitor the non-performing loans in the system more carefully, financial institutions were ordered to conduct qualitative reviews of their portfolios, both on- and off-balance sheet, and to submit a summary of the results to the BoT on a quarterly basis. In order to assist banks to recapitalize, on 14 August 1998 the BoT offered an assistance scheme for financial institutions which could not find partners for recapitalization. If financial institutions could comply with the new loan provisioning rules immediately, they would have the right to apply for assistance from the BoT to recapitalize their Tier 1 capital. Moreover, financial institutions were allowed to apply for assistance in recapitalizing Tier 2, if they undertook debt restructuring.

At the end of 1998, privately-owned asset management companies (PAMCs), which were set up by financial institutions solely or jointly with investors, were allowed to segregate their non-performing loans. The Thai Farmers Bank led the way by setting up its own PAMC, followed by Siam Commercial bank.

6 RESTRUCTURING AND REGULATORY REFORM

New Institutions Formed to Cope with the Post-1997 Financial Crisis

The Asset Management Corporation (AMC)

The AMC was established on 22 October 1997 in accordance with the Emergency Degree on Asset Management Corporations B.E. 2540. The corporation was established to take over and manage all the assets of the 56 closed finance companies left-over from the Financial Restructuring Authority (FRA) auctions or from the Property Loan Management Organization, as well as to purchase or receive non-performing assets from the Financial Institutions Development Fund. In order to help improve the quality of loans, it could also lend to debtors to enable them to continue in business. Initially, the capital fund of 1,000 million baht came from the Ministry of Finance, and it was given permission by the cabinet to issue bonds worth 12,000 million baht to finance the purchase of assets from the FRA.

In March 1999, the AMC purchased assets from the FRA with a principal outstanding value of 185 million baht for 31.2 billion baht, which was a steep discount. The AMC issued promissory notes of five years maturity in exchange for the assets purchased from the FRA. The AMC had a limited number of options in managing the assets, including debt restructuring and debt to equity conversion. It had to follow prescribed steps in order to help liquidate the assets purchased. First, it focused on debt-restructuring deals of about 5–10 billion baht with real estate developers. Second, it sold non-core assets such as vehicles, yachts and resort houses. Third, it sold factories, developed-land plots, and assets which could produce cash as soon as possible. Then it sold low-demand assets. For all the sales, the AMC made sure that all assets were sold to buyers on condition that the debtors could buy them back later. Lastly, the AMC calculated the value of non-collateralized assets in order to estimate the proportion of loans which would be converted to equity, rescheduled or written off.

Until about 2004, the AMC will manage the debts, given that some of the promissory notes mature by that date. Therefore, the AMC needs all the debtors to repay loans by 2004. In some cases, debtors need to issue debentures to cover payment to the AMC, which can then sell the debentures.

The private asset management companies (PAMCs)

The Emergency Decree on Asset Management Companies B.E. 2541 allowed a limited company that wished to register as a PAMC to apply for registration as an asset management company. The scope of business of PAMCs focused on the purchasing of the non-performing assets from financial institution and related businesses; this was limited to no more than either the outstanding debt in contracts or the appraised value of collateral, whichever value was lower. In order to rehabilitate the debtors, PAMCs were allowed to engage in any related businesses, such as lending, collecting interest and fees, securitization, restructuring, holding shares, debt for equity swaps, renting and leasing, as well as property development, or other businesses approved by the BoT. The sources of funds came from borrowing locally or abroad and the issuance of securities, including shares and debentures as well as debt instruments. The rationale behind the issuance of the Emergency Decree was that financial institutions had a lot of low-quality assets that obstructed their recapitalization and also had an adverse affect on their ability to lend. Full economic recovery was impossible unless non-performing loans were reduced and financial institutions were able to resume lending. So it was deemed appropriate to separate low-quality assets for sale or transfer to other legal entities. This allowed banks to manage non-performing loans more effectively and press borrowers to restructure credits. In order to attract the establishment of such legal entities, in October 1999 the cabinet deemed it appropriate to give waivers on transfer fees arising from debt restructuring and on specific business taxes levied on interest revenues gained from bank lending to management companies. In 1999, the Thai Farmers Bank started to operate a PAMC called the Thonburi AMC, and this was followed by the Jatujak AMC of Siam Commercial Bank.

The implication of the above experience is that the BoT has to enforce strict regulatory rules and monitor the PAMCs to ensure that their operations and the asset transfers are conducted in line with the regulatory standards. In cases where the commercial banks directly or indirectly hold shares in PAMCs of more than 50 per cent, the commercial banks have to draft consolidated balance sheets, and the assets transferred have to be sold by 2010.

The Radanasin Bank

The Radanasin Bank was established under the Commercial Banking Act B.E. 2505, as amended by the Commercial Banking Act (No. 3) B.E. 2535 on 23 February 1998. The initial registered capital of 4,000 million baht was fully paid by the Ministry of Finance. It was raised finally to 12,500 million baht at the end of December 1998. The Radanasin Bank was mandated to purchase the good assets of 56 closed finance companies from FRA. As well as managing the good assets from the closed finance companies, it could also lend to debtors to enable them to continue their businesses. However, because the Radanasin Bank had very limited resources, its main objective was not fulfilled.

As the financial crisis became severe, the status of financial institutions continued to deteriorate. Non-performing loans and the provisions that were made in accordance with the regulations of the BoT continued to increase. Some financial institutions remained unable to raise capital to meet the Basle capital adequacy ratio. The initial policy of maintaining Radanasin as a good bank had to be reviewed. The Financial Institutions Development Fund, on behalf of the government, had to intervene by taking over the ailing financial institutions, especially banks. It was decided to merge the newly acquired banks with the existing state-owned banks and finance companies. With the approval of the cabinet, the merger of the ailing Laemthong Bank with the Radanasin Bank took place on 16 November 1998 – the combined bank was called the Radanasin Bank.

In order to manage and rearrange shareholdings in financial institutions efficiently, on 16 March 1999, the cabinet approved the sale of the ordinary shares of Radanasin Bank, held by the Ministry of Finance, to the Financial Institutions Development Fund. The transfer took place on 26 July 1999. Furthermore, on 6 October 1999, the United Overseas Bank of Singapore made a 75 per cent acquisition of Radanasin Bank. Some 43 billion baht worth of non-performing loans were transferred to an AMC in exchange for bonds guaranteed by the FIDF. The AMC was set up by the FIDF and managed under a loss- or profit-sharing agreement by United Overseas Bank (UOB). Losses of the asset management company would be borne 85 per cent by the FIDF and 15 per cent by UOB; while gains would be shared 95 per cent by the FIDF and 5 per cent by the UOB. The UOB, in return, would receive a management fee equal to 0.1 per cent of the non-performing loans.

As of March 1999, the total assets of the new entity accounted for about 61,000 million baht, comprising mainly credit extensions; while the liabilities consisted mainly of deposits and capital funds (of 19.8 billion baht).

The Secondary Mortgage Finance Corporation (SMC)

The SMC was established on 27 June 1997 in accordance with the Emergency Decree on the Secondary Mortgage Finance Corporation B.E. 2540. The rationale behind the establishment of the SMC was that it was deemed necessary to rectify the problems of real estate businesses in the country, which were in a sluggish stage, by expanding credits on housing. This was considered as one of the measures for the rehabilitation of the national economy as a whole.

The securitization business was an important financial process which could be implemented to rectify the shortage of both short- and long-term capital of businesses. It also helped create a new, highly stable financial instrument, which could facilitate the development of the country's capital market and the mobilization of savings. It was therefore expedient to establish a government agency for the development of the secondary market for housing loans by using the securitization technique to raise funds to accommodate the expansion of demand for housing credit.

The SMC received an initial fund of 1,000 million baht as capital funds from the BoT on 2 February 1998. The major source of funds, however, came from its issuance of bonds, approved by the Ministry of Finance in early 1999, in exchange for the mortgage loans from financial institutions. The mortgage loans were securitized by the issuance of securities to be sold to investors, the returns on which depend on the inflows arising from the assets. By the end of September 1998, the total assets of the SMC amounted to about 1,100 million baht, mainly cash and deposits, with only 300 million baht of credit extension, while the liabilities consisted mainly of equity.

The FIDF and the Deposit Insurance Authority

When the crisis broke out, there was no formal deposit insurance scheme in Thailand. However, the FIDF was established under the Bank of Thailand Act B.E. 2485, as amended by the Royal Decree B.E. 2528, which took effect on 27 November 1981. The fund was set up as a separate legal entity managed by the BoT. The rationale behind the establishment of the FIDF was that financial crises had occurred several times in the past 30 years, such as when the RAJA finance company was in crisis in 1979 and when the 4 April 1984 'lifeboat' scheme was launched to save many banks. All these past crises had created deposit runs in the financial system and public confidence had to be restored. Thus the establishment of the FIDF was a combined effort of the private sector and the government and was created within the BoT to rehabilitate the financial institutions as well as to develop the financial system and restore solvency and stability.

The initial capital of 1,500 million baht came from the BoT, with further annual contributions to help cope with the financial crisis. The fund was empowered to collect annual insurance fees from financial institutions not exceeding 0.5 per cent of total deposits and borrowings. Initially, it began to collect fees of 0.1 per cent but, in 1998, it was raised to 0.2 per cent to compensate for the higher risk in the financial system. In addition, the government was responsible for the loss incurred by the fund since the fund operated in accordance with government policy. In addition, from time to time, the BoT allocated to the fund a suitable amount from its reserves.

The FIDF sold four nationalized banks. The first sale, on 10 September 1999, of Nakornthon Bank (which was wholly owned by FIDF) to Standard Chartered Bank, was worth 12.38 billion baht (75 per cent of equity) and was a major success in privatizing the nationalized bank. Furthermore, on 6 October 1999, the United Overseas Bank of Singapore sealed a 75 per cent acquisition of Radanasin Bank for 15,089 billion baht, equivalent to a price of 14.4 baht per share. Some 43 billion baht worth of non-performing loans were transferred to an asset management company in exchange for bonds guaranteed by the FIDF. The AMC was set up by the FIDF and managed under a loss- or profit-sharing agreement by United Overseas Bank. Losses of the asset management company were borne 85 per cent by the FIDF and 15 per cent by the UOB, while gains were shared 95 per cent by the FIDF and 5 per cent by the UOB. The UOB, in return, received a management fee equal to 0.1 per cent of the non-performing loans. Two more nationalized banks were privatized under the scheme: Siam City Bank and Bangkok Metropolitan Bank.

Since the FIDF had to issue a general letter of guarantee to all depositors and creditors in order to restore public confidence in the financial system in 1997, the burden directly impacted on the government, which was responsible for the loss by the FIDF. Therefore, the BoT Act was amended to reaffirm the government's commitment to underwrite the FIDF guarantees for depositors and creditors.

In the context of the above, the FIDF has played a complementary role to the traditional role of financial stability played by the BoT. Specifically, the FIDF has been instrumental in revitalizing ailing financial institutions throughout the economic crisis such that the burden of supporting financial restructuring has fallen on the FIDF rather than the BoT. Some of the FIDF's exposure has been converted into equity as part of the recapitalization of the restructured financial institutions. The government has promised to take full responsibility for the losses of the FIDF, by converting them into government debt. This has been a key component of Thailand's overall economic programme, which is supported by the IMF (IMF, 2000).

The Financial Sector Restructuring Authority (FRA)

The FRA was established on 24 October 1997 in accordance with the Emergency Decree on Financial Sector Restructuring B.E. 2540. The FRA was created as an independent body to oversee the rehabilitation of 58 finance companies – whose operations were suspended by order of the finance minister on 26 June 1997 (16 companies) and 5 August 1997 (42 companies) – and to safeguard the interest of *bona fide* depositors and investors.

Thus, the FRA provides a support role to the BoT in restoring financial stability to Thailand. Initially, the FRA focused on segregating the good assets from the bad assets of the banking sector. Then the FRA sold most of the good assets to Radanasin Bank in order to continue the operation of businesses. The bad assets were sold to the AMC in order to improve the value of the assets. However, as the government changed, the policy to deal with the assets of the 56 closed finance companies also altered. In order to attract more foreign currency and allow foreign investors to manage the assets, the government had to adopt a new policy to allow foreign investors to bid for the assets. After two years of operation, the FRA auctioned 648 billion baht of the 924 billion principal value of assets of the 56 defunct companies, with 583 billion baht as core assets and 64 billion as non-core assets. With the six past auctions of FRA, the value of the sold assets raised around 181 billion baht, about 27 per cent of the total principal value of 648 billion baht. Sales of core assets, loan contracts, yielded 25 per cent of the principal value, while the sale of the non-core assets, such as collateral and other property, yielded 53 per cent of the principal value. There were 229 billion baht of assets unsold, of which 219 billion baht were core and 10 billion baht were non-core. The FRA called for bids for assets valued at 23.8 billion baht and began distributing returns from the assets to creditors in November 1999.

With the financial crisis in Thailand now over, the FRA is expected to close its operations soon after paying creditors the money earned from the auctions of the 56 defunct companies.

The Property Loan Management Organization (PLMO)

The PLMO was established on 10 April 1997, in accordance with the Royal Decree on the Property Loan Management Organization B.E. 2540, in order to deal with the property market bubble that had burst in 1996. The oversupply of property was caused by a lack of reliable and comprehensive information on real estate projects, together with fierce competition among the developers. In order to resolve the problem, the BoT stepped in to remedy the property loans in the financial institutions that extended credits to the property sector.

The PLMO was established to purchase property loans with collateral from financial institutions for the purpose of managing and enhancing their value. The aim was to enable the financial institutions to improve the quality of assets while continuing to look after their borrowers through additional credit and a loan-monitoring process. The PLMO was not intended to directly extend credits to borrowers but was expected to arrange for a restructuring of debt so that property developers have flexibility to complete their project.

The initial capital of one million baht was appropriated from the government budget. Another source of capital was contributed by the 35 participating financial institutions, with an admission fee of one million baht for each financial institution. Its working capital, up to 100,000 million baht, was mobilized through the sale of government-guaranteed bonds as approved by the cabinet. The bonds were sold to general investors. The main objectives were to provide facilities for financial institutions to manage their property loans more flexibly, as well as to assist property developers to continue with their projects through a debt-restructuring programme. The PLMO's operating expenses were borne by both financial institutions participating in the scheme and the property developers whose loans had been transferred to the PLMO. Also, a management fee of 0.2 per cent per annum was charged equally to both financial institutions and the property developers.

As of December 1998, the total assets of the PLMO amounted to about 660 million baht, mostly consisting of short-term promissory notes issued by government financial institutions. From the beginning of its operation, the PLMO purchased only three property projects worth around 500 million baht. Since its members were mostly the 56 closed finance companies, therefore, the business was no longer viable. On 23 March 1999, the cabinet approved the proposal of the Ministry of Finance to revoke the operation of the PLMO.

Thus, the PLMO provided a short-term palliative measure for restoring stability in the mortgage finance market, thereby playing a supporting role to the efforts of the BoT in reversing the adverse effects of the financial crisis.

The Thai Credit Bureau Company

The Thai Credit Bureau Company, was set up in September 1999 as a joint venture between the Government Housing Bank (GHB) and the Processing Centre Company (owned by commercial banks), to operate under the auspices of the Finance Ministry. The aim of this body was to pool information about borrowers among different financial institutions. The information was expected to cover existing loans, payment and service history, and basic demographic information such as age, assets and dependencies. In the early stage, the bureau focused on consumer loans such as auto leasing, credit cards and personal loans. The bureau relied primarily on information gathered from the GHB's vast pool of mortgage borrowers. Information from other participating banks was expected to be put in the system by the end of 1999, adding to the GHB files already entered in the system. It was believed that the absence of a credit bureau was a major cause of poor credit risk management in the past, contributing to the financial crisis. There was limited customer information and hardly any credit scoring within the Thai banking system.

The Thai Bankers' Association also launched its own credit bureau, with support from the BoT, at the end of 1999. The bureau was owned by 13 Thai commercial banks with starting capital of 26 million baht. The bureau was expected to rely on the information from period reports on classified loans filed with the BoT, with the main focus on corporate loans. Banks were not permitted to access the information without authorization from customers. The status of the borrowers was noted in the records, for example, if they were under restructuring or in bankrupty proceedings. The bureau encouraged banks to change their lending practices from relationship-based connections and collateral-based values to analysis based on cashflow projections.

Thus, these credit bureaux have complemented the traditional role of the BoT in restoring financial stability in Thailand. It is expected that the bureaux will eventually lead to stronger financial institutions and increased lending as banks gain increased confidence in selecting promising customers. Access to credit files of the credit bureau is limited to participating financial institutions, and then only in cases where they are considering a new loan application. Customers approaching the banks for new loans will be asked to authorize lenders to access their files from the bureau databases. The credit bureau will help speed up loan requests, reduce costs and improve access to credit for customers with good credit histories. Customers with poor credit histories will also find access to credit more difficult in the future.

Achieving International Regulatory Standards

Basle capital adequacy ratio

In order to comply with the guidelines of the Basle Committee on capital adequacy, the BoT proposed to amend the Commercial Banking Act B.E. 2505, as amended by the Commercial Banking Act B.E. 2528, with the aim of upgrading the local banking standard to the international standard. The new capital adequacy ratio addressed both on- and off-balance sheet items. Since the implementation of the Basle Committee standards in 1993, Thai commercial banks have been permitted to include long-term subordinated debts and asset revaluation surpluses as supplementary capital.

During 1990–95, local commercial banks managed to accumulate their first-tier capital internally through the marked increase of retained earnings. To accomplish this, banks decreased their dividend payout to net profit ratio from 47 per cent in 1990 to 35 per cent in 1995. The banks also succeeded in accumulating second-tier capital. The increase in Tier 2 capital could be attributed to two main factors. First, Thai commercial banks were able to issue long-term subordinated debt in foreign currency denominations since early 1993, at a time when the Thai banking sector was very healthy. Second, the rapid expansion of branch networks of Thai banks in the past ten years had yielded a large number of new premises.

The BoT implemented the Basle ratios well before the crisis.[11] The Basle Capital Accord of 1988, which the BoT adopted, assigned weights for various types of assets, with greater capital required for riskier types of loans. Capital to be maintained is divided into two categories, first-tier capital, defined as equity and retained earnings, and second-tier capital, defined as subordinated debts and revaluation from assets such as bank offices. In June 1999, the Basle Committee on Banking Supervision issued a new capital adequacy framework aimed at replacing the 1988 capital accord. The objectives of the new capital accord were to strengthen the stability of the international banking system and ensure a level playing field among international banks. The minimum capital adequacy ratio was initially set at 7 per cent and was gradually raised to 8.5 per cent; the first-tier capital ratio was also raised to 6 per cent in October 1996. Following the devaluation of the baht in July 1997, the commercial banks faced increasing non-performing loans and had to set aside provisions to meet the requirements of the BoT. This capital to asset ratio duly fell below the Basle ratio and the commercial banks were forced to try to recapitalize, but the time was not ripe to do so. In order to solve the problem of continuing decreases in capital, especially Tier 1 capital, in August 1998, the BoT reduced the Tier 1 requirement from 6 to 4.25 per cent, but still maintained the overall risk-weighted capital adequacy ratio of 8.5 per cent. In addition, in March and June 1999, preferred shares with subordinated debts could be counted as part of Tier 1 capital, but subject to a limit of not more than 25 per cent of Tier 1 capital. This was in line with the Basle Committee's capital adequacy standards. Moreover, the 1 per cent provision requirement set in the case of normal lending, was also permitted to be counted as Tier 1 capital, but subject to a limit of 1.25 per cent of risk assets.

Asset classification, accrued interest and appraisal of collateral

In the past, the BoT allowed Thai commercial banks to include as assets accrued interest, in the form of revenues, given that the value of collateral covered total debt outstanding. However, the practice motivated banks to focus and rely on collateral (most of which is real estate) in their credit approval process. In an effort to follow international accounting standards, a more stringent income recognition rule for financial institutions was introduced in July 1995 when the BoT ruled that financial institutions could record accrued interest as income only up to six months, and if the loans and interest accrued were fully collateralized, accrued interest could then be recorded up to one year. Consequently, the period was reduced to six months, and since 1999 only three months accrued interest could be recorded in accordance with the 'three months past due' classification.

The classification and provisions of debts were amended. Previously, the BoT classified debts into four categories, namely, 'special mention', 'substandard', 'doubtful' and 'bad'. For doubtful debts, banks were required to set aside provisions of up to 50 per cent. In order to comply with international standards, in 1998 the classification of debts was improved by dividing them into four categories according to the past due date. If within three months past due, they were classified as 'special mention', if 3–6 months past due as substandard debts, 6–12 months past due as doubtful debts and if over 12 months past due as doubtful loss. In addition, the provisions were also adjusted: for doubtful debts they were raised to 75 per cent (100 per cent in 1995) while provisions of 20 per cent and 100 per cent were levied on substandard debts and doubtful loss in 1997, respectively, with provisions of 1 per cent for normal debts and 2 per cent for special mention being introduced in 1998.

Other Post-crisis Developments

Allowing BIBFs to be temporarily closed

As the economic conditions continued to deteriorate, the BIBFs in the provinces could hardly find customers to lend to. Therefore, they were allowed to close their operations temporarily until the economy had recovered. Moreover, the BIBFs that could not operate profitably, sought permission from the Ministry of Finance to cease operation.

In addition, due to the restructuring in the banking sector, some branches of domestic banks that could not operate profitably also sought closure in order to reduce costs.

Guidelines for equity holding for foreign investors in Thai financial institutions

The 1962 Banking Act prohibited foreign nationals from holding shares (or being directors) in Thai commercial banks in excess of one-quarter of the total shares. It also prohibited a director of one commercial bank from becoming a director in another commercial bank. As the financial crisis broke out in 1997, the public had no confidence in the financial system. The quality of assets was also deteriorating rapidly in line with the slowdown in the economy. It was difficult for financial institutions to raise their own capital. Therefore, in order to attract funds from abroad so as to enhance the stability of the financial system, the 1962 Banking Act was amended on 28 June 1997 to allow foreign entities or foreigners to hold shares in excess of the previous limit and to allow a director from one bank to be a director in another bank as well. However, the Ministry of Finance and the BoT also issued guidelines for equity holdings in financial institutions by permitting foreign entities that have a sound financial status and high potential to help increase the efficiency of the management of their financial institution, to hold equities in Thai financial institutions of more than 49 per cent of total shares for a period of ten years. After ten years, if the shareholding exceeded 49 per cent, the foreign entities would be allowed to continue to hold that amount of shares but they could not purchase or exercise the right to purchase any additional shares, unless the amount of shareholding was less than 49 per cent.

Regarding the policy statement, DBS Bank, ABN AMRO Bank, Standard Chartered Bank and United Overseas Bank were allowed to acquire shares in Thai banks of more than 49 per cent (and up to 75 per cent). Between 10 per cent and 49 per cent of shares in other banks, such as Bangkok Bank, Thai Farmers Bank and Siam Commercial Bank, could be acquired by foreign entities. Many other Thai banks, such as Bangkok Metropolitan Bank and Siam City Bank and so on, were put up for sale.

Mergers, acquisitions and the privatization of state-owned banks

Following the closure of 56 finance companies in 1997, the persistent economic slowdown and liquidity shortage in the money market caused the asset quality of financial institutions to deteriorate. Moreover, the requirement for financial institutions to set aside provisions against classified assets in line with international best practice resulted in many financial institutions experiencing losses, thus requiring recapitalization in order to strengthen their position.

In May 1998, the BoT ordered seven finance companies and four banks to write down their capital and reduce their par value per share to one satang (100 satang = 1 baht) to eliminate the loss of the companies. Moreover, in August 1998, the BoT further intervened in two banks and five finance companies using the same criteria. Thereafter, the financial institutions concerned were expected to raise sufficient capital to increase their capital adequacy ratio to 9 per cent, with the new shares to be sold to the FIDF. The BoT also ordered the removal of the board of directors and the appointment of new directors to oversee the management. Thereafter, Krungthai Thanakit Public Company Limited, a state-owned finance company, merged with 12 finance companies and the Union Bank of Bangkok and became Bank Thai, while the Leam Thong Bank was integrated with the Radanasin Bank. Another two banks, the Bangkok Bank of Commerce and the First Bangkok City Bank, were partially or fully acquired by Krung Thai Bank. Two other banks, including Bangkok Metropolitan Bank and Siam City Bank, were offered for sale by the end of the year 2000. These procedures were designed to reduce damage to the FIDF because of the potential profits from selling these shares to the private sector in the future.

Following the government's measures to resolve the corporate liquidity situation and strengthen financial sector soundness, the BoT on 14 August 1998 set the criteria whereby a bank or a finance company would be required: to write down capital to one satang per share; to remove management; and to seek recapitalization by the FIDF. The institutions would qualify for FIDF recapitalization if they had incurred large operating losses but they were able to present a clear and credible recapitalization plan.

In addition, due to slim future prospects of raising new capital to meet the Basle capital adequacy ratio, the government initiated the 'capital support scheme', to help recapitalize the financial institutions and provide incentives for the financial institutions (especially large commercial banks) to extend more credit to the corporate sector. The Financial Restructuring Authority Committee (FRAC) was set up with a 300 billion baht budget to help Thai banks recapitalize. The FRAC was expected to support any Thai commercial banks wanting to seek additional Tier 1 capital from the BoT in the form of preferred shares to fulfil their BIS capital adequacy ratio after setting aside the 100 per cent provisions required upfront in year 2000. Should the existing shareholders or management be concerned about the *dilution* effect, they would opt for a Tier 2 capital increasing scheme in order to boost corporate debt restructuring. This scheme is being run jointly with the BoT in a bid to facilitate the recapitalization of Thai banks.

Proposed banking and finance act reforms

The Commercial Banking Act and the Act on the Undertaking of Finance Business, Securities Business and *Credit Foncier* Business have been effective since 1962 and 1979, respectively. Both acts have been improved and amended several times during the 1976–92 period. When the financial crisis occurred in 1997, neither act was able to cope with the problems. The main objectives of amending the commercial banking and finance company acts were as follows:

- Banks and finance companies were separately supervised with different supervisory frameworks. This created difficulties in supervising them efficiently. In the amendment to the acts in 1992, the BoT sought to bring both acts to the same standard.
- Financial service conglomerates were permitted in order to modernize the regulatory framework for both banks and finance companies. It allowed financial services, such as insurance, leasing and securities companies and so on to be owned by holding companies. The BoT was responsible for supervising financial institutions while other agencies were involved in regulating the financial services.

Thus, the proposed amendments in the acts were designed to provide the BoT with more powers to tackle problems in financial institutions at an early stage. This would allow the central bank to tackle problems rather than avoid them. Previously, the Banking Act had left such matters to the discretion of the central bank governor, but the revised act called for prompt and thorough action in all cases, thus modifying the traditional role of the BoT in view of the financial crisis.

7 CONCLUSIONS AND LESSONS

One important lesson from the financial crisis is that, in Thailand, financial liberalization in an uncontrolled financial sector resulted in misallocation and mismatching of funds. In general, the Thai financial crisis reflected the failure of the banking sector, expressing itself partly in increasing current account problems but mainly in careless lending/borrowing and the accumulation of non-performing loans. When the real economy started to show signs of weakening, with sluggish exports and an increase in the current account deficit, 'hot money' flowed in and covered the deficit; but this also led to careless investments. Consistent with the conclusion by Lensink et al. (2000), it may be argued that political instability, indecisiveness and mismanagement at the political and administrative levels also contributed to capital flight and the financial meltdown in Thailand.

Lack of effective financial regulation played an important role in aggravating the financial crisis. Thus, the important lesson is that failure to impose proper regulatory and legal control over the operations of banks has serious consequences. In particular, excessive lending by domestic banks (sometimes financed by international investors) and a lack of control over the actions of the borrowers need to be addressed. Poor policy making at the central bank and within commercial banks, encouraged overinvestment and hence aggravated the fragility of the banking sector as firms were unable to service their debts.

One inevitable consequence of the financial crisis in Thailand has been the renaissance of informal credit in Thailand (Vatikiotis, 1998). New BoT rules introduced at the end of March 1998 to tighten borrowing led to interest rates rising sharply. The tougher regulations will mean a fundamental – perhaps painful – change in Thailand's business culture. For generations, Thais have taken out loans using assets, rather than cash flow, as collateral. To change all this may require more than a simple decree from the central bank. The personal nature of banking in Thailand means that local branches often act independently of head offices, setting their own interest rates and managing their own clients.

Another important lesson from this chapter is that, under a liberalized financial system, the central bank's role in supervision and examination of financial institutions is complex and demanding. Prudential regulation must be robust, up to date and well balanced in order not to hinder the future development of financial institutions and innovations. Regulation must also be effective in maintaining a stable and sound operation of financial institutions.

NOTES

* We thank Max Hall and Malee Sariddikul for useful comments on earlier versions of this chapter. We gratefully acknowledge financial support from the Department for International Development (DFID) under the 'Finance and Development Research Programme', Contract No. RSCI06506. However, the interpretations and conclusions expressed in this chapter are entirely those of the authors and should not be attributed in any manner to DFID.

1. The responsibility of the BoT as stipulated in the Bank of Thailand Act B.E. 2485 (1942) included the role of banker to the government.
2. Commercial banking in Thailand started in 1888 with the opening of a branch of the Hong Kong and Shanghai Bank. The banking system was thus heavily influenced by the British banking tradition. A branch banking system developed with a network of branches throughout the country.

3. Under the 1962 Act, the term 'commercial banking', is defined as 'the business of accepting deposits of money and of employing such money in one or several ways such as: (a) granting of credit; (b) buying and selling of bills of exchange or any other negotiable instruments; (c) buying and selling of foreign exchange'. In addition, commercial banks may undertake businesses such as collection of payments against bills, acceptance of bills, issuing letters of credits, providing guarantees or other business of a similar nature.
4. Possibly, the increase in bank lending to some sectors by 1998 compared to 1994 reported in Table 10.1 may be explained by the fact that the general lending practices of Thai banks were not primarily focused on collateral, such as land and premises, but on the feasibility study. If the business plan for the project was well prepared, the amount of the loan granted would be much higher than the value of the collateral.
5. The central bank also raised the limit on foreign exchange purchase for travelling expenses overseas to US$20,000 per trip. Commercial banks were also allowed to approve outward transfers of foreign exchange in small amounts not exceeding US$50,000, for the remittance of loans, the sale of securities and the liquidation of companies.
6. In addition, on 2 February 1994, further relaxation of the exchange control increased convenience for outward transfer of foreign exchange and baht currency for foreign investments, and lending to subsidiaries, with limits being raised from US$5 million to US$10 million; the repayment of foreign debt was also permitted.
7. The calculation of the MRR is based on the total cost of deposits, operational cost, and profit margin of 2 per cent. Every category of lending rate to retail customers must be related to the MRR, and commercial banks have to quote a lending rate for retail customers not exceeding the MRR.
8. This is an average of interest payable on the deposits of the five biggest banks.
9. The liquidity ratio allows commercial banks to substitute other securities for government securities, namely BoT bonds, and bonds issued by government organizations and state enterprises.
10. For example, to let their business premises temporarily, recommend insurance companies to their customers, conduct feasibility studies for investment decisions, engage in loan syndication and provide advisory services in merger and acquisition cases, provide safekeeping and custodian services, purchase or sell securities through office banking, and allow insurance companies to provide services through ATMs, tele-banking and office banking.
11. However, shareholders were able to receive the same dividend of about 3.32 baht per share over the previous five years due to high profits. The relatively low price to earnings ratio made bank stocks attractive to investors, thus the sale of stocks was a viable option for Thai commercial banks. Therefore, the high profitability in the banking sector enabled banks to increase their core capital via share issuance.

REFERENCES

Abdalla, I.S.A. and V. Murinde (1997), 'Exchange rate and stock price interactions in emerging financial markets: evidence on India, Korea, Pakistan, and the Philippines', *Applied Financial Economics*, **7**, February, pp. 25–35.

Bank of Thailand (1999), *Bank of Thailand Annual Report*, Bangkok: Bank of Thailand.

Doukas, J., V. Murinde and C. Wihlborg (1998), *Financial Sector Reform and Privatisation in Transition Economies*, Amsterdam: Elsevier Science B.V. (North-Holland).

Fry, M.J. and V. Murinde (1998), 'International financial flows and development: Editors' preface', *World Development*, **26** (7), July, pp. 1165–8.

International Monetary Fund (2000), *International Financial Statistics April*, Washingon, DC: International Monetary Fund.

International Monetary Fund (various), *IMF Survey*, Washington, DC: International Monetary Fund.

Lauridsen, L.S. (1998), 'The financial crisis in Thailand: causes, conduct and consequences?', *World Development*, **26** (8), 1575–91.

Lensink, R., N. Hermes and V. Murinde (1998), 'The effect of financial liberalisation on capital flight', *World Development*, **26** (7), July, pp. 1349–68.

Lensink, R., N. Hermes and V. Murinde (2000), 'Capital flight and political risk', *Journal of International Money and Finance*, **19**, 73–92.

McKinnon, J. and H. Pill (1998), 'International overborrowing: a decomposition of credit and currency risks', *World Development*, **26** (7), July, pp. 1267–82.

Vatikiotis, M. (1998), 'Culture shock', *Far Eastern Economic Review*, **161** (16), 54–6.

Vatikiotis, M. and F. Keenan (1999), 'Princely tradition', *Far Eastern Economic Review*, **162** (22), 44–5.

11. Financial reform in the UK

D.H. Gowland

1 CENTRAL BANK

The Bank of England, 1946–71

The Bank of England was nationalized in 1946; until then it had nominally been a private corporation, its status since its foundation in 1694. This change was largely but not entirely of symbolic importance. During the inter-war period the Bank of England had become an instrument of *dirigiste* policy designed to control and channel financial flows. These included controls on new issues of securities and measures designed to promote industrial restructuring but were primarily designed to restrict capital outflows. These were formalized and given statutory status in 1939. From 1946 to 1979 more Bank of England staff were employed in exchange control than in any other area of the Bank. For example, in 1971, 80 per cent of Bank employees were working in either exchange control or in the Registrar's Department; the administrative back-up to the Bank's debt management function. Nationalization was a reflection and a symbol of the extent to which the Bank of England was an arm of the Treasury, which executed a plethora of administrative controls on all aspects of finance. Details of these are given where relevant below.

Of course, nationalization of a central bank gave considerable comfort to the psyche of Clement Atlee's 1945–51 socialist government (1945–51); probably the only one Britain has ever had. Hugh Dalton, Chancellor of the Exchequer (finance minister), was responsible for nationalizing the Bank (Pimlott, 1985, pp. 457–61[1]). He went to an International Monetary Fund (IMF) meeting accompanied by the Governor of the Bank of England, flying by the then British Overseas Airways Corporation. Dalton made a famous quip about one nationalized industry lending wings to another. The governor reportedly grimaced and certainly the Bank rejected many of the implications of its new status. One aspect of this was that it fought hard against being held accountable to the House of Commons Select Committee on Nationalised Industries. Eventually the Bank was forced to accept investigation by this body. The chancellor responded to their reports as the responsible minister (for example, in December 1977, *Reply to the Seventh Report from the Select Committee on Nationalised Industries*, Cmnd 7032).

This dispute reflects something of the dichotomous nature of the Bank of England during this period. Most of its staff were employed in performing functions that were certainly 'civil service' in nature and relatively mundane. However, when people referred to the Bank of England they normally had a very different vision in mind. The mystique of the central bank was then at its height. Both critics and admirers felt that there was something almost mystical about central banks in general. The Bank of England was one of the high places of this cult. This was one of the reasons why the Bank opposed investigation by the House of Commons Select Committee on Nationalised Industries. The Bank believed that it would be more effective if as little as possible were known about its activities. Although the Bank eventually had to concede on the particular point it was largely successful in preserving the secrecy upon which its mystique was believed to rest. Indeed, a large part of changes in bank style and organization have reflected a gradual change from mystique to transparency. In the 1950s and 1960s, mystique made it possible for the governor to 'play the sterling card' (see below), his principal source of power. In 1957 the Labour Party's finance spokesman (Harold Wilson, the future prime minister) alleged that there had been a leak within the Bank of England about an intention to raise interest rates. He also argued that various City figures had benefited from consequent insider trading. It led to the establishment of a leak inquiry which was the basis of most contemporary analysis (Chapman, 1970). Of greater long-term significance, in combination with complaints about the impact of monetary policy by the Federation of British Industry, it led to the establishment of the Radcliffe Committee (Committee into the Workings of the Monetary System, Cmnd 827, 1959). Among other things this led to the Bank's third most important function in terms of number of employees: the collection of statistics. It also led to the establishment of the Bank of England *Quarterly Bulletin.*

So far, I have enumerated those functions of the Bank of England that employed the most staff: exchange control, the Registrar's Department and the collection of statistics. Collectively over 4,000 people were employed in this capacity in 1971. Perhaps a maximum of 50 people had involvement with the making of economic policy. Of course, some of the mundane administrative tasks could not be entirely separated from policy. From 1694 to 1997, the Bank of England acted as the UK government's debt manager: given the budget deficit, the debt manager has to decide how to finance this and any maturing debt. There is a natural connection between this and the administration of the debt subsequently created (although this is not inevitable; they have been separated in the UK since 1997). In the UK the debt management function was intimately connected with the setting of interest rates. Debt management decisions had a substantial impact on interest rates and vice versa. Again, the connection was severed in 1997 (see below).

As described above, most of the employees of the Bank of England worked in a number of 'civil service' departments. So far as economic policy was concerned the phrase 'Bank of England' might refer to any of three groups. Legally, the Bank of England was headed by the governor and a court of 16 directors. These were appointed by the Queen on the advice of the prime minister. Most of these (12 in 1971) were businessmen, bankers or trade union leaders. They acted as a source of economic intelligence for policy makers within the Bank but had little power or role; John Maynard Keynes famously decried his lack of influence in this capacity (Harrod, 1951, p. 517). Being a director of the Bank of England was an honour bestowed on the great and good rather than being an equivalent of membership of, say, the Federal Reserve Board. The court was a source of intelligence to the governor and might have been called an advisory board in the USA. The remaining directors (executive directors) headed the permanent Bank staff in the 1960s and 1970s; earlier this role had been performed by the chief cashier. One might compare the chief cashier, and later, the home finance director, with the permanent under secretary in a British ministry. Control in a British ministry is divided between the minister (a political appointment) and a permanent civil service head. In many ways the Governor of the Bank of England performed a role very similar to a minister. However, although effectively nominated by the prime minister his was not a political appointment in the usual sense of the term. The Conservative governments usually appointed investment bankers. Labour governments either reappointed investment bankers or (on one occasion) appointed a member of the Bank's permanent staff. However, all governors tended to behave in a similar fashion.

One of the Bank's official functions was the management of the Exchange Equalisation Account. Until the breakdown of the Bretton Woods Agreement this meant that it was responsible for the maintenance of the adjustable parity exchange rate system. The need to manage the foreign exchange market was a major determinant of interest rates during this period. There were periodic sterling crises (withdrawals of funds from London) that led to a significant rise in interest rates. Until 1971, the Bank of England fixed a rate called the bank rate. This acted as an equivalent of the US prime rate and commercial banks normally adjusted their lending and deposit rates accordingly. In fact, during the 1960s its direct importance declined with the growth of various wholesale money markets (the first being the Local Authority Market) and later the Euro Dollar Market. However, the impact of the change in the bank rate was always perceived to be at least as much psychological as through any direct economic effect, hence the desire of the Bank to maintain its mystique, referred to above. Governors of the Bank of England could 'play the sterling card'. Successive governors made dramatic visits to 10 Downing Street to inform the prime minister that sterling was in danger, that is it might not be possible to maintain the $2.80 parity. British governments in this period regarded devaluation as both (rightly) a political disaster and (less clearly) an economic policy to be avoided at all costs. The Governor of the Bank of England could demand changes in economic policy as being essential to maintaining the parity of sterling. Frequently the governor demanded cuts in public spending and/or rises in taxation as well as changes in interest rates and credit policy. In this period monetary policy was very much the Cinderella of economic management and was thought to have little significance. The Governor of the Bank of England, however, exercised enormous personal power. This stemmed from the perception in Whitehall that he embodied expertise as a man who understood financial markets. Moreover, he was responsible for raising the external borrowing necessary to maintain the parity and his *imprimatur* was necessary to persuade other central banks to provide funds, usually through the Basle meetings of the Bank of International Settlements.

This interacted with his other-self perceived role: that of being the representative of the City (that is, the London financial community) in Whitehall. In fact the Bank of England saw an important role as being the link between government and the financial sector. The Bank of England provided facilities and staff (usually the Secretariat) for all sorts of bodies within the City of London. Sometimes these had regulatory functions, on other occasions they had promotional functions. Sometimes they were designed to impose the will of the government on the financial community. On other occasions, they were very close to lobbying organizations. Frequently they combined all four without seeing any conflict among them. Many of the Bank's key permanent staff filled these secretarial positions as well as being part of the relatively small group concerned with managing economic policy. It is worth stressing the generalist nature of the Bank's vocation at this period. Until about 1980, the Bank of England employed only one or two economists who concentrated on monetary and financial matters. However, it normally employed at least a dozen who worked on industrial policy, labour policy and so on. The Bank of England at times appeared like a government in exile. Its Overseas Department was almost a shadow Foreign Office. The Bank sought involvement in all aspects of economic policy. It saw itself not as an expert on monetary and financial policy (which were regarded as unimportant in any case) but as the representative of the City in all aspects of economic policy.

A consequence of the structure and the points made above was that it was possible to distinguish very sharply between the influence of the governor of the Bank and of the Bank as an institution. Bank officials appeared to have become ever-less important in Whitehall committees throughout the post-war period. Even when monetary policy became more important after 1969, the Bank did not claim specialist expertise but a right of involvement in all decisions. Hence the Treasury became the executive arm of monetary policy, albeit with the Bank as the operational arm. There were various complex liaison committees to discuss the minutiae of policy, especially financial forecasting and so on. However it was very clear that the Treasury was boss. The Treasury could have issued directives under the Bank of England Act 1946 but never felt it necessary. These comments on the weakness of the Bank of England are in marked contrast with the power and influence that various governors of the Bank possessed.

The Transformation of the Bank of England, 1971–81

The Bank had enforced a series of direct controls on credit, especially that granted by banks. Some of these were quantitative: ceilings on lending. Others were qualitative: lending to the personal sector and property companies was restricted while shipbuilders, exporters and other groups were favoured. There were no clear legal underpinnings for these. The Bank had powers under the 1946 Act but these were never used. Moreover, some lawyers expressed doubts about whether the Bank had the legal power to enforce its controls on internal lending. The Bank relied on its influence (often called 'moral suasion' in this period), and a belief that it was foolhardy to cross it. Economic theory suggests such controls create an incentive to evade them: the black market argument. This happened in the 1960s through the emergence of new institutions, variously called fringe or secondary banks. Hence in 1971, the Bank said it would rely only on interest rates to control bank lending, promulgated in 'competition and credit control' (Bank of England, 1971), which became the name of the new policy (see also Bank of England, 1983).

Competition and credit control had important supervisory elements. The Bank had traditionally performed its supervisory functions in a very informal manner. Outsiders referred to the governor's eyebrow: raising it was supposed to deter misconduct. The Bank referred to itself as being like a marriage guidance counsellor or parish priest in rural Ireland (Blunden, 1975). The theme running through these analogies was simple:

all participants accepted the opinion of an unchallenged community leader who was perceived to know best. To a theorist, the system was essentially a closed one with participants being committed to a repeated game scenario with consequent rewards and penalties for establishing a reputation. Whatever the cause, participants felt that guidance from the Bank had to be followed even if it had no legal backing. This approach had some notable successes: for example, it deterred Cornfeld's Fund of Funds from operating in the UK (see Raw et al., 1972, ch. 13, who compare UK success with supervisory failures elsewhere). However it was put under insuperable pressure and was reformed on several occasions in the last 30 years of the century (see Section 3 below).

The Bank often operated through the club system. When a new activity arose in the City the Bank encouraged its practitioners to set up an association (club) with a Bank official as secretary. This body acted as regulator. The system was regarded as embodying self-regulation and voluntary regulation. The rules were largely enforced by the club and made by the club under Bank auspices. Hence, the 'self' epithet was justified. The 'voluntary' was less clear: institutions had a choice of joining the club or not operating at all. The system was avowedly non-statutory. In a sense the Bank made up the rules as it went along. Hence it took pride in operating the spirit of the rules rather than the letter. Given the rapid pace of financial innovation even in the 1960s there was a lot to commend such flexibility. It avoided the dialectic of innovation being driven by avoidance and the regulator constantly chasing an ever-changing world which was often alleged to characterize regulation in the 1990s. One survivor until 2000 was the takeover panel (a group of staff seconded from investment banks who policed takeovers so as to ensure that all shareholders received equal treatment) It was universally lauded until it fell victim to Brussels and was transformed out of recognition. However, the club system was open to criticism since:

1. corporations could not plan if they did not know the regulatory implications of their actions;
2. the system acted as an inducement to form cartels to enforce price fixing and deter or bar entry. The Clearing House was criticized on these grounds as preserving a cartel of large retail banks; and
3. the system presupposed a closed group of players. There were no sanctions for new entrants prepared to break the code and willing to hope for *ex post facto* admission to the club or accept withdrawal. This ceased to be either accurate as banks pursued global strategies or thought desirable; eventually (1978) the hit-and-run raider became the hero of William Baumol's contestable market approach.

In 1971, the Bank adopted 'competition and credit control'. As the name implied, this marked a switch to believing in competition and a desire to see new entrants in markets. Hence, out of a mixture of ideology and necessity, it opened the clearing house to new entrants and generally fostered competition. The spur to a new approach to supervision was – as usual in the UK – a scandal. Credit controls had prevented the clearing banks from satisfying the demand for credit. New institutions had filled the gap (the classic black market of the textbook). In 1973, various of these institutions failed (see Reid, 1982). The Bank was perceived to have mishandled the situation. For example, one bank was given enhanced status a week before it failed (Edward Bates). The Bank tried to rescue various banks through the First National Finance Corporation which subsequently failed itself. Reid claims that the resultant banking failures meant that NatWest was insolvent. Faced with this and the European Commission's (EC's) first credit directive, banking supervision was switched to a statutory basis with the 1979 Banking Act. A parallel Consumer Credit Act (1981) was promulgated to regulate the conditions on which loans were granted. Banks were allowed to enter the mortgage market.

These failures were the culmination of a period in which the money supply grew by 60 per cent in 27 months. Inflation peaked at 25 per cent. There is still debate about the precise role of oil prices, monetary growth and the collapse of the Heath incomes policy. However, the implication was that all elements of macro policy were reappraised. The incoming Labour government eventually introduced monetary targets. These were implemented with new administrative controls on the banking sector. This time, ceilings were placed on bank liabilities, not on lending; the corset or, more formally, ceilings were placed on interest-bearing eligible liabilities (IBELs) with penalties for breaching them. In 1979, the Thatcher government scrapped these and exchange control. The Bank would now control banks through interest rates. This was reaffirmed in 1981 after a reappraisal of techniques in response to pressure to introduce a *modus operandi* of monetary policy based on US methods.

To summarize, the Bank was at a crossroads in 1981. Many of its traditional functions had disappeared, notably, exchange control and direct controls on bank activities. The consensus was for managed floating not adjustable parities. It had traditionally downplayed the role of monetary policy and faced a government which was avowedly monetarist. This gave an enhanced role to the monetary targets introduced by Denis Healey in 1975–76. These were another move towards accountability and transparency and away from mystique. The Bank had believed in an informal approach rather than a legalistic one and had been forced to accept a statutory approach. The Bank had switched from a suspicion of market forces to a qualified acceptance, but now faced a government of enthusiastic believers in them in an era when bank culture had changed from regarding themselves as quasi-public utilities to zealously pursuing profit. I shall now trace these themes through the themes of this chapter.

The Bank of England's *Modus Operandi* for Monetary Policy

The (re-) discount rate has always been treated by textbooks as the key central bank instrument, that is, the price at which it guarantees to provide liquidity to the banking system by purchasing prescribed assets (in the UK, treasury bills and some categories of bank debt known as bank bills). The price is less than their value at maturity, hence the term 'to discount'. The Bank's rate was called the 'bank rate' until 1971. It also acted as the prime rate of the banking system. Hence time deposit rates were calculated as bank rate minus 2 per cent and loan rates as bank rate plus x, where x reflected a mixture of risk premium and market power. As part of competition and credit control these two were separated. Banks started to quote a base rate which was the equivalent of the US prime rate. The bank rate was replaced by the minimum lending rate (MLR). In part this was a reflection of reality. The Bank had only re-discounted one bill in the 1945–71 period; instead it lent against the security of such assets. The two are equivalent although interest rates on loans are calculated as a percentage of the amount advanced, not the amount repaid. Thus to purchase an asset which will be worth 100 in a year's time for 80 (discount rate 20 per cent) is the same as a one-year loan for 80 on the security of the asset at an interest rate of 25 per cent.

However, the MLR was also distinctive in that it was linked to the treasury bill tender rate. Every week the Bank offers a quantity of treasury bills for sale and market participants bid (tender) for them. The cut-off price was used to determine the MLR; the implicit interest rate rounded up to the nearest quarter per cent plus 0.5 per cent. The treasury bill tender is also unusual in that bidders pay the price they bid (thus there is no consumers' surplus). Until 1971, the discount houses agreed to submit a joint tender for the amount offered. This was abandoned as part of competition and credit control. Thereafter the discount houses agreed to tender for the whole amount but at prices of their choosing (each house entered several bids at prices of its choosing). Around 1980, this agreement was abandoned. It is convenient to deal with discount houses here. The houses borrowed large amounts from banks (at call or callable, that is they were demand or sight assets); the counterpart asset was the banks' main liquid asset. The discount houses invested these funds mainly in treasury bills (and accepted interest rate market risk). The Bank dealt only with discount houses. Hence if banks were short of liquidity they called money from the discount houses who in turn 'were forced into the Bank' for funds. In 1971, the Bank stated that it would henceforth deal directly with banks as well as through this distinctive mechanism. Slowly the discount houses lost their special role as Bank–bank dealings became more dominant. By 1990, open market operations in the UK had lost this special feature.

In 1975, the MLR ceased to be linked to the treasury bill rate and was once more fixed every Thursday by the Bank. In 1981 it was dropped (except for a brief reappearance in 1983) and replaced by an intervention rate, the rate at which the Bank would intervene in the treasury bill market. This was completely discretionary and was promulgated daily via Reuters' screens. This reflected the ultimate move from a highly-publicised (Bank) rate whose effect was believed to depend on mystique as much as markets to a flexible instrument of policy. In the 1950s the impact of the bank rate was symbolic and largely independent of market forces. Each change thereafter was designed to create a viable means of influencing markets. The Bank sought to be boring to quote an aphorism ascribed by Goodhart (1999) to Mervyn King, subsequently Deputy Governor; the bank rate system meant that interest rates could not be changed for technical reasons without media coverage and political pressure. From 1997 this intervention rate was complemented by an official rate fixed by the Monetary Policy Committee.

The other textbook instrument is reserve ratios. The Bank had always had a variety of liquidity ratios. It was never clear whether these were designed to achieve macro- monetary or supervisory goals. They were reinforced by a power to call for special deposits. In form these were like a variable reserve ratio although the Bank was careful to explain that they were anything but reserve ratios in the textbook credit multiplier sense. As part of competition and credit control, the Bank introduced a 12.5 per cent minimum reserve assets ratio (RAR). The Bank explained that this was a technique to manage interest rates, not a textbook reserve ratio:

> It is not to be expected that the mechanism of minimum reserve ratio and Special Deposits can be used to achieve some precise multiple contraction or expansion of bank assets. Rather the intention is to use our control over liquidity, which these instruments will reinforce to influence the structure of interest rates, the resulting change in relative rates of return will then induce shifts in the current portfolios of both the public and the banks (Bank of England, 1971).

> The RAR was never designed to serve as an officially controlled monetary base through which the pyramid of credit created by the banks might be directly limited. Instead, in conjunction with Special Deposits, the RAR was regarded as an element in the control of short term interest rates. (Chancellor of the Exchequer, 1980)

The precise mechanism was never elucidated, which perhaps explains why it was quickly abandoned:

> In the event, it quickly became apparent that use of joint RAR and Special Deposits requirements presented particular difficulties. . . . As a result, it became apparent to the authorities that it was better to put up interest rates directly rather than to use Special Deposits to achieve this effect less directly. (Chancellor of the Exchequer, 1980)

Hence these were scrapped in 1981. Thereafter, the only ratio was a requirement that banks hold a minimal quantity of deposits with the Bank so that the bank could cover its operating costs by on-lending these to the government; in effect and intention, a tax on banks. Originally this was 0.5 per cent but thereafter was reduced progressively.

In the era of monetary targets the Bank relied heavily on sales of government securities to the non-bank domestic sector. The Bank analysed monetary developments through the flow of funds, money creation or the supply-side counterpart equation:

$$\Delta Money \equiv PSBR + \Delta bank\ loans\ to\ non\text{-}banks - \Delta non\text{-}bank\ private\ loans\ to\ public\ sector + oversea\ effect$$

The Bank had treated this identity as a means of monetary control by assuming that each was determined independently of the rest and that by influencing any one it could thereby control the money supply. Frequently, this led to so-called 'overfunding', that is, sales of government securities to the non-bank private sector exceeded the budget deficit (public sector borrowing requirement, PSBR) so that a negative public sector contribution to monetary growth offset an excessive private sector one. Indeed from 1975 to 1985 much of monetary policy was the history of debt management. The Bank produced a cornucopia of devices to improve its ability to market government debt (for example, see Gowland, 1982, pp. 149 and 175ff. and 1992). These became of historical interest after Nigel Lawson abandoned overfunding in 1985. This has been excoriated notably by Congdon (1992, and in his *Lombard Economic Review*).[2] However, for good or ill, debt management ceased to be a tool of economic policy. Hence, the transfer of debt management from the Bank to the Treasury in 1997 was logical after 300 years, if regrettable. The government bond market was reformed in 1986 in parallel with the 'big bang' on the Stock Exchange (see Gowland, 1992) but the subsequent history of government bonds lies outside the scope of this chapter. The only feature of note is that the UK had introduced index-linked bonds, that is, both interest payments and capital were linked to the Retail Price Index. At the least, the price of these provides an estimate of market expectations of inflation. Nevertheless, they have proved to be 'a dog that didn't bark' (Kopcke and Kimball, 1999), despite economists' enthusiasm for them.

Henceforth, open market operations would be the main instrument of monetary policy designed largely to generate the level of interest rates the Bank felt necessary to achieve its objectives. Until 1971 (the Bretton Woods era) and in 1990–92 (the exchange rate mechanism era) it was clearly to maintain the parity of sterling. From 1975 to 1985, it was to meet a monetary target. After 1992, it was to meet an inflation target. In the intervening periods (1971–73 and 1985–90), there were no clear targets and it can be argued the macroeconomic consequences were disastrous on each occasion.

2 INSTITUTIONAL REFORM

Inflation Targets and Operational Independence of the Bank

The UK has been a pioneer in establishing a new approach to economic policy and in particular to the role of the central bank (*pace* New Zealand, which was the forerunner). In summary, the UK regime has three features: the central role of inflation targets, operational independence of the Bank of England and a very high degree of transparency. All these distinguish it from other systems such as the European Central Bank (ECB) and previous UK approaches. The difference between full central bank independence (the Fed or the ECB) and operational independence is very marked. In what follows, I have tried to explain the nature of all three, often by comparison with the ECB. My objective is to emphasize the nature of the system and to analyse arguments for and against only in so far as is necessary to explain the significance of the different regimes.

Following the UK's ignominious departure from the exchange rate mechanism (ERM) (of the European Monetary System) in 1992, the government announced a new approach to monetary policy. This survived until Gordon Brown radically transformed the operation of monetary policy shortly after he became Chancellor of the Exchequer in May 1997. He granted the Bank of England operational independence to set interest rates. He also announced proposals to transfer responsibility for the regulation and supervision of the banking system to the Financial Services Authority (see Section 3 below).

There were many common features to both the 1992–97 approach to monetary policy and to that which followed Chancellor Brown's granting of operational independence to the Bank of England. In effect, they are a formal incorporation of the Taylor Rule approach to setting interest rates.

Hence it seems important to start by analysing the common features before analysing the distinctive features of the 1997 regime. This approach to monetary policy can best be appreciated by describing and analysing it as a series of steps:

1. The authorities announce a target for inflation. Normally, it is set as part of a Budget speech. Typically the UK authorities have set all targets as a range, but in May 1997 it was set as a point: 2.5 per cent.
2. The authorities seek to produce a forecast of inflation with particular emphasis on its likely level 18 months to two years in the future. The authorities publish their forecast of inflation. Since 1997, the Bank of England is tasked to produce an independent forecast of inflation, which is published in its quarterly *Inflation Report*. This reviews and surveys the work of independent forecasters, academic, business and in the City. It also incorporates an analysis of inflation expectations as far as they can be deduced from the behaviour of financial markets or other action equivalent sources as well as surveys and so on. (All of these were also reviewed by a panel of independent economic advisers whose opinions were published in the 1992–97 period). However, a key element of the post-1997 approach is that the Monetary Policy Committee (MPC) of the Bank (see below) produces its own forecast. Indeed, this is the main change; the procedure is much more automatic and so transparent, but risks being mechanistic.
3. From 1992 to 1997, the Governor of the Bank of England and the Chancellor of the Exchequer met monthly to set the interest rate (frequently known as the Ken (Clarke) and Eddy (George) show, after the then chancellor and governor). They were supposed to compare the inflation forecast, described in 2 above, with the target. Now the MPC performs this task.
4. If the forecast of inflation were higher than the target, then the authorities are pledged to raise interest rates. In practice, during 1992–97, the governor and chancellor frequently disagreed about whether or not inflation would exceed its target. In these circumstances the chancellor's opinion prevails. However, the government was committed to publishing the minutes of the discussion between the governor and chancellor, normally about six weeks after the meeting. In consequence it became widely known that the chancellor had chosen to override the Governor of the Bank of England. Again, the element of discretion and uncertainty disappeared in 1997.

As described above, Gordon Brown announced in May 1997 that he would grant operational independence to the Bank of England and that the chancellor would continue to set an inflation target. The MPC was established, chaired by the Governor of the Bank of England. Its other eight members comprised four economists nominated by the chancellor and four Bank of England officials. This body was tasked to set interest rates so as to achieve as best it could the inflation target set by the chancellor. This was the sole difference from the 1992–97 approach. As described below this was a contractarian approach rather than granting independence to the Bank of England as understood in, for example, Germany and the USA, or as embodied in the Maastricht Treaty. Various measures were taken to render the Bank of England and the MPC accountable for their actions, as described below.

There are a number of important consequences and implications of both UK approaches. The first is that it gives inflation absolute priority as the target of monetary policy. It represents the culmination of the break with Keynesian orthodoxy with its emphasis on full employment. In part this is because of the modern view that a low rate of inflation is the only attainable objective of monetary policy but it also represents a view that unemployment will be caused by failure to maintain a low and stable rate of inflation. In other words, rather than seeing a trade-off between inflation and unemployment this view embodies the proposition that inflation causes unemployment. This proposition is outside the remit of this chapter and is considered elsewhere, for example, in Gowland (1991).

The second crucial departure from textbook orthodoxy is that there is no role for any intermediate target. In other words, the government has not chosen to commit itself to a monetary target or an exchange rate target or any of the alternatives. Indeed, it represents a desire to finesse the two longest-running and most bitterly contested debates in economics:

1. the choice between an internal target (such as the money supply or the budget deficit) and an external target (usually although not necessarily the exchange rate), and
2. the choice between rule and discretion.

This approach follows the spirit of the Taylor Rule literature (see the eponymous website (http://www.stanford.edu/~johntayl/PolRulLink.htm) for a bibliography and on-line versions of key references). Taylor argued that in practice central banks used a key short-term interest rate as their operational instrument. It was both descriptive and prescriptive (close to optimal) to model this as:

$$\text{Int rate} = \text{Int rate}^* + a\,(\text{inflation }(t) - \text{inflation}^*)^2 + b\,(\text{output gap})\,(t)^2$$

where * indicates target or long-run values; (t) is the time period.

This was a backward-looking rule; a forward-looking version substituted forecast values of inflation and the output gap. However, as a forecast of inflation would be based on current values of inflation and the output gap (the Friedman expectations-augmented Phillips curve), both versions meant that the UK approach was making explicit what had long been implicit and had a justification that went beyond the *ad hoc.* The inflation target approach became the focus of much attention amongst the academics and the policy community, usually laudatory.

Arguably, inflation targeting was more important than operational independence. Forder (for example, 1998a) has emphasized that there are two distinct strands of thought among those advocating the independence of the central bank. One group believes that central banks should be independent without qualification and *inter alia* they should be free to set interest rates at whatever level they wish. Such an approach is embodied in the Maastricht Treaty for both the ECB as well as for member states of the eurozone. This is based on German and American practice. Maastricht does entrench a clause that the independent central bank should seek to control the rate of inflation but it is left entirely free as to how best to achieve this.

The other branch of the 'independence' school has been termed 'contractarian' by Forder. This is embodied in its purest form in New Zealand but was the basis for the UK's approach. Contractarianism in origin is some mixture of the traditional doctrine of accountability to parliament with modern managerialist ideas such as performance-related contracts. The Chancellor of the Exchequer sets an inflation target on behalf of the government. Given this target, the MPC led by the Governor of the Bank of England must decide how best to achieve this. They are given but one instrument, the rate of interest.[3] This restriction was memorably described as being akin to playing one-club golf. It is not clear who first used this but Congdon was an early user.They are denied any role in determining other instruments of government policy: for example, fiscal policy or even debt management. They are held accountable to the House of Commons (through the Treasury Committee) for achieving the inflation target. The governor must supply (biannual) reports to the Treasury Committee and be subject to cross-examination by the committee. Furthermore if the inflation target is missed then the governor must supply a written report to the chancellor explaining where and why he and his committee went wrong. These details highlight the differences between the accountability of the MPC and the independence discretion and autonomy of the Fed, the Bundesbank and the ECB. This point is developed further below.

In terms of constitutional theory the objectives of the new regime are to introduce a responsible and an accountable government of monetary policy. These are perfectly proper and laudable objectives in their own right. However, they are not the same as independence and it is therefore necessary to examine whether or not they will achieve the alleged benefits of an independent central bank. Moreover, while the changes give the central bank more independence, in a certain sense they reduce the amount of discretion that it possesses, in the sense of achieving a depoliticized interest rate – the same prominence in UK newspapers as Australian rules football results. Goodhart (1999) following King, describes this as a desire to be boring. Only then could the Bank manipulate interest rates so as to achieve the goals of economic policy without any need to worry about the response of the popular press or the television news, and of politicians to the media. Some such model of a disinterested technician as policy maker certainly underlies the views of many advocates of central bank independence. However, if the Bank is to be held responsible and accountable then its degree of discretion is necessarily restricted and limited. So far this has not been a major problem because the MPC has been seen to be successful, but if crises occurred, then the Bank and the MPC would be subject to intense political scrutiny. Moreover, further revision would be necessary if the UK were to join EMU since Maastricht requires an independent central bank.

This is not the place to analyse the case for an independent central bank in either sense nor the alternatives (currency boards, fixed exchange rates, various constitutional rules such as a balanced budget). The argument is that such institutional reform will generate credibility. The argument for this may be based on empirical evidence or on the advantages of precommitment, discussed in the previous sections. A number of authors have argued that institutional change is neither sufficient nor necessary to attain credibility, notably Forder (1996). They argue that credibility is frequently the product of history (see, for example, Gowland, 1997). This interpretation seems to fit the ECB very well. It seems reasonable to argue that the ECB has not yet attained credibility. It may very well do so given sufficient time. (The implications of this are rather unpleasant for the UK. It is reasonable to assume that lack of credibility has been reflected in a low value of the euro and consequently in an overvalued sterling exchange rate.). One cannot attain credibility instantly by an act of institutional reform. Credibility has to be earned rather than inherited. Credibility is not simply a consequence of institutional structure. There are complex two-way causality patterns among history, social attitudes and institutional structures. Credibility implies that it is believed that one will avoid inflation at any price even if it seems unreasonable to pursue a particular policy; indeed its intellectual origins are shared with the madman theory of nuclear deterrence. All analysts stress that in its early years a new regime may need to practice overkill to acquire this reputation. Eijffinger (1997) and Forder

(1998a) have both suggested that the effects of credibility can be observed in financial markets but not in labour markets. The euro experience seems to confirm this; adverse effects of a lack of credibility are observed in foreign exchange markets but not in labour markets.

Most academic critiques of independent central banks assert that the major defect of such systems is the lack of coordination of monetary and fiscal policy, for example, Rankin (1998) and Forder (1998b). Suppose that the government believes that it is necessary to run a deficit to avert a recession. The independent central bank does not or is not allowed to share this concern so it raises interest rates. The government responds by increasing its deficit and the central bank with a further rise in interest rates and so on. More generally it can be argued that many economies suffer from an imbalance of monetary and fiscal policy. Some simultaneous adjustment of monetary and fiscal policy would yield substantial benefits but cannot be achieved because there are two independent policy makers: the central bank and the Finance Ministry. For example, in the UK during 1998–2000 there have been strong arguments for simultaneously tightening fiscal policy (for example, a rise in taxes) and reducing interest rates. The effect would be to leave inflationary pressure unchanged but to lower the exchange rate with benefits to the North, manufacturing and farming. The proposition is that it is impossible to devise a mechanism to permit coordinated changes in policy with an independent central bank. This appears plausible. In the early Reagan years, there were similar problems with very high (20 per cent plus) interest rates and a very large budget deficit. Goodhart (1999) has challenged this view. He argues that the critique is a coded attack on attributing primacy of demand management to fighting inflation. If the finance minister and independent central bank share this goal, the former can predict the reduction in interest rates if he (she) reduces the budget deficit and choose the mix of fiscal and monetary policy she (he) prefers. This assumes that the central bank is so transparent as to be perfectly predictable, otherwise Forder's (1998) analysis of a similar point by Michael Parkin applies. It also assumes that the finance minister agrees with the central bank's forecast of inflation. Suppose that the finance minister expects inflation to be less than the target whereas the central bank expects that the target will be achieved with current interest rates. The finance minister reduces taxes and the central bank responds with higher interest rates. Then the vicious cycle of ever-higher interest rates in response to ever-higher budget deficits would result. The standard criticism of schemes for European monetary union is that virtually all scope for economic policy (including fiscal policy) has been denied to member states without creating a central/federal authority with the power necessary to manage an economy. EU central spending is trivial and not financed by a deficit so the scope for fiscal policy is very small. In some ways this is an extreme version of the coordination problem. It might well be that the euro zone needs an increase in interest rates simultaneously with an increase in government spending. This might well raise the value of the euro and employment without raising any danger of inflation.

The designers of the ECB sought credibility at any price. The southern European states thought they had paid heavily because political instability had denied it to them whereas northern states regarded it as essential to compensate them for giving up the Bundesbank; not only Germany but other countries had been linked (credibly!) to the mark for many years. It seems that the new regime is less credible than expected so it is important to examine whether this is due to technical factors, since some commentators seem to suggest that in some sense Maastricht got it wrong. Comparisons can be odious but it is important to see whether the ECB would be more credible if differently designed, as many commentators have argued that the MPC was a better arrangement. As Friedrich (2000) has pointed out, it is fashionable to compare the ECB unfavourably and inconsistently with other central banks. To say 'The Bank of England MPC does x and the ECB does not' adds more heat than light to the debate, especially if the Fed is in the same position as the ECB. However, both the dangers and the fashionability of the comparison add to the point of a systematic analysis of the differences and their implications.

The ECB has discretion and autonomy to do what it wishes although Maastricht entrenches a need to pursue price stability as its goal. The Fed has similar freedom with the Humphrey–Hawkins Act filling a role analogous to the Maastricht Treaty. By comparison, the MPC is strictly bound to keep inflation as close as possible to the target level of 2.5 per cent. The MPC has to ignore exchange rate changes and asset price movements except in so far as they are deemed to be predictors of future inflation. Hence it is disingenuous for supporters of the MPC to criticize the ECB for ignoring exchange rates. The MPC cannot pay any attention to fears about the risk of a depression or a financial crisis. The ECB's position must be preferable unless the ambiguity contributes to lower credibility or to a fuzziness in perception about its future actions. The credibility school arguments are always redolent of the madman theory of deterrence: an effective foreign (economic) policy depends on other countries (economic agents) believing in an unreasonable response to threats (of inflation). However, if it is necessary to use nuclear weapons frequently to maintain credibility, then the argument loses its appeal. Similarly, the appeal of an overarching commitment to fighting inflation is that it reduces inflationary expectations not that it is desirable in itself.

The Fed and the ECB can achieve their goals as they wish. The ECB has decided that a broad money target (called a 'reference level') will play an important role in its deliberations. The MPC's *modus operandi* have no place for an intermediate target. It is committed to a methodology inherited from the arrangements introduced after the UK's ignominious departure from the ERM, which gives a central role to the generation of a forecast of inflation. Briefly, the MPC meets monthly and produces a forecast of inflation for two years in the future. If this is higher than the target level it raises interest rates by an amount sufficient to bring the inflation forecast down to the target level. If the forecast rate of inflation is below target then it should vote to reduce interest rates. The procedure is mechanistic and so is the central role of the forecast. As Goodhart (1999) emphasizes, the forecast is the collective responsibility of all members of the MPC unless they register a dissent; in other regimes staff members produce forecasts which are an input into decisions. In some sense, a member of the MPC would be acting *ultra vires* if he or she acceded to a forecast of 3 per cent inflation but did not vote to raise interest rates. Certainly their role is to generate forecasts not to exercise judgement about the desirable level of interest rates, unlike members of the Federal Open Market Committee (FOMC) or the ECB council. The problems this might create became clear early in 2001 when the possibility of an American recession loomed. Commentators regarded this as a reason for a cut in UK interest rates although strictly it was *ultra vires* for the MPC to consider it. If there were no danger of UK inflation exceeding its target it could cut rates but if, say, the pound were to fall against the euro, it would have to raise interest rates at a time when this was inappropriate or ignore its brief and risk losing credibility.

The need to generate a collective forecast imposes a heavy workload on the MPC (Goodhart, 1999). In consequence, even the independent members have become in effect full-time employees of the Bank of England, with no outside responsibilities (with the exception of Goodhart who performed his academic role but highlighted the discomfort thereof). The members of the FOMC and the ECB council include regional/national plenipotentiaries who can bring outside perspectives to their deliberations. The MPC can listen to anybody and its three-day seminar includes many representatives of industrial and regional opinion (especially through Bank of England agents). Nevertheless, there can be no direct representation of such views.

The comparison of the ECB with the MPC highlights the nature of the modern argument for an independent central bank. Traditional arguments emphasized the skill and expertise of the central banker. Modern ones emphasize only their commitment to fighting inflation. In the modern approach, selection criteria of policy makers are relevant only insofar as they affect credibility. The MPC approach makes process the means to achieve credibility not the nature of the decision maker as in the academic literature (this is consistent with its managerialist ideology). The Fed's history suggests the role of personality in the acquisition and maintenance of credibility, especially Paul Volker's and later Alan Greenspan's personality. The UK regime is based on the belief that procedure and transparency can achieve similar success.

Both the FOMC and the MPC publish minutes and voting figures. Like the Bundesbank, the ECB does not. It is essentially a federal body with the governors of the national central banks also acting as members of the central decision-making body. It has been argued that this lack of transparency has reduced credibility. Certainly it makes accountability impossible. However, the counterargument is that if it were known that the ECB were split then market confidence would be less, for example, if two or three key members of the decision-making body thought a cut in rates would cause inflation. Moreover it is consistent with a desire to maximize discretion revealed in ambiguity over its operating target or *modus operandi.* The architects of the ECB believe that secrecy will encourage central bank governors to act as members of a central body, rather than as delegates from their home country; at least secrecy protects a governor from pressure back home. Nevertheless, the contrast between the MPC and the ECB is marked. Many of the differences cited above stem from the difference between a contractarian MPC and a fully independent ECB. In addition, the former has opted for a transparency which is consistent with but strictly separable from accountability. All aspects of the MPC's procedures are open so one can see whether one agrees with their forecasting methodology, forecast and so on. It is possible to check and verify every stage of a mechanistic procedure but not of one involving judgement. Should one conclude that transparency is the golden route to credibility? Friedrich (2000) is sceptical and suggests that the current enthusiasm for the MPC may be a passing fad. However, to the extent that transparency is crucial, it strengthens Forder's (1998a, 1999) conclusion that the crucial issues in this debate concern the design of policy, not institutional structure. One can achieve transparency whether responsibility for setting rates lies with a central bank or a politician. Moreover, the MPC approach sacrifices the benefits of central bank judgement and mystique. Are the benefits of transparency greater than the costs of a mechanistic and tunnel-visioned approach?

The Private Sector

The major structural changes in the private sector involved the mutual savings bank sector. Like most countries, the UK had a system of mutual savings banks organized on a regional basis. In 1975, these were combined into the Trustee Savings Bank. In 1986, this was privatized. The new bank made some ill-judged takeovers in 1987, including those of an investment bank (Hill Samuel) and an investment management group (Target: purchased for £330 million and subsequently sold for £1). Largely in consequence it was taken over in turn by Lloyds in 1992. The bell wether of the British left, Tony Benn, had established a giro bank under state ownership in the 1960s which was sold to the Alliance and Leicester (see below) in 1993. The giro had never been more than a pale copy of its German model but this marked the effective end of publicly owned banks in the UK. As in other English-speaking countries, mortgage lending in the UK was dominated by mutually organized savings banks called building societies. These gradually shrunk in number through mergers. The difference between them and banks grew less. In part this was because of technology. They were pioneers of ATMs and so their deposits became much less distinct from 'bank' deposits. Regulatory reform extended their functions, especially the Building Societies Act 1986. This, for example, permitted consumer loans not secured by mortgages. More dramatically, many of the largest changed from mutual to shareholder ownership. The Abbey National converted, as the process was known, in 1989, followed by the largest, the Halifax, Northern Rock, Alliance and Leicester, Woolwich, National Provincial and Bradford and Bingley. Others were taken over by commercial banks: Midshires, Bristol and West, and Cheltenham and Gloucester (by Lloyds). All in all, mutuals saw their share of both mortgage lending and of retail interest-bearing deposits fall from over 90 per cent to less than 10 per cent between 1970 and 2000.

The commercial banking sector in the UK saw fewer changes, in part because of a negative attitude towards takeovers by the (then) Monopolies and Mergers Commission and by the Bank, expressed in the 1986 Loughborough lecture by the then governor.[4] A spate of mergers in the late 1960s left a big four (Lloyds, NatWest, Barclays and Midland) and a number of smaller, mainly Scottish, banks. The latter also operated in England; both the Royal Bank of Scotland and the Bank of Scotland made acquisitions at various times. One commercial bank (the Yorkshire bank) was owned by the big four. It was sold to the ANZ (Australia and New Zealand Bank) in 1984. This was precipitated by Midland's losses caused by taking over a Californian bank (Crocker) but helped all of the big four to meet their capital requirements. Further losses by the Midland led to its progressive takeover by the Hongkong and Shanghai Bank which shortened its name to HSBC. In 1999, The Royal Bank of Scotland took over NatWest. At the time of the Stock Exchange 'big bang', stock exchange firms were permitted to be owned by corporations rather than being partnerships.[5]

Most existing partnerships cashed in by selling out to a host of eager purchasers. These included the commercial banks who sought to diversify into investment banking, largely by acquisition. This was part of an overall strategy of seeking fee income, this in turn being part of the response to the Basle capital ratios. In 1998, both NatWest and Barclays pulled out of investment banking and it seemed that the era of diversification was over. Commercial banks had owned (life) insurance subsidiaries since the 1950s and this foothold was extended. Commercial banks had increased and extended their already dominant role in retail finance into both mortgages and savings products.

Foreign banks had always operated on a large scale in London but the big bang marked a new era as many foreign banks took over stockbrokers and/or became gilt-edged market makers. In the 1990s they absorbed all of the merchant banks except Rothschilds. (Merchant banks technically were members of the Accepting Houses Committee but the term implied blue-blooded investment houses.) Barings was rescued by ING after the Leeson affair. This probably speeded up the process whereby British-owned investment houses disappeared. Some would argue that it was a major cause (a sort of contagious run by shareholders) but most analysts felt that the merchant banks were too small and had too little capital to compete with, say, Goldman Sachs, but were too big and had too much history to become niche players. Fund management was an area where the success of London was accompanied by a large-scale transfer of ownership from UK to foreign. Indeed, London appeared to be ever-more successful as a financial centre but British-owned participation became ever less. Some argued that the meaning of a financial centre was nebulous as the ICT revolution meant that dealer and back office could be thousands of kilometres apart and two dealers could strike a deal booked in London while both were based in different continents from London and each other. Others argued that the changes showed the flexibility of London. Perhaps both were right but one thing was clear: there was no longer a distinctive cast of players in London.

'One Miracle at a Time': The Bank and Financial Innovation

The Bank of England had a sophisticated and complex attitude towards financial innovation. Innovation tends to increase efficiency but may threaten safety and stability. Hence, the German authorities discouraged it and, for example, barred certificates of deposit until 1989 (Wilson, 1993) whereas they were permitted in London soon after their appearance in New York in 1961. Thus, London generally welcomed innovation and put efficiency above safety as a goal of structural monetary policy. The Bank of England actively practised what continental central banks preached as positive regulation. For example, the establishment by the Bank of euro-clear played a major role in London becoming a major centre of the euro-bond market.

However, there was another aspect to the Bank's attitude encapsulated in (the later, Sir) Edward George's aphorism of the mid-1980s: 'one miracle at a time'. Hence the Bank could explain in 1993 why a repo market in government bonds (gilt-edged securities) was unnecessary but introduced one in 1996 and make the consequent interest rate the one fixed by the MPC. (The Bank had engaged in occasional repo transactions with banks since 1972 but had opposed an active market; it wished to be a party to all such transactions.)

3 SUPERVISORY REFORM

In 1997, responsibility for bank supervision was transferred from the Bank of England to the Financial Services Authority (FSA); the latter took up its new functions immediately although without statutory existence until the Financial Systems and Markets Act of 2000. Until then, the FSA acted as the delegated agent of the many (at least 11) bodies it replaced. The major innovation of the FSA was that it regulated all financial activities, that is, it combined being a bank supervisor with functions similar to those of the Securities and Exchange Commission (SEC). Hence there were two aspects to the change: the separation of bank supervision from central banking and the creation of a unified financial regulator. The separation of central banking and bank supervision was in line with the German and EU approaches and the nominal but not effective US position. It can also be argued that bank supervision should be politically accountable so separation is a concomitant of central bank independence. Alternatively, an independent central bank with responsibility for bank supervision is too powerful. Both central banking and bank supervision depend on credibility, of low inflationary expectations and in maintaining confidence, respectively. There can be negative or positive feedback between the two. There may have been negative feedback from the Bank's handling of supervision with the BCCI affair and from Barings (most would commend the eventual decision to let Barings fail, but not allowing it commit all its capital to an Asian venture or the Bank's handling of the crisis).[6]

On the other hand, bank supervision may provide information useful to monetary policy or vice versa.[7] Moreover, a central bank must be involved as lender of last resort. Following the US model, the legislation provided for close liaison between the Bank and the FSA. The growth of multi-product financial firms means that one must choose between regulation by function and by institution (for example, who regulates the insurance subsidiary of a bank – bank regulator (institution) or insurance company regulator (function)?). Whichever is chosen, problems will arise. Within a unified regulator, these do not disappear but arise within the organization and so there is a mechanism for resolving them.

The Bank's supervisory role had been subject to intensive scrutiny in the aftermath of the BCCI and Barings affairs. In response it had reformed and elucidated its practices (Bank of England, 1996). It introduced the RATE (Risk Assessment, Tools and Evaluation) system similar to the US CAMELS[8] approach. It expanded the role of on-site examination but the contrast with the US highlighted by Hall (1993) remained. The UK put most reliance on a process culminating in a meeting at the Bank between senior Bank staff and a bank's senior management (frequently compared to a *viva voce* examination) designed to ensure that the bank was aware of what it was doing, rather than on the US style on-site (bank premises) inspection by bank examiners. The importance of surveillance was emphasized, and in particular the role of bank auditors in providing information (see, for example, Bank of England, 1997).

The 2000 Act referred to above was the third major legislative reorganization, following the 1979 and 1986–87 package of legislation which included the 1987 Banking Act.[9] However, the main driving forces behind change were the need to implement EU banking directives and the interrelated Basle accords on capital adequacy, as extended and promulgated by the Basle supervisors.[10] Besides the content of the capital regulations, the process was important in introducing an effective system of international cooperation in banking supervision. The Bank's main innovations were in its attempt to find a solution to the problem of choosing between supervisory (or discretionary) and formulaic methods of determining capital requirements. The Bank and its successor the FSA operated a system of so-called 'base plus' requirements. Banks were required to maintain the minimum as laid down by the Basle formulae but were also required to maintain additional amounts of capital at the Bank/FSA's discretion. These were designed to meet market risk, operational risk and any other risk that the FSA felt was not covered by the Basle requirements. In calculating these the Bank/FSA gave full scope to such innovations as value-at-risk and other internal methods of calculating capital requirements.

4 FINANCIAL DEREGULATION

Financial deregulation in the UK started with competition and credit control and the 1974 Consumer Credit Act. However, the 'corset' re-introduced many constraints, so deregulation really starts with the Thatcher government, which abolished exchange control in 1979 and dropped virtually all direct controls on banks with the credit control notices of 15 November 1979 and 26 March 1980. This appears to have been accompanied by intimations that banks were free to enter the retail mortgage market. Thereafter, banks nominally operated in a completely deregulated environment, but on occasion the authorities intervened to order them to adjust interest rates or intimated that lending policies were in some sense undesirable from a macroeconomic perspective. The actions were unimportant but banks may not have believed that the era of controls was over. Barclays in particular engaged in off-balance sheet and offshore banking as a precaution against the reintroduction of controls. The 1979 Banking Act was neither deregulation nor increased regulation but the move towards a more formal system was in a sense deregulation. Between 1982 and 1987 a whole new code of financial regulation was established in seven acts.[11] A new set of regulatory bodies was introduced. This was described as deregulation and in particular building societies acquired new powers to make unsecured loans and to take wholesale deposits. However, banks lost freedom in some areas, for example, the polarization rules meant that they could offer savings products of all suppliers or offer only their own or be a designated agent of a single supplier. They could no longer choose, say, three suppliers and offer only their products. The acts introduced a mechanism of compliance officers and led firms to start taping phone calls to ensure a trail for regulators. This – and the complexity, of the new arrangements – meant that some regarded them as re-regulation. Others argued that the simplest rule is, 'No' so deregulation was bound to be complex. The new regime generated uncertainty, as besides an amending act (300 clauses of the 1989 Companies Act) and various institutional changes, the first head of the Securities and Investments Board (SIB) (Sir Kenneth Berrill) was sacked and replaced by David Walker who was in turn replaced by Andrew Large who compared the regime he inherited to that in East Germany. The creation of the FSA in 1997 led to further uncertainty. Minor acts of deregulation continued to reduce regulation of fund management and investment banking. Viewed *ex post* and objectively, deregulation was official policy from 1979 and government regulators and banks collaborated to enact it and to deflect pressure from either Brussels or the media to impose additional regulations. Viewed at the time and subjectively, the system was far from a liberal model because of the uncertainty.

5 CONSUMER PROTECTION

The major legislative framework for consumer protection, narrowly defined, was the 1974 Consumer Credit Act. The various banking acts and the 2000 Financial Systems and Markets Act made some minor changes, notably replacing codes of practice with statutory regulation of mortgages in 2000. The 1979 act introduced a system of bank deposit insurance administered through a guarantee fund. This meant that the fund could *ex post* levy banks to meet its requirements rather than like the FDIC (Federal Deposit Insurance Corporation) charge an explicit premium. The government was protected from having to underwrite the fund as with the thrifts débâcle in the USA, while the banks felt they would normally pay less than with an explicit premium. The system incorporated both partial and co-insurance (75 per cent of the first £10,000 of a deposit); building societies had a separate and more generous scheme. These arrangements also satisfied the EU directives on the matter.

The most distinctive feature of the UK system was that much of consumer protection was delegated to specialist bodies called ombudsmen; there were seven of these, covering various aspects of finance, including banking, later (2001) amalgamated into one.

NOTES

1. Pimlott ascribes more substantive importance to the change than the conventional wisdom; for example, Cairncross, 1985, p. 465.
2. Congdon's Lombard Economic Review is a monthly publication which is distributed by Lombard Economic Research and widely read in the city and policy community.
3. It is an unusually pure example of the assignment of one instrument to one target as discussed in the 1960s 'Tinbergen' literature.
4. *Bank of England Quarterly Bulletin*, Vol. 26, No. 4, 1986, pp. 499–508.
5. See, for example, Thomas (1986), Reid (1988).
6. Truell and Gurwin (1992) describe the BCCI affair. It was investigated by the House of Commons and in the Bingham Report. References and an analysis of both reports and reactions can be found in Hall (1993). The Barings crisis is described in Gapper and Denton (1996).
7. For a discussion of the issue, see Goodhart and Schoenmaker (1995), Peek et al. (1999) and Briault (1999)
8. Camels are a composite rating of banks produced by US supervisors based on on-site examination. The acronym stands for Capital adequacy, Asset quality, Management quality, Earnings, Liquidity risk exposure and Sensitivity to market risk.
9. Banks were subject thereafter to financial services regulators as well as the Bank for various activities.
10. The most accessible sources for these are the Europa and BIS (www.BIS.org) websites.
11. Lloyds Act 1982, Police and Criminal Evidence Act 1984, Corporate Securities (Insider Trading Act) 1985, Financial Services Act 1986, Banking Act 1987, Criminal Justice Act 1987 (strictly two acts: CJA (1) and CJA (2), and Building Societies Act 1987.

REFERENCES

Bank of England (1971), *Competition and Credit Control*, London: Bank of England.

Bank of England (1983), *The Development and Operation of Monetary Policy*, Oxford: Clarendon Press.

Bank of England (1996), *The Bank's Review of Supervision*, London: Bank of England.

Bank of England (1997), *Bank's Internal Controls and the Section 39 Process*, London: Bank of England.

Blunden, Sir G. (1975), 'The supervision of the banking system', *Bank of England Quarterly Bulletin*, Vol. 15, No. 2, p. 188.

Briault, C. (1999), *The Rationale for a Single National Financial Services Regulator*, FSA Occasional Paper No. 2, London: FSA.

Cairncross, Sir Alec (1985), *Years of Recovery*, London: Methuen (University Paperback).

Chancellor of the Exchequer (1980), *Monetary Control*, Cmnd 7858, London: HMSO.

Chapman, R. (1970), *Decision Making*, London: Routledge & Kegan Paul.

Congdon, T. (1992), *Reflections on Monetarism*, Aldershot: Edward Elgar.

Eijffinger, S.C.W. (1997), 'Introduction' to Eijffinger (ed.), *Central Banks and Economic Performance*, Cheltenham, UK and Northampton, MA, USA: Edward Elgar.

Forder, J. (1996), 'On the assessment and implementation of institutional remedies', *Oxford Economic Papers*, Vol. 48, pp. 39–51.

Forder, J. (1998a), 'Central bank independence: conceptual classifications and interim assessments', *Oxford Economic Papers*, Vol. 50, No. 3, pp. 307–34.

Forder, J. (1998b), 'The case for an independent European Central Bank: a reassessment of evidence and sources', *European Journal of Political Economy*, Vol. 14, pp. 53–71.

Forder, J. (1999), 'Central bank independence: reassessing the measurements', *Journal of Economic Issues*, Vol. 33, No. 1, pp. 23–41.

Friedrich, K. (2000), 'The European Central Bank', *Newsweek*, 23 July.

Gapper, J. and N. Denton (1996), *All that Glitters*, London: Hamish Hamilton.

Goodhart, C.A.E. (1999), 'Recent developments in central banking: some special features of the Monetary Policy Committee and the European System of Central Banks', Financial Markets Group (LSE) Special Paper No. 118, London: London School of Economics.

Goodhart, C.A.E. and D. Schoenmaker (1995), 'Should the functions of monetary policy and banking supervision be separated?', *Oxford Economic Papers*, Vol. 47, No. 4, pp. 539–62.

Gowland, D.H. (1982), *Controlling the Money Supply*, London: Croom Helm.

Gowland, D.H. (1991), *Money Inflation and Unemployment*, Brighton: Harvester Wheatsheaf (second edition 1995).

Gowland, D.H. (1992), 'The UK Bond Market', *Economia*, Societa e Istituzioni, **IV** (1), pp. 7–41.

Gowland, D.H. (1997), *Banking on Change*, London: Politeia.

Hall, M.J.B. (1993), *Banking Regulation and Supervision: A Comparative Study of the UK, USA and Japan*, Aldershot: Edward Elgar.

Harrod, Sir Roy F. (1951), *The Life of John Maynard Keynes*, London: Macmillan.

Kopcke, R.W. and R.C. Kimball (1999), 'Inflation-indexed bonds: the dog that didn't bark', *New England Economic Review*, January, pp. 3–24.
Peek, J.S., E.S. Rosengren and G.M.B. Tootell (1999), 'Is bank supervision central to central banking?', Working Paper 99-13, Federal Reserve Bank of Boston.
Pimlott, B. (1985), *Hugh Dalton*, London: Macmillan.
Rankin, N. (1998), 'Is delegating half of demand management sensible?', *International Review of Applied Economics*, Vol. 12, pp. 437–94.
Raw, C., B. Page and G. Hodgson (1972), *Do You Sincerely Want to be Rich?*, Harmondsworth: Penguin (also Andre Deutsch, 1971).
Reid, M.I. (1982), *The Secondary Banking Crisis*, London: Macmillan.
Reid, M.I. (1988), *All-Change in the City*, London: Macmillan.
Thomas, W.A. (1986), *The Big Bang*, Oxford: Philip Allan.
Truell, P. and L. Gurwin (1992), *BCCI*, London: Bloomsbury.
Wilson, J.S.G. (1993), *Money Markets*, London: Routledge.

12. Financial sector reform in Vietnam

Rainer Klump and Klaus Gottwald

1 INTRODUCTION

For more than a decade the Socialist Republic of Vietnam has been undergoing a 'double transition'. The country, which has suffered from war and division, has made enormous efforts to escape economic underdevelopment by repeating the growth miracles of other Southeast Asian nations. This ambitious aim could, however, only be achieved by breaking with the economic model of rigid state planning and control which had been practised in North Vietnam since independence in 1954 and which was introduced in the South immediately after reunification in 1975. Disastrous economic results at the end of the 1970s forced the Vietnamese government to implement substantial reforms which were enacted after 1986 as part of a new policy approach called *doi moi* (renovation). Similar to the development in the People's Republic of China the liberalization of the economy was not, however, accompanied by a fundamental change in the political structure, which is still characterized by the undisputed supremacy of the Communist Party.

The Vietnamese financial system clearly reflects the successes and problems of this particular strategy of transformation. On the one hand, it was understood that a fundamental reform of the country's monetary and financial system, including external financial relations, was a crucial prerequisite for becoming a dynamically growing market economy. Thus the socialist monobanking system was changed into a two-tier banking system with the state bank conducting the function of a central bank. A multitude of state-owned as well as private, local and foreign banks have been permitted to operate in the country. Furthermore an interbank market, an interbank foreign exchange market and a treasury bond market have emerged. Even a stock market was established. On the other hand, the economic heritage of the old system – the dominance of state-owned banks, the inefficiency of most state-owned enterprises and strong political influence in all economic matters – is the main reason for the lasting fragility of the Vietnamese financial system. Thus the recent Asian crisis, which has contributed to an even larger instability of the entire financial sector, has not only slowed down Vietnam's ambitious development efforts but has also delayed the country's progress towards a well-functioning market economy (Klump and Spitzenpfeil, 1998, p. 335).

2 ECONOMIC TRANSFORMATION IN VIETNAM

The new policy of *doi moi* which the Communist Party of Vietnam instituted at its Sixth Party Congress in 1986 was intended to combine courageous economic and cautious political reforms. After various but failed attempts to carry out currency reforms in 1976, 1979 and 1985 (Hauskrecht, 1998, p. 46), inflation reached ruinous heights of 775 per cent in early 1986 (Ngo, 1997, p. 121), leading to widespread pauperization of large parts of the Vietnamese society. As a result of this critical situation the government was forced to start with reforms of the price and rationing systems, the exchange rate system and retail trade. It also granted greater autonomy for state enterprises. With its Law on Foreign Investment of December 1987, the government lowered the barriers for foreign companies to enter the Vietnamese market. After two more years of experimentation, economic reforms went into full swing in 1988. The most important reform steps included the formation of market prices and fundamental changes in the agricultural sector, changing the basis of farming from the collective to the household. The household and private sectors were given legal recognition and the autonomy of state enterprises was extended. In 1989 the collapse of the Eastern European countries forced the government to seek new markets and to focus on reforms of foreign trade: the multiple official exchange rates were unified at a level which was in line with the parallel market rate; export subsidies as well as a number of import duties and export taxes were abolished. In 1990, important laws – the Law on Private Enterprise and the Law on Companies – were passed, followed in 1993 by the Law on Bankruptcy and the Law on Domestic Investment (Fforde and Goldstone, 1995, pp. 7 ff.). The state-owned enterprises (SOEs) were given substantial autonomy regarding price setting, selection of inputs and outputs and determination of investments. In order to make them more efficient they were exposed to greater competition and harder budget constraints. Most direct subsidies for SOEs were cut. After the closing of about 6,000 unprofitable SOEs the 'equitization' of the remaining 6,000 state companies started in 1992. 'Equitization' is the government's preferred term for its policy of partial privatization, meaning that the state will keep a significant share of the newly equitized state enterprises. This process, however, proceeded rather hesitantly with no more than 17 SOEs equitized during 1992–97. After official data suggested that 60 per cent of SOEs were running losses or were only marginally profitable, the equitization programme has gained some momentum since 1998 with 130 SOEs (mainly small and medium sized) being equitized during the 15 months to March 1999 (IMF, 1999).

In 1992 the Vietnamese economy emerged from the transition period without pervasive direct subsidies or controls on prices and output. Inflation decreased to 17.5 per cent and the economy grew at an annual rate of 8.7 per cent. In the period from 1992 to 1997, GDP growth ranged between 8.1 per cent and 9.5 per cent, making Vietnam one of the fastest-growing and most auspicious markets in the developing world (Fforde and Goldstone, 1995, p. 11, figures for 1992–94; EIU, 1997, p. 10, figures for 1995–96; and Kyodo News Service, 1998, figure for 1997). Because of the government's tight monetary and fiscal policy, inflation could be further reduced from 14.4 per cent in 1994 to 3.6 per cent in 1997 (Fforde and de Vylder, 1996, p. 301, figures for 1986–92; SBV, 1998, p. 71, figures for 1993–97). Between 1992 and 1996 the official dollar target rate of the national currency, the Vietnamese dong (VND), could be stabilized at a level of VND 11,000 with a tolerated trading band of +/−0.5 per cent, which was sufficient to maintain external competitiveness (Dodsworth et al., 1996, pp. 38ff.). Due to the macroeconomic successes, as well as to Vietnam's strategic location and the dynamic development of other Asian countries, many foreign companies and banks considered that Vietnam would become the next 'Asian Tiger' and greatly increased their activities in the country at the beginning of the 1990s. In 1995 Vietnam became a member of the Association of South East Asian Nations (ASEAN) and is supposed to enter the Asian Free Trade Area (AFTA) not later than 2003. Vietnam concluded a bilateral trade agreement with the United States by the end of 1999 and also became an observer of the World Trade Organization (WTO). This means that negotiations for WTO membership are expected to start within five years.

In spite of single-digit inflation rates and a record level of realized foreign direct investment (FDI) in 1997, there were clear signs of an economic slowdown, not least as a consequence of the Asian financial crisis and Vietnam's close economic ties with its neighbours. The growth rate plunged to 5.8 per cent in 1998 and 4.8 per cent in 1999. New FDI commitments decreased dramatically in 1998 and 1999, and it could be observed that companies from the crisis-shaken Asian countries, which generally lead the list of foreign investors in Vietnam, reduced or even cancelled their planned investments. In addition, the ongoing financial crisis of many of the SOEs, which still contribute nearly two-thirds to total industrial output and 40 per cent to GDP (CIEM, 1999) will reduce future development prospects and make growth rates ranging between 4 per cent and 5 per cent in 2000 and

2001 likely. Moreover, investors have become increasingly cautious since long-lasting problems such as an inefficient bureaucracy (sometimes labelled the worst in Asia), unfavourable and shifting regulations, official corruption and an inadequate legal and physical infrastructure still dramatically hamper business activities in Vietnam. Some big companies have already felt the consequences. For example, the Australian oil company BHP and the American car company Chrysler, which planned to build a $192 million plant in Vietnam to assemble Dodge Dakotas and Cherokee Jeeps, left the country in 1997 (Huus, 1998). Meanwhile, the government reacted to the growing unrest among the business community by calling a meeting with foreign investors in March 1999. At this meeting the issues of dual pricing, business licensing fees and regulations on wages were discussed extensively. As a result of the conference, from July 1999, foreigners will enjoy the same price for clean water supply and telephone installation as the Vietnamese, the excessively high business licensing fees will be reduced and the minimum wage will be determined and paid in dong instead of US dollars. Whether these measures will prove sufficient to restore confidence in the business environment, however, is not yet predictable (Dang Hong Nga, 1999, pp. 6ff.).

In fact since 1993 the Communist Party has instituted only minor economic reforms. The reigning triumvirate of Party General Secretary Le Kha Phieu, President Tran Duc Luong and Prime Minister Phan Van Khai has already announced a slow pace of economic reforms rather than risk political and social instability with hasty 'shock therapies'. The expected social unrest due to possible high unemployment rates, higher inflation and rising costs for imported goods leaves the government reluctant to implement radical reform steps (Huckshorn, 1998). It must be doubtful whether this gradualist approach is still adequate to ensure continued high economic growth and to fulfil the expectations of rising prosperity that were raised in large parts of the Vietnamese population during the first half of the 1990s (Klump and Spitzenpfeil, 1998, p. 338).

3 THE STRUCTURE OF THE VIETNAMESE FINANCIAL SYSTEM

In 1954 after the French colonial period and the partition of the country, all financial institutions in the North were nationalized and merged to form the State Bank of Vietnam. The same happened after reunification in the South. The banking sector was an integral part of the planning system and in charge of the implementation of the public sector's credit and cash plans. The banking system had a passive role and the government paid little attention to monetary issues (Teufel, 1997, p. 79; Rana and Hamid, 1995, p. 366). In 1958 and 1963, respectively, two state-owned specialized banks were established, the Bank for Investment and Development and the Bank for Foreign Trade. They were not independent banks but only functional departments of the state bank.

With *doi moi* it was recognized that the financial sector plays a key role in economic development by financing trade activities, mobilizing saving funds and channelling them to profitable investments. The reforms initiated in 1988 were promulgated in two important laws issued in October 1990. The first, the Law for the Vietnamese State Bank, confirmed the shift to a two-tiered banking system. It provided for the separation of the state bank from its former commercial functions which were transferred to the state commercial banks (the two banks already mentioned) as well as the Vietnam Industrial and Commercial Bank and the Bank for Agriculture and Rural Development, both newly created in 1991. The second law was the National Law on Banks, Cooperative Credit Institutions and Financial Institutions, which gave the state commercial banks greater autonomy, permitted operation of private commercial banks (joint-stock banks, joint-venture banks, credit cooperatives) and allowed the opening of foreign bank branches or representative offices (Fforde and Goldstone, 1995, pp. 34ff.). It soon became obvious that the existing rules needed to be streamlined and clarified for greater financial transparency. In December 1997 after two years of discussions the National Assembly finally passed two revised banking laws – one dealing with the state bank and one affecting other intermediaries – which became effective on 1 October 1998. The new banking laws include some provisions for credit approval procedures as well as measures for interest control and internal auditing, but some contentious points lack the clarifying details and therefore need to be supplemented by later legislation. The expectations of foreign bankers for a broader scope of operations, particularly with regard to security of local assets, were also not fulfilled (*Asia Pulse*, 1997).

The State Sector Banks

The State Bank and the Bank of the Poor

The State Bank of Vietnam (SBV) is authorized to manage and control all monetary, credit and banking activities, to issue banknotes and coins and to act as the bank for other banks and for the state. Monetary policy instruments, however, are still heavily influenced by the past planned economy to the extent that prices and quantities in the banking system are very largely determined by direct intervention of the state bank. Market-economy instruments of monetary policy, such as minimum reserve requirements, rediscount policy and open market policy are only gradually being developed (Klump and Spitzenpfeil, 1998, p. 340). Hence, the most popular instrument of steering the money supply is interest rate policy. Until January 1996 interest rates were applied according to deposit type, tenor and depositor. In 1996, banks were given some discretion in setting specific interest rates subject to a maximum spread of 0.35 per cent per month. Although the state bank has been very successful in restricting total money supply and fighting inflation during the 1990s, its independence from political pressure is far from being realized since it is organizationally closely linked to the government and its activities are largely controlled by the prime minister's office and the Politburo (Marshall, 1998).

The Bank for the Poor, jointly owned by the SBV and the Bank for Agricultural and Rural Development, was established mainly as a distribution channel for development funds and started operating in January 1996. Essentially it is a non-profit credit organization with the objective of mobilizing capital and giving preferential financing and lending conditions only to underprivileged classes and rural areas (Murray, 1999, p. 19; Wolff, 1999, p. 53).

State-owned commercial banks (SOCBs)

The state-owned Vietnam Bank for Foreign Trade (Vietcombank) is the largest bank in the country. It is involved mainly in banking services in foreign-related sectors, financing import-export activities and carrying out international settlements. In 1996 it held a share of 60 per cent of total foreign transactions (Freeman, 1996, p. 68).

The Vietnam Bank for Investment and Development (VBID) concentrates on financing state-investment projects. It is funded by the state budget and invests in infrastructure projects as well as technological and economic development projects.

The Vietnam Industrial and Commercial Bank (Incombank) operates mainly in lending to several industries, such as transport, communication, commerce and services.

The Bank for Agriculture and Rural Development (Agribank) remains the most important financial institution for rural areas and specializes, as its name suggests, in the agricultural sector and provides loans and other banking and consulting services for farming, forestry and fishery businesses through its wide network of 2,654 local branches (Asian Development Bank, 1996, p. 10). The Agribank increasingly relies on group loans and such intermediaries as cooperatives and the farmers' association to reduce transaction costs in the small loan business.

The Bank for House Development in the Mekong Delta is a joint-stock bank and started operating at the end of March 1998. The government contributed VND 500 billion to the bank's charter capital and an additional VND 100 billion to a number of SOEs in Ho Chi Minh City. The new bank will primarily provide loans to peasants for the building and repairing of houses and for investments in production, livestock raising and cultivation (VNA, 1998).

The Private Sector Banks

Joint-stock banks (JSBs)

The first joint-stock banks (or share banks) came into existence in 1990 (McReynolds, 1998, p. 30). Some of them are owned jointly by the state and private groups and individuals, while others are completely in private hands. In the beginning, the majority of stock was held by SOEs which were trying to diversify their business activities. Meanwhile, there are some share banks that have a majority of private ownership. The headquarters of these banks are mostly located in Ho Chi Minh City. The major ones are the Vietnam Export-Import Bank, the Maritime Commercial Bank and the Saigon Bank for Industry and Trade. According to the annual report of the state bank, there are currently 51 joint-stock commercial banks operating in Vietnam, 41 of which are privately owned (SBV, 1999, p. 55). After experiencing rapid growth during the past nine years, some of these private banks are now encountering a multitude of difficulties – a low capital base, poor risk management and the use of outdated technology – and therefore have to undergo a period of consolidation. Observers are convinced that if the process of restructuring JSBs is mastered successfully, then the private banks – despite their limited size – might play an increasingly important role in the country's banking industry since they react with more flexibility and innovation to the demands of the market. Some own warehouses so that durable consumption goods, for example, motorcycles (Irvine, 1998, p. 23) can also be mortgaged as collateral for credit (Nguyen and Guretzky-Cornitz, 1996, p. 277). Among the banks under special control by the state bank are Viet Hoa Bank, Ficombank, Que Do Bank and Nam Do Bank.

Joint-venture banks (JVBs)

The four joint-venture banks in Vietnam, Indovina Bank (established in 1990 as the first bank of this kind), VID Public Bank, Firstvina Bank and Vinasiam Bank are all characterized by a mixture of foreign capital and local expertise. They are 50:50 joint ventures between the state-owned commercial banks (Incombank, VBID, Vietcombank and BARD) and foreign banks (Bank Dagang Nasional Indonesia, Public Bank Malaysia, Korea First Bank & Daewoo Securities and the Thai Siam Commercial Bank and

Charoen Pokphand Group). Indovina Bank is the best known of the four JVBs and enjoys a good reputation. The JVBs focus mainly on the financing of foreign trade activities (Nguyen and Guretzky-Cornitz, 1996, p. 277).

Foreign Banks

The history of foreign banks in Vietnam actually reaches back to the colonial period. Before 1975 there were many French and American banks operating in the South. After reunification most left, but they returned with Vietnam's move towards economic liberalization. The first foreign bank branch licence was given to the French bank Indosuez in 1991. At the end of the 1990s there were 24 foreign bank branches operating in the narrow Vietnamese market (SBV, 1999, p. 55). Trade financing, providing letters of credit for import and export as well as remittance processing are the most important parts of the foreign banks' daily business. However, due to intensive competition among the many banks in the country, the rewards are small and risks are fairly high (N.N., 1996, p. 11). In addition, foreign bank operations are constrained by not being allowed to accept land as security. The foreign banks' predominant customers used to be joint-venture companies or foreign companies, but since the beginning of 1997 they also attract more and more of the profitable SOEs by providing better service and large loans. Loans by foreign banks to SOEs in Ho Chi Minh City doubled during the first six months of 1997, while state-owned banks had an increase of only 4 per cent in lending to the state sector (N.N., 1997, pp. 32ff.). In the first nine months of 1997, all bank loans amounted to VND 49 trillion ($4.2 billion) and 49 per cent of the total was approved by foreign banks (Keenan, 1997b, p. 72). Foreign banks' efforts to attract funds were equally successful. Total fund mobilization by the foreign banks and joint-venture banks totalled VND 21 trillion ($1.62 billion) or 19 per cent of all funds raised by the banking system (*Asia Pulse*, 1997). The many representative offices of foreign banks operating in Vietnam (in 1998 there were 79) have to limit their activities solely to business negotiations and are not allowed to carry out financial transactions actively.

The presence of numerous foreign bank branches and JVBs in Vietnam has already brought about some positive changes to the entire industry by putting domestic banks under pressure to optimize their operations. For example, in March 1995, 13 Vietnamese banks started to conclude their international payments through the SWIFT network, a move carried out earlier than at some banks in the Philippines or Indonesia (Nguyen and Guretzky-Cornitz, 1996, p. 277).

Cooperative Associations

Credit cooperatives

Credit cooperatives are unions of private persons or enterprises contributing capital to a common fund in order to provide credit services to their members. Between 1988 and 1990 there were about 7,900 credit cooperatives. At the beginning of 1990 a number of these credit cooperatives tried to attract deposits by offering rates sometimes as much as four times as high as the banks. Since there was no deposit insurance and the cooperatives did not hold any reserve assets, some of them went bankrupt. After the first cases became public, depositors lost faith in the cooperatives and withdrew their money, which resulted in the closing of most of the credit cooperatives and about 2,000 small private firms. As a consequence of this first crash in the banking sector, the government recognized that the secondary credit market also needed regulation and thus the Law on Banks, Cooperative Credit Institutions and Financial Institutions of 1990 implemented stricter controls for the licensing and supervision of the credit cooperatives. The number of credit cooperatives then decreased to a mere 82, and their importance continued to decline (Klump and Spitzenpfeil, 1998, p. 343).

People's credit funds

To supplement the activities of the Vietnam Bank for Agriculture and Development (Agribank) in rural finance, in 1993 the state bank created a system of credit cooperatives, the so-called 'people's credit funds', which, apart from a few small semi-private rural shareholding banks, are the only alternative to the Agribank in the rural areas. They are approved by the state bank and managed by local villagers, but often the staff lack banking training and technical equipment (Rana and Hamid, 1995, pp. 367ff.; Asian Development Bank, 1996, p. 48). The People's Credit Funds have so far been able to mobilize only a small volume of savings capital and therefore depend on refinancing funds from the state bank or the Agribank. These problems were not unexpected, considering the failure of the credit cooperatives in the early 1990s and hence, considerable confidence-building efforts are needed if more local savings capital is to be mobilized in the medium term. Nevertheless, these new financial institutions seem suitable for rural financing mainly because, being so close to their clients, their collateral requirements are less stringent. Today there are about 950 of these mainly province-based institutions aiming to set rural financing on new foundations (Wolff, 1999, pp. 53ff.).

Financing Institutions and Insurance Companies

Financing institutions can be either public or private owned. Their major purpose is to give credit for purchases and sales of goods and services (Nguyen and Pham, 1994, p. 87). To date, there are two joint-stock finance companies, three corporation-subordinated finance companies and eight leasing companies operating in Vietnam (SBV, 1999, p. 55). In the insurance sector the state insurance Bao Viet held a monopoly until 1995. Since then four local companies have been established but Bao Viet still holds a market share of about 65 per cent and has an interest in several joint ventures and joint-stock companies (Levine, 1998, p. 38). Already in 1993, foreign insurance companies were given permission to operate in the local market but only three international companies have since set up joint ventures with Bao Viet or with Bao Minh, the second-largest of the Vietnamese insurers. Until early 1999, foreigners had been forced to sign joint-venture arrangements with domestic entities since 100 per cent foreign-owned insurance companies were forbidden by law (Murray, 1997, p. 191). However, this situation changed recently when the Politburo reaffirmed its endorsement that insurers can obtain 100 per cent foreign-owned licences (Levine, 1998, p. 38). In August 1999, the first of such wholly foreign-owned insurance companies – a joint venture between Canada's Manulife and Taiwan's Chinfon Group – started operations in Ho Chi Minh City.

Financial Markets and the Foreign Exchange System

The Vietnamese interbank market was established in July 1993 for both foreign exchange and short-term domestic currency transactions (Murray, 1999, p. 20). The banks have since been able to trade their liquid resources among themselves without any interference from the state bank (Wolff, 1999, p. 46). For foreign banks whose local-currency-gathering activities are restricted, the market has become the principle source of funding. Although the domestic banks appear quite active, the market is still very limited. Its fragile nature was highlighted during the first months of 1998 when the interbank market for foreign exchange nearly ceased to function. The daily volume of interbank exchange transactions, in 1996 more than $8 million, plunged to under $200,000 early in 1998 because of massive dollar hoarding preceding an expected devaluation of the Vietnamese dong (Dow Jones, 1998). In the second half of 1998, in addition to exchange rate adjustments, this situation relaxed and the market operated positively with transaction volume rapidly increasing to a daily volume of approximately $20–30 million (SBV, 1999, p. 35). The Treasury also developed a retail market for government bonds and runs branches all over the country where two-year bonds with values as low as VND 100,000 can be bought. Treasury bill auctions by the state bank began only in 1995. Bidders are mainly Vietnamese state-owned banks and insurance companies. Participation by joint-stock, joint-venture and foreign banks is still limited to testing the market. But due to a lack of a secondary market the Treasury's practice of issuing minimum bidding prices and restrictions on the participation of foreign banks, bill auctions still have only a minor role. In 1996, treasury bonds worth only $759 million were sold, with just 2 per cent of the sales resulting from treasury bill auctions (Duc, 1997, pp. 32ff.).

A particular feature of the Vietnamese economy is the large use of the US dollar as a parallel currency. In the decade prior to 1985 there were no significant holdings of foreign currency in Vietnam (Leung and Duc, 1999, p. 84). During the 1980s, Vietnam's trade was predominantly conducted with the former Soviet bloc on a convertible rouble basis and there was no incentive for trading firms to optimize their portfolio holdings. This situation began to change in the wake of economic liberalization in 1986, with the expansion in foreign currency holdings becoming particularly pronounced in 1989. Today, official sources acknowledge a total circulation of $600 million, but unofficial estimates are of about $3 billion or even more (Freeman, 1998); (Party Secretary Le Kha Phieu cited a figure of $5 million); gold holdings are supposed to be of about the same value. This high degree of dollarization in the Vietnamese economy was brought about by certain institutional changes that made it easier for firms and households to hold US dollars. First, in 1988, the legal ban on holding dollars was ended as foreign exchange surrender requirements were lifted and the use of foreign currency holdings within the domestic banking system was liberalized for companies and individuals. Since May 1991, banks have also been allowed to offer foreign currency time deposits, for which they guarantee conversion back into the currency of deposit. Second, with the collapse of the former Soviet Union and the changes in trade and FDI, transactors began to use dollars to make international payments. Third, in 1989, with an effective fivefold devaluation in the official exchange rate and with further devaluations expected to come, the holding of dollars provided a useful substitute for the domestic currency as a store of value. It is therefore not surprising that these developments together with the hyperinflationary experience of 1986–88, when the average inflation rate (general retail prices) reached 356 per cent per annum, led to an upward shift in dollar holdings. The (official) foreign currency deposits in Vietnam rose from $135 million in 1986 to $815 million in 1992, an amount corresponding to 31 per cent of M2 compared to 2 per cent in 1986 (Leung and Duc, 1999, p. 85).

4 STRUCTURAL DEFICITS AND RECENT REFORMS

Structural Deficits of the Vietnamese Financial Sector

Even after a decade of transition, the structures of the Vietnamese financial system are still characterized by a remarkably low financial intermediation ratio, a continuously high importance of dollarization and a very pronounced and dangerous bias of capital allocation towards the SOEs. The legal uncertainty of private property rights in a socialist market economy as well as the ongoing strong influence of the state in the whole financial system can be identified as a common source of these structural deficits.

The ratio of M2 to nominal GDP in Vietnam amounted to 27 per cent in 1997, compared to more than 90 per cent in Malaysia and about 80 per cent in Thailand (Kubota, 1998, p. 3). Only about 5 per cent of the Vietnamese used a bank account or any other banking service; the overwhelming majority preferred to accumulate savings in the form of gold stocks, buildings and houses or dollar cash holdings. The 1992/93 household survey discovered that about three-quarters of savings were accumulated outside the banking sector. Potential customers deeply mistrust domestic financial intermediaries for several reasons: they fear the type of wealth losses which had been experienced with the breakdown of many credit cooperatives and which may arise at some of the joint-stock banks; they also wish to protect private income streams and financial asset holdings from state control (and taxation) and they eschew banks because of poor service and low real returns on deposits (Klump and Spitzenpfeil, 1998, p. 9). At the same time, domestic banks themselves do not have strong incentives to compete for increasing dong deposits. Due to the state bank's regulation of lending rate ceilings and given the banks' generally high operating costs, they cannot expect additional profits from attracting new deposits by offering higher deposit rates (Murray, 1997, pp. 174ff.). Because of the low profitability of most Vietnamese banks and inadequate bank supervision, the World Bank has proposed a limitation on the total number of banking licences in order to increase the banks' efforts to mobilize local capital (World Bank, 1995, p. 8). Concerning credit cooperatives, this proposal has already been turned into reality: in 1999 and 2000 new licences were given to this branch of the local financial market.

The high degree of dollarization sets additional limits on the banks' activities. Since about one-fifth of demand and time deposits was denominated in foreign currencies, mainly in US dollars (SBV, 1997, p. 17), the attractiveness of dong deposits required that in real terms dong interest rates had to be higher than dollar interest rates. During the period of disinflation, which was also a period of relative exchange rate stability, the legal acceptance of currency substitution by the Vietnamese government appeared to be a very helpful strategy in order to restore and maintain confidence in the future value of the domestic currency. With lower domestic inflation the attractiveness of the dong as a store of value increased and the higher domestic demand for dong then contributed to a further fall in inflation rates (Dodsworth et al., 1996, p. 31). The hysteresis of currency substitution, even at the present low level of domestic inflation, can be explained by three factors: first, by the fear of future reinflation given the strong personal and functional linkages between the state bank and the Vietnamese government; second by the effects of Vietnam's exchange rate policy over the last two years. Since November 1996 the state bank has been forced to devalue the dong against the dollar in several steps by varying the official dollar target rate as well as by widening the trading band and further devaluations are expected, which will increase the demand for dollars (Keenan, 1997a, p. 95). Third, the dollar is expected to remain a popular medium of transaction given the very small denominations of the dong notes – the highest denomination (VND 50,000) is worth $3.50 – and because the Vietnamese lack familiarity with the use of credit cards and cheque accounts. As Vietnam's financial sector and its payments system will continue to develop, the transaction motive can be expected to diminish as well as the dollarization of the economy (Leung and Duc, 1999, pp. 84f.).

The ratio of overdue loans in the entire banking sector accounted for 3.5 per cent of the total outstanding loan balances in 1995. This ratio soared to 13.6 per cent in 1997 and to around 16 per cent in 1998 (Kim Chi, 1999, p. 17). The state bank claims that overdue loans in the state-owned bank sector average 9.4 per cent with a range of 2.4 per cent to 19 per cent; however, foreign bankers say these figures are only the 'tip of the iceberg' (Schiffrin, 1999, p. 29). For joint-stock banks this ratio is significantly higher: about 17 per cent of credit assets are classified as overdue with some private joint-stock banks recording overdue loans of more than 90 per cent of total credit (Murray, 1999, p. 20). A central bank study found that overdue loans at Nam Do joint-stock bank in Ho Chi Minh City comprised 94.3 per cent of all outstanding loans. To avoid customer panic, the state bank allocated cash to the ailing JSB and called on other banks for support. Finally, Nam Do was taken over by the state-owned Investment and Development Bank. Because of the relatively higher proportion of impaired assets some analysts claim that the risk of financial crisis in Vietnam's banking system, however small, does exist. But these fears probably overstate the real dangers for the Vietnamese economy. While the ratio of non-performing loans to total loans is higher than in some Asian countries (that is, in

Malaysia 5.7 per cent; in Indonesia 9.2 per cent), the ratio of non-performers to GDP – an indicator of systems vulnerability – is very low at just 3 per cent of GDP (Malaysia 23 per cent; Indonesia 43 per cent) (Allen, 1998, p. 50. These figures are valid for September 1997). Nevertheless, many of the figures concerning impaired loans in the Vietnamese banking sector are necessarily based on estimates, since accounting methods do not conform to international standards. All banks in Vietnam complain about the lack of both solid financial information and tangible assets to secure loans. A lack of interbank communication and credit checking still makes it easy to mortgage a single property to several banks. Therefore Vietnamese banks have always had a natural preference for loans to the SOEs, hoping that the government will ultimately discharge their debts (Klump and Spitzenpfeil, 1998, p. 347).

Until early 1998, loans were not classified as impaired until they were overdue by at least 360 days. Since January 1998, banks have been required to analyse the quality of their loans and to classify them according to four categories (Murray, 1999, p. 20): (i) performing; (ii) past due by 180 days; (iii) past due by 181 days to 360 days and (iv) past due by more than 360 days. But non-performing assets are still not publicly disclosed and the classifications do not, however, mirror the propensity of losses. Hence there is urgent need to revise these regulations. Loan classification and loan-loss provisions must reflect stricter time-based classification. The current capital-asset ratio of 5 per cent is too low (compared to 8 per cent in Thailand and Korea and 10 per cent in Malaysia) and is not even assessed on a risk-weighted basis. A first step was to improve the prudential standards of the Vietnamese financial system and to address the credibility deficits at the joint-stock banks in late 1998 when these institutions were forced to increase their minimum capital requirements to VND 70 billion.

Recent Reforms in the Vietnamese Financial Sector

Although the cautious, gradualistic approach to reform adopted by the Vietnamese government during the 1990s has proved successful in some respects – the number of banks has risen substantially and confidence in the stability of the currency and the banking system is slowly improving – Vietnam is none the less still far from having a modern market-economy financial regime.

In the past the Vietnamese government too often showed a tendency to postpone necessary reforms. But the shock of the Asian crisis that led to the breakdown of numerous overleveraged credit institutions in neighbouring countries, intensified the pressure on the country to overhaul its ailing banking system in order to prevent a similar experience in Vietnam. As a result of these efforts, new banking legislation was introduced in October 1998 and measures to tackle the severe weaknesses of the joint-stock banks and the state-owned banks were taken in the same year. We shall now examine in greater detail the reforms initiated since the outbreak of the Asian crisis in 1997.

Central bank reform

The new Law on the State Bank of Vietnam (LSBV) (Socialist Republic of Vietnam, 1998a), which was introduced on 1 October 1998, was highly controversial. Whereas some analysts regarded the codification of new banking regulation as an important milestone in the development of the market (Murray, 1999, p. 17) or at least as a step in the right direction, the vast majority of observers inside and outside Vietnam rather speak of a serious setback in the process of financial reform. According to the law, the state bank's operations will 'facilitate the socio-economic development in a manner consistent with socialist orientation' (Art. 1.3). Furthermore, the state bank will conduct the state's management over monetary and banking activities which include ensuring the leading role of state-owned credit institutions in monetary and banking activities, maintaining the socialist orientation and the national sovereignty (Art. 2). The state bank governor is supposed to be a member of the government (Art. 11). Accordingly, the governor, Nguyen Tan Dung, who was elected in May 1998, continued his previous functions as one of the deputy prime ministers of Vietnam and was at the same time a member of the Politburo (Irvine, 1998, p. 22). Although Dung was considered to be a reformer, who initiated long-awaited reforms among the joint-stock banks, his membership of one of the most powerful political bodies of the country underlined the strong functional and personal linkage between the SBV and the central government. In addition, the plan for the national monetary policy and the estimated annual inflation rate is prepared by the government and approved by the National Assembly. The state bank provides annual advances to the state budget whose amounts are coordinated by the Ministry of Finance and the prime minister (Art. 6.2).

The organizational structure of the state bank comprises branches in every one of Vietnam's 61 provinces. Hence, tightening this extensive network in order to achieve greater centralization of regional organization is in fact one important reform issue for the coming years which will be pursued enthusiastically by the SBV. Nevertheless, it is doubtful whether the ambitious plan will be realized in the short run since it goes against the interest of local and regional policy leaders.

The new legislation did not provide for profound changes in the way monetary policy is carried out. The supremacy of control-oriented rather than market-based instruments is still largely intact, even if the use of credit ceilings as a regular instrument in conducting monetary policy came to an end in the second quarter of 1998. The SBV, however, continued managing the interest rate in the monetary market by regulating the ceiling of the lending rate in dong and foreign currencies, forcing banks to allocate credit on some basis other than market interest rates. Differential pricing based on risk and tenor is therefore not widespread among the domestic banks. Hence, credit may not flow to those activities where it is most productive or obtain the highest return.

The introduction of open market operations as an instrument of monetary policy is an important issue on the reform agenda of the SBV. According to the state bank report it was planned to put the open market into operation in 1999, but at the moment this plan seems rather too ambitious considering the still quite narrow and fragmented nature of the Vietnamese financial sector. Although the number of regular auctions of treasury bills has risen considerably and the state bank intends to issue more state bank bills to provide additional instruments for open market operations, daily interventions by the SBV to control the monetary base are still not practicable. Therefore, it will take some time before the money and capital markets are sufficiently developed for the state bank to be able to operate an open market regime as an alternative to the prevailing direct control of the money supply. Similarly, the liberalization of interest rates will be possible only when the banking system has a sounder basis of capital resources (Wolff, 1999, pp. 53ff.).

Since the early stages of financial reform during the late 1980s, the bank supervision function has been performed by the state bank. The LSBV confirmed the supreme role of the SBV in the field of inspection and auditing (Arts 50–57). Nevertheless, there are plans to transfer the banking supervision function to independent private auditing companies in the future. Yet, only one joint-stock bank – the small but strong Asia Commercial Bank (ACB) – has been audited by an international accounting firm (Irvine, 1999, p. 18).

Commercial bank reform

The new Vietnamese Law on Credit Institutions (LCI) (Socialist Republic of Vietnam, 1998b) took effect on 1 October 1998 and specifies a model of the Vietnamese banking system, provisions on prudent operations of the banking system and powers and responsibilities of credit institutions as a legal basis to conduct monetary operations. In its first chapter (especially Arts 1–10), the law is even more characterized by anti-reformist rhetoric than the law on the state bank. In the preamble the law expresses the will to contribute 'to a socialist-oriented multisector market economy operating under the state management'. The law emphasizes the state's power to issue special credit policies in favour of the state-owned enterprises and the cooperatives, which will play a leading role and become the foundation of the national economy (Arts 6 and 7). Also, preferential credit policies in favour of the agricultural sector, needy areas and regions and underprivileged persons are made possible (Arts 8–10). The role of the private sector and private banks in the development of a 'multisector market economy' is not mentioned explicitly in the law.

Growing rapidly during the 1990s, the (privately owned) joint-stock banks – at present they represent about 10 per cent of the system's assets – have recently been subject to severe stress. Most of these private banks have failed to develop a business plan and therefore lack a clear strategy. They suffer from a weak interest rate and credit risk management caused by the traditionally close relationship between the borrower and the bank's management. Additionally, the use of outdated technology has limited the ability of many JSBs to compete with highly sophisticated foreign banks (McReynolds, 1998, p. 30). In early 1998, two Ho Chi Minh City-based joint-stock banks – Nam Do and VP Bank – were in severe trouble after signing company guarantees without the required mortgages and only immediate support by the state bank and some other banks prevented them from going bankrupt (N.N., 1998, p. 20). Hence, there is urgent need for restructuring these institutions. The SBV started the process of rehabilitating JSBs in early 1998. The plan involves convincing the four state-owned banks to take a stake of up to 10 per cent in the ailing JSBs in order to strengthen the latter's financial base. But at present the SOCBs seem to be reluctant to bail out the JSBs because they are not in a position to make such loans and they fear the weakening of their own financial base. Thus, the reforms have fallen behind schedule and the aim of finishing the clean-up by the end of 1998 could not be realized (Schiffrin, 1999, p. 28). In Decree 82, issued in October 1998, JSBs are required to meet stricter minimum capitalization and loss-loan provisioning standards. Minimum capital requirements for JSBs amount to VND 70 billion, for financial cooperations VND 50 billion and for SOCBs VND 1,100 to 2,200 billion. JVBs are required to have a minimum capital of $10 million. Credit institutions which cannot meet the requirements are encouraged to merge or to close (World Bank, 1999, p. 29). Since autumn 1998, at least seven JSBs in Ho Chi Minh City have done so. In addressing the issue of troubled JSBs, avoiding depositors' panic at all cost is of great concern. The breakdown of numerous credit cooperations in Ho Chi Minh City in 1990 is still fresh in people's minds and an experience of a similar kind would be a setback to emerging confidence in private financial institutions. Another issue of great concern to advisers is to maintain the right incentives during the process of restructuring JSBs, meaning that losses must be allocated first to shareholders and to large depositors. Bailing out shareholders in poorly run banks – as seen in the case of Nam Do and VP Bank – is not likely to send the right signals and would provide strong incentives for mismanagement in the future, thus encouraging the rise of moral hazard behaviour (Irvine, 1998, p. 23). Furthermore, current shareholders must be given time to raise additional capital. If they are not able to raise this capital, the government must take control and decide to close down banks that are insolvent and restructure those that are potentially viable (World Bank, 1999, p. 24).

Observers are, however, more worried about the situation at the large state-owned banks which account for the vast majority of the country's bank lending, compared to only 10 per cent for the joint-stock banks. Regarding credit allocation, the Vietnamese financial system still acts rather one-sidedly. Historically, the state-owned bank sector has been used as an instrument of public policy and much of its lending is still influenced by non-economic criteria. Although reforms have resulted in increased lending to private firms, the SOEs – which dominate the key industries but have to deal with problems of low productivity and bad debt – remain the key recipients of credit from state-owned banks. This credit is often unsecured and provided at concessionary interest rates (Murray, 1999, p. 19). On a formal level, in Article 15 of the Law on Credit Institutions, all banks are granted the right 'to refuse any request for credit extension, capital contribution, provision of banking service if such a request is considered unjustified or not in compliance with the laws'. However, the government has continuously pressed them to lend to troubled state companies, resulting in an even greater amount of bad debts. A demonstration of government intervention in favour of the SOEs could be observed after the state-owned banks cut off loans to the SOEs following several fraud cases. To avoid financial difficulties for the companies concerned, the state bank issued a regulation in May 1997 abolishing the requirement of the SOEs to post collateral for loans. Instead, the state-owned banks are now permitted to approve loans only on the basis of creditworthy business plans (N.N. 1997, pp. 34ff.). To prevent such concessional lending in the future, the government is planning to separate politically motivated lending from regular banking activities at the state-owned banks. Therefore, the creation of a special policy bank based on the already existing Bank of the Poor is envisaged, concentrating all concessional lending activities of the SOCBs in this new organization. Provided that the transformation is carried out successfully, the state-owned commercial banks are to lend only on the basis of commercial criteria and to manage their business more efficiently. It is doubtful, however, whether this ambitious intention will ever be realized, as many executives of the state-owned banks strongly oppose the plan. They fear a loss of influence and power and thus prefer to maintain the status quo. Another issue on the reform agenda for state-owned banks is their recapitalization. The government has already spent $300 million in 1998 and 1999 to add to their chartered capital in order to ensure the banks' financial capability. At the same time, it is imperative that recapitalization efforts include structural measures (such as transferring concessional lending to 'policy banks') as well as operational measures (that is, reorganizing management and improving staff training). Recapitalizing SOCBs without restructuring banks' objectives and operations is unlikely to work and would probably lead to an even greater amount of debt (World Bank, 1999, p. 26).

Financial deregulation

After ten years of reform, Vietnam's financial sector is still highly regulated – at least according to Western standards – although some remarkable progress has been achieved in creating a modern and flexible business environment. We have already mentioned that a money and foreign exchange market was developed as an interbank market from 1991 to 1993 and a securities market also began to emerge in the mid-1990s. The breakdown of sector specialization and the dismantling of restrictions on geographical areas of operation in the early 1990s have set the stage for increased competition and improved efficiency (Murray, 1999, p. 19). Since 1993, foreign insurance companies are allowed to operate in Vietnam and a stock exchange on which bonds and shares are traded is planned to start operations in late 1999.

The fixed exchange rate regime, prevailing during the 1990s, was abandoned in February 1999. Since then, Vietnam has employed a so-called crawling-peg system. The official rate is set daily and allowed to move in a 0.1 per cent band. Thus, the exchange rate is no longer fixed by the state bank but set on the interbank market for foreign exchange according to supply and demand. Nevertheless, the SBV is still the most powerful market participant and therefore able to influence the value of the Vietnamese dong.

Although there is ample need for further liberalization in the Vietnamese financial system in order to make full use of domestic as well as foreign sources of capital, many observers argue that at present further deregulation should not represent the top priority for Vietnam's policy makers. Instead of opening the foreign exchange market more fully or even loosening administrative controls on banks – hence increasing Vietnam's financial vulnerability – the government should give priority to resolving internal deficiencies. Thus, the creation of a sound domestic financial infrastructure must be awarded an outstanding position. This task comprises strengthening the legal framework for the financial sector and advancing the process of institution building (for example, banking associations, auditing firms and deposit insurance funds) (Klump and Gottwald, 1999, p. 25).

Consumer protection and the modernization of banking technology

The experience of 1989/90, when numerous overleveraged credit cooperatives broke down in rural Vietnam and many savers not only lost their money but also their trust in an ill-designed banking system, is still vivid in people's minds. Since then, protecting customers' savings at domestic commercial banks has become an issue of growing concern to officials in the state bank while they are trying to improve public confidence in the financial sector and to accelerate mobilization of domestic funds. With the amount of savings and credit to the economy constantly growing, the necessity to set up a deposit insurance and compensation scheme has increased over the past years. Hence – according to Hoang Nghia Tu, the general secretary of the government's State Finance and Monetary Council – such an institution will be in operation in the near future as well as a 'risk fund' intended to deal with the non-performing loans (Schiffrin, 1999, p. 28). Participation in this deposit guarantee or deposit insurance fund will be compulsory for all credit institutions dealing with the public (LCI, Art. 17.1). It is planned to raise a compulsory member's fee from the credit institutions corresponding to their size and the structure of their credit portfolio. Information about the insurance coverage – expressed as a percentage of a bank's total deposit – which a bank is required to pay into the fund is not yet available but will be stipulated by the government (LCI, Art. 17.1). Furthermore, the government is supposed to 'create favourable conditions for deposit and withdrawal of money by customers upon request to ensure full and timely payment' (LCI, Art. 17.2).

Since Vietnam is predominantly a cash economy with people eschewing banks and accumulating wealth principally outside the (official) financial sphere, the SBV is eager to modernize banking technology and promote the usage of non-cash payment instruments in order to improve the efficiency of the whole system and to convince more Vietnamese people to use banking services. At present, banking payment instruments being used are not abundant and are mainly based on documents. According to a state bank study, among the various payment instruments being used, cash accounts for 40 per cent of total payment conducted through banks and 60 per cent are non-cash payment instruments. The largest share of non-payment instruments is occupied by payment orders (67.8 per cent), followed by payment notes (21.1 per cent) and cheques (9.9 per cent) (SBV, 1999, p. 53). Since May 1996 (Government Decree 30/CP) a uniform cheque format was applied for both individuals and firms and cheques became negotiable. Nevertheless, the scope of payment with cheques is still limited due mainly to the underdeveloped payment system. Cheque payment among commercial banks is still difficult because of the lack of a countrywide cheque-clearing centre. As a contribution to the process of modernization of banking technology, payment cards were developed on a pilot basis and are being issued by four domestic commercial banks, namely Vietcombank, Asian Joint Stock Bank, EximBank and First Vina Bank. According to specialists, payment cards have a big potential in Vietnam as they can be conveniently used in payment of retail goods and services. At present, however, a lack of technical equipment and information technology as well as the fact that only a few merchants accept bank payment cards prevent this device from becoming popular (SBV, 1998, p. 45). A project to upgrade banking payment systems has been started since the end of 1994 and is financed by the World Bank to a total value of $53 million. At the end of 1998, the state bank concluded the second phase of bidding for a subproject on the modernization of the interbank payment system. This subproject is urgently needed to accelerate the development of the interbank money market since the existing payment system is obsolete and therefore cannot meet the demand for fast payment transactions from credit institutions (SBV, 1999, p. 51).

The emergence of a new market: the Vietnamese stock market project

The creation of Vietnam's first stock market has been a matter of concern since 1992. However, it was not until November 1996 that efforts to create such an institution gained momentum and the establishment of the State Security Commission (SSC) under the direction of its chairman Le Van Chau was completed. In mid-1998, the SCC issued the first preliminary legal instruments (Government Decree 48) for the operation of a securities market and for the establishment of share trading centres (STCs), dealing with such issues as the criteria for an initial public offering of shares, foreign participation, prohibited practices and the state administration of the securities market (Nguyen Viet Ha, 1998, p. 35). In March 1999, the SCC announced further decisions on securities companies, investment funds and clearance, settlement and registration procedures (VLU, 1999, p. 16). The stock exchange finally opened on 28 July 2000.

Much of the delay in proceeding to open Vietnam's first stock market can probably be attributed to the Asian crisis. In late 1997, when financial markets throughout the region recorded severe losses and short-term portfolio investment fled Southeast Asia, Vietnam's officials were obviously relieved that the stock market was not yet in operation. But now, the government seems ready to proceed and willing to implement reforms aimed at mobilizing capital. However, there remain many unsolved problems which are in part – beside the Asian crisis – responsible for the slow progress of the stock market. Probably the most pressing issue is the slowly proceeding equitization of the SOEs and the fact that most of the equitized enterprises do not meet the minimum requirements to obtain a licence from the SSC in order to issue shares in the market. In order to obtain a licence, a shareholding company must clear a number of hurdles, including existing equity of at least VND 10 billion (about $710,000) and recording profit for the past two years. According to a recent survey conducted by the Ministry of Finance and the SSC, only 12 of 29 equitized enterprises could meet minimum listing requirements (Nguyen Viet Ha, 1998, p. 37). As a consequence, the supply of shares is very limited. It is estimated that a maximum number of ten shareholding companies (Irvine, 1999, p. 18; VLU, 1999, p. 17) will list on the STC and this low number could imply a danger of speculation and high volatility of share prices. Nevertheless, there is hope that the stock market will speed up the equitization process. For a while, however, bonds are likely to trade more heavily than shares, as shareholding companies take advantage of the new avenue for raising debt financing. Derivate trading will be several years away (VLU, 1999, p. 17). Furthermore, the training of brokers and the selection of staff for the administration of the future stock exchange is not yet completed. Some trainees have already spent three to six months abroad to improve their economic knowledge and to gain experience of the functioning of a stock market. An additional issue of concern is the need to disseminate information via the media about the nature of stock investments since the Vietnamese population has to date no experience of the functioning of a stock exchange. In this context, the SSC will presumably play an active role in educating the public about the operations of the STC and about the benefits and risks of investing in Vietnamese securities (Spitzenpfeil and Gottwald, 1999, p. 15). Minor problems are expected when the STC opens. However, settlement procedures and the other mechanics of the market should become established fairly quickly (VLU, 1999, p. 17).

The success of the stock market – as with all markets – will mainly depend on availability and timeliness of information. Companies must be required to publish disclosures and announcements, and be penalized if they ignore this regulation. Furthermore, internationally accepted accounting standards will need to be applied to companies whose shares are listed if Vietnam's securities market is to attract lasting amounts of investment. Hence, the SSC was right in taking its time to construct a consistent legal framework and to give priority to enhanced investor protection (for example, stipulating strict rules against insider trading) in order to sow well the seeds for the future industry. An overhasty approach would have been of no use for Vietnam. Finally, one should not forget that the sooner Vietnam adds this market-oriented institution to its financial sector, the sooner the national economy will begin to derive the benefits. A security market can help Vietnam to accelerate its economic development by providing additional domestic capital resources and new sources of foreign capital (Klump and Gottwald, 1999, p. 17).

5 OUTLOOK

Since the beginning of *doi moi*, the Vietnamese government has undertaken decisive steps to create a financial system which simultaneously satisfies the need for an emerging market economy and contributes to the country's ambitious plans of catching up. On the whole, the sequencing of reforms can be described as successful: basic regulatory reforms from 1988 to 1990, consistent stabilization since 1992, cautious liberalization and institutional reforms over the whole period. Nevertheless, it should be said that the present financial infrastructure in Vietnam is still inefficient in mobilizing capital, particularly from domestic sources, and in distributing it to the most productive and profitable investments. There is even the danger that structural problems of the financial sector might act as a brake on Vietnam's future path of development.

The effects of the severe financial and economic crises which have hit many countries in the region are still being felt in Vietnam. Since foreign investors from other Asian countries have cut back their investments dramatically in Vietnam (while American and European investors mainly follow a 'wait-and-see' strategy), high growth rates have to rely even more on the internal mobilization of funds. Inefficient regulations, lack of knowledge and the economic heritage of socialism, including the huge problem of SOE debts, impede the necessary expansion of the Vietnamese financial system. The bad debt crisis and the problems of many commercial banks (state owned as well as private) can only be solved if the government grants massive financial support to most of the commercial banks. The low intermediation ratio and the high degree of dollarization are signs of a still widely shared distrust towards domestic financial assets in Vietnam. Dollarization also limits the feeble options of exchange rate policy to cope with the present crises. Any devaluation of the dong not only will increase Vietnam's external debt, eventually causing problems of servicing and repayment, but also works against the attractiveness of dong holdings within the domestic banking system.

Thus, the focus of adjustment measures has to be on domestic reforms which not only enhance the competitiveness of the Vietnamese economy but also improve the stability and soundness of the country's monetary and financial infrastructure. Only if this task is carried out successfully, can a sustained growth process be induced, thus enabling the country to catch up with its neighbours and to fight widespread poverty effectively. Right now, there are three crucial issues on the reform agenda for Vietnam which should receive priority in the short run: (i) the bank supervision function, which is performed by the state bank, must be strengthened, (ii) the legal framework for the financial system has to be developed continuously, in particular a clear definition of property rights and the judicial enforcement of claims is needed and (iii) the process of institution building (banking associations, auditing firms) must be advanced without question. The opening of local financial markets to international flows, that is, opening the foreign exchange market more fully or allowing for short-term capital flows, is expected to become an issue of concern in the future stages of reform (Klump and Gottwald, 1999, pp. 24ff.).

This challenge comes into conflict, however, with the basic ideological inconsistency of Vietnam's 'double transition' strategy. The socialist government wants to transform the economic system yet at the same time resists significant changes in the political and social institutions. Thus every cautious reform step is a compromise between socialism and capitalism (Román, 1995, p. 131). But it seems that if the Vietnamese government continues its 'go-slow attitude', in particular with regard to the further development of the internal financial system, it might risk the outbreak of a financial crisis followed by a severe economic slump.

REFERENCES

Allen, Peter (1998), 'It can't happen here', *Vietnamese Business Journal*, Vol. 6, No. 5, October, pp. 50–52.

Asia Pulse (1997), 'Vietnam's new banking laws still leave doubts', 23 December, internet: http://viet.simplenet.com/vietnews/archives/dec97/vb578G.html.

Asian Development Bank (1996), 'Socialist Republic of Vietnam – Rural Finance Project', *Staff Appraisal Report* No. 15088 VN, January, Manila.

Central Institute for Economic Management (CIEM) (ed.) (1999), *Vietnam Economy in 1998*, Hanoi: Education Publishing House.

Dang Hong Nga (1999), 'New measures to attract FDI', *Vietnam Economic News*, Vol. 9, No. 13, March/April, 6–7.

Dodsworth, John R., Erich Spitäller, Michael Braulke, Keon Hyok Lee, Kenneth Miranda, Christian Mulder, Hisanobu Shishido and Krishna Srinivasan (1996), 'Vietnam. Transition to a Market Economy', International Monetary Fund Occasional Paper 135, March, Washington, DC.

Dow Jones (1998), 'Vietnam's devaluation fails to revive its foreign-currency market', 18 February, internet: http://viet.simplenet.com/vietnews/archives/feb98/vb636B.html.

Duc Tan (1997), 'Bond sales – government securities edge forwards', *Vietnam Economic Times*, November, 32ff.

Economic Intelligence Unit (EIU) (1997), *EIU Country Report Vietnam*, 2nd Quarter, London: EIU.

Fforde, Adam and Anthony Goldstone (1995), *Vietnam to 2005 – Advancing on all fronts*, London: EIU.

Fforde, Adam and Stefan de Vylder (eds) (1996), *From Plan to Market – The Economic Transition in Vietnam*, Oxford: Westview Press.

Freeman, Nick (1996), 'Realism reigns', *The Banker*, June, 65ff.

Freeman, Nick (1998), 'Market reality', *Vietnamese Business Journal*, Vol. 6, No. 5, October, 31–3.

Hauskrecht, Andreas (ed.) (1998) *Monetäre Aspekte des Transformationsprozesses – Eine Fallstudie Vietnams*, Studien zur monetären Ökonomie; Bd. 23, Marburg: Metropolis-Verlag.

Huckshorn, Kristin (1998), 'Vietnam to go slow on economic reform, *Mercury News Vietnam Bureau*, 25 March, internet: seasia-l@msu.edu.

Huus, Kari (1998), 'Investors turn cold on Vietnam', *MSNBC*, 18 March, internet: vnnews-l@postbox.anu.edu.au.

International Monetary Fund (IMF) (1999), 'IMF concludes Article IV consultation with Vietnam', Public Information Notice No. 99/46, 8 June, internet: http://www.imf.org/external/np/sec/pn/1999/PN9946.HTML.

Irvine, Reed (1998), 'Exchanging times', *Vietnam Business Journal*, Vol. 6, No. 6, December, Vol. 3, 22–3.

Irvine, Reed (1999) What happened to the funds?', *Vietnam Business Journal*, Vol. 7, No. 3, July, 14–19.

Keenan, Faith (1997a), 'Don´t look now. Vietnam's bad debt could be worse than officials say', *Far Eastern Economic Review*, 23 October, 95.

Keenan, Faith (1997b), 'Reversion to type, Vietnam's coercive monetary policy spells trouble', *Far Eastern Economic Review*, 20 November, 72.

Kim Chi (1999), 'Overcoming challenges – assessing the performance of banking operations in 1998', *Vietnam Economic News*, Vol. 9, No. 9, March, 17–19.

Klump, Rainer and Klaus Gottwald (1999) 'Financial reform in Vietnam: lessons from the Asian crisis', Discusssion Papers in Economics, University of Ulm, Department for Economic Policy.

Klump, Rainer and Annette Spitzenpfeil (1998), 'Vietnam: the financial system of an economy in transition', in: Lukas Menkhoff and Beate Reszat (eds.), *Asian Financial Markets*, Baden-Baden: Nomos Verlag, pp. 335–52.

Kubota, Akira (1998), 'Current trends and issues in Vietnamese economy', in Bank of Tokyo-Mitsubishi (ed.), Tokyo-Mitsubishi Review, February, pp. 1ff.

Kyodo News Service (1998) 'Vietnam's '97 GDP growth lower than estimated', 17 April, internet: http://coombs.anu.edu.au/vern/vnnews-list.html.

Leung, Suiwah and Ngo Huy Duc (1999) 'Dollarization and financial sector developments in Vietnam', in: Suiwah Leung (ed.), *Vietnam and the East Asian Crisis*, Cheltenham, UK and Northampton, MA, USA: Edward Elgar, pp. 83–95.

Levine, Joshua Jake (1998), 'Ensuring success', *Vietnam Business Journal*, Vol. 6, No. 6, December, 38–9.

Marshall, Samantha (1998), Senior Minister will be named Chief of Vietnam's Central Bank, *The Wall Street Journal* 7 May.

McReynolds, Drew (1998), 'Growth funds', *Vietnam Business Journal*, Vol. 6, No. 6, December, 30–31.

Murray, Alison (1999), 'Regulation and reform for Vietnamese banks', *Standard & Poor's Credit Week*, 10 February, 17–21.

Murray, Geoffrey (ed.) (1997) *Vietnam: Dawn of a New Market*, Bath, UK: St. Martin's Press.

N.N. (1996), 'Banking on future returns', *Vietnam Economic Times*, May, 11.

N.N. (1997), 'Losing it, foreign banks win over major state-owned customers', *Vietnam Economic Times*, September, 32 ff.

N.N. (1998), 'Red hot money – cracks in the banking system are beginning to show through', *Vietnam Economic Times*, June, 20–21.

Ngo Tuan Kiep (1997), 'Die Reform des Bankensystems im Transformationsprozeß, in: State Bank of Vietnam (SBV) and Deutsche Gesellschaft für technische Zusammenarbeit (GTZ) (eds), *Zentralbankpolitik in einer Transformationsökonomie*, Hanoi: GTZ Verlag, pp. 107ff.

Nguyen Duc Thao and Pham Dinh Thang (1994), Vietnam: banking system and its payment modalities, Hanoi: New Word Publishers.

Nguyen Khac Q. Tung and Gerdpeter von Guretzky-Cornitz (1996), 'Das vietnamesische Bankwesen', *Die Bank*, Vol. 36, No. 5, May, 274ff.

Nguyen Viet Ha (1998), 'Buy low', *Vietnam Business Journal*, Vol. 6, No. 6, December, pp. 35–7.

Rana, Pradumna B. and Naved Hamid (eds) (1995), *From Centrally Planned to Market Economies: The Asian Approach, Lao PDR, Myanmar and Viet Nam*, Vol. 3, Oxford/New York: Oxford University Press.

Román, Lisa (1995), 'An institutional challenge: transition in the Vietnamese banking sector', in Björn Beckman, Eva Hansson and Lisa Román (eds), *Vietnam: Reform and Transformation*, Stockholm: SIDA, pp. 121ff.

Schiffrin, Anya (1999), 'Cleaning house', *Vietnam Business Journal*, Vol. 7, No. 3, July, 28–9.

Spitzenpfeil, Annette and Klaus Gottwald (1999), 'Vietnams Börse läßt auf sich warten', Discussion Papers in Economics, University of Ulm.

State Bank of Vietnam (SBV) (1997), *Annual Report 1996*, Hanoi.

State Bank of Vietnam (SBV) (1998), *Annual Report 1997*, Hanoi.

State Bank of Vietnam (SBV) (1999), *Annual Report 1998*, Hanoi.

Teufel, Hariolf (1997), 'Banken und Finanzmärkte in Vietnam', *Zeitschrift für das gesamte Kreditwesen*, Vol. 50, No. 2, February, 77ff.

Vietnam Legal Update (VLU) (1999), 'Update on opening of Vietnam's new securities market', Part 4 (Equitization Issues), August, 16–17, Ho Chi Minh City: Phillips Fox Lawyers.

Vietnam News Agency (VNA) (1998), Bank for House Development in Mekong Delta set to open; 5 March, internet: http//viet.simplenet.com/vietnews/archives/feb98/vb6341.html.

Wolff, Peter (ed.) (1999), *Vietnam – The Incomplete Transformation*, London: Frank Cass (published in association with the German Development Institute, Berlin).

World Bank (ed.) (1995), *World Bank Perspective: Financing Development in Vietnam*, Bangkok: World Bank.

World Bank (ed.) (1999), 'Vietnam: rising to the challenge', *An Economic Report of the World Bank, Consultative Group Meeting for Vietnam*, 7–8 December 1998, Hanoi.

Legal Documents

Socialist Republic of Vietnam (1998a), *The Law on the State Bank of Vietnam*, Hanoi: National Political Publishing House.
Socialist Republic of Vietnam (1998b), *The Law on Credit Institutions*, Hanoi: National Political Publishing House.

Index